Boris Ford is the General Editor of the New Pelican Guide to English
Literature (in 11 vols) which in its original form was launched in 1954.
At the time it was being planned he was Chief Editor and later
Director of the Bureau of Current Affairs. After a spell on the
Secretariat of the United Nations in New York and Geneva, he
became Editor of the Journal of Education and also first Head of Schools
Broadcasting with independent television.

Following a period as Education Secretary at the Cambridge University Press, Boris Ford, until he retired in 1982, was successively
Professor of Education at the Universities of Sheffield, Bristol and
Sussex, where he was also Dean of the School of Cultural and
Community Studies. He edited Universities Quarterly from 1955 until
1986. He is General Editor of The Cambridge Guide to the Arts in Britain
(in 9 vols, 1988–91), editor The Cambridge Cultural History of Britain
(1992), and of a forthcoming series of 10 volumes on the arts and
civilization of the Western world. He has edited Benjamin Britten's

From Blake to Byron

VOLUME

5

OF THE NEW PELICAN GUIDE TO
ENGLISH LITERATURE

EDITED BY BORIS FORD

PENGUIN BOOKS

PENGUIN BOOKS

Published by the Penguin Group
Penguin Books Ltd, 27 Wrights Lane, London w8 5tz, England
Penguin Putnam Inc., 375 Hudson Street, New York, New York 10014, USA
Penguin Books Australia Ltd, Ringwood, Victoria, Australia
Penguin Books Canada Ltd, 10 Alcorn Avenue, Toronto, Ontario, Canada m4v 3b2
Penguin Books (NZ) Ltd, 182–190 Wairau Road, Auckland 10, New Zealand

Penguin Books Ltd, Registered Offices: Harmondsworth, Middlesex, England

First published in *The Pelican Guide to English Literature* 1957
This revised and expanded edition published 1982
Reprinted in Penguin Books 1990
Reprinted with revised Appendix 1998
1 3 5 7 9 10 8 6 4 2

Printed in England by Clays Ltd, St Ives plc
Filmset in Monophoto Bembo

500 485117

CONTENTS

CONTENTS

PART IV

Appendix: compiled by Hilda D. Spear

GENERAL INTRODUCTION

The publication of this *New Pelican Guide to English Literature* in many volumes might seem an odd phenomenon at a time when, in the words of the novelist L. H. Myers, a 'deep-seated spiritual vulgarity ... lies at the heart of our civilization', a time more typically characterized by the Headline and the Digest, by the Magazine and the Tabloid, by Pulp Literature and the Month's Masterpiece. Yet the continuing success of the *Guide* seems to confirm that literature – both yesterday's literature and today's – has a real and not merely a nominal existence among a large number of people; and its main aim has been to help validate as firmly as possible this feeling for a living literature and for the values it embodies.

The *Guide* is partly designed for the committed student of literature. But it has also been written for those many readers who accept with genuine respect what is known as 'our literary heritage', but for whom this often amounts, in memory, to an unattractive amalgam of set texts and school prizes; as a result they may have come to read only today's books – fiction and biography and travel. Though they are probably familiar with such names as Pope, George Eliot, Langland, Marvell, Yeats, Dr Johnson, Hopkins, the Brontës, they might hesitate to describe their work intimately or to fit them into any larger pattern of growth and achievement. If this account is a fair one, it seems probable that very many people would be glad of guidance that would help them respond to what is living and contemporary in literature, for, like the other arts, it has the power to enrich the imagination and to clarify thought and feeling.

The *Guide* does not set out to compete with the standard Histories of Literature, which inevitably tend to have a lofty, take-it-or-leave-it attitude about them. This is not a Bradshaw or a *Whitaker's Almanack* of English literature. Nor is it a digest or potted version, nor again a portrait gallery of the great. Works such as these already abound

7

and there is no need to add to their number. What it sets out to offer, by contrast, is a guide to the history and traditions of English literature, a contour map of the literary scene. It attempts, that is, to draw up an ordered account of literature as a direct encouragement to people to read widely and in an informed way and with enjoyment. In this respect the *Guide* acknowledges a considerable debt to those twentieth-century writers and critics who have made a determined effort to elicit from literature what is of living value to us today: to establish a sense of literary tradition and to define the standards that this tradition embodies.

The *New Pelican Guide to English Literature* consists of eleven volumes:

Most of the volumes have been named after those writers who dominate or stand conveniently at either end of the period, and who also indicate between them the strength of the age in literature. Of course the boundaries between the separate volumes cannot be sharply drawn.

Though the *Guide* has been designed as a single work, in the sense that it attempts to provide a coherent and developing account of the tradition of English literature, each volume exists in its own right and sets out to provide the reader with four kinds of related material:

(i) *A survey of the social context of literature* in each period, providing an account of contemporary society at its points of contact with literature.

(ii) *A literary survey* of the period, describing the general characteristics of the period's literature in such a way as to enable the reader to trace its growth and to keep his or her bearings. The aim of this section is to answer such questions as 'What *kind* of literature was written in this period?', 'Which authors matter most?', 'Where does the strength of the period lie?'

(iii) *Detailed studies* of some of the chief writers and works in the period. Coming after the two general surveys, the aim of this section is to convey a sense of what it means to read closely and with perception; and also to suggest how the literature of a given period is most profitably read, i.e. with what assumptions and with what kind of attention. This section also includes an account of whichever one of the other arts particularly flourished at the time, as perhaps throwing a helpful if indirect light on the literature itself. In this volume this chapter is on landscape painting.

(iv) *An appendix of essential facts for reference purposes*, such as authors' biographies (in miniature), bibliographies, books for further study, and so on.

Thus each volume of the *Guide* has been planned as a whole, and the contributors' approach to literature is based on broadly common assumptions; for it was essential that the *Guide* should have cohesion and should reveal some collaborative agreements (though inevitably, and quite rightly, it reveals disagreements as well). They agree on the need for rigorous standards and have felt it essential not to take reputations for granted, but rather to examine once again, and often in close detail, the strengths and weaknesses of our literary heritage.

BORIS FORD

PART I

PART I

THE SOCIAL SETTING (1780–1830)

EDGELL RICKWORD

It is rarely that the perceptible limits of a literary 'period' coincide so closely with crucial political events as is the case with what we call the Romantic Movement. The name is convenient; but it would be misleading to give it any narrow meaning or to equate it with an 'escapist' or a past-ward yearning. Almost all the 'romantic' writers were acutely aware of their environment, and their best work came out of their impulse to come to terms with it.

The historical upper limit of this period is unmistakably the outbreak of the Colonists' rebellion in North America, their successful defence and their achievement of independence. 'A large proportion of society here at home,' says Wraxall, had wished for such a conclusion, 'because they dreaded lest the British Constitution itself would not long survive the increase of power and influence that the Crown must necessarily derive from the subjugation of the Colonies beyond the Atlantic.'

There was an appreciable sensation of 'thaw' in the political atmosphere. The autocratic system which the Hanoverian kings tended to foster was challenged at home as well as overseas. Wilkes was a portent. The group round Charles James Fox (which included Edmund Burke and R. B. Sheridan) set out a programme for reform of abuses which if implemented must have led to a measure of democratization. The middle class was growing in assurance and competence, the corrupt and extravagant system which prevailed did not suit them. Wedgwood, the great potter, after reading James Thomson's *Liberty*, writes to a friend: 'Happy would it be for this Island were his three virtues the foundation of British Liberty: Independent Life, Integrity in Office, and a passion for the Common Weal, – more strictly adhered to amongst us.'

That was in 1762, and by the eighties the war taxation and its secondary effects had further aggravated the situation and emphasized the need for reformation.

The American victory was a stimulus to those who for one reason or another felt confined by the existing institutions – the Dissenters, kept down by civil disabilities; the manufacturers, harassed by the archaic system (one could not begin on a making of paper, a batch of starch, or a brewing of vinegar till the excise man had been along to see that the quantities were correctly recorded in the books); the farmers by tithe and game laws; the lower middle and working classes by indirect taxes which weighed on every article of common use as well as on luxuries.[1] All this was imposed by a Parliament in which there was no representation of the ordinary people, the productive classes, neither of masters nor men. Not a penny of the money collected was returned as social services.

Men recalled the expectations latent in the Glorious Revolution a century earlier. There was again, more widely spread, an air of expectancy, of revival. The formalized system that had moulded Augustan taste was splitting open. The poems of Burns and of Blake reveal the imminence of a transition from convention to nature. Note Blake's indictment of contemporary versifying:

> The languid strings do scarcely move!
> The sound is forc'd, the notes are few!
> (*Poetical Sketches*, 1783)

This renewal is to be felt in the exquisitely truthful wood-engravings of Bewick, in the lyrical grace which refines Rowlandson's robust humour, in the carefree insolence of Gillray's immense grotesqueness.

In other social spheres, like that of costume, the same trend is visible. Gentlemen wore their own hair instead of wigs. Ladies' dresses were allowed to outline the body. The use of cosmetics was much reduced in fashionable circles. The simple elegance of domestic architecture and furniture provided the appropriate setting.

So the assembling of the States-General at Versailles in 1789 was realized here to portend great changes and the outcome was awaited with sympathetic optimism. The fall of the Bastille was widely greeted as a symbol of the regeneration of France and as opening a prospect of friendship and common progress. The evidence of printed matter, in verse and in prose, leaves no doubt about the favourable response to the measures for the eradication of feudal privileges. The promise of this outset of the Revolution was the illumination, the Fairy's gift (and ambiguous as all such), bestowed on the infant talents of all the earlier Romantics. How that promise was blighted, and withered for many, in the long ordeal of the wars against the Republic and the Empire is a matter of common knowledge. Waterloo was as decisive a landmark for the younger generation (Byron, Shelley, Keats) as the Bastille had been for Blake, Wordsworth, and Coleridge; but any promises Waterloo might have offered were dishonoured in the increasing disorder and distress of war's aftermath. The ensuing decade was a confused struggle between the growing forces of liberalism and an inefficient oligarchy with dictatorial powers. By the passing of the Reform Bill of 1832, the larger industrial and commercial interests received a share of that power, which had been monopolized up till then by the large landowners.

Material and Industrial Changes

The social developments in the last decades of the eighteenth century decisively ensured the emergence of Britain as the first nationstate of a new type, that form of industrial-capitalist democracy which reached maturity about the end of the nineteenth century. The transition from our older economy of agriculture and domestic handicrafts was quite spontaneous, not directed from above or regulated in any way except by the laws inherent in the new system of production. In no long time, the cumulative effect of the introduction of mechanical improvements provoked an upheaval affecting the community at all levels. From the eighties onwards, the scale and tempo of change were visibly increasing, and in a single generation the mode and manner of living which had fostered the brief splendour of a native classicism had become incompatible with social reality.

A sense of change had been in the air for some time. It was stimulated from many sources, from the writings of the French Enlightenment which circulated freely here, from the spread of interest in scientific discoveries and their possible applications, from the American example in setting up a constitution without hereditary legislators, from speculations as to the perfectibility of man. Stability and contentment had inspired the glow in the Augustan bosom; an iridescent perspective of unlimited human progress awoke the enthusiasm of the Romantic generation. The resignation or quietism so perfectly in key in *The Traveller* –

> How small, of all that human hearts endure,
> That part which laws or kings can cause or cure,

would have been repugnant to most of the significant writers, at any rate in their earlier lives, for they could not remain unaffected by the turmoil of social and political changes which succeeded one another in these fifty years, and all were led, some lightly and some profoundly, to reappraise the aims and function of literature.

When Defoe had toured Great Britain it was with the consciousness of a man of business that he enjoyed the countryside. The gentlemen's mansions, the neat farmsteads, and stout cottages seemed to him a natural reward for industry and enterprise. Wealth appeared to be a secretion from the process of exchange, whether it concerned a luxury from the Far East or a farmer's crop brought to the local market. It was a process by which everybody gained (though some gained much more than others), excepting the idle, the extravagant, and the afflicted. The idle and extravagant brought their punishment on themselves, they were bound to 'break'; the afflicted, since they suffered by decree of Providence, ought to be relieved by private charity. It was a world which admitted extreme contrasts between the lots of individuals and violent fluctuations of fortune, but it was basically simple and apparently permanent. There were no teasing questions.

Some speculations there had been in the seventeenth century as to the origin of national well-being. A plentiful 'treasure' or hoard of the precious metals was widely believed to be its basis. The realities of production and exchange were hardly inquired into; the spinning-wheel, the hand-loom, the pack-ponies, the miry tracks were so familiar that they were hardly seen when looked at. Yet in this sector, technology, there lurked the fatality which was to break up the relatively harmonious country life into hostile factions of rich and poor, with the middle class, the writers' main audience, uneasily aware of the tension this polarization set up.

Wordsworth wrote in 1817:

I see clearly that the principal ties which kept the different classes of society in a vital and harmonious dependence upon each other have, within these thirty years, either been greatly impaired or wholly dissolved. Everything has been put up to market and sold for the highest price it would buy.[2]

Small technical improvements had been made in most industries throughout the century. An acute observer, Josiah Tucker, remarked in 1757, 'Few countries are equal, perhaps none excel, the *English* in the Numbers and Contrivances of their Machines to abridge Labbour ...'[3] He mentions great improvements in mining and metalworking, and noted already the moves towards technical innovation in the linen and cotton industries, which were to prove decisive in breaking up the old economy. This lay some twenty years ahead of his observations. But in 1765 Matthew Boulton laid out his famous Soho works:

a noble range of manufactories, constructed at a cost of £9000 ... with connecting workshops sufficiently extensive for the accommodation of 1000 workmen ... All the best machines and newest mechanical contrivances to save labour and perfect workmanship, which were then extant, had been introduced.[4]

Among these contrivances, James Watt's improved steam engine was soon to be included.

Although steam-power is the most spectacular of the innovations of the time, it was not the effective instrument of the great change, though these engines' clangour and belching of smoke and flame made them appropriate symbols of a baleful modernity. The textiles which broke down the local market economy were produced mainly by water-power, often in mills in romantic valleys such as Wordsworth describes in *The Excursion* (Book the Eighth).

Cheap textiles were fatal to the country people because their standard of living depended on augmenting the produce of their land with that of some home industry, spinning, weaving, or knitting. Samuel Bamford, best known for his *Passages in the Life of a Radical*, gives a somewhat idyllic picture of this sort of domestic economy just before the invention of the machinery which led inevitably to the setting-up of the large-scale factory system:

Their working hours, whether at the loom or on the farm, were, as compared with those of modern operatives and labourers, spent in leisure. There was often great irregularity in their observance of working hours, and their duration varied much, according to the wants, or habits, of individual workers, or of families ...

The almost universal breakfast of the working classes, and indeed of the middle also, consisted of oatmeal porridge, and milk, with an oaten-butter-cake, or a piece of cheese and oatcake, to make up. Dinners generally consisted of dumplings, boiled meat, broth and oaten bread. Potato pies were not un-common, but then, besides a substantial crust, they were seasoned with a scant-less mixture of beef or mutton ... After dinner came an hour and a half or two hours' play, or lounging; and in the afternoon, oat-cake and cheese, or butter, sufficed for bagging; supper was the same as breakfast, and then play was allowed till bed-time.

But soon a change was destined to come over this scene of homely labour and plenteous living. In 1769, a patent was taken out for a machine to spin cotton by rollers; in 1770 the spinning jenny was patented; in 1785 appeared improved carding, drawing and roving machines ... then came a wonderful facility of production, and a proportionate decrease of the cost, whence fol-lowed an increase of demand, an increase of population, a crowding towards the great hive, of many people of all industrial classes, and from all parts of the kingdom and the world.[5]

Allowing that Bamford takes an exceptionally well-situated family, the contrast between the hours of labour in the early factories and the living conditions he describes gives a solid foundation to the charge that the health and happiness of the working-people suffered a grievous deterioration in these decades.

There was one other important cause of the decline of living stand-ards. This was the enclosure of the commons and the 'waste', to which the smallholders and cottagers had had access as grazing for their few beasts and as source of fuel. From *The Deserted Village* (1769) to Clare's lament for the loss of Swordy Well (in the 1820s), this cruel process has left ample traces in our literature. The few commons that have survived to our day were allowed to do so because they were so gravelly or otherwise infertile that they were not worth the cost of fencing. We do not naturally realize what a substantial loss the en-closure of the common lands meant to their habitual users. This is brought home by a passage in Thomas Bewick's autobiography. He was fortunate in having been brought up on the edge of a common some miles long, which he lovingly describes:

It was mostly fine, green sward, or pasturage, broken, or divided, indeed, with clumps of 'blossom'd whins', foxglove, fern, and some junipers, and with heather in profusion, sufficient to scent the whole air ... On this common – the poor man's heritage for ages past, where he kept a few sheep, or a Kyloe cow, perhaps a flock of geese, and mostly a stock of bee-hives – it was with infinite pleasure that I lay and beheld the beautiful wild scenery ... and it is with the opposite feelings of regret that I now find all swept away.

He comments that when this waste was divided (in 1812) 'the poor man was rooted out, and the various mechanics of the villages deprived of all benefit of it'.[6]

Bewick adhered to no political ideology. He was just naturally, like Cobbett, *with* the people, and felt their grievances. Such inconsiderate proceedings were going on all over the country, and must have been a general source of resentment against the landlords. One need make no attempt to deny the eventual benefit of these changes, enclosures, or inventions. It is their impact on the creative writer that concerns us here. Plenty of references can be quoted to show that the Romantics recognized the deep alteration taking place in the national way of life and that they judged it to be inimical to man's truest interests. This holds for the Tory Southey as for the revolutionary Shelley.

Whether they are explicit on the subject or not, that is their background, and it is responsible for the fact that they could not, and did not, persist in the attitudes and techniques of their immediate literary predecessors. Our English Romanticism was not in origin or intention escapist; its impulse is to be truly representative of human life in the broad sense, not merely the expression of a cultivated minority. The times were exciting, the prospects vast; it seemed impossible that it should not soon be within the power of men to eradicate the flaws and errors of society.

Opening New Worlds

There was abundance of evidence to justify optimism. Great and apparently beneficial developments were taking place in all sectors. In that of geography, the recent circumnavigations had revealed new worlds, no less astonishing than those that the Elizabethans had discovered. Captain James Cook's three voyages were the most impressive. In the second of them he discovered Australia and the Sandwich Islands and crossed the Antarctic Circle. Numerous works and editions, including one in eighty sixpenny weekly parts, attest the popularity of this subject. Enticing descriptions of the Earthly Paradises found in the South Seas gave fresh impetus to the current theorizing on the nature of society, and encouraged the comparative study of political systems, with corrosive effect on established ideas.

More materially, the voyages were remarkable for Cook's accurate charting of coast-lines. Since the chronometer had now been perfected so that the navigator could determine his longitude at sea with an extremely small possibility of error, ocean travel lost much of its hazard. From now on the profitable trade with the East Indies and the systematic penetration of the Indian sub-continent proceed at increasing tempo. The trial of Warren Hastings drew attention to the vast profits, or easy plunder, to be had there. It was the Age of the Nabobs, who could outbid most competitors for a rotten borough. The huge Indian market greatly stimulated the growth of the cotton industry.

The expansion of commerce raised the demand for all kinds of nautical gear. The rivalry between England and France for the most profitable share of the new-found territories gave an impulse to the metallurgical industries. Larger ships required heavier anchors; cannon increased in calibre. To satisfy the demand for coal deeper seams had to be worked, and this brought the need for a more efficient pumping engine than the Newcomen, which had been little improved since it had been first utilized in 1712. James Watt's earliest engine embodying his great invention, the separate condenser, began work in 1776. It had only rectilinear motion, and was used to supply the blast for an iron-works. A few years later, the engine's usefulness was greatly extended by being adapted to rotary motion. Even so, it seems that of the five hundred Watt engines manufactured by Boulton by the end of the century most were employed for pumping and less than a hundred installed in textile factories. Many were at work in isolated districts, but one of them was for some years a notable sight in London. It operated the Albion Flour Mills in Southwark. Though burnt down in 1790, it might have been visited by Coleridge and Wordsworth, and it was certainly familiar to Blake. The snorting ear-shattering monster must have been impressive in action, and may have helped to condition the poets' attitude to the new technology.

The rapidly increasing output of goods required a new communications system for its distribution. The roads were notoriously bad, and until this was remedied manufacturing centres could not much expand if far from the coast or a navigable water-way. The opening up of the Midlands by canals was the achievement of a great con-

structional engineer, James Brindley, with the support of an enlightened landowner, the Earl of Bridgewater. At one stage he was helped
by the active participation of Josiah Wedgwood, whose fragile wares
were particularly vulnerable to the hazards of the ill-kept roads.
Even there, however, considerable improvements were effected, at
least on the traffic arteries, and by the 1820s the most rapid coaches
could complete the journey from London to Liverpool, Leeds, or
Manchester in about twenty-four hours.

This opening up of the inland districts fostered the growth of industry in the already existing towns. Between 1800 and 1830 many
of these towns doubled their populations; e.g. Birmingham rose from
71,000 to 144,000; Sheffield from 46,000 to 92,000; Leicester from
17,000 to 41,000; and so on. Since nothing was done to expand the
amenities or to plan accommodation for these migrants (beyond the
haphazard gambling of the speculative builder), the manufacturing
towns became notorious for over-crowding, insanitary squalor, and
grimy ugliness. 'Town' ceased to denote the apogee of civil organization; to the poets especially it came to denote greed and evil.

The shift of population from the villages to the towns was co-
incident with that general rise in population which added some three
million in thirty years. As emigration was not yet a relieving factor,
this meant intense pressure on the existing resources of food and
shelter. Swiftly as industry expanded, there was always a supply of
labour surplus to requirements which depressed the rate of wages of
those at work. The very rapid accumulation of capital which resulted
from these low wages and absence of taxation of manufacturing
profits assisted the further development of industry. In periods of
market stagnation such as 1819 and 1825–6, a very high proportion
of the labouring classes were in acute physical distress, and this caused
grave anxiety among the more fortunately placed sections of the
community.

If the circulation of goods was immensely speeded up by the new
facilities of communication, the dissemination of ideas could not but
benefit also. Local self-sufficiency gave place to interdependence and
local issues to national ones. If information and discussion are the
bases of a political democracy, then the material conditions were ripe
for one to come into existence. The pamphlet had been the main
vehicle for controversy ever since the Martin Marprelate tracts of

Elizabethan notoriety, and the enormous output of them during the Civil War has been already noted. In the first part of our period, the pamphlet reached a height of influence which has never been surpassed. The great debate on the French Revolution, which was formally initiated by Burke's *Reflections* (1790) with the intention of discrediting those who championed that cause, was carried on by pamphlets, and Thomas Paine's rejoinder, *The Rights of Man* (Part I, 1791), became immediately the rallying-point for those dissatisfied with the present state of things. After the turn of the century, the speedier traffic favoured the periodical as the organ of opinion. From the daily newspaper to the book-size quarterlies, every publication had its political bias, for or against the Government; in favour of some measures of reform, or adamantly opposed to the extension of the franchise by a single thorn bush.[7]

The daily newspapers seldom had a circulation of more than two or three thousand. *The Times* did not touch five thousand until 1815. Even so, the Government thought them sufficiently influential to desire a firm hold over their expression of political opinions, and tried to effect this by an unsystematic application of cajolery and coercion. The first would be exercised by the channelling of departmental advertisements, by priority of information, and by hard cash.[8] Recalcitrant editors would find, first, that the *douceurs* would be withdrawn and, next, that they might have to face a prosecution. At the end of the long Napoleonic wars there had grown up a wide-spread consciousness of the unfairness of prohibitions enforced on the lower orders, and this was naturally accompanied by a desire to communicate these feelings to all in a similar position. But the Government quickly realized the dangers for them of the growth and spread of such a movement, and the radicals were hampered in every possible way – first by fines, and for second offences possibly by imprisonment or even deportation. Amongst the various obstacles put in the way of unfettered expression of opinion, was the Stamp Duty, originally a clumsy revenue-collecting device invented during the wars against Louis XIV, and which by 1815 had been heavily increased. Newsagents and street sellers could be fined for lending copies of stamped newspapers, and imprisoned for selling copies of unstamped ones. During the great battle of the unstamped there were some seven hundred and fifty convictions, mainly for selling newspapers. Even more important was the Publications Act or 'Act to subject certain publications to the Duties upon newspapers ...' As William H. Wickwar says in his book *The Struggle for the Freedom of the Press*:

> This was directed against the cheap weeklies. In the preamble it was declared that 'pamphlets and printed papers containing observations upon public events and occurrences, tending to excite hatred and contempt of the Government and constitution of these realms as by law established, and also vilifying our holy religion have lately been published in great numbers and at very small prices: and it is expedient that the same should be restrained'.

The aim of this measure was not simply to lessen the number of readers of these popular radical and rationalist works, but also by so doing to make their publication in the first instance quite unprofitable.

Legal sanctions were more frequently employed against the weekly periodicals. These had much larger circulations, covered the whole country, and were very attentively read. John and Leigh Hunt's *Examiner*, Carlile's *Republican*, Wooler's *Black Dwarf*, Hone's pamphlet-parodies are only the most notable of the many publications expressing 'democratical' views which were brought before the Courts. The reports of such trials were usually published *in extenso* and sold in large numbers, so that the opposite of the Government's intention was in fact achieved.[9]

But the greatest stimulant to and organizer of the popular reform movement was Cobbett's *Political Register*. Year in, year out for some thirty years, Cobbett put the case for common humanity against trickery and brutality, usury, stock-jobbery, and cant, the instruments of privilege. When at last he sat for Oldham in the first reformed Parliament he felt out of place. This was not what he had meant his work to do. Yet his writing, or much of it, is as alive today as ever, since it is the romantic protest against the basic fact of exploitation.[10]

The Milieu of the Writer

The increase in the literate and relatively well-to-do sections of the population so enlarged the market for books that printers and publishers had incentive to undertake large-scale productions involving heavy capital investment. From the early years of the eighteenth century much enterprise had been shown in the publication of works of information and reference. John Harris's *Lexicon Technicum* had appeared in 1710, Chambers's *Cyclopaedia* in 1728, and the first edition of the *Encyclopaedia Britannica* in 1771. Johnson's famous Dictionary (1755) was not a pioneering effort in publishing. World atlases, though not so decorative as those of the Antwerp masters, testified to native skills of a high order. Many of such ambitious publications were issued in parts, unbound, at stated intervals, thus greatly enlarging the number of prospective buyers. Recent research has shown this practice to have been much more general than was previously supposed,[11] and the successful management of such a complicated enterprise argues for a high level of organization of the book trade throughout the country. Of course, every town then had its binder or binders, who would bind the completed work in leather at an acceptable charge. Calf bindings were not then a luxury (unless executed by a specialist) but normal usage, as most books were sent out merely protected by a thin paper wrapper.

Since extensive undertakings could not be dependent on the impulse to authorship, publishers had to resort to commissioning writers to compose or compile something that they believed would be profitable. Then as now, long runs from the same setting of type were more profitable than short ones, hence the search for subjects which would create a wide demand independent of such an incalculable factor as public taste. The bread-and-butter lines were works of information or instruction, almanacs, school books, devotional manuals. Poetry, works of scholarship, and *belles-lettres* were necessarily speculative but, so long as the outlay was not heavy, one winner would compensate for quite a number of failures.

It was these conditions which created the demand for writers of a higher standard of performance than the Grub Street hack of Pope's day. The basis for the emergence of a class of professional writer was established, and this hastened the disappearance of that usually (though not invariably) degrading intermediary between the writer and his public, the patron.

Under these new conditions it was no longer the case, as it had been in the mid eighteenth century, that writers were not solely men of letters. Previously they had had careers at Court, in the Church or the armed forces, but in this period there is no outstanding writer who greatly distinguished himself in any other walk of life.

Thus originated a race of men and women who lived, or endeavoured to live, by the pen, considering their intellectual production sufficient justification for claiming a place in society. This assumption of a specialist function involved a narrowing of the opportunities for social experience; none of these writers was intimately associated with those holding political power, none had moved so close to the control-room of the State as had Swift and Prior, Milton, Marvell, or Donne. This estrangement from the personnel and practices of government was in the main due to a mutual revulsion, a motive which by and large continued throughout the century. To it we owe a greater grasp and penetration of the subjective, a keener analysis of sense perceptions. Deriving from it, perhaps, is the increasing tendency of poets to dwell, or to hope to dwell, in remote places. Only Byron moved for a time in the great world, by the twin rights of birth and genius, and the effect of the experience is apparent in the adultness, the maturity of attitude, of his best later work.

Of course not every writer was able to live on the earnings of the pen. Far from it. But the possibility of so living did exist, as Southey and Hazlitt proved the hard way. Scott's poetry brought him a moderate fortune, his novels a great one. Byron could have achieved independence had he needed to, and Thomas Moore did so. But these last three had the quite unpredictable good fortune to strike the public taste at the right moment. In the ordinary run of things, it was regular access to the periodical press which could alone ensure a living wage.

The relation between publisher and author was now frankly that of buyer and seller (only Byron made sometimes romantic gestures of throwing his copyright to Murray, which the publisher was sensible and generous enough not to take seriously). But the royalty system had not been adopted, and instead of receiving so much per copy sold, it was usual for the author to receive a payment down for the first edition of a specified number. If subsequent editions were called for, he received a specified sum for each. Another common system was that of sharing the profits of an edition between author and publisher – a practice providing innumerable opportunities for dispute, and often unsatisfactory with even an honest publisher. John Clare, although his first collection of poems sold well, found himself twenty pounds in debt when he at last received a statement.

The high and rising prices of new books encouraged the formation of circulating libraries and reading-rooms. These might be run for the membership of some philosophical society such as few of the older towns were without; or merely by a dozen or so people in friendly association.

Novels were excessively costly. After Waterloo, the regular price for the often poorly produced three volumes duodecimo, in stiff paper boards only, was £1 11s. 6d. So in most shopping centres, and of course at every seaside resort and inland spa, there would be commercial lending libraries, located usually on the premises of a stationer's or a milliner's. The appetite for this kind of reading had been growing since the eighties, and reviewers uselessly complained of the insipidity and sameness of most of these publications. Since the rewards of authorship might be as low as £5,[12] it is not surprising that a flagging invention should have been sustained by repetition and an inflationary style. One publisher in particular exploited this market, Mr Lane of the once legendary Minerva Press.[13] He combined publishing acumen with a genius for distributive resourcefulness which the later Mudie could only repeat in an age of much easier communications. He opened his central library in Leadenhall Street, in the City, about 1770. In 1790 his lending stock was around 10,000 titles; in 1802 it had risen to 17,000. He had a principal agent in every considerable town, who supplied the lesser libraries.

In the four decades to 1810 he published respectively 91, 214, 236, 192 works of fiction. Some representative titles were: *Miseries of an Heiress; Bride and No Wife; Black Robber; Mysterious Baron; Chamber of Death; Homicide; German Sorceress; Horrors of Oakendale Abbey.*

Leigh Hunt, Shelley, De Quincey, Macaulay were some of the writers-to-be who in their young days were addicted to this kind of stimulant. The borrowing charge was as much as 2d. a day for each volume.[14]

Theatre-going was the greatest delight to townspeople, and full-blooded entertainment was provided, by the audience as well as by the players. It was an age of great or very talented performers, whose interpretations preserved the continuity of the drama at a time when contemporary dramatists were few and second-rate. In view of the opportunities, it is surprising that none of the Romantics was able to achieve a successful acting play. Coleridge's *Remorse*, although it ran for twenty nights and so constituted a record for that circle, was never revived, Godwin's tragedy *Antonio* was damned outright, as was Lamb's farce, *Mr H.* – but both survive in Lamb's ludicrous account of the occasion. On the credit side, Leigh Hunt and Hazlitt originated modern dramatic criticism, which they raised to a permanent achievement in spite of its ephemeral nature. And Coleridge was to illuminate Shakespeare with flashes of profound insight.

To most Dissenters, Quakers, and the Evangelical section of the Church, theatre-going was still a reprehensible pastime. They found a congenial and innocuous substitute in attending lectures, of which there was a fair choice during the winter season. Not all the audience would be in these puritanical categories, of course, but enough of them would be to require the lecturer to be chary of giving offence. To these institutions we owe much of Hazlitt's literary criticism. It must, however, have been an arduous way of earning money – there was no comparison with the grandiose returns for such activities that the United States was soon to offer.

Gentlemen and Writers

The caste privileges which attached to the most minor degree of nobility in the still feudal European states had been effectively eliminated in the Civil War. However, wealth and social status still perpetuated gradations, which were obstacles, if not insuperable ones, to the intercourse of the classes. These centred in the aristocracy and the bishops (themselves mostly from titled families), and were enforced by their *de facto* position on the local bench of magistrates. That is why the democratic constitution of America, then in its pristine innocence, made such an appeal to the middle class and the intellectuals. America was a promise to the politically conscious Englishman in the 1790s as to the Pole and the Russian a century later. Witness Blake's poem *America* or the hero of Robert Bage's *Hermsprong*. Godwin's *Caleb Williams* and the novels and plays of Thomas Holcroft are also critical of the survival here of feudal attitudes. There was not, then, a perfectly free commingling of social groups, which was significant for the middle-class writer, since his profession was not in itself a passport to gentility. Indeed, Francis Jeffrey had to insist that the gentlemen who contributed to his *Edinburgh Review* should not refuse payment. And Sir Joseph Banks, deploring the irascible character of a botanist whose professional career he had advanced, comments: 'Had he been a gentleman he would have been shot long ago in a duel.'

Failing the tradition of the literary *salon* (with the exception of the Holland House hospitality and banker-poet Samuel Rogers's literary breakfasts), writers tended to gravitate towards their economic nodes, a publisher and/or a review. A publisher's shop and his regular or occasional dinner-parties were the usual ground where acquaintances were formed and relations established. Naturally, these gatherings took on a political coloration from the prevailing divisions. Thus at Joseph Johnson's in the early 1790s there could have been assembled William Godwin, Thomas Paine, Mary Wollstonecraft, William Blake, and even young William Wordsworth, for this publisher was responsive to the blowing wind of innovation. Twenty years later, when the rising publisher John Murray moved west to Albemarle Street, his afternoon drawing-rooms would be crowded with the aristocracy of fashion and literature. There might be gathered together four of the most lauded and best rewarded poets of all time, Scott and Byron, Campbell and Moore. 'You offer 1,500 guineas for the new canto [of *Don Juan*]. I won't take it. I ask 2,500 guineas for it, which you will either give or not, as you think proper. If Mr Moore is to have 3,000 for "Lalla" [Rookh] &c., if Mr Crabbe is to have 3,000 for his prose or poetry, I ask the aforesaid price for mine.' Byron had his way, and it is figures such as these which led other poets to hope that they might through their poetry achieve a reasonable independence. Such were John Keats and John Clare. But soon after this the bottom dropped out of the poetry market.

Apart from Murray's glittering circle and the meteoric Shelley, our writers had their origin in one of the innumerable gradations of the middle class. Sneered at by Mr Blackwood's character-assassins as the Cockney School (though they were no School) they were certainly at home in London. Even the Lakers had close ties with their metropolitan colleagues. The homogeneity, in the social sphere, of such diverse talents and personalities is remarkable, when we consider that over some thirty years everyone who had written anything of note might have been met with at William Godwin's house or at Lamb's Wednesdays (imperishably described in Hazlitt's *On the Conversation of Authors*). The only front-rank absentees that come to mind are Jane Austen and Walter Scott. Henry Crabb Robinson, a barrister of literary tastes, has left in his diaries a remarkably vivid and intimate picture of the day-to-day intercourse amongst the intellectuals.[15] One is particularly aware of the frequency of their domestic hospitality and the easiness of their relations, decorum without starchiness. They also associated, though with less easiness, with those of a higher social grade, who, without being patrons in the eighteenth-century sense, could yet give a valuable assistance, directly or indirectly, through political influence. Snobbery, of course, was a powerful segregator, but its vagaries were a source of comedy – tragic only to the social climber.

Jane Austen's novels draw much of their motivation from a subtle playing on the gradations of status amongst the nobility and gentry. In *Emma* (published 1816) the differentiation of social position is carried further. For instance, Emma considers that a tenant farmer is quite beneath consideration as husband for her pretty protégée. And there is the superb delineation of Mrs Elton, prophetically ruffled at the encroachment on her genteel preserves of the new type of self-enriched industrialist:

'I have quite a horror of upstarts [Mrs Elton proclaims]. Maple Grove has given me a thorough disgust to people of that sort ... People of the name of Tupman, very lately settled there, and encumbered with many low connexions, but giving themselves immense airs, and expecting to be on a footing with the old established families ... They came from Birmingham, which is not a place to promise much, Mr Weston. One has not great hopes from Birmingham. I always say there is something direful in the sound; but nothing more is positively known of the Tupmans, though a good many things, I assure you, are suspected.'

The innuendo is that Mr Tupman had started life as a tradesman, a small master, and progressed from grimy Birmingham to the fringe of gentility by his own exertions. Birmingham was the centre of the light-metal and trinket industry and shared in the stimulus to trade given by the wartime demand. Competition between these small masters was intense; success required ability, luck, and a hard heart.

Mr Tupman has his place here as showing the early emergence from the new conditions of a type soon to become familiar, the brash, self-opinionated, uncultivated manufacturer whose philistinism looms ominously over the literature and art of the Victorian age.

Epilogue

In 1830, the July Revolution in France undid the work which for twenty years had cost Europe an unparalleled expenditure of lives and wealth. Charles X, whose Bourbon blood had qualified him to restore the principle of 'legitimacy', was unceremoniously deposed. Waterloo was nullified on the barricades of Paris.

Though here it did not come to a show-down, the achievement of the French middle class greatly stimulated the movement for Parliamentary Reform. Ruling circles did not all sympathize with the obduracy of the Duke of Wellington in refusing to countenance any suggestion of any reform at all. And there were many in both parties who thought that the rotten boroughs should be done away with and representation given to the large towns which lacked it. These measures and the enfranchisement of the ten-pound-a-year householder (a middle-class qualification), were all that was eventually pushed through Parliament, with the backing of the greatest mobilization of public opinion that had ever been undertaken.

In 1830, the people generally were willing to believe that Reform would improve their sorry conditions of work and wages; but at the same time many were looking to other, extra-parliamentary, means of bettering their lot. Robert Owen's successful New Lanark community and his advocacy of the replacement of competition by co-operation was beginning to influence opinion. In 1827, one of his supporters, William Thompson, challenged the accepted political economy of Malthus and Ricardo and sought to prove that the so-called 'iron laws', which kept the masses poor, were merely a symptom of the capitalist system of production for profit.[16] A couple of years later, Owen's ideas were reflected in the precursor of many socialistic romances, John Minter Morgan's *The Revolt of the Bees*.

In 1824 the temporary repeal of the Anti-Combination laws encouraged the growth of trades unionism. The association for economic purposes was soon expanded to include political aims as well, and out of this tendency Chartism was to develop. In 1830 Henry Hetherington was preparing to launch the first working-class newspaper in defiance of the law requiring the payment of Stamp Duty. In this perspective of democratization from below, the enfranchisement of the ten-pound householder does not appear to have a shattering significance.

These were some of the effects of the ferment into which the Romantics had been born. If the closing years of the period are barren of major works, it may be due not at all to any slackening of impulse but to the mere combination of accidents responsible for the death of three major poets in three years. For with only the normal expectation of life, Byron, Shelley, and Keats should all have been writing vigorously well after the accession of Queen Victoria in 1837, when none would have yet been fifty years old. Their loss is not compensated by the longevity of the generation senior to them, whose creative powers were now flagging. Blake, it is true, retained his genius to the last, but it was expressed in design not poetry. Cobbett's virile prose was as alive as ever when he denounced the crushing of the helpless labourers. There is the wry humour of the picaresque in J. J. Morier's *Adventures of Hajji Barba* (1824); a vein of authentic poetry in Thomas Hood's *The Plea of the Midsummer Fairies* (1827); but these, with some other talents, do not amount to a succession. This dramatic period, in which such a rich, vital, and various literature was created draws to a close in a muted mood, on a note of expectancy. There was wide awareness that a new world had come into being, and boldly and ruthlessly, with much optimism and little forethought, men set about the exploitation of its vast potentialities.

NOTES

1. 'It has been proved by me, but, which is better for us, it has been expressly acknowledged by Mr *Preston*, who is a lawyer of great eminence, the owner of a large estate in Devonshire, and a Member of Parliament for a *Borough*, that the labourer who earns 18 pounds a year, pays 10 pounds of it in taxes. I have before observed, but I cannot repeat it too often, that you pay a tax on your shoes, soap, candles, salt, sugar, coffee, malt, beer, bricks, tiles, tobacco, drugs, spirits, and, indeed, on almost all that you use in any

way whatever. And, it is a monstrous cheat in the corrupt writers to attempt to persuade you, that *you* pay *no taxes*, and, upon that ground to pretend, that you have no right to vote for Members of Parliament.' Cobbett, *Political Register* (1816). Quoted by Cole: *The Opinions of William Cobbett.*

2. *Letters of William Wordsworth*, selected by P. Wayne (London, 1954), 149.

3. *Instructions for Travellers.*

4. Meteyard, *Life of Josiah Wedgwood* (1866).

5. *Dialect of South Lancashire*, or *Tim Bobbin's Tummus and Meary* (Manchester, 1850).

6. *A Memoir of Thomas Bewick*, written by Himself (1866).

7. One rotten borough, Old Sarum, which returned two members to Parliament, was entirely uninhabited, and it was popularly alleged that the franchise was exercised by its thorn bushes. A substantial proportion of seats in the House of Commons was filled by the nominees of peers. Thus Robert Southey found himself a Member of Parliament without having known that he was a candidate – Lord Radnor, approving of views he had expressed unfavourable to Catholic Emancipation, put him into one of the family seats. *Letters of Robert Southey*, a selection by M. H. Fitzgerald (London, 1912), 409ff.

8. See A. Aspinall, *Politics and the Press c. 1780–1850* (London, 1949).

9. See W. H. Wickwar, *The Struggle for the Freedom of the Press 1819–32* (London, 1928).

10. See Cole: *The Opinions of William Cobbett* (n. 1 above).

11. R. M. Wiles, *Serial Publication in England before 1750* (1957).

12. Fanny Burney, however, was to receive £1,500 for the first edition of *The Wanderer*, £500 for the second, and £250 for subsequent editions.

13. Now most ably factualized. See Blakey, *The Minerva Press* (1939), to which I am indebted for the information given here.

14. H. A. Eaton (ed.), *A Diary of Thomas De Quincey* (1803). (London, 1927.)

15. E. J. Morley (ed.), *Henry Crabb Robinson on Books and their Writers*, 3 vols (London, 1938).

16. *Labour Defended – the Claims of Labour and Capital Conciliated; or How to Secure to Labour the Whole Products of its Exertions.*

PART II

PART III

THE CHARACTER OF LITERATURE
FROM BLAKE TO BYRON

D. W. HARDING

The distinctive quality of the period in which the Romantics wrote
will be obscured if we allow our view to be taken up too much with
the Romantics themselves. The period is notable not only on their
account but because so much else, strongly contrasting with them,
was going on at the same time; it is remarkable for the diversity of
the outlooks and systems of value that were held together, in spite
of mutual antipathies and revulsions, in a common English culture.

The social life and the literature of a period can be seen as a continuous process of reciprocal sanctioning and challenging – of course
mainly implicit – among the members of a social group. Our every
action, every formulation of opinion or expression of emotion, has
some slight influence on those around us, either to confirm them in
familiar modes of feeling and behaviour or in some degree to question
them. Every culture is concerned to defend its established system of
values, and the extent to which challenges by its individual members
are tolerated or welcomed is always limited. But the limits vary from
one period to another, and the range of permissible behaviour and
opinion, of permissible interest and sentiment, is a vitally important
characteristic of any culture or period. How the limits come to be
defined and what produces contractions and expansions of that range
are questions that have hardly been asked yet, let alone answered.
Outside the limits, deviant behaviour may be dealt with in two main
ways. The familiar one is the use of material penalty and physical
force, a method reserved for what is regarded as intelligible though
not permissible. For what is unintelligible, the judgement of 'abnormal' is available, serving to insulate the deviant behaviour or
opinion, denying it social relevance and excluding it from the net-
work of mutual support and mutual control that makes up society.
A milder form of the same social insulation is provided by the label
'eccentric'. If the range of the intelligible and the permissible is large,

there may at the same time be intense conflict between representatives of diverse permissible viewpoints; mutual antipathy, ridicule, and abuse are evidence that both sides recognize the other as socially relevant, in some sense part of the same culture and within its range of normality, however wrong-headed.

The earlier eighteenth century of Pope, Addison, and Johnson gives the impression of having had a compact area of normality, with a small range of permissible interest and sentiment. The limits of good sense and decency were clear and soon reached. Outside the range of intelligible good sense, such people as Smart and Cowper with their psychotic episodes, and Chatterton with his improbable degree of romanticism, could be almost disregarded. They were not of sufficient serious interest to count in the culture of the time. In the last decade of the eighteenth century and the first quarter of the nineteenth, this compact normality was breaking up, and interests and inclinations that had previously either not appeared or not mattered could no longer be excluded from the social context. The more influential critics might regard the Romantics as silly or wicked, but they had to take serious account of them, for currents of interest had set in which kept open a route between them and the more conventional nucleus of their social group. Equally the Romantics themselves could feel that they had some place in the society of their time, however hostile its chief representatives might be. They and the conventional were closely enough in touch for mutual antagonism; they were not socially irrelevant. From this point of view the period appears not simply as an age of transition in which the values of the Romantics gradually ousted the earlier scale of values, but as a time during which many English people enlarged their outlook to include some understanding of the appeal both of the Romantics and of much that was antagonistic to them.

The earlier period's range of permissible interest and sentiment had been that of the self-controlled reasonable adult, urbane according to the standards of his prosperous contemporaries and accepting their conventional morality. Implicitly it had belittled several areas of human experience and interest, most important among them being the less controlled forms and degrees of emotion; the less conscious parts of experience, beyond justification by the standards of reason; the child's experience; contrasting ways of life, whether of distant peoples or of the poorer social classes, especially in the rural areas; much of the historical past; and the individual questioning and testing of scales of value and moral codes. This is to simplify drastically. But much of the new spirit of the late Georgian period can be understood as a willingness to explore – or to give sanction to others to explore – these neglected possibilities of outlook, interest, and behaviour.

Blake and the New Period

An aspect of the difference in compactness between the norms of the two periods as they appeared in literature may be seen in two statements on the same subject, one by Johnson, one by Blake, sharply contrasting and yet each conveying good sense. They deal with the moral effect on the reader of descriptions of behaviour. Speaking of the influence of novels, Johnson said:

...When an Adventurer is levelled with the rest of the World, and acts in such Scenes of the Universal Drama, as may be the Lot of any other Man; young Spectators fix their Eyes upon him with closer Attention, and hope by observing his Behaviour and Success to regulate their own Practices, when they shall be engaged in a like Part ... If the Power of Example is so great, as to take Possession of the Memory by a Kind of Violence, and produce Effects almost without the Intervention of the Will, Care ought to be taken, that ... the best Examples only should be exhibited.

(*The Rambler* 4)

The same point of view is expressed *ad nauseam* about television today. But now listen to Blake on the examples offered by the Bible:

None can doubt the impression which he receives from a book of Examples. If he is good he will abhor wickedness in David or Abraham; if he is wicked he will make their wickedness an excuse for his & so he would do by any other book.

(Annotations to Bishop Watson's *An Apology for the Bible in a Series of Letters addressed to Thomas Paine*)

Johnson's point of view expresses a broad social truth, that literature affects conduct by the behaviour that it chooses to display as attractive. Blake sees that the effect of literature on an individual mind can be predicted only out of a full knowledge of the tendencies and qualities of that mind. Out of Blake's basic truth we can reach Johnson's position by adding that, after all, individuals have a good many resemblances to each other and enough in common to justify generalizations about broad social influences. But the difference of emphasis and starting-point is characteristic of the change from the one period to the next. The society of those who wrote books and read them became less compact and less susceptible of general description.

Blake is the great exemplar of the individual testing of standards in all directions, revealing the value and the dangers of a consistent refusal to accept the ready-made. The greater part of his writing bears witness to his individual testing of the wisdom, morality, and theology of his time. In the end his convictions were not far removed from what many other people capable of living seriously have believed before and since Blake's time, though he phrased them in forms that were then a violent challenge to conventional habits of thought. He reached his scale of values by an infinitely more strenuous route than most people, and possessed it as a personal achievement. At the same time, the consequence of being too continuously private in one's thinking and idiom of writing is revealed in the laborious obscurity of much of the 'Prophetic Books'.

In other ways, too, besides that of testing the conventional values personally, Blake reveals characteristics of the period that was coming in. He felt the significance of childhood experience; he accepted eagerly the glimpses he gained, sometimes in the form of hallucination, of unconscious process; he turned away from his contemporary culture's dependence on the classical past to his own version of history and pre-history in order to draw on the dynamic resources of what seemed early and primitive; he valued strong emotion, notably anger, as the tool or weapon of a healthy mind.

Coming at the beginning of a new period, Blake was to a great extent isolated, and only very precariously in the social context at all. In the later years of the period, the narrow compactness of the earlier 'normality' gave way increasingly, and it was possible to make excursions outwards from the established bases of thought and feeling without incurring, or needing, as much social isolation as Blake.

The Non-Rational in Literature

As the period went on there was further use of fantasy as a means of giving expression, with some degree of control, to emotional experience not sanctioned by the conventional good sense of the previous age, and perhaps not strictly accountable to reason. As with all the trends of the time, precursory movements had appeared, in such forms as the Gothick of Walpole and the fantasy-macabre of Fuseli's drawings; mysterious danger and sexually-tinged evil were the first features of experience to advance into the foreground out of the unnatural distance at which reason and good principles try to place them. With Coleridge it was subtler states of feeling, including depression and an irrational sense of guilt, that found an outlet in fantasy, supremely in *The Ancient Mariner*. This poem and *Kubla Khan* incorporate in their texture (as Livingstone Lowes has shown) a great deal of material that was organized unconsciously, and they stand at a far remove from any writing that can be simply para-phrased in alternative terms provided by the vocabulary and structure of reasoned thought. The fiction of the supernatural was important because it demonstrated the effectiveness of the non-rational and non-discursive in literature as a vehicle for communicating states of mind and feeling that cannot readily be justified in explicit statement. It was thus easier for Wordsworth, in some ways a more reasoning writer, to take seriously and convey to the reader the impression made by such events as the moon's sudden dropping behind Lucy's cottage, or the mountain's apparent growth in accusing menace against his boyish offence in 'borrowing' a boat. There was an enlargement of the extent of experience that could be taken seriously.

Such an enrichment was the valuable aspect of the cheaper and widespread fascination in what lay beyond reason, including the glimpses revealed by narcotics. *The Concise Cambridge History of English Literature* may possibly be right in saying:

> The prose rigmarole in which Coleridge tells the story of the coming and going of the vision called *Kubla Khan* is a characteristic piece of self-deception. So far from being an opium dream, *Kubla Khan* is the product of one un-expected lucid interval before the fumes closed up once more the expression of the spirit . . .

Whether valid or not, this confident comment misses the significant fact that Coleridge could in this period expect sympathetic interest when he suggested that something of great value had emerged from the dream state induced by a narcotic. De Quincey's *Confessions of an English Opium Eater*, having appeared as articles in *The London Magazine*, were worth collecting and publishing as a book in 1822.

And A. M. Terhune notes in his *Life of Edward FitzGerald* that, in 1831, a Cambridge student could still record: 'Talked with FitzGerald about Opium, Shakespeare, Sir Thomas Browne, and Pictures.' These were signs of the willingness of educated people to pay serious attention to those gleams of mind which had not been directed through the facets cut by reason.

The Insights of Childhood

A willingness to explore the less conscious aspects of feeling and interest was accompanied in the Romantic period (though not necessarily in the same person) by a more serious concern with the experience and insights of childhood than many previous periods would have thought reasonable. Basil Willey makes this point in writing of Coleridge's belief that a fusion of

'the sense of novelty and freshness with old and familiar objects' could be achieved especially by carrying on 'the feelings of childhood into the powers of manhood', by combining 'the child's sense of wonder and novelty with the appearances, which every day for perhaps forty years had rendered familiar'.[1]

An intense conviction of the importance of childhood is seen in Blake, who is also poignantly aware of the terror and hostility of conventional adult society in face of some features of the child's outlook. But the 'child' was for Blake primarily an aspect or possibility of every human personality. Lamb (1775–1834) reflects the growing interest in childhood in a way that keeps nearer, perhaps, to observable children, though being more sentimental. A modern reaction to his characteristic quality appears in the comment by Dyson and Butt:

Like so many of his contemporaries, there is an eternal immaturity about Lamb. None of them made this often irritating quality so rich a source of delight ... He was most at home in his imagination amidst the years when terrors and pleasures alike spring from slight matters and endure long. He reminds us that our childhood is real and is not quite extinguished.[2]

De Quincey (1785–1859), too, put explicitly, if sentimentally, his conviction of the vital and lasting importance of early experience:

The bewildering romance, light tarnished with darkness, the semi-fabulous legend, truth celestial mixed with human falsehoods, these fade even of themselves as life advances. The romance has perished that the young man adored; the legend has gone that deluded the boy; but the deep, deep tragedies of infancy, as when the child's hands were unlinked for ever from his mother's neck, or his lips for ever from his mother's kisses, these remain lurking below all, and these lurk to the last.[3]

In John Clare, who himself notes apologetically that 'childhood is a strong spell over my feelings', the immaturity (or the failure to adopt the conventional manner of maturity) merged with his extraordinarily close and sensitive attention to the wild things, the flowers, and the simpler human pursuits of the countryside he knew. He enjoyed them for themselves rather than for moral or spiritual meanings to be read into them. As a boy and a young man he found them vividly and unquestionably valuable; but he went through the experience, common and distressing in later life, of seeing that their radiant significance had faded. The losses inflicted by the enclosures, bitterly as he lamented them, his acute nostalgia in having to leave his native village, these distresses arising from external change counted for less than his inner loss of a sense that the pleasure he took in natural things was intensely important. *Decay* expresses with simple directness this basic experience – of perceiving the vision splendid 'fade into the light of common day' – out of which Wordsworth elaborates the *Ode: Intimations of Immortality from Recollections of Early Childhood*.

Implied in *The Excursion* and conveyed with more detailed retrospection in *The Prelude*, Wordsworth's theme of the lasting importance of childhood impressions, especially of natural forces, met with sharply opposed judgements from the readership of the period. In the *Quarterly Review*, October 1814, Lamb wrote of *The Excursion*:

If from a familiar observation of the ways of children, and much more from a retrospect of his own mind when a child, he has gathered more reverential notions of that state than fall to the lot of ordinary observers ... his verses shall be censured as infantile by critics who confound poetry 'having children for its subject' with poetry that is 'childish', and who, having themselves, perhaps, never been children, never having possessed the tenderness and docility of that age, know not what the soul of a child is – how apprehensive! how imaginative! how religious!

In contrast here is Jeffrey's (1773–1850) comment on the same poem, in the *Edinburgh Review*, November 1814:

An habitual and general knowledge of the few settled and permanent maxims, which form the canon of general taste in all large and polished societies – a certain tact, which informs us at once that many things, which we still love and are moved by in secret, must necessarily be despised as childish, or derided as absurd, in all such societies – though it will not stand in the place of genius, seems necessary to the success of its exertions . . .[4]

The *Oxford English Dictionary*'s entry for 'childlike', as an adjective referring to the good qualities of childhood, quotes Wesley in 1738 for the first use of the word, and then jumps to Southey, 1825, and to De Quincey, 1840, who makes explicit distinction between the childish and the childlike. It was in this period, too, that a change came over the books published for children: the moral-laden and puritanical stories of such writers as Mrs Trimmer and Mrs Sherwood, with their aim of giving children the staidness and wisdom of adults as soon as possible, gave way to books of the kind published in the first decade of the nineteenth century by John Harris, catering 'for the vast majority of children who just wanted to be amused, without having to pay the penalty of continual reminders to keep their faces clean, their hair tidy, and everything else up to scratch, including their morals'.[5] In this simple and practical way, as well as in serious literature, the claim for the all-sufficiency of rational adult standards was being relinquished.

Conventional Society and the Individual

The significance attributed to childhood by serious authors implied a relatively diminished respect for the later and more public influences by which an individual was shaped to the standard pattern of his group, the influences that Lord Chesterfield, for instance, would have considered decisive. In this respect the concern with childhood was part of a broader tendency to re-emphasize the significance of the individual and the possible validity of individual judgement even when they clashed with conventional opinion. Lamb, whose review already quoted is a compendium of the Romantic outlook, writes:

The causes which have prevented the poetry of Mr Wordsworth from attaining its full share of popularity are to be found in the boldness and originality of his genius. The times are past when a poet could securely follow the direction of his own mind into whatever tracts it might lead. A writer, who would be popular, must timidly coast the shore of prescribed sentiment and sympathy.

The truth was, of course, that Wordsworth's poetry and Lamb's review themselves testified to the increasing vigour of the unconventional at this period. In political philosophy Godwin's (1756–1836) anarchism expressed an extreme form of the individualist viewpoint. In literary criticism the reviews battled to uphold the conviction that established authority, the authority of the group, was a more reliable guide than individual judgement.

Much of the open conflict in the intellectual life of the time centred on the claim of individual people to defy the standards and expectations of conventional society. As commonly happens, literary preferences were entangled in this conflict with political convictions, and the ferocity of the attacks on Keats and Shelley were in part a reaction against the political tendencies of Leigh Hunt (1784–1859) and Godwin. Nor has this association of political and literary outlook proved to be a transient thing peculiar to that age. A century later Courthope, the Professor of Poetry at Oxford, exemplified it again.

Courthope states much the same case against the Romantics as did their contemporary adversaries. John Wilson, reviewing Tennyson's early poems (which were regarded as products of the influence of Keats and Shelley) in *Blackwood's*, May 1832, complained, 'What all the human race see and feel, he seems to think cannot be poetical; he is not aware of the transcendent and eternal grandeur of commonplace and all-time truths, which are the staple of all poetry.'[6] And when *Lamia* was discussed in *The Monthly Review*, July 1820:

> The reviewer found fault with Keats's selection of images as 'according to the tenets of that school of poetry' which held that 'any thing or object in nature' is a fit material on which the poet may work; forgetting that poetry has a nature of its own, and that it is the destruction of its essence to level its high being with the triteness of everyday life.'[7]

Any idea that the attitude of *Blackwood's* was something that the 'Romantic revolution' ousted from English literature is corrected by such passages as the following from Courthope in 1910:

> ... in their theory, as well as in much of their work, Wordsworth and Coleridge departed altogether from traditional practice. They placed the source of poetical inspiration exclusively in the mind of the individual poet, without reference to those active fountains of social feeling, thought, and language, from which the reader as well as the poet had been accustomed to derive his imaginative ideas.

PART TWO

The perennial clash between two fundamentally opposed outlooks is evident. What was to Courthope the tried and tested was to the Romantics the second-hand.

The complexity of the period appears, however, in the impossibility of ranging the writers neatly on either side in the conflict. Byron notably fails to go into one category or the other. Violently antipathetic to the work of Keats and Wordsworth, for instance, he was in many ways far more in harmony with the conventional aristocratic attitudes of his time than with the Romantics, and some of his verse, especially in *Don Juan*, is close to the spirit of *The Anti-Jacobin*. To superficial appearance, at all events, Byron's role of rebel and outcast went against the grain and came to him by accident. But when it came he clearly accepted it as one of the roles, almost one of the theatrical roles, which have their necessary place in a society. *Childe Harold* (especially the opening of Canto Three) gives the impression of a man who realizes that in leaving his country and people and wandering as an outcast, he still performs a function for the society of his time. Writing for it fluently, certain of being bought and read, he gives paradoxically the impression of being much more thoroughly embedded in his society than many of the other poets of the period; and, compared with Shelley's, his conviction of the lonely rebel's place and function is robust and free from narcissism. This came about in part from his being actively involved in the wider movement of rebellion against despotism and established authority throughout Europe; in such broad features of political outlook he was in sympathy with much that the Romantics stood for, just as in moral matters and religion he defied or questioned the conventional views of the time. But he remained highly socialized: he never appeared to be proclaiming individual self-sufficiency of the kind that irritated and still irritates the conservative antagonists of the Romantics.

The Foreign and the Savage

Byron's conviction of having a role in his society was supported by the fact that much of his writing was a reporting back to his own country observations made among other peoples, a form of journalism for which English readers had a keen appetite. The conventional European tour had supplied a different need, educating the traveller

44

(and the readers of his journals and letters) along the lines of an accepted model, confirming the cultural ideals already established in England. In Byron's time the current interest in travel welcomed something more challenging; not only the picturesque and formidable in scenery, but the remote and unfamiliar in custom and social outlook. The less urbane parts of Europe and – for Lady Hester Stanhope – the Near East had the appeal of being strange, unpredictable, and unamenable to polite control. Here again the earlier part of the eighteenth century had established the trend and provided materials, Anson's *Voyages* being evidence of the interest in remoter travel and adventures, and in ways of life not serving to sanction the urban civilization of England and not within the scope of its standards. In Cowper's *Castaway*, and more richly in Coleridge's *Ancient Mariner*, this material is used as a symbol for other modes of human experience in which danger and disaster, adventure and the inexplicable, were very much closer at hand than eighteenth-century rationality had implied.

Admittedly there was not much understanding that distant peoples might have features of culture that could seriously challenge our own. Omai, the Tahitian whom one of Cook's captains brought to London in 1774, was seen as a possible messenger of civilization when he should be returned to his people.[8] The savage, noble or quaint, remained for long a generalized figure, and it was not until the twentieth century that social anthropology tried to show with any particularity the relevance of actual primitive cultures to an understanding and appraisal of Western civilization. Yet the germ of this kind of interest, though embedded in fantasy, was to be found in Rousseau and those whom he influenced.

The Poor and Unlettered

The educated and urbane people of the period around 1800 had a challenge nearer at home in the way of life of the poorer sections of their own nation. The effectiveness of this challenge in political and economic terms is a question for social historians. Cobbett, in hard-hitting, robust prose, gave insistent attention to the economic conditions of working life, especially of the farm labourers. Denouncing the enclosures and the landowners, but little interested in political abstractions, he was moderate and (in view of the facts of the time) realistic in his hopes of reform. Schooling, for instance, was to be a poor second to preparing labourers' children for their working tasks, even if that meant that a few exceptional children must wait for a later opportunity of developing themselves, 'and, if they never have that opportunity, the harm is not very great to us or to them'. The descendants of labourers might become gentlemen, but only after several generations of effort, for 'the path upwards is steep and long'.

For earlier eighteenth-century writers the rural poor might be objects of compassion, and their life valued for simpler virtues lost in the ostentation and insincerities of the city, but they were to be appraised, certainly not learnt from, by a literary culture that emphasized rationally moderate morality, order, and elegance. Yet even people whose taste had been moulded by Augustan standards began to see its limitations. Mrs Chapone, one of the bluestockings, complained:

> It is only from the ignorant that we can now have anything original; every master copies from those that are of established authority, and does not look at the natural object.[9]

For readers who felt this jadedness the appeal of Burns is understandable. The welcome given his work, written from direct contact with the poor and illiterate, is evidence of a readiness to extend the range of cultivated interest to the experience of people in the lower social strata, not out of compassion but for the life that was in them. The welcome, however, was confused, and the conventionally decorous were strongly enough entrenched in Edinburgh to edit away much of the distinctive quality from the collections of Burns's verse that were published in his lifetime. The unhappy history of his life and work, the confusion of values that probably prevented the development of his full range, reflect the contrasts held uneasily together in the literary culture of his time. His poverty and his temperament put him at the mercy of the conflict. Clare was still more vulnerable. The brief public success of his rural poems ('corrected' by his publisher) was followed by a neglect that left him in limbo, without a role in town or country other than that of an amenable patient in a kindly mental asylum.

In this respect, as in so many others, Wordsworth expressed a contemporary trend in a more considered, assimilated form, or a form muted by a reflective mind. Whether what he found in the rural poor was really there hardly matters. What is important is that he and other people of his time were able to believe that a segment of valuable human experience was lost in the sophisticated urban civilization of the prosperous. In his review of *The Excursion*, Lamb puts this point too when he describes the contemporary restrictions placed on the poet:

If from living among simple mountaineers, from a daily intercourse with them, not upon the footing of a patron, but in the character of an equal, he has detected, through the cloudy medium of their unlettered discourse, thought and apprehensions not vulgar; traits of patience and constancy, love unwearied, and heroic endurance, not unfit (as he may judge) to be the subject of verse, he will be deemed a man of perverted genius by the philanthropist who, conceiving of the peasantry of his country only as objects of pecuniary sympathy, starts at finding them elevated to a level of humanity with himself...

Even if the life of villages and farms as Wordsworth presented it was largely fiction, it was a fiction that sustained the exploration of real possibilities of human experience and gave an effective means of defining human values.

Clare and Cobbett had a simpler relation with natural things than Wordsworth's. Poles apart in personality and literary gifts, they both saw the countryside as their own ordinary habitat; it was neither a backdrop of the picturesque nor yet to be yielded to with quasi-religious awe. They were fully aware of its economic realities for farmers and cottagers, but they could also enjoy features of the landscape not shaped for agriculture and take pleasure in plants and animals other than those that served the farmer or the sportsman. In his *Rural Rides* it was only in the Fens that Cobbett found land devoid of 'waste' and totally at the mercy of the farming methods then available: '*Here* the grasping system takes all away, because it has the means of coming at the value of all.' And, again, amid the agricultural richness of Lincolnshire which he greatly appreciated he yet lamented as a deficiency 'the want of *singing birds*' and described with enthusiasm (and accuracy) the birdsong of the southern counties. Clare, even more, lived in affectionate familiarity with the natural things around him.

A more sombre view of rural life appeared in the poems of Crabbe; and the fact that in the spirit and technique of his verse he was much nearer the earlier eighteenth century makes it all the more significant that his readers had enlarged their range of interest to include a presentation in some detail of the form taken by the fundamentals of human experience in the lives of very poor people and of un-educated farmers and tradesmen.

Several of the motifs of the period are brought together in Mary Shelley's (1797–1851) *Frankenstein*, one of those second-rate works, written under the influence of more distinguished minds, that some-times display in conveniently simple form the preoccupations of a coterie. The narrator is on a voyage of discovery to the North Pole:

This expedition has been the favourite dream of my early years ... You may remember that a history of all the voyages made for purposes of dis-covery composed the whole of our good uncle Thomas's library.

And he attributed his passionate enthusiasm for 'the dangerous mysteries of ocean' to the influence of Coleridge's *Ancient Mariner*. The story of Frankenstein is given a background of typically ro-mantic Swiss scenery with melancholy as one of its keynotes:[10]

It is a scene terrifically desolate. In a thousand spots the traces of the winter avalanche may be perceived, where trees lie broken and strewed on the ground; some entirely destroyed, others bent, leaning upon the jutting rocks of the mountains, or transversely upon other trees ... The pines are not tall or luxuriant, but they are sombre, and add an air of severity to the scene. I looked on the valley beneath; vast mists were rising from the rivers which ran through it, and curling in thick wreaths around the opposite mountains, whose summits were hid in the uniform clouds, while rain poured from the dark sky, and added to the melancholy impression I received from the objects around me.

The monster whom Frankenstein creates is a variant of the noble savage. He does evil only in response to the social injustice he suffers. After rescuing a girl from drowning, he is shot by a terrified country-man:

This then was the reward of my benevolence! ... The feelings of kindness and gentleness which I had entertained but a few moments before gave way to a hellish rage and gnashing of teeth. Inflamed by pain, I vowed eternal hatred and vengeance to all mankind.

The benevolence of the individual so long as he is unharmed by contact with social injustice is one of the axioms of the book. The monster wants love, but finds himself unjustly repelled because he is hideous. The repulsed love turns to hate and destructiveness; and the longing for communion with his creator, denied because of the monster's wicked deeds, becomes a determination to harry him perpetually until both are annihilated.

> Everywhere I see bliss, from which I alone am irrevocably excluded. I was benevolent and good; misery made me a fiend. Make me happy and I shall again be virtuous ... Believe me, Frankenstein: I was benevolent, my soul glowed with love and humanity: but am I not alone, miserably alone?

It is not difficult to see among these characteristics of the monster some aspects of the Byronic role; and Byron of course was one of the party of friends who encouraged Mary Shelley to write the story.

Social injustice is the other side of the picture. The monster watches an idealized version of the simple life in rural surroundings, lived by a cultivated family who had once been affluent but were ruined by their defiance of the government in rescuing from prison a Turkish merchant, condemned only because of the greed and religious prejudice of the authorities. Once ruined, they were despised and abandoned by the merchant, himself equally prejudiced and materialistic. The hostility of the merchant classes to things of the mind is displayed again in the father of Frankenstein's friend, Clerval, who longs to study at a university:

> His father was a narrow-minded trader, and saw idleness and ruin in the aspirations and ambitions of his son,

who was, none the less, resolved 'not to be chained to the miserable details of commerce'. Naturally, too, in a book by Godwin's daughter, the iniquity of class differences is emphasized:

> 'I learned', said the monster, 'that the possessions most esteemed by your fellow-creatures were high and unsullied descent united with riches. A man might be respected with only one of these advantages; but, without either, he was considered, except in very rare instances, as a vagabond and a slave, doomed to waste his powers for the profits of the chosen few!'

And again:

> The republican institutions of our country [Switzerland] have produced
> simpler and happier manners than those which prevail in the great monarchies
> that surround it. Hence there is less distinction between the several classes of its
> inhabitants; and the lower orders, being neither so poor nor so despised, their
> manners are more refined and moral. A servant in Geneva does not mean the
> same thing as a servant in France and England ... does not include the idea of
> ignorance, and a sacrifice of the dignity of a human being.

History and Imaginative Reconstruction

The refusal to restrict cultivated interest to the prosperous strata of
civilized Europe was at this time paralleled by a reaching out of sympathetic and appreciative interest into periods of history contrasting
sharply with the eighteenth century. Once again an earlier fashion,
the medievalism of Walpole (1717–97) and other writers, had introduced an interest that the later period assimilated more seriously.
The assimilation consisted partly in a reaction against the early extrava-
gances of fantasy, a reaction to be seen in one form in Jane Austen's
Northanger Abbey. More positively it involved efforts of revival like
Percy's (1729–1811) *Reliques*, and most notably, the serious effort of
imaginative reconstruction seen in Scott's novels. A modern historian
has assessed the importance for the writing of history of the development that occurred at this time:

> ... if the Romantic movement went too far and led to aberrations – led, for
> example, to visions of a medieval world that could never have had any exist-
> ence – one must not imagine that the mental exercises that were involved in
> the romantic endeavour were without their significance in the development
> of historical study ...
>
> It was said of Scott that 'He had something like a personal experience of
> several centuries'. He so soaked himself in the Covenanters that he did not need
> to remember things about them – he could think their way and feel what they
> would do or say in various kinds of situations ... Even if nobody ever reads
> him any more he will remain significant in the history of historical science
> not for the light which he throws on any age of history, but because he re-
> vealed so much concerning those operations which are possible to students of
> the past for the achievement of historical-mindedness.[11]

The Expression of Emotion

The importance for general literature of this imaginative effort, as
of all the other enlargements of interest, lay in its effect on the sentiments and emotional life of the time. The extended range of respons-

iveness made it difficult to maintain the earlier ideal of narrowly reasoned control in emotional life. The passage already quoted from De Quincey illustrates, in extreme form, the freedom of emotional expression which could by this time find a place in the mental life of literate people. A great change is evident here since the time of Johnson and the uneasy truce he kept with emotions. Mrs Thrale reports 'he always said he hated a *Feeler*', and in a letter of 8 November 1779, he wrote:

> You shall not hide Mrs [Byron] from me. For if she be a feeler, I can bear a feeler as well as you; and hope, that in tenderness for what she feels from nature, I am able to forgive or neglect what she feels by affectation.[12]

Disapproving embarrassment at unrestrained emotion by no means disappeared, any more than it has since, but its secure authority as the only civilized response was broken. Keats's letters, even more than the best of his poetry, show what free emotional expression was then possible in private to a young man, even one with eager claims to literary education.

The embarrassment felt about emotion is often connected with the seeming simplicity and ordinariness of the events that arouse strong feelings; they are often events (such as partings, reunions, sudden sights of natural beauty, examples of injustice, scenes of suffering) for which everyday conventions provide alternative responses that soft-pedal the emotion. The clichés and customary reactions are useful and partly adequate, but if nothing else is permitted the result is a gradual desiccation of life. There was a feeling after the Augustan period that the emotional side of life was getting lost. Blake, of course, saw it clearly:

> Men are admitted into Heaven not because they have curbed and govern'd their Passions or have No Passions, but because they have Cultivated their Understandings. The Treasures of Heaven are not Negations of Passion, but Realities of Intellect, from which all the Passions Emanate Uncurbed in their Eternal Glory.
>
> (*A Vision of the Last Judgement*)

Burns's willingness to express spontaneous warmth of feeling about ordinary events was another way out of the desiccation.

It is understandable that this way out was not acceptable to everyone; it was only too easy, after such a drilling as the Augustan age prescribed, to regard intense emotion about ordinary events as still being out of the question, even though one wanted to feel intensely about something. So we have Mrs Montagu, another bluestocking, saying that Pope, much as she admired him, was lacking in

that something which makes a poet divine, that lifts him 'above the visible, diurnal sphere', that gives him visions of worlds unknown, makes him sing like a seraphim, tune his harp to the musick of the spheres, and raise enchantments round him.[13]

The admirers of Shelley in the Edwardian and later Victorian periods would have seen him as typically the poet to fill the want that Mrs Montagu felt. In the twentieth century the revulsion against his work between the first and second German wars drew attention to the nebulousness of the experiences around which his emotions gathered. The adverse view of his work amounts largely to the suggestion that he put the cart before the horse, by aiming first at a state of emotional responsiveness and then finding something that would nearly enough justify it, whether something of direct experience or some product of intellectual elaboration. It seems possible, however, that the obscure relations between feeling and other parts of mental life are not yet fully enough understood to allow of a thoroughly adequate account of Shelley. It is at any rate clear that he offered his period something that sympathetic readers could regard as an escape from the prosaic belittlement of life by good sense and sound principles.

Confidence in a very simple idea of reason and its power to regulate the rest of the personality had encouraged the sharp divorce of the insane from ordinary people, typified by the Londoners' entertainment of going to watch the Bedlamites. In the later eighteenth century, however, the sort of kindness, rather patronizing, with which Samuel Johnson had spoken about Christopher Smart's madness had developed into a more widespread humaneness in caring for the insane, partly as a result of George III's spells of madness.[14] Among writers, John Clare in Northampton Asylum, and Charles Lamb's sister Mary in a small mental home, could hardly have had gentler and more considerate treatment, given their condition and the medical resources of the time.

It is true that in some quarters the older ideals of strict rationality and the control of emotion within the bounds approved by reason were still confidently expounded. They guided the vigorous writing of *The Anti-Jacobin*, the journal in which political conservatism allied itself with the older standards of literary good sense and decorum in attacking revolutionaries and Romantics. Both in political thought and (with *Blackwood's* and *The Quarterly Review*) in literary criticism, the writers of *The Anti-Jacobin* felt a profound mistrust for individual judgement that disregarded or defied the segments of tradition enshrined in contemporary orthodoxy. Godwin was one of *The Anti-Jacobin*'s chief targets; his anarchism invested heavily in the notion of the individual who could do without external authority, and because of his influence on the romantic poets he remains a figure of interest in connection with the political and literary tensions of the time.[15]

Rousseau and his disciples were almost equally good targets, with their over-developed emotionalism, their claim to individual self-sufficiency by which the effects of social ridicule could be nullified, and their conviction of finding in Nature the sanction Society denied. *The Anti-Jacobin*'s satire on Sensibility, from which Courthope quotes with understandable satisfaction, glances at all these characteristics:

> Sweet child of sickly Fancy! – her of yore
> From her loved France Rousseau to exile bore;
> And, while midst lakes and mountains wild he ran,
> Full of himself, and shunned the haunts of man,
> Taught her, o'er each lone vale and Alpine steep,
> To lisp the story of his wrongs, and weep ...

But the contrasting attitude to wild natural scenes and the emotions they support is to be found in – once more – Lamb's review of *The Excursion*:

If he has the fortune to be bred in the midst of the most magnificent objects of creation ... he must conceal his love, or not carry his expressions of it beyond that point of rapture, which the occasional tourist thinks it not overstepping decorum to betray, or the limit which that gentlemanly spy upon Nature, the picturesque traveller, has vouchsafed to countenance. He must do this, or be content to be thought an enthusiast.

It is the highly explicit tensions, the vigorous development of contrasting values within a common culture and in continuing contact with each other, that make the period so noteworthy, and one of the chief tensions was between conflicting attitudes to emotion and the expression of sentiment. The one valued calm and the seeming security achieved by checking and regulating emotional expression, the other valued the heightened sense of living brought about by a free and even exaggerated expression of emotion. In the period around 1800 the range of permissible values in English culture included the two extremes; exponents of either might deride or abhor the other, but each had its place in the culture of the time and, though attacked, could not be ignored.

Jane Austen and Moral Judgement

Behind, and much more important than, the public polemics, lay the private tension felt by cultivated people between the two contrasting outlooks on emotion. It is given admirable expression by Jane Austen in *Sense and Sensibility*, where the two devoted sisters represent contrasting points of view. Jane Austen (who admired Crabbe to the point of saying that she would have been willing to marry him) undoubtedly comes down in favour of Apollonian sense, but she is able to see its limitations and to show sympathy and understanding for some part of the 'sensibility' of Marianne; it seems likely, of course, that the sisters represented contrasting aspects of herself and probably of other people of her time. She can ridicule the excesses of sensibility without doubting the genuineness of the personality traits that lead to it and without losing sympathy with the person whose emotional life is organized in this way. It is perhaps in the complex attitudes of Jane Austen, whose control may tempt us to overlook her intense vitality, that the gradual change of outlook among people who were neither revolutionary nor defensively reactionary can best be seen. She remained fully committed to the good sense and moral principles of the previous generation but she lightened its ponderousness and checked its moral and sentimental generalities against her own direct observation and spontaneous feeling.

It is characteristic of her work that its extraordinarily amusing, entertaining quality is fused intimately with moral seriousness (which rarely lapses into moralizing), and that she has the manner of assuming the same seriousness in her readers. It has, strangely, been possible for readers and critics in the past to overlook this quality, and to discuss her work as if it offered no more than delicately entertaining studies of the surface of polite society and its trivial doings amidst the costumes and architecture of advertisers' Regency. One of the more fatuous of several standard misunderstandings is the complaint that she shows no interest in the great social events of the time – by which is meant the Napoleonic Wars. Apart from the doubt whether these national cataclysms are the important social events, the suggestion itself is inaccurate, for Jane Austen's work in fact gives a convincing impression of the impact of public events on the ordinary lives of middle-class people of the time. There are the militia and the camps, with their effects on the local girls, in *Pride and Prejudice*; the regular Army as a career in *Pride and Prejudice* and *Emma*; still more the Navy as a career, in *Mansfield Park* and *Persuasion*, with the use of influential acquaintance to get the midshipman promoted, young men making their fortunes from prizes, 'this peace' turning them ashore, the hope of another war to bring further promotion and prize-money, their disablement from wounds, the life of their wives and families waiting for them or accompanying them, and the jealousy of established families at the sudden social ascent of successful officers. Nor are the wars the only great social events to be reflected in their natural contemporary light. The importance of West Indian estates to English incomes has its ordinary unemphasized place, in *Mansfield Park* and *Persuasion*, together with the hazards of the journey when the Antigua estate has to be visited. The abolition of slavery echoes in a form that reveals exquisitely the readjusted social attitudes it produced, when Mrs Elton(whose brother-in-law Mr Suckling has his fortune from Bristol) shows her over-sensitiveness on the subject by seeing a reference where none was made and replying '... if you mean a fling at the slave trade, I assure you Mr Suckling was always rather a friend to the abolition'. And a pervasive influence in *Mansfield Park*, mentioned explicitly only once (in Mary Crawford's sneer), is the challenge of Methodism to the serious people among the clergy of the Established Church.

Yet these direct references to contemporary conditions and events are a small part of Jane Austen's claim to a fundamentally serious concern with society. More important is her constant preoccupation with the moral basis of social relations, and the implicit judgement she passes on the social context of the experiences she shaped into entertainment.

Despite her manner of expecting from her readers a moral outlook and social good taste to match her own, she was far from feeling herself comfortably embedded in a society whose standards were acceptable to her. It is true that her novels were highly successful (and enjoyed by the Prince Regent among others) and that she lived an affectionate life with her family. But her work reveals, sometimes explicitly, sometimes more subtly, how little she supposed the greater part of her social world to live up to her standards of moral taste and cultivated intelligence. The possibility of holding a low opinion of people to whom one is bound by affection is stated in *Pride and Prejudice* as if it were commonplace – in one of those scarcely noticed sentences of devastating implication which Jane Austen camouflages amidst more ordinarily acceptable or light-hearted remarks. Elizabeth is talking, half laughingly but with fundamental seriousness, to her sister Jane, who tries to think well of everybody: 'Do not be afraid of my running into any excess, of my encroaching on your privilege of universal goodwill. You need not. There are few people whom I really love, and still fewer of whom I think well.' A conflict of values between the heroine and her close associates, a conflict muted and generally known only to the heroine herself, is an intrinsic part of most of the novels, and because the heroine is also attached with genuine affection to those around her the tension is an inner one.

Romantic love gave Jane Austen a focus where individual values could achieve high definition, usually in conflict with the social code that condoned marriages for money and social standing. Such marriages were not just romantically distasteful, they were morally repugnant to Jane Austen. *Persuasion*, in some ways the most gravely reflective of the novels, deliberately states the obligation to treat love as the only allowable basis of marriage. The moral issue is summed up in Anne Elliot's discussion with her lover, to whom she has been reunited after the years that were lost to them when she gave in to the prudent persuasions of middle age and broke off her engagement. He tells her how afraid he had been that she might be persuaded into marrying her wealthy and highly eligible cousin by the same devoted godmother who had persuaded her to break her first engagement.

'You should have distinguished,' replied Anne. 'You should not have suspected me now; the case so different, and my age so different. If I was wrong in yielding to persuasion once, remember that it was to persuasion exerted on the side of safety, not of risk. When I yielded, I thought it was to duty; but no duty could be called in aid here. In marrying a man indifferent to me, all risk would have been incurred, and all duty violated.'

More lightly and ironically the same view is implied in *Mansfield Park* when the fashionably brought up Mary Crawford describes the situation of one of her smart friends:

'. . . I look upon the Frasers to be about as unhappy as most other married people. And yet it was a most desirable match for Janet at the time. We were all delighted. She could not do otherwise than accept him, for he was rich, and she had nothing . . . Poor Janet has been sadly taken in; and yet there was nothing improper on her side; she did not run into the match inconsiderately, there was no want of foresight. She took three days to consider of his proposals; and during those three days asked the advice of everybody connected with her, whose opinion was worth having; and especially applied to my late dear aunt, whose knowledge of the world made her judgement very generally and deservedly looked up to by all the young people of her acquaintance; and she was decidedly in favour of Mr Fraser.'

The necessity to continue in amicable relations with one's associates in spite of holding essentially different standards is shown again and again in Jane Austen's work. For the heroine, it is true, the moral obligation to resist a loveless marriage may lead to actual conflict with her family, most notably in *Mansfield Park*. But equally the heroine must make the best of the fact that those to whom she is greatly attached may have no such standards. In *Pride and Prejudice* Elizabeth reflects on her friend Charlotte's marriage to Mr Collins solely in order to have an establishment of her own:

She had always felt that Charlotte's opinion of matrimony was not exactly like her own, but she could not have supposed it possible that, when called into action, she would have sacrificed every better feeling to worldly advantage.

But she retained this friend ('a friend disgracing herself and sunk in her esteem'), and came to feel a sort of respect for the self-control with which Charlotte tolerated her impossible husband and his patroness.

Although loyalty to the ideal of love between individuals was central to Jane Austen's social morality, she was reticent about their sexual attraction, taking it for granted as part of the total pattern of romantic love without giving it special emphasis. But she was far from being prudish or prim. Her cheerfully matter-of-fact attitude to childbirth, flippant once or twice in her letters, still shocks spinster minds, male and female. But bearing children was an everyday fact of social life, and she treated it without sentimentality or smirking, though well aware of the more usual quality of the gossip it provided; she refers, for instance, to '... the situation of Mrs Weston, whose happiness it was to be hoped might eventually be as much increased by the arrival of a child, as that of all her neighbours was by the approach of it'.

The novels make a similarly straightforward and entirely unprudish acknowledgement of loose sexual behaviour as an ordinary though deplorable human fact. Illegitimacy features in a matter-of-fact way in *Sense and Sensibility* and *Emma*; seduction and attempted seduction in *Sense and Sensibility* and *Pride and Prejudice* (with a duel fought on account of it in one and threatened in the other); adultery in *Mansfield Park*, and the open keeping of a mistress in *Mansfield Park* and *Persuasion*; and these things, though condemned, are taken as familiar, regrettable facts and never treated with a hush and a blush. Nor are the men and women who are guilty of them presented as monsters; most of them are well-bred, attractive members of polite society, with good qualities marred through faulty upbringing or mercenary marriage.

Her treatment of sexual attraction is in line with her general view that strong impulses and intensely emotional states should be regulated and controlled. *Sense and Sensibility*, of course, provides the simplest illustrations of the need for control and the refusal (on Marianne's part) to exert it. 'This violent oppression of spirits continued the whole evening. She was without any power, because she was without any desire of command over herself.' The control that Jane Austen respected was not to be exercised in favour of some abstract standard of 'reason', but in consideration for one's immediate companions. It fulfilled a social obligation, as Marianne shows in her self-reproaches after she has recovered from her serious illness, and as Mr Knightley implies when, sympathizing with what he supposes Emma to feel at the loss of Mr Frank Churchill, he says: 'Time, my dearest Emma, time will heal the wound. – Your own excellent sense – your exertions for your father's sake –...' And again in *Pride and Prejudice*, concern for the effect of one's emotions on others ranks equal with good sense as a means of control:

Having never fancied herself in love before, her regard had all the warmth of first attachment, and from her age and disposition, greater steadiness than first attachments often boast; and so fervently did she value his remembrance, and prefer him to every other man, that all her good sense, and all her attention to the feelings of her friends, were requisite to check the indulgence of those regrets which must have been injurious to her own health and their tranquillity.

Tumultuous experiences of any sort, joyful or disagreeable, have to be brought to order by private reflection until one is fit for society again, and the heroine's 'reflection' in her own room after a crisis or a climax is a usual feature of the novels. The importance of understanding and coming to terms with one's private feelings is never doubted; when that has been done, the heroine returns and takes her ordinary part in the commonplace of social intercourse. The separation of important private feelings from the routine of social behaviour, even amidst the family and its close associates, not only safeguards the comfort of others but allows the heroine's personal judgement to establish itself and secures her own moral autonomy. Moral autonomy is a striking feature of Jane Austen's heroines; although she never fails to pay tribute to the vital importance of sound upbringing and the early inculcation of good principles, yet her heroines are always required to make sounder judgements than those around them (including their parents) or like Emma, to correct their errors through their own experience and not through submission to the advice of others.

She makes this autonomy and judgement possible, in spite of the close pressure of society, by imagining for her heroines a social context in which indifference, impercipience, or considerate reticence allow their feelings on important matters to be very little known even to their near associates. Closely as the sisters of *Sense and Sensibility* and of *Pride and Prejudice* are attached to each other, great reticence is maintained between them. And when the Gardiners, Elizabeth Bennet's civilized uncle and aunt, observe with astonishment Darcy's attentions to her, she hurries away 'fearful of enquiries or hints':

But she had no reason to fear Mr and Mrs Gardiner's curiosity; it was not their wish to force her communication. It was evident that she was much better acquainted with Mr Darcy than they had before any idea of; it was evident that he was very much in love with her. They saw much to interest, but nothing to justify enquiry.

This is the positive ideal that she sets over against the prying intrusions of Mrs Jennings in *Sense and Sensibility*. And in *Persuasion* Anne and Lady Russell, in spite of their intimate and affectionate relation, have never in seven years alluded to the broken engagement, and Lady Russell has no knowledge of what Anne may feel about her former lover. Jane Austen was here no doubt exaggerating and idealizing current conventions of her society. The effect was to make possible for her heroines a striking degree of private judgement (and often condemnation) of conventional values while still preserving outward amenability.

Not only do her heroines maintain the forms of politeness to those they dislike, as Emma so scrupulously does with Mrs Elton, but they may be detached even from their close friends by private reservations and concealments. Emma, for example, finds that her party to Box Hill is to be spoilt by the inclusion of the intolerable Mrs Elton at the invitation of Emma's thoroughly amiable friend Mr Weston, who hopes she has no objection:

> Now, as her objection was nothing but her very great dislike of Mrs Elton, of which Mr Weston must already be perfectly aware, it was not worth bringing forward again: – it could not be done without a reproof to him, which would be giving pain to his wife; and she found herself therefore obliged to consent to an arrangement which she would have done a great deal to avoid; an arrangement which would probably expose her even to the degradation of being said to be of Mrs Elton's party! Every feeling was offended; and the forbearance of her outward submission left a heavy arrear due of secret severity in her reflections on the unmanageable goodwill of Mr Weston's temper.
>
> 'I am glad you approve of what I have done,' said he very comfortably. 'But I thought you would. Such schemes as these are nothing without numbers. One cannot have too large a party. A large party secures its own amusement. And she is a good-natured woman after all. One could not leave her out.'
>
> Emma denied none of it aloud, and agreed to none of it in private.

This kind of tension between the woman of genuine good taste and moral fastidiousness and even those to whom she is sincerely attached is characteristic of Jane Austen's work. *Emma*, which shows polite concealment carried very far, also shows the dilemma it creates for those who value sincerity but know that a frank definition of their own values would seem a slight or a reproof to many of their friends. When Frank Churchill professes to be 'the wretchedest being in the world at a civil falsehood', ' "I do not believe any such thing," replied Emma. "I am persuaded that you can be as insincere as your neighbours, when it is necessary ..."' And the full significance of the exchange depends on the fact that Frank Churchill is at this very time occupied in acting out with the utmost skill a serious falsehood by which Emma herself is being thoroughly taken in. So, too, there is an ironic contrast between Emma's own readiness for keeping her opinions to herself and her great dislike of Jane Fairfax's 'reserve'; it is Emma, so skilled in holding her tongue, who exclaims to Jane, when the disclosure of the secret engagement makes reserve no longer necessary, 'Thank you, thank you. – This is just what I wanted to be assured of. Oh! if you knew how much I love everything that is decided and open!' Early in the book she supposes that after his marriage Mr Elton has made Harriet's ill-starred infatuation for him 'a sacrifice to conjugal unreserve'. But at the end of the book Emma looks forward with relief to Harriet's marriage with her farmer so that she herself can at last give up the reserve she has had to maintain with her own husband-to-be about Harriet's affairs. The inconsistencies, whether or not intended as deliberate ironies by Jane Austen, point to the dilemma of a subtle and sensitive woman who had to come to terms with the moral and intellectual mediocrity of a society on which she was dependent and of friends and relations with whom she had the closest and most affectionate ties. The detachment and autonomy of the individual as a centre of self-responsible moral judgement, which she maintained unswervingly, was in fact another variant of that reaction against submission to ready-made social codes which marks Blake, Shelley, Wordsworth, and even Byron.

New Tools of Language

The new tasks attempted by many of the writers of the period demanded new tools of language, especially in poetry. The more conservative poets Rogers (1763–1855), Crabbe, Southey (1774–1843), Moore (1779–1852), for example, were content with language and verse forms that flowed with ease of habit through minds trained on Pope. Byron's aims in poetry were also compatible with the language of the older school in essentials, in spite of the flippantly colloquial style he used in Don Juan. He was devoted to the work of

Pope, and it was Keats's disparagement of Pope as a poet that cost him Byron's regard:

> Had I known that Keats was dead – or that he was alive and so sensitive – I should have omitted some remarks upon his poetry, to which I was provoked by his *attack* upon *Pope*, and my disapprobation of *his own* style of writing.
>
> *(Letter of 26 April 1821 to Shelley)*[16]

In a letter to Thomas Moore (1 June 1818) he ranges himself explicitly with the poets who used the older verse forms, retorting angrily to Leigh Hunt's suggestion that Wordsworth was recognized by contemporary poets as being pre-eminent among them:

> He is the only one of us (but of us he is not) whose coronation I would oppose. Let them take Scott, Campbell, Crabbe, or you, or me, or any of the living and throne him; – but not this new Jacob Behmen, this — whose pride might have kept him true, even had his principles turned as perverted as his *soi-disant* poetry.

Wordsworth's statement in the Advertisement to the *Lyrical Ballads* (1798) that he had tried 'to ascertain how far the language of conversation in the middle and lower classes of society is adapted to the purposes of poetical pleasure' received disproportionate attention in his lifetime and for long afterwards. As H. W. Garrod suggests, Wordsworth was surprisingly unsuccessful in this kind of writing, and the use of everyday language was not an important feature of the innovating verse of the period. Clare, it is true, freely used the cottagers' vocabulary and grammar, which were his own, but he so readily adopted standard schemes of metre and rhyme that the movement of his poetry suggests Augustan verse rather than a language of conversation. Wordsworth's Advertisement (and the modified statement of his views in the Preface to later editions of the *Lyrical Ballads*) had great influence because it was taken as an extreme statement of the revolt against the poetic diction of Pope and his followers. But the actual poetry of the Romantics evinced a revolt only against the donnish conventionality of the earlier poetic diction: the triteness of its metaphor, the pompousness of simile, its failure to record direct observation, and the rigidity of the verse form in which it was cast.

There was no avoidance of non-conversational and non-prosaic idioms in romantic verse. Livingstone Lowes, when he discusses the archaisms in *The Ancient Mariner*, shows what a strong and fashionable appeal archaic forms of the language had at the time, and how swamped with them the early versions of Coleridge's poem were. Keats drew on Spenser and for a time came under Milton's influence. He felt later that '*Paradise Lost*, though so fine in itself, is a corruption of our language ... A northern dialect accommodating itself to greek and latin inversions and intonations ... Chatterton's language is entirely northern. I prefer the native music of it to Milton's cut by feet.' (Letter to George Keats.) But Chatterton's is not the language of everyday; nor is the second *Hyperion*, which Keats wrote in reaction from the influence of Milton. All that can be said – and this perhaps not of Shelley – is that the Romantic poets at their best made far more use of speech rhythms than the previous generation to modify their verse line and avoid the subjugation of rhythm to metre. They were far from 'the language of conversation', and in fact it was the poetic diction of the Romantics (and still more of their debilitated successors) against which the verse innovations of the first quarter of the twentieth century were largely directed.

More characteristic features of the Romantics' language were connected with their view of the poet as *vates*, seer and prophet, as well as speaker; far from wishing their poetry to be 'what oft was thought but ne'er so well expressed', they believed in the poet's function of illuminating, revealing, and inciting. Byron was at one with them in making his poems incitements to action and conviction. But he had no wish to illuminate and reveal, and his use of language was consequently nearer to Pope's in one fundamental characteristic, namely the rather simple subjection of language to reasoned thought. If it could ever be true to regard speech and writing as thought 'clothed in' words, it would be true of the writing of Pope and his followers. They might almost make it plausible to suppose that a thought existed fully formed in some non-verbal mode and then, in a subsequent process, was 'expressed in' words. We get that impression because we feel that in such writing the sense could be expressed pretty accurately in a paraphrase, or translated with comparatively slight loss. In fact, in his objections to Tennyson's early poems (*Blackwood's*, May 1832), John Wilson explicitly spoke of translation as a test of poetic excellence:

All human beings see the same light in heaven and in women's eyes; and the great poets put it into language which rather records than reveals, spiritualizing while it embodies . . . Scott, when eulogizing our love of our native land, uses the simplest language, and gives vent to the simplest feelings –

> Lives there the man with soul so dead,
> Who never to himself hath said,
> This is my own, my native land?

What less – what more, could any man say? Yet translate these three lines – not omitting others that accompany them equally touching – into any language, living or dead – and they will instantly be felt by all hearts, savage or civilized, to be the most exquisite poetry.

Byron's continental popularity in part reflects this quality of his writing; it is largely understandable without a native's intimate feeling for the English language.

The contrasting quality found in different degrees in much of the Romantics' writing is the welcoming of effects secured by verbal overtones and subtleties of association, effects which convey a large part of the 'meaning' of the poem although they are lost in a paraphrase of the 'sense'. It seems doubtful whether I. A. Richards's analysis of 'meaning' in *Practical Criticism* can help us very much at this point. What the unreasoned aspect of the Romantics' language conveys is not the 'feeling', 'tone', or 'intention' that Richards distinguishes, but something of the 'sense', though not the translatable or paraphrasable sense. An example is given by Wordsworth's lines

> . . . and add the gleam,
> The light that never was, on sea or land,
> The consecration, and the Poet's dream.

This in his deadened years (though later again he restored the original lines) he changed to

> . . . and add a gleam
> Of lustre, known to neither sea nor land
> But borrowed from the youthful Poet's dream.

The revised wording gives a sense fitting better with the later stanzas, in which the 'Poet's dream' is seen less as a consecration than as an illusion, but the original form conveys the value that the 'Poet's dream' still had for Wordsworth in spite of his willed submission to 'a new control'; it reveals the division of mind, the valuable flaw in his more reasoned judgement. Apart from this, it gives the impression of some mysterious natural phenomenon. 'The gleam', 'the light that never was', something intrinsic to the scene; whereas in the second version 'a gleam of lustre' is at once recognized as a metaphor for a merely subjective impression 'borrowed' elsewhere and superadded to the scene.

Hard as it is to analyse the effect, it seems clear that the accident of the word-arrangement in the first version half suggests that the poet's vision (or illusion) is a quality of the world of nature outside him. Such an idea put into the form of explicit statement would have had to carry more weight than it could bear; hinted at through overtones of the words, it gives the lines a complexity of sense that makes them fascinating and conveys feelings that the simpler paraphrasable sense would not support.

It might be thought that overtones of this kind would depend too much on casual, personal associations to be usefully treated as part of the poem. But in their fortunate moments the Romantics lighted upon an ordering of overtones that was so closely controlled by the traditional behaviour of the language as to have much the same extra-rational sense for vast numbers of English readers. Any one reader's attempt to analyse the effect may be only partly convincing to others, but it still seems likely that some more or less common impression has been received.

A willingness to trust their language to produce such effects – sought for but not preconceived – is evident in Blake, Keats, Shelley, Wordsworth, and Coleridge. Where Pope and his followers used language as a tool for their purposes, these Romantics treated it rather as a material or medium and to some extent submitted their purposes to it. Their exact intention could not be formulated in advance; it reached definition only in what the language actually produced when they worked in it, rather as a sculptor's exact intention cannot exist apart from the materials that define it. This attitude to language harmonized well with the romantic conception of the poet as *vates*. But it also links the Romantics with the Elizabethan poets and with many contemporary twentieth-century writers. Few contemporary poets would claim or accept the role of seer, but they are at one with the Romantics in not treating the language as simply amenable to their purposes; instead of merely using it, they collaborate with it. In this respect the Romantics recovered a characteristic quality of

English poetry that had in the main been lost by their immediate predecessors.

NOTES

1. *Nineteenth Century Studies* (London, 1949).

2. *Augustans and Romantics: 1689–1836*, Vol. III of *An Introduction to English Literature*, ed. Bonamy Dobrée (London, 1940).

3. Quoted by Edward Sackville-West in *A Flame in Sunlight* (London, 1936).

4. Both quoted from *Contemporary Reviews of Romantic Poetry*, ed. John Wain (London, 1953).

5. Percy Muir, *English Children's Books* (London, 1954).

6. Wain, in *Contemporary Reviews of Romantic Poetry*.

7. Dorothy Hewlett, *A Life of John Keats* (London, n.d.; first published as *Adonais*, London, 1937).

8. See E. H. McCormick, *Omai: Pacific Envoy* (Auckland and Oxford, 1977).

9. Quoted by M. Wilson in *The Life of William Blake* (London, 1927).

10. For the tendency of women writers of the period to luxuriate in melancholy, see Sylvia Norman's essay in *On Shelley*, by Edmund Blunden *et al.* (Oxford, 1938).

11. Herbert Butterfield, *History and Human Relations* (London, 1951).

12. Quoted by K. C. Balderstone, *Thraliana* (Oxford, 1951).

13. Quoted by Wilson, in *The Life of William Blake*.

14. See Ida Macalpine and Richard Hunter, *George III and the Mad Business* (London, 1968).

15. Cf. A. E. Rodway, *Godwin and the Age of Transition* (London, 1952).

16. *Byron: a Self-portrait*, ed. Peter Quennell (London, 1950).

PART III

PART III

WILLIAM BLAKE

D. W. HARDING

One of the difficulties in coming to Blake's poetry is to know where to focus attention. So formidable a mass of exegesis and comment has accumulated during the twentieth century, and some of it so little less obscure than Blake himself (1757–1827), that on first approaching the poetry (or returning to it after a nonage acquaintance) the reader is liable to feel baffled. If we read only those short poems that seem fairly comprehensible, we may lose much of their meaning by ignoring their relation to the obviously esoteric writings, and if we struggle with the 'Prophetic Books' and the commentators' quasi-religious exegesis, we may well miss the distinctive enjoyment of Blake as a poet. How far to follow the journeyings of the commentators as they get more and more distant from the poem Blake wrote is a central problem for literary criticism. For those who could read there was an impressive and valuable quality in the poems long before their esoteric meanings were taken seriously. *The Tyger* was widely popular even among Blake's contemporaries in eighteenth-century London. Later on, Edward FitzGerald, Rossetti, and Swinburne were all responsive to the quality of his work as soon as they met it. An appreciation of Blake's power as an English poet, not as a preserve for initiates, must remain the nucleus to which we assimilate more or less of the remoter significance that his writing can be shown to possess.

The remoter significance has been studied, if not exhaustively – for the elaborations it invites seem inexhaustible – at least at stupefying length. An array of books devoted to his moral, religious, and political doctrines testifies to the profound importance of the topics that exercised Blake and to the power and suggestiveness of a symbolic treatment that still fascinates good minds and seems worth struggling to comprehend. Yet the need for all this exegesis, its own obscurity, and the divergent views of different commentators point

to the disturbing feature of Blake's writing: his failure to achieve sufficient control of his readers' response, even the response of those
particularly well equipped for reading him.

The Tyger serves as well as any poem to illustrate the problem of
drawing the line between critical elucidation and doctrinal exegesis:

> Tyger! Tyger! burning bright
> In the forests of the night,
> What immortal hand or eye
> Could frame thy fearful symmetry?
>
> In what distant deeps or skies
> Burnt the fire of thine eyes?
> On what wings dare he aspire?
> What the hand, dare seize the fire?
>
> And what shoulder, & what art,
> Could twist the sinews of thy heart?
> And when thy heart began to beat,
> What dread hand? & what dread feet?
>
> What the hammer? what the chain?
> In what furnace was thy brain?
> What the anvil? what dread grasp
> Dare its deadly terrors clasp?
>
> When the stars threw down their spears,
> And water'd heaven with their tears,
> Did he smile his work to see?
> Did he who made the Lamb make thee?
>
> Tyger! Tyger! burning bright
> In the forests of the night,
> What immortal hand or eye,
> Dare frame thy fearful symmetry?

At simplest reading the poem is a contemplation of the fact that,
besides peacefulness and gentleness, the world includes fierce strength
terrifying in its possibilities of destructiveness but also impressive and
admirable, a stupendous part of creation and seemingly a challenge
to the idea of a benign Creator. To see that the tiger's fierceness and
the lamb's gentleness are also contrasting qualities of the human mind
is a very slight extension beyond the simplest literal sense. The theme
is a commonplace, and also a fact of supreme human importance,

the focus of sharp psychological conflict in individual minds and of unending theological and philosophical discussion. What Blake's fine poem does, is allow us to contemplate the facts in their emotional intensity and conflict, and to share his complex attitude of awe, terror, admiration, near-bafflement, and attempted acceptance.

The commentators' extended but limiting interpretations sacrifice Blake's combination of a very general, complex meaning with a vivid phrase-embodied symbol. It is important for an understanding of Blake as a poet (rather than a teacher in parables) to see that he presents the fierceness of nature not through a symbolic object – a tiger – but through that object embodied in particular language. The description 'burning bright', for instance, has important uncertainties of meaning: we may (in view of the second stanza) think primarily of the two burning eyes in the darkness, but the phrase itself makes the whole tiger a symbol of a 'burning' quality – wrath, passion, ardour perhaps; but then again the word 'bright' modifies the kind of burning suggested: it may convey incandescence, white heat, and it brings a sense of light, something glorious and shining in the quality symbolized. The essential thing is to recognize how such a cluster of half-activated associations and potential feelings and attitudes is stimulated by the symbolic language, and how inadequately it can be expressed through an elaboration of formulated and organized ideas.

Extended interpretation along an ordered line of thought raises doubts and divergences of opinion. Take, for instance, the fifth stanza of *The Tyger*. The words have a wide range of echoes and half-allusions in each mind, but the central sense needed for the mere construing of the poem is explicit and unambiguous once we see that the stanza refers to the effect of the tiger's creation. Blake asks, with scarcely believing awe, whether the Creator smiled with satisfaction at what he had made when in fact its ferocious strength was so appalling that even the stars abandoned their armed formidability (the spears suggested by their steely glitter) and broke down in tears.

The commentators, however, each following up the allusions and associations that mean most to him, elaborate far beyond this. Gardner suggests that the stars, symbols of material power, cast aside the instruments of strife and take on pity; and the Creator, now become the God of Innocence, 'smiles upon the triumph of the Lamb'. He amplifies by saying: 'The stanza of the Lamb is the only one in which not only the tyger of wrath and rebellion is brought to harmony, but the universe of stars and night as well. The tyger lies down with the Lamb.' The exegesis of Wicksteed, always honestly explicit, goes further. He thinks the theme is the Incarnation, the stars symbolizing 'the hard cold realm of Reason and war, that held the earth before Compassion came with Christ'. At the end of his long commentary, after the convincing suggestion that the tiger is 'nothing less indeed than the Divine spark, the fiercely struggling individuality . . .', he concludes:

And yet when we ask ourselves, Is it good to be alive and to burn with quenchless desire, with love half-realized and with purpose ever imperfectly fulfilled? the incarnate heart of Deity in ourselves responds, with the smile of daybreak, that the spirits which discern and divide and contend in labour and agony, are but glimpses of the Great Light that shall unite and heal in strength and tenderness and joy.

The objections to this kind of writing as comment on Blake are first that it imports into the poem intellectual meanings that are too remotely and indirectly derived from the words, if they can claim to derive from them at all, and second that the parish-magazine quality of sentiment it expresses is totally foreign to the tautness and strength of the state of mind Blake invites us to share.

Yet it would be a worse mistake to ignore the deep seriousness of Blake's preoccupations and his constant concern with fundamental questions of human life. This quality of his work is put beyond doubt by any responsive reading of the symbolic books; and even an inkling of what he was attempting there reflects back on our reading of the shorter poems, not mainly in throwing light on particular symbols but in putting beyond question the spirit in which he approached poetry. It is obvious that for Blake any separation of art from moral problems and belief would have seemed ridiculous; the understanding and evaluation of human experience, especially in certain crucial situations, was his constant object in writing.

The short poems as a whole are finer than the long books as a whole, not only for their more secure control of the readers' response (their better 'communication' if we care to use that uncertain term), but for their more direct statement of human experience in place of the too-cosmic or cosmologized disguise of experience in the books.

They include some in which Blake makes a direct moral comment on the London world of his time, using his simple metres to give force and emphasis, as in the *Holy Thursday of Songs of Experience* (1794):

> Is this a holy thing to see
>   In a rich and fruitful land,
> Babes reduc'd to misery,
>   Fed with cold and usurous hand?
>
> Is that trembling cry a song?
>   Can it be a song of joy?
> And so many children poor?
>   It is a land of poverty!

More usually, however, Blake is wrestling with the psychological and moral problems of us all, those that are inescapable in family life and in the contact of old with young and men with women. These problems and their effects on our personality are the ultimate material of the symbolic books, too, but in the short poems they receive clearer statement. *Infant Sorrow* imagines the protest of the child at birth, its first experience of danger and constraint, its rage and its reluctant submission:

> My mother groan'd! my father wept.
> Into the dangerous world I leapt:
> Helpless, naked, piping loud:
> Like a fiend hid in a cloud.
>
> Struggling in my father's hands,
> Striving against my swadling bands,
> Bound and weary I thought best
> To sulk upon my mother's breast.

For Blake, the father (and any God in which he saw the image of the father) was a figure of oppression and jealousy, and the mother was obliged to join the father in his terrified and tyrannous control of the child. So in *The Book of Urizen* (1794), when Enitharmon has borne the child Orc to Los:

> They took Orc to the top of a mountain.
> O how Enitharmon wept!
> They chain'd his young limbs to the rock
> With the Chain of Jealousy
> Beneath Urizen's deathful shadow.

The perpetual cycle of conflict thus initiated between young and old is expressed in the dream-like poem *The Mental Traveller*, which also illustrates his sense of the conflict and mutual exploitation in sexual attraction, a theme expressed simply in *The Golden Net* and in subtler forms recurrently throughout his work.

In Blake's eyes the possessiveness of sexual love and the constraint exercised by the old each contributed to the creation of an abstract moral code, and with it a sense of guilt. Contrasted with all that these things implied, he kept in mind the state of Innocence, the 'contrary state of the human soul', and throughout his work he was exploring the relation between the perfect possibilities he felt in human life and the lamentable confusions and imperfections that appear in actual experience. Faced with the sources of conflict and sin in his own personality, he dealt with the problem of guilt by developing his conviction that there is nothing to be afraid of in the human personality.

> Mutual Forgiveness of each Vice,
> Such are the Gates of Paradise,

he wrote in denouncing the abstract Commandments, and asserted in *The Marriage of Heaven and Hell* (*c.* 1793) that 'The road of excess leads to the palace of wisdom'. In *The Book of Los* (1795) the introductory stanzas put forward the same ideas in describing the condition of innocence:

> O Times remote!
> When Love & Joy were adoration,
> And none impure were deem'd:
> Not Eyeless Covet,
> Nor Thin-lip'd Envy,
> Nor Bristled Wrath,
> Nor Curled Wantonness.
>
> But Covet was poured full,
> Envy fed with fat of lambs,
> Wrath with lion's gore,
> Wantonness lull'd to sleep
> With the virgin's lute
> Or sated with her love:
>
> Till Covet broke his locks & bars
> And slept with open doors;

> Envy sung at the rich man's feast;
> Wrath was follow'd up and down
> By a little ewe lamb,
> And Wantonness on his own true love
> Begot a giant race.

It was out of these basic problems and attitudes that Blake built his moral and quasi-religious system, and it was in the attempt to express adequately the complexity revealed in an extended and subtle exploration of them that he developed his intricate mythologies.

But neither vast mythopoeic cosmologies nor brief and clear-sighted statements of basic psychological problems could by themselves have given him any importance as a poet. For that his extraordinarily fine handling of language was needed. His rhythms deserve more attention than the length of this essay permits. In his best work they are at the same time forceful and supple, some based on ballad metres, some metrically free and influenced by the Bible, but all returning again and again to the rhythm of speech. Notice the style of folk rhyme and incantation ('Double, double toil and trouble') in Blake's poem about being dogged by his 'Spectre':

> He scents thy footsteps in the snow,
> Wheresoever thou dost go
> Thro' the wintry hail & rain.
> When wilt thou return again?

And in the later stanzas of the poem observe the supple variety in what is deliberately repetitive and might have become tum-ti-tum:

> Seven more loves weep night & day
> Round the tombs where my loves lay,
> And seven more loves attend each night
> Around my couch with torches bright.

> And seven more Loves in my bed
> Crown with vine my mournful head,
> Pitying & forgiving all
> My transgressions great & small.

In the short poems an outstanding quality is the immense compression of meaning, sometimes of a simple kind – as in 'Old Nobodaddy' for the God of the churches, or the 'Marriage hearse' of *London* – and sometimes far more complex. A closely related feature of his writing, often a means of compression and notably contrasting with the contemporary practice of his time, was the trust with which he launched himself into imagery and ideas that carried symbolic implications scarcely susceptible of reasoned exposition, and that gained their coherence and ordered effect through unexplicit associations and incompletely formulated reference:

> Never seek to tell thy love
> Love that never told can be;
> For the gentle wind does move
> Silently, invisibly.
>
> I told my love, I told my love,
> I told her all my heart,
> Trembling, cold, in ghastly fears –
> Ah, she doth depart.
>
> Soon as she was gone from me
> A traveller came by
> Silently, invisibly –
> He took her with a sigh.

The suggestions are of something too terrifying in the ultimate nature of love to be disclosed, of the man's need nevertheless to try to establish full knowledge between them, of the woman not able to bear it, lost to him and taken by some invisible agency that moves gently, perhaps regretfully, but irrevocably. The 'traveller' who takes her may carry echoes of 'time' and 'death', but all we know is that when the man tries to break down the conventional limits of the communicable some silent, invisible agency comes into action, ends their union, and puts the woman beyond his reach. We could go on to speculate that the silent, invisible traveller might be just some aspect of fear-inducing conventionality, for Blake's lines to the God of the churches refer to the same characteristics:

> Why art thou silent & invisible,
> Father of Jealousy?

There is the obvious psychoanalytic interpretation in terms of the oedipal situation, and among the commentators Wicksteed and Gardner offer yet other views, both plausible and each different. The fact seems to be that these speculative 'meanings' all isolate one or two harmonics from the note. Left to itself the poem half evokes these and probably many other ideas; repeated listening, with strict moderation in the use of intellectual ingenuities, seems the likeliest way of getting from the words something of the effect that led Blake to find them satisfying.

The risks in such an approach to obscure poetry are clearly evident, especially the risks of wasting time on the charlatans of emotion and incantation. But unless we take them we shall miss the enjoyment of poems whose obscurity, in T. S. Eliot's words,[1] 'is due to the suppression of "links in the chain", of explanatory and connecting matter, and not to incoherence, or to the love of cryptogram'. 'Such selection of a sequence of images and ideas', he continues, 'has nothing chaotic about it. There is a logic of the imagination as well as a logic of concepts.'

Blake can be seen suppressing expository links in a simple way in *The Tyger*. The exclamation now on its own as the end of a stanza –

> And when thy heart began to beat
> What dread hand & what dread feet

– was in the early draft the opening of a sentence that went on:

> Could fetch it from the furnace deep
> And in thy horrid ribs dare steep
> In the well of sanguine woe?

As Blake revised, the broken sentence seemed to convey the meaning far enough, besides preserving the full exclamatory force.

A more complex and extremely fine example of his method is provided by the 'Introduction' to *Songs of Experience*, and *Earth's Answer* which follows it. Certain familiar themes are used, their ordinary associations recalled but unexpectedly modified, and they are set in relation – but not an explicitly defined relation – to totally different and unfamiliar ideas. The 'Introduction' might seem at first glance a straightforward treatment of the Fall, with its reference to

> The Holy Word
> That walk'd among the ancient trees,
>
> Calling the lapsed Soul,
> And weeping in the evening dew;
> That might controll
> The starry pole,
> And fallen, fallen light renew!

Even here the word 'ancient' for the trees unexpectedly modifies the
ordinary notion of Eden; it is taken up again in *Earth's Answer*
when, in denouncing the jealous, love-chaining God, Earth calls him
'the father of the ancient men'. The 'weeping' is given an implication
of helplessness by the next two stanzas of the 'Introduction' in which
the Holy Word is shown as pleading with Earth, in effect wooing
her to come to him in the permitted period of darkness:

> 'Turn away no more;
> Why wilt thou turn away?
> The starry floor,
> The wat'ry shore,
> Is giv'n thee till the break of day.'

With this helplessness is contrasted the power of the Creator to reverse, if he would, the darkness of the Fall,

> And fallen, fallen light renew!

The effect is already to convey not only the usual sense of boundless
loss and the grief of the Creator, but with it an astringent hint of
something questionable in the power of renewal not exercised. Moreover, the lapsed soul is not man but 'Earth'. In *Earth's Answer* it
becomes clear that Earth is feminine and is being wooed for her love,
including her sexual love. The Holy Word has now become

> 'Selfish father of men!
> Cruel, jealous, selfish fear!'

And the denunciation of his imprisoning jealousy is combined with
Blake's hatred of the conventional restriction of sexual activity to
darkness, with its implications of shame and secrecy:

> 'Can delight,
> Chain'd in night,
> The virgins of youth and morning bear?
>
> 'Does spring hide its joy
> When buds and blossoms grow?
> Does the sower
> Sow by night,
> Or the plowman in darkness plow?'

The fallen light of the 'Introduction' thus gathers a further meaning. Behind the two poems, moreover, there lurks the idea which

Blake developed in the Prophetic Books that the Creation was a division in God and itself constituted the Fall:

> Six days they shrunk up from existence,
> And on the seventh day they rested,
> And they bless'd the seventh day, in sick hope,
> And forgot their eternal life.
> (*The Book of Urizen*, IX, 17–20)

But that is not made explicit here, and the exegesis is perhaps not needed. What the two poems offer is an unexpected handling of the Fall, with its sexual aspects, in a way that links God's relation to the world with that of men to women, associates the Creator with the jealous patriarch and with the selfish fear in us all, and at the same time shows him helplessly defeated by the refusal of his creation to submit to jealous control and accept atonement on his terms.

Even a brief discussion of Blake's use of language brings up the nature of his ideas. To balance what was said before, no skills and subtleties in the handling of language would have given him much importance as a poet if it were not for the significance of the concerns that held him and the worth of his insights and judgements. They are not, however, judgements that can be adequately examined in paraphrase, detached from his modes of presentation – among them his use of symbols. The nature of his work exposes it to every passing aberration of critical endeavour[2] but modern criticism includes at least one valuable study, by D. G. Gillham, of the meaning Blake gave Innocence and Experience and his reasons for putting a Song into one series rather than the other. Although Experience, with its caution, abstract rationality and firm general principles, is unavoidable and necessary, it is an inferior state of being to Innocence, the possibility we sometimes glimpse of merging spontaneously and selflessly with an occasion and what it offers. Gillham sees the Songs as utterances not of Blake but of characters he has created. The innocent *Nurse's Song* issues from spontaneity and trust in life; the experienced Nurse conveys anxiety and a shrinking from the risks of joy, the dangers of tomorrow always damping today's zest. And however convincing and sensitive some of the *Songs of Experience* may seem to be they express, according to this view, a state of mind falling short of 'a better spirit' represented by innocence, and Blake must be taken as tacitly criticizing the supposed speaker. So, for instance, the experienced observers of *The Chimney Sweeper* and *Holy Thursday* are to be seen as warped in some degree – theirs are generalized truths applied to the situation instead of being 'a lively outcome of the circumstance itself'. Even the wanderer who denounces what he meets in *London* is shut off in his desolation: 'He must accommodate himself to abstractions and institutions, but cannot reach out to the persons whose cries of distress penetrate to his solitude.'

Yet it seems difficult to believe that Blake always presents experience as a dereliction of innocence. In some of the explicitly paired poems, *Holy Thursday*, *Infant Joy* and *Infant Sorrow*, *The Chimney Sweeper*, the two outlooks seem to be mutually corrective; and the innocent version strikes twentieth-century readers, who take more readily to the bitter than the sweet, as one-sided, leaning towards sentimentality and credulity. It may also be doubted whether the dramatic device of a speaker distanced from Blake himself is adopted in every Song of either series. It is more likely that in poems like *London*, *Infant Sorrow*, and *The Tyger* Blake conveyed what for the time being he himself wholeheartedly felt, even if he decided later that it reflected less than his ideally whole self. But Gillham's work effectively emphasizes the fact that Blake had a serious intention in assigning a poem to Innocence or to Experience; and although we may rightly enjoy any of the Songs by itself we have probably not seen its full implications until we set it in the framework of the contrary states that he created.

Blake's symbolism, defeating in some of its later elaborations, can best be approached by way of the so-called Rossetti manuscript.[3] The poems he wrote in this manuscript book were evidently personal documents in which he expressed and tried to come to terms with his own psychological problems and foci of intense emotion. The nature of the poems and their sequence are what would be expected when a writer of genius used a verse form for self-analysis. At some points the topic he handles is dealt with compactly and completely enough, and in symbols near enough to public intelligibility, to create a publishable poem; from poems of this sort he selected *Songs of Experience* for engraving. At other points in the manuscript what he wrote reflects more fragmentary and shifting states of mind, often expressed incompletely and in symbols too uncertain or unprofitably

ambiguous for publication. Something like free association is evident at times, as in poems XV and XVI of the manuscript: the first
is an obscure four lines beginning 'O lapwing thou fliest around
the heath', and the second switches to 'Thou hast a lap full of
seed'.[4]

Such a flow of important and less important material is nowadays
familiar enough in psychoanalysis; the symbolism thrown up in
dreams, waking fantasy, and free association has sometimes to be
guessed at, sometimes serves mainly as a bridge from one important
topic to another, and only occasionally offers an effective and tolerably
certain statement of an important theme. Commentators on Blake,
whether wittingly or not, have adopted very much the psychoanalytic method in interpreting further and further the possible
implications of phrases, associations, and symbols. They may use the
traditional symbolic meaning attached to an idea or they may concentrate on Blake's private symbolism, and they illuminate one passage by reference to similar words or images in another part of his
work. In the attempt to understand the long symbolic writings (the
so-called Prophetic Books) this recondite interpretative analysis is
carried to extreme lengths.

In these books, Blake's communing with himself about problems
of his own personality, seen in manageable form in the Rossetti
manuscript, now appears on a vaster literary scale. When he reached
some definite standpoint on a problem, he expounded it in the spirit
of a religious teacher and in language clear enough, as for instance
when he teaches forgiveness in *The Ghost of Abel* (1822). But this is
uncharacteristic; most of the writings reflect his struggles to establish
order among apparently conflicting aspects of his own personality
expressed as symbolic figures and situations. The uncertainties and
conflicts play as big a part as the ordering he achieves, and he
sometimes gives the impression not of reporting the resolution of
conflicts previously examined but of discovering and threshing out
his problems in the process of writing. The personal issues with which
he wrestled seemed to him to be also the salient problems of human
life. They included questions of the proper place of intellectual control in the total economy of the personality, the place of impulse,
the relations between authority and those it controls (and therefore
between elders and children), the relations of the sexes, the folly of

moral generalities (one law for the lion and the ox), the poison of jealousy, and the overwhelming importance of forgiveness.

The parallel between the Prophetic Books and Blake's struggle to understand and harmonize features of his own personality is illustrated from the letter to Hayley of 23 October 1804, quoted by Sloss and Wallis and compared with passages of *Jerusalem* and *The Four Zoas*. To Hayley he exclaimed:

> O Glory! and O Delight! I have entirely reduced that spectrous fiend to his station, whose annoyance has been the ruin of my labours for the last passed twenty years of my life. He is the enemy of conjugal love, and is the Jupiter of the Greeks, an iron-hearted tyrant, the ruiner of ancient Greece ... Oh! the distress I have undergone, and my poor wife with me; incessantly labouring and incessantly spoiling what I had done well ... I thank God with entire confidence that it shall be so no longer – he is become my servant who domineered over me; he is even as a brother who was my enemy.

Sloss and Wallis compare this with *The Four Zoas*, VII, 335ff.:

> Los embrac'd the Spectre, first as a brother,
> Then as another Self, astonish'd, humanizing & in tears,
> In Self-abasement Giving up his Domineering lust.

> 'Thou never canst embrace sweet Enitharmon, terrible Demon, Till
> Thou art united with thy Spectre, Consummating by pains & labours
> That mortal body, & by Self annihilation back returning
> To Life Eternal ...'

Other passages in *The Four Zoas* and the opening pages of *Jerusalem* refer to the same struggle with the 'Spectre' (by which Blake seems to have meant something like dependence upon abstract, analytic reasoning). Uncertain as the dating of the later writings must be (owing to Blake's protracted revisions), it seems clear that *The Four Zoas*, at least, was written before the ecstatic letter to Hayley, and it therefore looks as if the illumination he celebrates in that letter occurred after he had been struggling with the problem for a considerable time in the symbolic writings. The likelihood that they were not *records* of psychological struggles but to a great extent the form in which the struggles found expression while they actually occurred helps to explain their obscurity and inconsistencies.

An early and unfinished symbolic book, *Tiriel* (*c.* 1789), shows that there were interesting possibilities in this self-exploratory writing, and that outlandish names and a privately concocted mythology need not have been insuperable barriers to communication. Whatever its inadequacies, *Tiriel* is successful in conveying promptly, and without the need for a wide search through this and other poems, the essential features of its persons and situations: Tiriel, the tyrant father facing death, the sons and daughters reduced by his treatment to futile hatred of him, an alternative form of age in Har and Heva with their childish abdication of any attempt at self-responsibility and control of others, the creature Ijim of tremendous animal vitality confused by the dissemblings and mental complications of Tiriel and his offspring, the witless Zazel reduced to menial tasks and servitude by his cunning brother Tiriel. The poem indicates the promise of the method Blake was experimenting with. It gives him people who are 'real' enough to have intense feelings: they represent figures of family life of deep psychological importance, and at the same time they are hinted at as aspects of every personality, or possibilities of personality development, each with plausible justifications for itself while being in violent conflict with the others. Though Blake reaches no solution, he expresses in more or less dramatic form the diverse qualities and aspects of personality and the situations of conflict in which they meet, and he conveys his sense of the vast importance, the violence, and the confusedness of their struggles.

The nature of the failure met with in the later books is also forecast in *Tiriel*. The persons and action hover uncertainly between intellectually controlled allegory on the one hand, and on the other the representation of concrete situations taken seriously in their own dramatic right but with overtones of symbolic meaning to enrich them; the poem is neither a deliberated allegory like *The Faerie Queene*, nor a plunge into the emotional reality of a symbol-charged incident such as *The Ancient Mariner* takes. In the more massive books the same ingredients appear, but the allegory becomes increasingly obscure and the figures and incidents less immediately significant. Personae and places are introduced abruptly, without sufficient context to establish their meaning and feeling-quality; and the commentators are therefore sent searching through the rest of Blake's writings for a clue to the cipher he is using. Instead of reading a poem in his own language the reader finds himself studying a cabbala, and the rewards he meets will be, in the main, not the rewards of poetry. A passage from *Jerusalem* will illustrate the division of aim between poetry and doctrine, the fumbling between cipher and symbol:

> And Los beheld his Sons and he beheld his Daughters,
> Every one a translucent Wonder, a Universe within,
> Increasing inwards into length, and breadth, and heighth,
> Starry & glorious: and they, every one in their bright loins,
> Have a beautiful golden gate which opens into the vegetative world;
> And every one a gate of rubies & all sorts of precious stones
> In their translucent hearts, which opens into the vegetative world;
> And every one a gate of iron dreadful and wonderful
> In their translucent heads, which opens into the vegetative world.
> And every one has the three regions Childhood, Manhood, & Age.
> But the gate of the tongue, the western gate, in them is clos'd,
> Having a wall builded against it: and thereby the gates
> Eastward & Southward & Northward are incircled with flaming fires.
> And the North is Breadth, the South is Heighth & Depth,
> The East is Inwards, & the West is Outwards every way.
>
> And Los beheld the mild Emanation Jerusalem eastward bending
> Her revolutions toward the Starry Wheels in maternal anguish,
> Like a pale cloud arising from the arms of Beulah's Daughters,
> In Entuthon Benython's deep Vales beneath Golgonooza.
>
> (1)

The failure – in large part – of the prophetic writings is not due to the method of allegory or even to the inconsistencies in the cipher, but to Blake's failure in embodiment. A repeated decoding, deliberated and often needing the aid of an external key, has to take the place of an immediate conviction of meaning and feeling. And when Blake takes existing names – London, Highgate, Conway, Albion, etc. – and puts them to his private allegorical purposes, we are worse baffled, since we now have to undo the ordinary associations before trying to tack on his.

Doubtful as must be the rewards of wrestling with the long symbolic books, it would still be a loss not to know some of the passages in which states of mind and dramatic situations are given expression of a fully intelligible and effective kind, even while the symbolic scaffolding around them is baffling. Unexpectedly, too, the verse of the long books has a cumulative appeal in spite of so much that repels. Quotation cannot convey that, but something of the variety and effectiveness of the language and rhythms may be indicated. Though the biblical echoes are prominent in the following passage, for instance, the completely new, individual note (besides a concern with comtemporary social fact) is there too:

> 'Shall not the King call for Famine from the heath,
> Nor the Priest for Pestilence from the fen,
> To restrain, to dismay, to thin
> The inhabitants of mountain and plain,
> In the day of full-feeding prosperity
> And the night of delicious songs?
>
> 'Shall not the Councellor throw his curb
> Of Poverty on the laborious,
> To fix the price of labour,
> To invent allegoric riches?
>
> 'And the privy admonishers of men
> Call for Fires in the City,
> For heaps of smoking ruins,
> In the night of prosperity & wantonness,
>
> 'To turn man from his path,
> To restrain the child from the womb,
> To cut off the bread from the city,
> That the remnant may learn to obey,
>
> 'That the pride of the heart may fail,
> That the lust of the eyes may be quench'd,
> That the delicate ear in its infancy
> May be dull'd, and the nostrils clos'd up,
> To teach mortal worms the path
> That leads from the gates of the Grave?'
>
> (*The Song of Los*, Asia, 9–32)

Again, the whole of Enion's lamentation in Night II of *The Four Zoas* is worth reading for the sake of the dramatic rhetoric, whether or not we know what Enion represents, for here Blake's power is unquestionable and we glimpse the possibilities that might have been realized if he could have handled his dramatic themes more lucidly and with more convincing embodiment. The causes of his relative failure in the Prophetic Books were multiple and can only be guessed at. The influence of *Ossian* may have led him to rely too readily on the acceptability of an outlandish mythology. Boehme and Swedenborg suggested the possibility of new mystical and religious systems, and seemed to sanction extreme obscurity of utterance.

Above all stands the fact of his having had no adequate reading public whose adverse criticism or lack of comprehension he could have taken seriously. His pugnacious attitude to the dimly conventional figures of his time led him to take the line he indicates in a letter to Dr Trusler, whose writings he was asked to illustrate and who objected to the obscurity of the designs. 'You say,' writes Blake, 'that I want somebody to Elucidate my Ideas. What is Grand is necessarily obscure to Weak men. That which can be made Explicit to the Idiot is not worth my care. The wisest of the Ancients consider'd what is not too Explicit as the fittest for Instruction, because it rouzes the faculties to act. I name Moses, Solomon, Esop, Homer, Plato.' However, if we sympathize with this line of justification we are checked by a further assertion in the same letter: 'But I am happy to find a Great Majority of Fellow Mortals who can Elucidate My Visions, & Particularly they have been Elucidated by Children, who have taken a greater delight in contemplating my Pictures than I even hoped. Neither Youth nor Childhood is Folly or Incapacity.' Blake, like many who are unappreciated, seems to have been divided between defiant justification of the obscurity of his work and the belief that people of unspoiled intelligence would find none. He wanted to be understood, but not at the cost of trimming down his meaning to the assimilative capacity of conventional minds. The Hayleys, Truslers, and Crabb Robinsons must always set the tone of cultivated society – of which educated mediocrity necessarily forms the greater part – and in the complacent literary culture of his early life Blake could have scarcely a hint of any effective minority of readers who in his own time or later might understand and value his work. The miracle is that he produced such work at all. He represents a tremendous opportunity in English literature that was largely wasted owing to the reading public's restricted capacities for response; and the combination of greatness and failure in his work is a reminder that a literature consists not of writers only but of their readers too.

NOTES

1. Preface to T. S. Eliot's translation of St-J. Perse's *Anabasis* (London, 1930).

2. Harold Bloom's view of *London* as an inverted rewriting of Ezekiel, ch. 9, with far-fetched readings based on the remote etymology of some of the words, has been disposed of by S. H. Olsen ('On Unilluminating Criticism', *British Journal of Aesthetics*, 21, 1; winter 1981) with a thoroughness and patient rationality that it may not altogether deserve.

3. Reproduced, with a commentary, by Wicksteed.

4. Geoffrey Keynes (ed.), *Poetry and Prose of William Blake* (London, 1927), 92.

GEORGE CRABBE'S VERSE-TALES

FRANK WHITEHEAD

Although it was in the England of Dr Johnson that Crabbe (1754–1832) first gained recognition as a poet, his best work was almost exactly contemporary with that of Jane Austen. Not that he was merely an eighteenth-century poet who happened to live on into the Romantic age. He does indeed retain many features which bear the unmistakable stamp of the earlier period – his almost unfailing attachment to the heroic couplet, his continued use of conventional and highly artificial poetic diction, the predominantly Augustan quality of his poetic sensibility and values; yet at the same time his tales are a highly original achievement in a wholly new art-form, and one which was only possible to someone who had exposed himself, sensitively though not uncritically, to the new currents of feeling which were stirring around the turn of the century.

Of the poems which Crabbe published as a young man, only *The Village* (1783) is of any living interest today, and even this shows less individual distinction than has sometimes been claimed for it. The gulf which separates these early non-narrative poetical essays from his mature work is more understandable when we remember that they were separated in time by an interval of no less than twenty-two years – a period during which Crabbe wrote incessantly, destroyed almost all that he wrote, and published nothing. When he appeared in print again (at the age of fifty-three) he had discovered the narrative bent which from then on shaped the character of all his poetry. In his next three volumes we can trace the rapid growth of this narrative mode, from the brief and pointed anecdotes which illustrate many of the character-sketches in *The Parish Register* (1807), through the various Letters of *The Borough* (1810) in which tales with a moral loom increasingly large, to the final flowering in the masterly and complex short stories in verse of *Tales* (1812). In each of these volumes, too, what is immediately striking (and innovatory) is the specific and highly particularized detail which Crabbe selects with such unerring skill to give both concreteness and psychological reality to his portrayal of individuals.

In *The Parish Register* the narrative voice is that of a village clergyman meditating on the entries in his parish register for a single year, grouped under the headings 'Baptisms', 'Marriages' and 'Burials'. While character-sketches predominate, there are also six fully-developed narratives which prefigure in miniature Crabbe's later achievement. Widely different in mood, the finest of these are perhaps 'Lucy the Miller's Daughter' and 'Sir Richard Monday', both in Part I. *The Borough* takes the form of twenty-four letters from 'a residing burgess in a large sea-port' describing various aspects of life in a borough which is clearly identifiable with Crabbe's native Aldeburgh. Typically the discursive argument of a Letter is rounded off by an illustrative anecdote which may be longer than those in *The Parish Register* but rarely shows any advance in narrative technique. Towards the end of this very long and rather formless poem, however, Crabbe makes a sudden breakthrough with the introduction of seven Letters which proclaim themselves to be exclusively the history of a single individual – either one of the 'Inhabitants of the Alms-House' or one of 'The Poor of the Borough'. In the background of the poet's development at this stage is the eighteenth-century 'progress piece', with the influence of Hogarth's great Progresses at its most clearly apparent in *Clelia* (Letter XV), which traces the moral and social decline of an incurably trivial-minded provincial flirt in a sequence of four distinct 'scenes' each separated by a ten-year interval. In these 'progresses', however, satire has modulated into didacticism, and as he compassionately yet relentlessly depicts the inexorable consequences of vice and folly, Crabbe's moral judgement is at its most harsh and hortatory.

Unique among this group of tales is *Peter Grimes* (Letter XXII), a life-history culminating in madness, in which the poet has set himself the difficult task of making convincing the operation of something akin to remorse in a mind so unfeeling as to appear incapable of it. Here any initial didacticism has been transmuted into an almost Shakespearean moral horror at what a human mind can be capable of, but the essential driving-force of the tale's poetic vision is an unrelenting realism, both sociological and psychological. Though

Peter Grimes has its local patches of weak writing, the intensity of this vision makes it by far the most powerful of Crabbe's various portrayals of insanity.

The twenty-one separate and unrelated tales in the 1812 volume are notable for their tautness of structure and economy of narrative line, yet within their self-imposed limits (most of them are between 300 and 500 lines in length) they encompass a wealth of incident and characterization. The incident is realistic in tone and presentation, while the characterization is marked by the same shrewd psychological insight which Crabbe had started to deploy in the later tales in *The Borough*. It is noticeable that whereas the tales in *The Borough* dealt wholly with the poor or with those who had come down in the world, in *Tales* the characters belong mainly to the middle rank of society. Again, most of the 1812 tales (unlike the single-character histories of *The Borough*) deal with the interplay of two or three leading characters, and the action arises out of some conflict of values which provides the focus of moral concern at the heart of the tale. It is, indeed, this moral focus which determines, in varied ways, each tale's structure. Most typically, a tale starts with an expository passage in which the theme is announced, and there follow at least two extended and vividly-realized 'scenes', the concrete visualization of which is usually aided by some realistic if slightly stylized dialogue. These 'scenes' are placed in a significant relationship to each other in such a way as to define the moral issues in more specific terms, often by means of contrast, or parallelism, or both combined. Since development over time usually plays a role in the tale's structure, the highlighted 'scenes' tend to be linked by highly compressed narrative which spans the years in a series of condensed and laconic cameos, a technique in which Crabbe's talent for concise expression shows to full advantage. However, each tale is unique, and in a short essay it seems best to concentrate on two contrasted examples.

Arabella opens with admirable (and characteristic) economy:

> Of a fair town where Dr Rack was guide★
> His only daughter was the boast and pride;
> Wise Arabella, yet not wise alone,
> She like a bright and polish'd brilliant shone;
> Her father own'd her for his prop and stay,

★ Spiritual guide, or vicar.

> Able to guide, yet willing to obey;
> Pleased with her learning while discourse could please,
> And with her love in languor and disease:
> To every mother were her virtues known,
> And to their daughters as a pattern shown;
> Who in her youth had all that age requires,
> And with her prudence, all that youth admires.

For all its sprightliness of tone, this is thoroughly Augustan in its poetic texture. It is clearly the work of a poetic sensibility which addresses itself 'to the plain sense and sober judgement' of its readers rather than 'to their fancy and imagination'.[1] The movement of the verse and the marshalling of the ideas are both controlled by a mind which finds it natural to subordinate all its perceptions and intuitions to a conscious rational order. Each word, each phrase, each element in the formal pattern (a pattern strongly reminiscent of Pope in its use of balance and antithesis) submits itself readily to conscious critical scrutiny, as if securely aware of playing its part in the precise considered statement of the whole. (Notice, for instance, that the balancing of 'admires' against 'requires' in the final couplet is not a perfunctory verbalism, but compels us to notice a relevant distinction between youth and age.) The aptness of the simile is of the same order; we feel certain that Crabbe knew exactly what he was doing in introducing, through the image of 'a bright and polished brilliant', the idea of a scintillation which removes from Arabella's wisdom and learning any sense of heaviness, together with the suggestion of personal attractiveness, a high degree of deliberate cultivation, and a readiness for public display.

Arabella's accomplishments, which are described in detail, are, in fact, those of a typical bluestocking of the period; as so often in Crabbe's characterization, the concrete and highly particularized realization of an individual goes hand in hand with a keen sense of the socially typical. But his characters are also (and quite designedly) typical on a more fundamental level: they are 'just representations of general nature' in the Johnsonian sense, so that the moral issues and conflicts which they embody have a universal and timeless significance. In the case of Arabella, Crabbe's moral theme is the intricate mixture of virtue and self-regarding pride which motivates her conduct. The pride is soon apparent in the exacting 'store of virtues' which she openly demands of any prospective husband. Three contrasted suitors offer themselves and are rejected; the treatment of the last of these is worth quoting to show the flexibility which the heroic couplet assumes in Crabbe's hands:

> On Captain Bligh her mind in balance hung –
> Though valiant, modest; and reserved, though young:
> Against these merits must defects be set –
> Though poor, imprudent; and though proud, in debt:
> In vain the Captain close attention paid;
> She found him wanting, whom she fairly weigh'd.
>
> (110–15)[2]

The movement of the first four lines admirably enacts the judicial balancing and weighing, and is in sharp contrast to the brisk decisiveness of the succeeding couplet; the effect is unobtrusive, but wholly successful in its economic forwarding of the narrative. Next comes Edward Huntley, who appears to fill the bill satisfactorily; but because her ideal suitor 'his passions must command/And yet possess', she repeatedly postpones their marriage in face of his impatient entreaties, and before the appointed date a young woman whom he has seduced appears on the scene with her illegitimate child. Huntley's mother appeals on her son's behalf to Arabella's 'reason':

> 'It well becomes thee, lady, to appear
> But not to be, in very truth, severe . . .'
>
> (157–8)

but this worldly conception of reason is clearly not shared by the poet. Although Crabbe does undoubtedly judge the remorselessness of Arabella's repudiation of Huntley to be unreasonable, this is partly because it is too extreme a reaction (and 'excess' is always for Crabbe almost as much a term of reproof as 'folly'), and, more particularly, because it proceeds from impure motives. As Crabbe puts it in his note to the poem, 'motives may in a great measure be concealed from the mind of the agent: and we often take credit to our virtue for actions which sprang originally from our tempers, inclinations, or our indifference'. This mingling of motive is vividly and convincingly presented in Arabella's indignant reply:

'Say that the crime is common – shall I take
A common man my wedded lord to make? ...
Shall I forgive his vileness, take his name,
Sanction his error, and partake his shame?
No! this assent would kindred frailty prove,
A love for him would be a vicious love:
Can a chaste maiden secret counsel hold
With one whose crime by every mouth is told?
Forbid it spirit, prudence, virtuous pride ...'

(165–75)

The self-regarding pride which reveals itself (quite unknown to the speaker) in such expressions as 'partake his shame' and 'one whose crime by every mouth is told' is rendered with consummate skill and insight. Arabella is, in fact, one of those

... who feel, when young, the false sublime,
And proudly love to show disdain for crime;

(194–5)

and we may note, in passing, that 'the false sublime' is a phrase which indicates very clearly the basis of Crabbe's cautious distrust of exalted notions and ardent feeling.

We are now shown (as Crabbe puts it in one of those transitional passages in which he excels):

... the gradual change in human hearts
That time, in commerce with the world, imparts;
That on the roughest temper throws disguise,
And steals from virtue her asperities.

(212–15)

Twelve years later ('Twelve brilliant years .../Yet each with less of glory than the last') Arabella has accepted the attentions of Beswell (whose social status as a merchant represents in itself a decline from her former pretensions), and the course which their courtship follows is in ironic contrast to the earlier courtship of Huntley:

Now was the lover urgent, and the kind
And yielding lady to his suit inclined:
'A little time, my friend, is just, is right;
We must be decent in our neighbours' sight':
Still she allow'd him of his hopes to speak,
And in compassion took off week by week;
Till few remain'd, when, wearied with delay,
She kindly meant to take off day by day.

(250–57)

93

At this point Arabella's spinster-friend comes to her with the information that Beswell is secretly keeping a coloured mistress who has borne him 'a spurious race' of 'brown ugly bastards'. This time Arabella tries at first to discount or minimize the crime and then proclaims her intention of marrying the culprit in order to reclaim him.

> She spoke, nor more her holy work delay'd;
> 'Twas time to lend an erring mortal aid.
> 'The noblest way,' she judged, 'a soul to win,
> Was with an act of kindness to begin,
> To make the sinner sure, and then t'attack the sin.'
>
> (333–7)

In these concluding lines it is not the action itself that excites ironic disapprobation but, once again, Arabella's self-deception about her own motives.

It can be seen, even from this foreshortened summary, that there is no disablingly narrow didacticism about Crabbe's pervasive moral interest. It is true that he writes always in the spirit (the thoroughly eighteenth-century spirit) of his own lines from *The Parish Register*:

> And could I well th'instructive truth convey,
> 'Twould warn the giddy and awake the gay.
>
> (I, 281–2)

But, secure in his conviction that the 'Nature' to which art is required to be faithful is itself the supreme repository of moral law, he can feel no temptation to distort the facts as he sees them; the 'truth' is itself bound to be 'instructive'. In almost all his tales[3] we can trace an explicit moral purpose, but in his best work the centre of interest shifts increasingly to the attempt to define the complexity of the moral issues involved, and with this there goes a corresponding increase in the complexity of poetic organization of the tale itself. Most typically this complexity is a matter of holding a just balance between two conflicting attitudes, each of which has something to be said for it, a balance which is not merely *stated* but is also (as in *Arabella*) *enacted* in the tale's actual narrative structure. In *Arabella*, of course, the balance has to be struck somewhere between the extremes of condoning the sin and condemning the sinner; and this is a preoccupation which recurs frequently in one form or another.

Crabbe, in general, holds firmly to the Augustan values of sense, judgement, balance, and moderation; yet at the same time he shows (like Jane Austen) a fascinated awareness of all that is irrational and inexplicable in human behaviour, and a robust determination to explore it, understand it, and bring it within his own framework of values. Elsewhere this readiness to face and examine the non-rational shows itself in the Romantic themes (dreams, madness, childhood, even ghosts) to which he reverts so frequently, though always treating them from his own essentially reasonable standpoint; in *Arabella*, as we have seen, it takes the form of acute insight into human motivation, and as such gives rise to a kind of ironic comedy which must have been part at least of what Jane Austen found to admire in Crabbe. And actually, of course, Crabbe has over Jane Austen one advantage: as we can see even from *Arabella*, he is not at all inhibited by moral squeamishness, so that his portrayal of the England of his day is a remarkably frank and comprehensive one.

The Lover's Journey is one of the tales in which Crabbe deals, from his own point of view, with a Romantic theme, in this case the extent to which the perception of natural beauty is dependent upon the subjective frame of mind of the beholder. Perhaps the most characteristic Romantic enunciation of it is to be found in Coleridge's lines:

> O Lady! we receive but what we give,
> And in our life alone does Nature live.[4]

We may contrast with this Crabbe's opening statement:

> It is the soul that sees; the outward eyes
> Present the object, but the mind descries;
> And thence delight, disgust, or cool indiff'rence rise:
> When minds are joyful, then we look around,
> And what is seen is all on fairy ground;
> Again they sicken, and on every view
> Cast their own dull and melancholy hue;
> Or, if absorb'd by their peculiar cares,
> The vacant eye on viewless matter glares,
> Our feelings still upon our views attend,
> And their own nature to the objects lend;
> Sorrow and joy are in their influence sure,
> Long as the passion reigns th' effects endure;
> But love in minds his various changes makes,
> And clothes each object with the change he takes;
> His light and shade on every view he throws,
> And on each object, what he feels, bestows.

We see at once that Crabbe's way of putting it assumes tacitly that the object is there, fully there, whether the mind perceives it or not; and that his metaphors firmly though unobtrusively assign the subjective vision to a decidedly lower level of reality. The mind 'casts', 'throws', or 'bestows' something on the object, 'lends' or 'clothes' (and it is worth noticing that each of these verbs takes an additional stress through the position it occupies in the line). Already we are aware of a suggestion that what the soul sees is in some sense illusory, and the suggestion is kept alive by the poet's method of presenting the succeeding narrative.

The lover sets out on a visit to his loved one, riding at first through unenticing stretches of bleak countryside – 'a barren heath' which gives way to the 'meagre herbage' of 'a common pasture wild and wide' and is followed in turn by the sterile vegetation of a salt-marsh; yet his feelings of joy and anticipation lead him to see all this as delightful and even beautiful. Arriving at his beloved's house he finds that she has left a message asking him to follow her elsewhere, so he completes his journey through a green, fertile and well-kept valley – but now his disappointment and vexation cause him to detest the lushness which surrounds him:

> 'I hate these long green lanes; there's nothing seen
> In this vile country but eternal green;
> Woods! waters! meadows! Will they never end?'
> (260–62)

At each stage we are given first a superbly vivid and detailed description of the natural scene, and then the lover's idealizing or denigrating vision of it; the effect of this contrast is to convince us that the subjective viewpoint is inescapably unreliable and delusory. For good measure the tale ends with the lover retracing the whole of his journey, but this time his mood is such that he does not even notice the countryside he passes through. During the first stage his 'Laura' is with him, and since his mind is preoccupied with her presence his eye does no more than 'rove o'er the fleeting views'. Subsequently, when alone, his mind is 'absent' (dwelling on recollections of the immediate past) and consequently his 'vacant eye' merely 'wanders o'er viewless scenes'.

Characteristically enough, Crabbe adds a further moral dimension to the theme. During the first part of his journey the lover comes upon a sordid gipsy encampment, and the poet's condemnation of a way of life which he presents as vicious and ill-regulated is tempered only by the compassion with which he foresees their inevitable end. After describing the 'brown boys' already adept at begging, the 'light laugh and roguish leer' of their already corrupted twelve-year-old sister, the slatternliness of the wife, and the 'steady falsehood' of expression worn by the fortune-telling mother, the passage concludes:

> Last in the group, the worn-out grandsire sits
> Neglected, lost, and living but by fits;
> Useless, despised, his worthless labours done,
> And half protected by the vicious son,
> Who half supports him; he with heavy glance
> Views the young ruffians who around him dance;
> And, by the sadness in his face, appears
> To trace the progress of their future years:
> Through what strange course of misery, vice, deceit,
> Must wildly wander each unpractised cheat!
> What shame and grief, what punishment and pain,
> Sport of fierce passions, must each child sustain –
> Ere they like him approach their latter end,
> Without a hope, a comfort or a friend!
> But this Orlando felt not; 'Rogues,' said he,
> 'Doubtless they are, but merry rogues they be ...'
>
> (182–97)

The lover's idealizing vision has here betrayed him into a dangerous insensitivity to the moral aspect of human character and conduct. 'Nature' for Crabbe embraces the whole of the created universe, including mankind; the truth which it offers for our contemplation is inseparable from the objective and universal moral law, and it is folly to allow our feelings to falsify or distort this truth. The point is reiterated with telling force in the second part of the journey by the fatuity of Orlando's reaction (in his bad-tempered mood) to another human feature of the landscape, this time a wedding.

Taken as a whole, this tale is of outstanding interest. Its intrinsic achievement is that of treating the typically Romantic theme in a way that does full justice to the phenomenon while at the same time 'placing' it in a wider and more objective setting; and the penetration of the comment upon a dominant Romantic trend will bear a good deal of pondering. In addition, it offers a clue to the sources of the energy and tension which characterize almost all Crabbe's mature poetry, qualities which make it very different from anything which eighteenth-century Augustanism had to offer and which clearly owe a good deal to the challenging contact with the Romantic environment.

Widely though they differ from each other, these two examples can give no idea of the remarkable variety of themes and purposes to which the tale lends itself in Crabbe's hands. This range should be studied in the 1812 volume as a whole, though a good start could be made by reading, for instance, *Procrastination*, *The Frank Courtship* and *Advice*. In *Tales* (1812) Crabbe's art is, in fact, at its most masterly. In the succeeding volume, *Tales of the Hall* (1819), he has moved towards a more natural everyday vocabulary, but the verse texture is more relaxed and meandering, while the organization of the individual tale tends on the whole to be slacker and more diffuse. This more leisurely and expansive style undoubtedly has its successes, most notably in *Delay has Dangers* (Book XIII) which is among the very best of Crabbe's tales; but elsewhere it is accompanied at times by an over-dependence upon coincidence, or even by an occasional lapse into melodrama. *Posthumous Tales* (1834) opens with the wholly admirable *Silford Hall* in which the influence of Wordsworth is clearly evident; but the *Farewell and Return* sequence which makes up the bulk of the volume is thin and uninteresting, offering melancholy if unsurprising evidence of the decline in Crabbe's powers in the last few years of his long life.

During his later period Crabbe was held in remarkably high esteem by critics and reading public alike, and almost all the important writers of his day have left on record some expression of their veneration for his work. Now that he has begun to be read again after a long period of neglect, it still remains extremely difficult to formulate a just assessment of his stature. It is certainly true that, unlike Blake or Wordsworth, he did not initiate any new forms of sensibility, any radically new mode of thought or feeling; his originality lay in his success in making a new synthesis of already existing elements, and his art is that of a short-story writer in verse, a medium in which he is excelled by Chaucer alone. In this sense Crabbe is, in his tales at least, a major poet who can hold his own, for permanent interest and value, alongside any of the Romantics.

NOTES

1. The words quoted are from Crabbe's Preface to *Tales* (1812).

2. Quotations are from the 1823 edition of *The Works of the Reverend George Crabbe* in 8 vols (John Murray, London, 1823).

3. Notable exceptions are *The Parting Hour* in *Tales* (1812) and *Silford Hall* in *Posthumous Tales* (1834).

4. From *Dejection: an Ode*, first published in *The Morning Post*, 4 October 1802.

BURNS AND ENGLISH LITERATURE

JOHN SPEIRS

Burns (1759–96) the man and the symbol have been much talked about in the world. The poetry, on the other hand, appears to be as imperfectly known as ever. Certain of the songs that most appealed to nineteenth-century taste have lodged in the anthologies and now stand for Burns's poetry as a whole. Meanwhile the body of his achievement, the comic and satiric poetry of the Kilmarnock edition (1786), remains comparatively neglected.

The greater part of this body of Scots verse was composed in a single year (1785) and in the early months of the following year. The 1785 vintage included such characteristic pieces as *Death and Dr Hornbook*, *Address to the Deil*, *The Jolly Beggars*, *Halloween*, *Holy Willie's Prayer*, *The Holy Fair*, *The Ordination*, *To a Mouse*, *To a Louse*, and the *Epistles to Lapraik*, *to Smith*, and *to Simpson*. *Scotch Drink*, *The Earnest Cry and Prayer*, *The Twa Dogs* followed in 1786. These (when the poet was twenty-six) represent the full vigour and maturity of Burns's Scots genius. Apart from the body of the songs – the best of which associate most closely with the comic and satiric verse – and apart from *Tam o' Shanter* (1790), Burns added little in later years to this achievement.

The essential characteristics of Burns's Scots verse, though not its total range, will become apparent in a reading of any one or two of his best pieces. There is no space here to attempt more than that and to add a few generalizations about his poetry as a whole. But though two pieces only must here serve as specimens, the Scots poems so belong together that they should all be read as parts of a single whole. Then only is it possible fully to apprehend the animating life of this body of comic poetry, the fine recklessness and powerful out-flow of genial and generous sympathies, the spirited independence and vigour of judgement, the warmth and generosity of regard for intrinsic human worth. Then it can be recognized, too, that the satire arises from the natural recoil of these same sympathies against things that thwart the creative energies and potentialities of life and pervert the essential nature of man.

The poems here chosen for illustration, *To a Louse* and *Holy Willie's Prayer*, are virtually dramatic monologues, though in the first the poet himself is the character speaking or has assumed this role. The opening of *To a Louse* is as dramatic as Donne:

> Ha! whare ye gaun, ye crawlin ferlie!
> Your impudence protects you sairly:
> I canna say but ye strunt rarely,
>   Owre gauze and lace;
> Tho', faith, I fear ye dine but sparely
>   On sic a place.

The manner is that of the traditional 'flyting', yet it is clear that abuse is mingled with admiration for the amazing agility and strut of the creature. The poet cannot help having a certain sympathy even with a louse, which like 'mice and men' also 'maun live'. Gauze and lace are very fine but not edible. They are no more use to the louse than was the jewel on the dunghill to the cock of the fable. But the impudence of the louse rouses the poet's indignant fury:

> Ye ugly, creepin', blastit wonner,
> Detested, shunn'd, by saunt an' sinner,
> How dare ye set your fit upon her,
>   Sae fine a lady!
> Gae somewhere else, and seek your dinner
>   On some poor body.

The comic poetic imagination magnifies and multiplies the diminutive creature into whole populations of its kind all in a state of vigorous animation, whole nations in a beggar's rags:

> Swith, in some beggar's haffet squattle;
> There ye may creep, and sprawl, and sprattle
> Wi' ither kindred, jumping cattle,
>   In shoals and nations;
> Whare horn nor bane ne'er dare unsettle
>   Your thick plantations.

In the development of this poem the shifts of attention and sudden excitements of the observer are reproduced in his speaking voice and correspond dramatically to the movements and struggling upward progression of the indefatigable, intrepid creature till it reaches the summit of Jenny's new bonnet:

> Na, faith ye yet! ye'll no be right
> Till ye've got on it,
> The vera tapmost, tow'ring height
> O' Miss's bonnet.

The observer is curious to see how far it will get until it overtops the summit of pride.

At this point in the poem there is a shift of attention to Jenny herself. The irony is that no doubt she thinks she is making a grand impression in church in her new bonnet and Sunday finery, unaware of the indignity being imposed on her by the louse. The old traditional feeling about 'pride and vanity' is here again in the impression of Jenny giving herself airs, proud Jenny:

> O, Jenny, dinna toss your head,
> An' set your beauties a' abread!
> Ye little ken what cursed speed
> The blastie's makin'!

The poem is both a comedy – based on the incongruity of louse and fine lady – and a moral fable:

> O wad some Pow'r the giftie gie us
> To see oursels as others see us!

Holy Willie's Prayer, perhaps the finest of Burns's satiric poems, is a dramatic monologue in which the mounting fervency of Willie's eloquence, as he himself is more and more carried away by it, is itself comic, an aspect of the whole grand effect of ironic comedy. The irony is that in his eloquent outpouring Willie completely exposes his own nature and instincts without exposing himself to himself, without disturbing his own inordinate self-conceit. The poem is thus, among other things, a study in unconscious hypocrisy. Willie kneels at the centre of his little parochial world, so vividly present in the imagery, in direct relation with his God – and what a God! The poem's implied criticism of the character of Holy Willie is at the same time a criticism of the Calvinism that shaped the character; they stand and fall together. Holy Willie's is a God who pleases himself and, in doing so, damns ten times the number of people he saves all for his glory:

> O Thou, wha in the Heavens dost dwell,
> Wha, as it pleases best thysel',
> Sends ane to heaven and ten to hell,
>   A' for thy glory,
> And no for ony guid or ill
>   They've done afore thee!

> I bless and praise thy matchless might,
> When thousands thou hast left in night,
> That I am here afore thy sight,
>   For gifts an' grace,
> A burnin' an' a shinin' light
>   To a' this place.

Salvation has no relation to one's moral conduct, but depends on 'election' – and Willie has no doubt that he is one of the elect. It is a damning criticism of Willie that he can 'bless and praise' a God thus conceived. But Willie is sublimely unconscious of the figure he cuts. His arrogance is so unbounded as to amount to caricature. While thousands are lost in darkness (such is his vision of mankind), Willie is 'a burnin' an' a shinin' light'. His 'humility' is a form of pride:

> What was I, or my generation,
> That I should get sic exaltation?
> I, wha deserve sic just damnation
>   For broken laws ...

The laws were not broken by Willie, but before he was born:

> Five thousand years 'fore my creation,
>   Thro' Adam's cause.

Thus even Willie's faults are not his responsibility but are part of the divine plan for his benefit, since he is 'chosen'.

> When frae my mither's womb I fell,
> Thou might hae plunged me in hell,
> To gnash my gums, to weep and wail
>   In burnin' lake,
> Where damned devils roar an' yell,
>   Chain'd to a stake.

Though the effect throughout the poem is of course 'comic', the imagery that Willie conceives here is as inhuman, as unnatural as Lady

Macbeth's when she is doing violence to her own nature as a woman, and it reveals how far the Calvinist Holy Willie has deviated from nature and sense. Yet, even at this point he can rise to a sublimity of complacent self-satisfaction:

> Yet I am here a chosen sample,
> To show thy grace is great and ample;
> I'm here a pillar in thy temple,
>   Strong as a rock;
> A guide, a buckler, an example
>   To a' thy flock.

God's grace excludes the greater part of mankind, but so long as it includes Willie it is 'great and ample'.

Willie goes on to reveal in what respects he is 'an example'. He speaks of his own sins of the flesh as if they were ills of the flesh, afflictions sent to him which he must bear. After declaring and apparently believing that he is not as other men who drink, swear, sing, and dance, the opposite begins to come out – and that he is in his way a lusty fellow:

> But yet, O Lord! confess I must,
> At times I'm fash'd wi' fleshy lust.

He excuses himself for one of his lapses by saying that that night he 'was fou'. After what he had just said about his immunity from the local drinking habits, we thus learn incidentally that there are occasions when he is not so. But his sins are of course not Willie's personal affair, not his responsibility; they are inflicted on him, sent to save him from pride.

> Maybe thou lets this fleshy thorn
> Beset thy servant e'en and morn,
> Lest he owre high and proud should turn
>   'Cause he's sae gifted.

Willie remains unshakably convinced of his own exceptional merits, and thus continues to exemplify the pride that he presumes himself to be saved from.

The 'prayer', as it goes on, reveals a Holy Willie full of most un-Christian feelings towards his neighbours, full of envy, malice, and all uncharitableness, particularly towards those among them who have in some way offended Willie himself and the small band of the 'chosen'. A fierce energy, a ferocity of personal vindictiveness and spite kindles the eloquence of his prayer against them. His concern is that they should *not* be spared, that they should get their deserts:

> Lord, mind Gaun Hamilton's deserts,
> He drinks, an' swears, and plays at cartes . . .
> An' whan we chasten'd him therefore,
> Thou kens how he bred sic a splore,
> As set the warld in a roar
>   O' laughin' at us;
> Curse thou his basket and his store,
>   Kail and potatoes.

The world that laughs – a laughter not to be borne – is Willie's own small parochial world, the world of his neighbour's 'basket and store, kail and potatoes'. The God of all mankind is called upon fervently, in Old Testament phraseology, to curse Gaun Hamilton's basket, store, kail and potatoes, and also to curse the Presbytery of Ayr. The comic satiric effect depends on the disproportion:

> Thy strong right hand, Lord, make it bare
>   Upo' their heads;
> Lord, weigh it down, and dinna spare.

Willie's God might here be the village schoolmaster.

With the repetitions of 'dinna spare' and of 'Lord' (as, earlier, of 'chosen') Willie's eloquence rises to a climax, which is sublime in manner but comic in effect:

> But, for thy people's sake, destroy 'em,
>   And dinna spare.

He sees his neighbours as the Philistines of the Old Testament, the enemies of God's chosen. The mercies which at the same time Willie asks for himself are both 'temp'ral and divine', both 'gear and grace'. It is clear that for Willie the increase of temporal blessings, the multi-plication of earthly goods ('gear'), is the way the divine grace favours the chosen. Worldly prosperity is the visible and outward sign and effect of the divine grace. Willie expects to have it both ways, to prosper both in a material and a spiritual sense.

Burns's Scots verse evidently does not belong to the context of the English literature that was contemporary with him. It comes at the end of a tradition of verse-making in Scots that had been

continuous since Henryson and Dunbar (for the eighteenth-century
Scots verse of Ramsay and Fergusson was rather a development than
a revival), and the differences between the Scots and the English languages imply differences of life as well as of conversation, different
kinds of communities. Burns's Scots verse is that of a poet very consciously alive in his contemporary local world – which was not, however, the world either of his English urban or his English provincial
contemporaries. It is almost by what seems an accident that Burns
is a contemporary of the English authors of the eighteenth century.
It was in many ways a misfortune that Burns's Scots verse had to
be appreciated first by a late eighteenth-century 'polite' taste, then
by the nineteenth-century 'romantic' taste. Burns has never properly
recovered from the effects of these 'appreciations'. Had the nature
of Burns's poetic achievement been more clearly apprehended, it
could perhaps have made a difference to the English poetry of the
nineteenth century itself. But it is impossible to find that the Scots
verse of Burns and his predecessors had any appreciable effect on
English poetry (unless possibly on the Byron of *Don Juan*); there
was no place for his comic and satiric poetry any more than for Pope.
The Burns who took the fancy of the nineteenth century is the Burns
of the songs, particularly of those that could be felt to be the Scotch
equivalent of Tom Moore's Irish Melodies.

Burns's comic and satiric verse, like the best English poetry and
the novel of the eighteenth century, deals with human nature and
behaviour, not with landscape or the poet's own personal feelings.
There are, of course, important distinctions between Burns and the
eighteenth-century English authors, even apart from the differences
of language and tradition. For example, Burns's vision of human life
is a comic one, unlike that of Johnson or Crabbe which, though witty
and satiric, is profoundly tragic. Nevertheless, these authors have at
least this in common that their subject is man and society, whether
urban (London) society as in Pope and Johnson, or particular kinds
or levels of rural or provincial society, as in Crabbe and Jane Austen
– and Burns.

Burns was not, as he has sometimes been portrayed, an unlettered
peasant, an inspired artless folk-singer. He read not only the Bible,
Shakespeare, and Pope, but also the *Spectator*, Richardson, and Sterne,
besides the lesser poets, Thomson, Shenstone, and Gray. He had

little Latin; but he read French, and his French reading included Racine. Nevertheless, his English and French reading proves to have been finally irrelevant to his work as a Scots *lettered* poet, as well as to the Burns of those songs which are properly to be regarded as in the folk-song tradition. At an early age he had read the Scots verse of Allan Ramsay. But it seems to have been that of Robert Fergusson, when he at last became acquainted with it, that precipitated that sudden efflorescence of Burn's Scots genius which, from a wider point of view, the lives and speech of a whole people had been preparing. For Burns's individual achievement was possible because there was a living tradition of verse-making in his own Scots language, an art being practised. Burns must have been familiar from an early age with the practice of verse-making in Scots − including the custom of exchanging verse epistles − since it was still prospering.

But above all the people provided him with a spoken language that was itself almost his own poetry, the speech of a complex community having its own very old traditional life.

> The words come skelpin, rank and file,
> Amaist before I ken.

For copiousness and fertility of surprising phrase and image, the nearest parallels in English to Burns's Scots language are Elizabethan colloquial English − Falstaff's English − and, indeed, Chaucerian English. Burns's Scots seems to grow out of a rich underlying life, nourishing the roots of the spoken language; and he shares, through his language itself, a conscious sense of the complexity of life, a shrewd humorous knowledge of human nature and human weakness tempered with generous kindliness, an old proverbial wisdom.

Burns's comic and satiric poems are not just comedy and satire; they are a body of comic and satiric *poetry*. There is no such thing as the comedy or the satire apart from the poetry − and apart from the language out of which the poetry is made; they are inherent in the whole imaginative, creative process. It is a process working, as poetry does, through rhythm and imagery to create a sense of a world or community of particular characters behaving, talking, in particular scenes. Burns's comic and satiric poetry is like Chaucer's *Canterbury Tales* in this respect at least that it is the nearest thing to a kind of dramatic poetry. We listen not only to dialogues and monologues, to characters talking, but to the poet himself talking characteristically, as eye-witness and shrewdly humorous commentator on the life that he is presenting and of which he is himself a part; for Burns is, on the whole, more engaged in the human comedy, to him a dance rather than a procession, than is Chaucer. Like Chaucer, too, Burns transcends the distinction between prose and verse. Prose fiction never developed in Scots; it might almost be said that it did not need to, because the kind of interest out of which the eighteenth- and nineteenth-century novel developed was to some extent provided for in the verse. The *Epistles* again, intimate though they are, are a kind of extension of conversation between friends and neighbours, a social art, intelligent, lively, and witty commentary on various subjects connected with their lives, amusements, and work. In the *Epistles*, incidentally, Burns is his own best literary critic.

Poetry made, as are these poems, out of a spoken language – and such a language as was eighteenth-century Scots, entirely free from poetic diction and consequently from 'poetical' subjects – is almost necessarily counter to pretension and affectation both literary and moral. There is a relation between Burns's 'realism', including his satire of hypocrisy and pretence, and his unaffected familiar idiom.

Burns's poetry rises from a conversational level, from small market-town and village talk about various subjects that include the affairs of kirk and kingdom, but are always related to personal and local interests, rises from that level in rhythms that have a relation also to dance and dance-tunes. The comic verve and flow of Burns's poetry is indeed such that it is as if the rhythms of the dance had got into the blood of the talkers, animating the talk into witty phrases and images both humorous and fanciful. Several of the poems are specifically related to the fairs and rustic holidays, the folk festivals that were still a traditional part of the life of Burns's Scottish community, and it is scarcely too much to say that at a deeper level the whole of his comic and satiric Scots verse is related to this side of Scottish life. It is both bucolic and bacchanalian in the sense that conviviality is associated with spring and harvest, fertility and fruitfulness, and so with the perpetual struggle against sterility and barrenness, not only in the fields but in the minds and feelings of men. Sense and shrewdness are associated with generosity and kindliness. These values are expressed not in abstract generalizations but in impressions of individual human behaviour in a particular community which is that of the eighteenth century in Scotland.

Burns's Scots verse is still contemporary with the modern reader who in reading relives it and shares its viewpoint and criticism of human life. His comic and satiric poetry thus brings a community, of which there are few traces now left, immediately to the imagination of the modern reader − without idealization, though with a genial realism − so that he almost seems to be living in it, listening to the very accents of the talk. It is, in short, the best kind of social history. But it is also far more. It is a poetry that creates a comic world, and in doing so presents its own unique vision and criticism of our human life − at a particular place and time.

VARIETIES OF ENGLISH GOTHIC

GILBERT PHELPS

There is a tendency in histories of English literature to treat the Gothic novel as an unfortunate aberration, a diversion from the main thrust of development. It is an understandable attitude in view of the fact that this curious cultural phenomenon was associated with a sharp decline from the high promise represented, in varying degrees, by such eighteenth-century pioneers of the English novel as Defoe, Richardson, Fielding, Smollett and Sterne, and with the advent of new methods of composition, publication and circulation designed to cater for a different kind of readership which demanded, above all, novelty and sensationalism. But it is impossible fully to understand the Romantic Movement – and the decadence that followed it – without paying attention to the Gothic novel, which in fact is not divorced from the mainstream of English fiction.

What exactly, though, does the term Gothic mean as applied to this particular type of fiction? The word originally implied anything wild and barbarous, and destructive of classical civilization. In particular, the adjective came to be applied to the pointed arch in ecclesiastical architecture between the twelfth and fourteenth centuries – and by degrees to any style of building that was not classical, and from there to almost anything medieval. In the early part of the eighteenth century, when classical values reigned supreme, Gothic was a term of contempt, but when the reaction against Classicism set in the word took on positive implications. It was this defiant anti-Classicism that in part explained the growing craze for Gothic architecture and ruins, actual or contrived. Indeed, the most constant feature of the Gothic novel was the presence of a medieval building of some sort, with secret corridors and labyrinthine underground passages. The other main ingredients were various supernatural manifestations; a mysterious crime, usually of an illicit or incestuous nature; a villain who in many cases has pledged himself

110

to diabolical powers; persecuted maidens or fatal, Medusa-like women; charnel-houses, tombs and graveyards; and nature itself conspiring to produce effects of gloomy terror.

The label Gothic as applied to the novel is not, however, a very precise one. Generally speaking there are three main lines of development, springing from Horace Walpole's *The Castle of Otranto* which, in 1764, launched the genre in England. First there was Gothic-Historical (or rather pseudo-historical), practised by such disciples of Walpole as Clara Reeve in *The Old English Baron* (1777) which is set in what purports to be the fifteenth century – and which was entitled *The Captive of Virtue, a Gothic Story* in its first edition; the Lee sisters, and especially Sophia with *The Recess, or a Tale of Other Times* (1785); and Charlotte Smith in *The Old Manor House* (1793). Secondly there was the School of Terror, in which superstitious dread is aroused by a series of apparently supernatural manifestations; this was initiated by Mrs Ann Radcliffe with her highly influential *The Mysteries of Udolpho* (1794). Third was the School of Horror, partly derived from German and French models, of which the chief exemplar was Matthew Gregory Lewis, with *The Monk* (1796).

But these categories often overlap. In Charles Maturin's *Melmoth the Wanderer* (1820), for example, the streams of terror and horror intermingle. There are, too, a number of novels commonly labelled Gothic which would fit just as comfortably into other pigeon-holes. The Penguin *Three Gothic Novels*, for example,[1] includes, in addition to *The Castle of Otranto* and Mary Shelley's *Frankenstein* (1818), William Beckford's *Vathek* (1786), which is in large part an oriental tale with quite different antecedents, though it has a decidedly Gothic core. And William Godwin's minor masterpiece *Caleb Williams* (1794), though included in most studies of the Gothic novel, is primarily a novel of ideas with a few Gothic accretions.

The general purpose of the more traditional Gothic fiction is aptly summed up by William Hazlitt (in his essay 'On the English Novelists') when he says of Mrs Radcliffe that she has mastered 'the art of freezing the blood ... harrowing up the soul with imaginary horrors, and making the flesh creep and the nerves thrill'. Why this should be regarded as a necessary or desirable aim is one of the questions any inquiry into the Gothic novel must seek to answer. Exploitation of the public by cheap sensationalism is not by itself an adequate explanation. To begin with it must be remembered that, ludicrous though they must seem now, the ingredients listed above do not belong exclusively to the Gothic novel. A number of them had made their appearance well before the reaction against the prevailing classicism of the earlier eighteenth century had begun. Gloom, melancholy, death and the graveyard had, for example, inspired Thomas Parnell's *Night Piece on Death* as early as 1722; Edward Young's *Night Thoughts* (1742), Robert Blair's *The Grave* (1743) and Thomas Gray's *Elegy Written in a Country Churchyard* (1751) also contain 'Gothic' elements. The earlier eighteenth-century novel itself, moreover, contained aspects which could fairly be described as Gothic. Jane Austen's *Northanger Abbey* (1818) is not only a parody of what she herself termed 'horrid books' (horrid in the sense of horrendous) such as Mrs Radcliffe's *The Mysteries of Udolpho*, but an ironic commentary on a wide range of eighteenth-century novelists, including not only other 'horrid' writers like 'Monk' Lewis but also Samuel Richardson. Richardson is of particular interest here. The novel Jane Austen singles out is *Sir Charles Grandison* (1753), as a particularly insipid example of the novel of sensibility. But his *Clarissa Harlowe* (1747–8), great novel though it is in most respects, contains elements of a more specifically Gothic nature. There is, for example, the dream of Clarissa (a classic example of the persecuted maiden) in which Lovelace,

seizing upon her, carries her into a churchyard; and there, notwithstanding all her prayers and tears, and protestations of innocence, stabs her to the heart, and then tumbles her into a deep grave ready dug, among two or three half-dissolved carcases; throwing in the dirt and earth upon her with his hands, and trampling it down with his feet.

In the course of the eighteenth century, moreover, there were attempts to accommodate to current aesthetic theory the kind of emotions to be exploited by the Gothic novelists, notably by Edmund Burke in his *A Philosophical Inquiry into the Sublime and the Beautiful* (1756), when he declared:

whatever is fitted in any sort to excite the ideas of pain, that is to say, whatever is in any sort terrible ... is a source of the sublime.

In other words, there were elements within the Classical or Augustan period which lent themselves to the new sensibility from which the

Gothic novel sprang. Not that there was anything new in these elements in themselves; such preoccupations are as old as man. As Charles Lamb acutely observed in his essay 'Witches and Other Night Fears':

Gorgons, and Hydras, and Chimaeras – dire stories of Celaeno and the Harpies – may reproduce themselves in the brain of superstition, but they were there before. They are transcripts, types – the archetypes are in us and eternal.

There are important differences, though, between the horrors of the earlier writers (the Jacobean dramatists, for example, or the meta-physicals) and those of the Gothic novelists. For one thing, the former were controlled by various literary and cultural conventions such as the paradox and the conceit. Far more important, they operated in the context of a still powerful and vital religion, which incorporated the supernatural in a positive and life-enhancing form and, so to speak, took care of primitive fears, cravings and guilts by means of its rituals and symbols, and the overall concept of a Saviour who took upon himself the world's cruelties and sufferings. One of the reasons for the popularity of the Gothic novel was that, with the weakening of the sustaining and containing religious framework, it provided something of an alternative outlet and repository for many impulses of the Romantic revival which had not yet been properly assimilated at a more serious level. To some extent it was an inevitable process. To quote Herbert Grierson's famous distinction:

Classical and romantic, these are the systole and diastole of the human heart in history. They represent our need of order, of synthesis, of a comprehen-sive yet definite, therefore *exclusive* as well as inclusive, ordering of thought and feeling.[2]

The Gothic novelists were employing a kind of shock-tactics directed against the complacency of the Augustans, and against their exclusion of certain areas of experience and feeling. The Augustans were quite aware of these exclusions, but for the most part they accepted them because they ensured the continuance of other values which they prized more highly.

However, a time came when the sense of exclusion became in-tolerable and the repressed emotions began to break through, and it was the Gothic novel that to a large extent provided a conduit for them. There are occasions, admittedly, when one is tempted to use that term in its most debased sense, in view of the material that made its way into some of the Gothic novels. For although the liberation of emotions that took place during the Romantic revival was largely beneficial and productive of some of the finest literature in the English language, the Romantic doctrine of the divine right of passion had implications, too, of a dangerous and sinister nature. It is no coincidence that the 'infernal novels' of the Marquis de Sade were appearing in France at about the same time that the English tale of terror flourished. The central challenge, indeed, that faced the writers of the Romantic period was how to come to terms with the flood of new emotions that had been released, which, at the same time that it greatly extended the bounds of the imagination, also let loose negative and destructive forces. To a considerable extent their stature *as* creative writers is to be measured by the degree to which they refused to surrender to these forces. The later phases of the Romantic revival exhibited unmistakable symptoms of such a surrender, and in the decadence of the late nineteenth century it was (with a few exceptions) almost complete.

To what extent, though, did the Gothic novel itself surrender? The answer is not as clear-cut as some literary historians have suggested. Distinctions and differentiations between intention and degrees of awareness have to be made. Walpole's *The Castle of Otranto* did little more than bring together the Gothic *dramatis personae*, atmosphere and machinery, including a castle which bears a decided resemblance to Walpole's own mock-Gothic castle at Strawberry Hill, Twickenham. It is difficult to credit now that Thomas Gray and his Cambridge friends were 'afraid to go to bed o' nights' after reading the novel. Yet even this gimcrack production is not altogether devoid of importance in the history of serious English fiction. Walpole tried to relate his novel to the realistic tradition, by the common device of casting his story within the framework of a newly discovered medieval manuscript, by attempts at realistic characterization, and by a self-consciously 'Shakespearean' blending of high and low through the presence of various servants commenting on the action. He played some small part in the creation of the genuine historical novel and had some influence on Sir Walter Scott.

Mrs Radcliffe's *The Mysteries of Udolpho* (her fourth novel) was

hailed as the natural successor to *The Castle of Otranto*. It contains
the usual pseudo-historical setting – the end of the sixteenth century.
The heroine is the orphaned Emily St Aubert, who is wooed by
Valancourt, a young man of good family but moderate means. But
her despotic aunt and guardian, Madame Cheron, has more ambitious
plans for her niece. Madame Cheron has married a sinister Italian,
Montoni, and the two of them carry Emily off to Montoni's sombre
castle of Udolpho in the Apennines. There all kinds of dark dealings
are carried on, connected with the Montonis' marriage plans for
Emily, in the midst of the usual Gothic apparatus of sliding panels,
secret passages, abductions and the hint of supernatural happenings,
though ultimately Mrs Radcliffe always produces natural explanations. Eventually Emily escapes, meets Valancourt again, and after
further vicissitudes is finally united to him, while Montoni, revealed
as the chief of a band of robbers, is captured and executed. Mrs
Radcliffe handles her Gothic material in *The Mysteries of Udolpho*
more successfully than Walpole, creating a more convincing sense of
mystery and suspense, so that, for what it is worth, it can probably
be called the first modern thriller. It is with her natural back-
grounds, however, that Mrs Radcliffe is most original. When she
wrote *The Mysteries of Udolpho* she had travelled no further abroad
than London and Bath. The exotic settings in which Emily has her
adventures were entirely derived from paintings, travel-books and
theatrical back-drops. Oddly enough they gain from this, taking on a
kind of surrealist quality, something like that of the steel-
engravings in numerous early Victorian books, which are so often
more effective than the contents themselves. What is more, these
imagined scenes are closely and successfully integrated with Emily's
state of mind, continually modifying her sensibility.

In this connection Ellen Moers, in her stimulating and perceptive
book *Literary Women*,[3] offers a number of fresh ideas about the
importance of 'the travelling heroine' of the day in the context of the
whole question of the position of women in contemporary society.
She suggests that Mrs Radcliffe used the form of the Gothic novel in
large measure as a 'a device to send maidens on distant and exciting
journeys without offending the proprieties' as a kind of 'feminine
substitute for the picaresque'. In many respects *The Mysteries of
Udolpho* can be considered not so much as a Gothic novel, but as one

in the Richardson tradition. Emily is very much a persecuted maiden of the Clarissa pattern; she too is a model of sensibility and propriety. What is especially interesting is that Mrs Radcliffe introduces a definite critique of sensibility. Early on in the novel Emily's father warns her against its dangers:

'Above all, my dear Emily, do not indulge in the pride of fine feeling, the romantic error of amiable minds ... Beware of priding yourself on the gracefulness of sensibility ... Always remember how much more valuable is the strength of sensibility ...'

and it is this kind of strength in her heroines which forms the major theme of Mrs Radcliffe's fiction. In *The Mysteries of Udolpho*, too, this strength is often deployed in a social context, concerned with matters of decorum, class mobility and differentiation – and, in particular, with property. The start of Emily's misfortunes is the financial ruin of her family, and much of the book after her aunt's death deals with Emily's efforts to consolidate her inherited fortune and property in the face of Montoni's diabolical machinations.

Before mentioning *The Italian* (1797), generally acknowledged to be Mrs Radcliffe's best novel, it is necessary to say something about Matthew Gregory Lewis, because the two are linked in an uneasy literary relationship. Lewis's novel *The Monk* (written when he was only nineteen) had many sources, including various contemporary French and German romances. But Lewis was also strongly influenced by Mrs Radcliffe, and Ambrosio, the central character of *The Monk*, was derived from Montoni. In the process, however, the character underwent profound changes. Lewis's Ambrosio, the seemingly near-saintly Superior of the Capuchins of Madrid, is in fact a slave to secret sexual desires, the repression of which is in itself a perversion. The instrument of his downfall is a seductive young girl named Matilda, with magical, witch-like powers, who enters his order in the guise of a male novice and then plays upon his secret longings. It is in a sepulchre deep beneath the monastery, among bones and decaying corpses, that he acts them out. With the help of Matilda's magic he also gets into his power the young novice, Antonia (who turns out to be his own sister), rapes her and then kills both her and her mother. Eventually he is discovered, tortured by the Inquisition and sentenced to death, but escapes from the *auto-da-fé* by making a Faustian pact with the Devil, only to meet with a more horrible fate at his hands.

Lewis employed most of the Gothic devices already introduced by Walpole and Mrs Radcliffe. But in addition he gave full rein to the darkest elements implicit in the Gothic genre. It is quite likely that he had read de Sade's *Justine*, the third edition of which was published in 1792 when Lewis himself was in Paris. (De Sade was, incidentally, an admirer of Mrs Radcliffe's work.) Certainly Lewis, like de Sade, had seized upon the perversely cruel elements latent in the whole theme of the persecution of innocence, from Richardson onwards. As with de Sade, Lewis was exploring the notion of man's almost unlimited capacity for evil. Although, therefore, Lewis's book, with its gross melodrama, lascivious lingering over horrors, and inflated, rhetorical style has little to recommend it as a work of art, it was perhaps the first in England to use the Gothic mode – and especially the paraphernalia of underground dungeons, cells and tombs – as a metaphor for descent into the most primitive depths of the subconscious. As such *The Monk* had a considerable influence not only on Lewis's near-contemporaries – among them the German writer Hoffmann in his *Elixire des Teufels* (1815–16) – but also on many later writers.

Mrs Radcliffe, however, was dismayed by Lewis's Ambrosio and his possible derivation from the Montoni of *The Mysteries of Udolpho*, and it was in part as a riposte that she wrote *The Italian, or the Confessional of the Black Penitents*, creating in Schedoni her own version of an evil monk. Like Ambrosio, Schedoni veers between iron self-control and surrender to evil impulses. His intended victim is Ellena, yet another persecuted maiden, who is incarcerated in a convent deep in the Abruzzi Appenines by the vengeful Marchesa di Vivaldi. It is Schedoni, employed by the Marchesa to murder Ellena, who is the most memorable figure of the novel. There is no attempt to minimize his crimes, or even the sexual aspect of his passions (though these are dealt with in a much more genteel fashion than in Lewis's *The Monk*). But whereas Ambrosio's character is irretrievably damned, and his fate irreversible, once he has sold his soul to the Devil, Schedoni, in spite of his preposterous Gothic aspects, remains a character in whom good impulses are not altogether dead and in whom conscience still operates. In her own way Mrs Radcliffe was attempting psychological analysis in the tradition of Richardson. In other words, she wrote *The Italian* both in defence of her genre, as she conceived it, in face of the threat posed by Lewis's *The Monk*, and, once again, with the aim of maintaining continuities with earlier fictional traditions. The comparisons and contrasts between Mrs Radcliffe and Monk Lewis (as he was nicknamed) pinpoint the clash between the still comparatively harmless and traditional tendencies within the Gothic novel and those pathological elements which were certainly *not* harmless – unless they could be absorbed into and controlled by an unusually profound imaginative and moral vision.

There are a number of critics who have argued that this is the case with Charles Maturin in his *Melmoth the Wanderer* (1820). Some very big claims have been made for him – comparisons, for example, with Coleridge, Dostoyevsky and Kafka. Certainly Maturin is a more powerful writer than Walpole, Mrs Radcliffe, Lewis or any of their followers. This passage, describing a shipwreck, has a kind of hallucinatory intensity reminiscent of the drug-induced visions of Thomas De Quincey:

The whole shore was now crowded with helpless gazers, every crag and cliff was manned; it seemed like a battle fought at once by sea and land, between hope and despair. No effectual assistance could be rendered – not a boat could live in that gale, – yet still, and to the last, cheers were heard from rock to rock, – terrible cheers, that announced that safety was near and – impossible; – lanthorns held aloft in all directions, that displayed to the sufferers the shore all peopled with life, and the roaring and impassable waves between; – ropes flung out, with loud cries of help and encouragement, and caught at by some chilled, nerveless, and despairing hand, that only grasped the wave, – relaxed its hold, – was tossed once over the sinking head, – and then seen no more.

Melmoth himself, an amalgam of Cain, the Wandering Jew, Milton's Satan, Faust, the Ancient Mariner and the Byronic hero, is a powerful creation. Like Faust[4] he has pledged his soul to the Devil in return for a prolonged life, but there is a twist to the pact: Melmoth can be released from the bargain if he can persuade one other person to take it over. The novel consists of a series of separate stories of extreme suffering, whose protagonists are all offered release by Melmoth – on condition that they take over his bargain with the Devil. Each of them, even the wife who loves him devotedly to the end, refuses, and eventually the term of the compact comes to an end and devils hurl Melmoth from a cliff into the sea. Taken together, these stories fit into each other to produce a kind of tunnelling effect, reaching down to deeper and deeper levels of despair. Melmoth is a terrifying figure, always aware of the shrivelling away of his soul, his cynicism and incapacity to experience real human feelings. His predicament gives him a devil's-eye view of the panorama of human suffering, cruelty and depravity. His is the vision of the madman, of the extreme outsider. Maturin (who was a Protestant clergyman) enters fully into his character's longing for redemption – a longing which, because it is hopeless and essentially corrupt, has a genuine tragic dimension. But although his handling of the usual Gothic elements was less mechanical than that of Walpole, Mrs Radcliffe, or Lewis, producing effects that look forward to Edgar Allen Poe, Maturin is not creatively in full control of the chaos of negative emotions released by his theme.

The two other novels which must be discussed are Mary Wollstonecraft Shelley's *Frankenstein: or the Modern Prometheus* and her father William Godwin's *The Adventures of Caleb Williams*. Though separated by some twenty-four years, it is convenient to begin with the later work, because it is obviously much more closely related to the central Gothic tradition. *Frankenstein*'s genesis was itself attended by all kinds of Gothic circumstances. It arose in the first instance out of a discussion on ghosts and the supernatural that took place at the Villa Diodati near Geneva, between Byron, Shelley, Mary Godwin (she was not yet Shelley's wife), and Monk Lewis who was visiting Byron. Later, when Shelley and Mary were again with Byron and his young Italian physician Polidori, Byron suggested that each of them should write a ghost story. In the Introduction she wrote for the 1832 edition of *Frankenstein*, Mary Shelley also describes a conversation between the four of them at which the experiments in galvanism of Dr Erasmus Darwin (one of Shelley's heroes at the time) were mentioned, prompting the speculation:

Perhaps a corpse could be reanimated; galvanism had given a token of such things: perhaps the component parts of a creature might be manufactured, brought together, and endued with vital warmth.

That night, Mary Shelley records that she had a waking dream in which she

> saw the hideous phantasm of a man stretched out, and then, on the working of some powerful engine, show signs of life, and stir with an uneasy half-vital motion. Frightful it must be; for supremely frightful would be the effect of any human endeavour to mock the stupendous mechanism of the Creator of the world.

When she woke the next morning, she realized she had the story she had been challenged to write, and at once began work on it.

Frankenstein has entered so thoroughly into popular folk-lore and in the process there have been so many distortions of it – simplifying and cheapening the author's intention – that the complex structure and course of the plot are often forgotten. The novel is epistolary in its basic form (true both to Gothic and to earlier eighteenth-century traditions), consisting of letters from Robert Walton, an explorer in Arctic regions, to his sister in England. Frankenstein's story is related to Walton on board ship, and his account includes a further narration from the monster to his creator. These documents reveal how Frankenstein, a Genevan student of natural philosophy, learned the secret of imparting life to inanimate matter, constructed a creature from materials collected from charnel-houses, cemeteries and mortuaries, and succeeded in giving it life. The creature, endowed with supernatural strength, but revolting in appearance, inspires loathing in anyone who sets eyes on it. Filled with hatred for his creator, who has condemned him to a life of misery and loneliness, he escapes, and murders Frankenstein's bride and his infant brother. Frankenstein, determined to destroy his terrible creation, sets off in pursuit, eventually tracking it down in the Arctic region. But there he is himself killed by the monster, who then disappears into the wastes of the frozen north to seek his own release from the life that had been forced upon him.

It is obvious enough that Mary Shelley made full use of many of the basic attributes of Gothic fiction. But she was right when, in her preface (dated September 1817) to the original edition of her novel, she asserted: '... I have not considered myself as merely weaving a series of supernatural terrors'. In fact she handles these terrors to much better purpose than most of the Gothic writers; in particular, the moment when Frankenstein's monster first stirs to life is something more than a cheap thrill, striking as it does at some atavistic nerve, and possessing something of the same myth-like quality as the moment when Robinson Crusoe first finds a human footprint in the sand. But there are also intentions of a very different nature. Mary, after all, was not only the wife of Shelley but also the daughter of Mary Wollstonecraft, authoress of *The Vindication of the Rights of Women* (1792), and of William Godwin, whose *Enquiry Concerning Political Justice* (1793) was probably the most influential single work of the whole period. Mary Shelley dedicated *Frankenstein* to Godwin, and it contains many of the ideas held by her parents, as well as those of her husband, as the sub-title 'The Modern Prometheus' indicates – Shelley's *Prometheus Unbound* was published in 1820. There is an element of irony in the sub-title, though, in that the Prometheus of the myth suffered his torments because he had benefited mankind, whereas Frankenstein, consumed by pride and self-glorification, and prepared to sacrifice his friends and even his fiancée for the sake of his scientific obsession, is in effect an enemy and traitor to the human principle.

In a sense, Frankenstein has made a Faustian pact – but it is with that part of himself which exalts his experiments above everything else. He is the first modern embodiment of the theme of the scientist's responsibility to mankind. The responsibility of the individual for his own decisions and actions, independent of the dictates of society, was in fact one of William Godwin's prime doctrines. Implied in it was the inalienable right of the individual to develop at his own rate, and according to his own innate abilities. Frankenstein's crime is to have created irresponsibly a creature with human attributes but of such terrible appearance that he is condemned to wander the face of the earth, unloved and unable to give love. The monster conforms, too, to Godwin's belief that man is endowed with innate goodness, which is frustrated and distorted by the interference of the laws, prejudices and conventions of society. The monster, because he is patched together out of human parts, including a human brain, initially possesses this instinct. He yearns for human society; at one stage he begs Frankenstein to create a mate for him – and Frankenstein in fact begins to do so but this time recoils from the task. When the monster, after escaping from Frankenstein's care, rescues a young girl from drowning, he is shot at by the peasant who sees him with the girl in his arms.

'This was then the reward of my benevolence!' [he later tells his creator] 'The feelings of kindness and gentleness which I had entertained but a few moments before gave way to hellish rage and gnashing of teeth.'

So Frankenstein has compounded his crime by driving his creature (as, in the Godwinian philosophy, society so often did) to hatred and evil.

Frankenstein's monster can also be seen as a symbol of social and racial intolerance. It is significant that among the subjects discussed at the Villa Diodati during Lewis's visit was that of slavery. Lewis's own wealth derived from plantations in the West Indies but he was well known for the unusually generous arrangements he made for the treatment of his slaves, and for his strong opinions on the subject. Frankenstein, however, has sought to create a creature that belongs to him, in effect a slave. Again one is reminded of Crusoe's Man Friday. But this was the period not of economic individualism and nascent colonialism, but of the French Revolution and of egalitarianism, and one of the reasons why the monster commands sympathy is that he refuses to be Frankenstein's thing.

There are other elements of a less theoretical kind, though, in Mary Shelley's *Frankenstein*. It is indirectly a commentary upon the split between intellect and feeling. Personal emotions, from deeper levels of her being, undoubtedly entered into Mary Shelley's story as well. It has been suggested, for example, that it was to some extent an unconscious critique of her husband's excessive fondness for abstraction. There is also the theory[5] that *Frankenstein* is a species of birth myth (directly related to Mary's early traumatic experiences of birth, illegitimacy and infant death). The presence of all these elements gives Mary Shelley's novel, in spite of the fact that the writing is often undistinguished, a depth of texture that ensures its survival as a minor classic of the Romantic revival.

To turn to her father's novel, *Things As They Are, or the Adventures of Caleb Williams*. Most writers on the eighteenth-century novel include it in the Gothic category, but as its full title indicates it was conceived in ideological terms. Earlier writers, of course, had used the forms of fiction in order to convey their ideas; for instance, Swift's *Gulliver's Travels* (1726) had embodied his views on the politics and society of his time, though in the process it spread out into a more savage and universal indictment. But none of them had been so deliberately and specifically ideological in intention and execution. As Godwin stated (in an Introduction to the 1832 edition), *Caleb Williams* 'was the offspring of that temper of mind in which the composition of my *Political Justice* left me'; and the Preface to the first edition was so uncompromising in its expression of the anarchistic political views which the novel sought to expound that the frightened publishers insisted on omitting it – though it was restored in the second edition, after the treason trials of 1794 ended in acquittals.

The full title of Godwin's philosophical work is *The Inquiry concerning Political Justice, and Its Influence on General Virtue and Happiness* and the novel is, at the ideological level, a sustained commentary on it. The hero is the new man, naturally intelligent but ordinary in his aspirations, who seeks only individual fulfilment but finds himself hounded and nearly destroyed by the forces of authoritarianism. To begin with Caleb Williams is secretary to a wealthy and cultured landowner, Ferdinando Falkland, for whom he has great admiration. His master appears kindly and considerate, but is obviously labouring under some secret guilt. Williams learns that some years before Falkland had come into conflict with a neighbouring landowner, Barnabas Tyrrel, a typical representative of the privilege of birth and wealth in its most brutal form. He had done his best to protect the victims of his neighbour's tyranny, among them a yeoman farmer named Hawkins and his son. Some time later Tyrrel had been found dead. At first Falkland had been suspected, until strong circumstantial evidence had pointed to Hawkins and his son, who had been arrested and hanged. Falkland had been a melancholy recluse ever since.

Williams comes to suspect that Falkland was indeed Tyrrel's murderer, and eventually Falkland confesses. Williams assures him that his secret is safe with him, and protests his undying devotion. But he has badly miscalculated: the natural relationship of friendship with Falkland which he has yearned for is impossible; instead he finds himself his master's slave. For Falkland, in spite of his culture and genuinely noble propensities, is inevitably as much a representative of the system as Tyrrel. Escaping, Williams falls in with a band of robbers whose leader, Raymond, is so patently a man of innate goodness that Williams urges him to give up his life of crime. Raymond, however, extols the kind of civil disobedience he and his fellows are practising. If, under the laws of their kind of society, innocence can be punished as well as guilt, surely any man of spirit will defy them. Williams rejects the argument, but sees clearly that outlaws like Raymond possess a certain energy from which mankind could benefit, but which is utterly wasted by the traditional state. Pursued by Falkland's agent, Williams becomes a wanderer and an outcast, (as surely as Frankenstein's monster) the very symbol of 'natural man' hounded by the tyrannies and injustices of an unnatural system. Bitterly aware that Falkland's secret which he carries has made him vulnerable to all traditional authority, Williams comes close to madness, crying out in his despair:

'Here I am, an outcast, destined to perish with hunger and cold. All men desert me. All men hate me ... Accursed world! that hates without a cause ... Why do I consent to live any longer? Why do I seek to drag on an existence, which, if protracted, must be protracted amidst the lairs of human tigers?'

It is a cry which echoes that of Robinson Crusoe alone on his desert island, with two great differences: whereas Crusoe has lost a society in which he can believe, Williams is a castaway in a far more radical sense, rejected and hated by a society he knows to be morally wrong and corrupt; and whereas Crusoe has his religious faith to sustain him, Caleb must seek his salvation within himself, and not in any of the consolations of tradition. What is surprising is that somehow Williams's cry also rings true, in spite of the rhetoric and in spite of (perhaps because of) the accretions of the Godwinian doctrine with which it is engrained.

Eventually, as a last resort, Williams lays a formal charge of murder against Falkland. Before the magistrates he makes an impassioned speech which reveals his own agony of soul in being now forced to betray the trust of a man he had loved and revered. It is not, of course, the law that vindicates Caleb Williams, but the innate goodness still residing in Falkland's own soul. When Williams has finished speaking Falkland throws himself into his arms, begs his forgiveness and publicly confesses to Tyrrel's murder. He is taken to prison, and dies there a few days later. But Williams can feel no triumph. He should, he feels, have made the 'just experiment' – that appeal, from the uncorrupted core of his own heart, to the innate goodness of man that also resided at the core of his enemy's. As it is, the noble qualities of Falkland, and whatever potentialities for good Williams himself possesses, have been wasted. So it must always be in society as it is at present constituted. The most remarkable feature of *Caleb Williams* is that in spite of the underlying argument, which threads through it with the utmost consistency, it is a real novel and not a mere doctrinaire thesis cast in fictional form. Godwin himself was well aware that he was writing something more than a fictionalized tract. He certainly wanted to convey the ideas of his *Political Justice* in fictional form, but only as they genuinely fired his imagination. He frequently referred to the unusual inspiration that attended the writing of *Caleb Williams*, insisting that he 'wrote only when the afflatus was upon me'. He planned the novel with the greatest care, adopting an unusual and original procedure in its composition. He began with the climactic third volume, 'then proceeded to my second, and last of all grappled with the first'. The result is that the earlier volumes, pregnant as they are with the ultimate denouement, generate a disturbing tension, while the climax itself gains in concentration and a sense of inevitability. This method, moreover, also has the effect of reducing the tendentious elements of the argument and throwing the emphasis onto a genuine dramatization of it. In addition, it leads to shifts in time, place and narrative angle which are, on the whole, technically most effective, and it would perhaps be no exaggeration to see in *Caleb Williams* a pioneer of the Jamesian point of view.

Equally effective technically is the double-take in the relationship between Williams and Falkland. To begin with Williams is in effect the hunter and Falkland his victim, as Williams tries to worm his secret out of him. Then the situation is reversed, and Williams becomes his victim's victim. This, together with the curious affinity that exists between the hunter and the hunted, is something over and above the demands of the ideological thesis, and again Godwin was aware of the fact:

The thing in which my imagination revelled most freely was the analysis of the private and internal operations of the mind, employing my metaphysical dissecting knife in tracing and laying bare the involutions of motive, and recording the gradually accumulating impulses ...

If there are some Gothic elements in the novel, the only equivalent to the Gothic castle is the dark interior of man's mind. There is no gloating over cruelties for the sake of a Gothic thrill: they are present, but they belong to the chase with its primordial, mythical undertones. In writing *Caleb Williams* Godwin, almost in spite of himself, was gripped by the wider imaginative implications of his theme, so that the abstract theories, though passionately held, were transformed into a private nightmare of the lonely individual utterly at the mercy of outside forces. In consequence he wrote the one novel of the period which successfully combined most of its fictional modes and the philosophical ideas generated by the French Revolution, and at the same time (and most important) showed how terror could be absorbed into psychological realism.

The Gothic novel, then (to use the term in its wider sense), produced one near-masterpiece in *Caleb Williams*, and one minor classic in *Frankenstein*. Mrs Radcliffe will probably continue to have her admirers, and William Beckford's *Vathek* a cult following. It is not a rich harvest. The Gothic phenomenon lasted about sixty years – from Walpole's *The Castle of Otranto* to Maturin's *Melmoth*. Many of its constituents, of course, poured into the fiction of the period immediately following and were often to surface again later – as in the decadence of the late nineteenth century and, more recently, in the 'southern Gothic' of American writers like William Faulkner and Carson McCullers. But Jane Austen's mockery in *Northanger Abbey* in effect marked the end of a specific Gothic school in England.

At the same time it must be remembered that, unassailable though Jane Austen's position is to the central tradition of English fiction, other dimensions had to be added if, within a rapidly changing social and economic context, the novel was to make further significant progress, and in making this possible the Gothic school had played a part. However naïvely, however crudely, it had been trying out methods of dealing with a range of human experience that had not been rendered in fiction before. Its medieval castles, for example, with their underground passages, were metaphorical gropings towards an exploration of the unconscious and subconscious mind, and represented in consequence the possibilities of an extension of realism, just as the various Gothic supernatural manifestations, ludicrous though they so often are, represented a first step towards encompassing the irrational and surreal. In other words, the elements which the Gothic novelists introduced were ones which the English novel needed, and which would be exploited and consolidated by writers of genius: before long Emily Brontë in *Wuthering Heights* (1847), and Charles Dickens in a whole series of novels from *Oliver Twist* (1837–8) onwards, were to show how even the most obvious and negative Gothic stereotypes (including the grotesque, the macabre, and the cruel) could be incorporated into a comprehensive poetic vision.

NOTES

1. *Three Gothic Novels*, ed. Peter Fairclough, with an introductory essay by Mario Praz (Penguin, 1968).

2. 'Classical and Romantic', in *The Background of English Literature and Other Collected Essays and Addresses*, H. G. C. Grierson (London, 1925).

3. 'Travelling Heroinism: Gothic for Heroines', in *Literary Women*, Ellen Moers (New York, 1963; London, 1977; 2nd edn, London, 1978).

4. The first part of Johann Wolfgang Goethe's *Faust* was published in 1808, and had a considerable influence on the later Gothic novelists.

5. By Ellen Moers in 'Female Gothic', ch. 5 of *Literary Women* (see above). Her interesting argument needs to be read in its entirety.

WALTER SCOTT

PATRICK CRUTTWELL

Walter Scott (1771–1832) was a thorough Scotsman who wrote
for a public overwhelmingly outside Scotland – a public which became, indeed, in his own lifetime more international than any
writer's before him. He was basically an Augustan, heir to the culture
of Dryden and Dr Johnson, who found himself a leader of Romanticism and who conquered a public which was abandoning and dis-
integrating that classical culture. He was a convinced and
old-fashioned Tory, who became the most popular writer of an age
of revolution. In these contradictions lie the secrets of both his greatness and his weakness.

He came from one of the greatest of the Border clans. The Scotts,
a race of many families who all owed an allegiance more or less
shadowy and claimed a kinship more or less remote to the Dukes of
Buccleuch, had for centuries been leading exponents of that Border
warfare which gave birth to the finest corpus of ballad-poetry in
English. The warfare itself had ended by Scott's time, but the folk-
songs and poems it inspired had not; they were still alive, though
dying, and they came to the child Scott in the right way – by word
of mouth, by hearthside and family telling. They formed the basis –
never forgotten, for his memory was prodigious – of the whole
structure of his imagination. They came to him together with
another potent stimulus; the tales of Highland Jacobites who had been
'out' in the Forty-five. Those tales brought him into personal contact
with a piece of history both living and alien, local and remote; for the
Forty-five was a clash of civilizations as much as a political movement, it was the last great foray against the modern world by a Gaelic
civilization which had not changed in essence for centuries. For
Scott's mind those veterans' tales did two things of capital importance. They laid the foundations of his romantic and traditional
Toryism; they bent his sympathies towards the Episcopalian-Tory-

Jacobite side of Scottish history (though the adult Scott was far too sensible and un-crankish to remain a Jacobite when the cause was irredeemably lost) and away from its opposite, the Presbyterian-Covenanter-Whig. And they – together with the Border ballads – gave him his vision of history: a vision intimate and local, seen in terms of human individuals.

Alongside this, Scott was receiving an orthodox eighteenth-century schooling – that is, a Latin schooling. For that he had always a basic respect, and for his own deficiencies in it he felt a certain shame, often expressed and perfectly genuine. But his real education was not there: it lay in the vast miscellaneous reading which he describes as his hero's in *Waverley* – a huge mass of chronicles and romances, ballads and plays. His tone is apologetic when he tells of it; for it scarcely accorded with his critical tastes. Those tastes were firmly Augustan. Dryden and Swift were the authors he chose to edit (he was scholar and man of letters as well as poet and novelist), and he worked on them both, as he said himself of Swift, '*con amore*'. When (in his *Life* of Dryden) he writes a survey of English poetry, he sees it in entirely Augustan terms; the 'false wit' of the metaphysical poets is scourged by the exact canons of Addison and Johnson. To the poetic experiments of his own time he was always lukewarm; admiring Wordsworth and Southey as men, he had no liking for the innovations and inbred fanaticism (as he saw it) of the 'Lake poets'. Crabbe, among his contemporaries in verse, was his favourite – the poet whose works he made his children read (instead of his own, which he thought were bad for their tastes) and asked to have read to himself on his deathbed. And Crabbe was the last Augustan.

With all this as the raw material and bent of his mind, Scott, as a young man apprenticed to the law, entered the society of legal and literary Edinburgh in the closing years of the eighteenth century. It was a society of great intellectual brilliance, certainly the liveliest that Britain could then exhibit; it was intensely argumentative, full of a debating-society kind of cleverness, prolific in bright ideas and even more in words to express them. It was a society of clever, loquacious, and ambitious young men, of whom the cleverest, the most loquacious, and the most ambitious were Whigs, tilting at the rigid Toryism which then, under the dictatorship of Pitt's Scottish henchman Melville, held all the posts of advantage. Scott, comparatively slow of wit and expression, never at home in the realms of abstract argument, with a mind which he felt to be ill-trained and ill-equipped for such purposes, reacted against this society in two directions. His Toryism was confirmed, and he acquired a lifelong distrust of clever and 'progressive' intellectuals.

Settled thus upon a firm Augustan and Tory basis – which in Scott, as well as in Johnson, Crabbe and Jane Austen, was allied to a Christianity as firm and as un-fanatical – Scott could give himself freely to the new materials of romanticism. For him as for so many others, the reading of Percy's *Reliques of Ancient English Poetry* was a decisive moment, recorded with loving particularity;[1] so was the moment of encounter with German 'Gothick' romanticism, in the form of Bürger's *Lenore*. They met and encouraged the strong element of the antiquarian that was in him. He had, as he said himself in a letter to Robert Surtees (26 April 1808), been 'an antiquary many years before [he] thought of being a poet', and the quality of his antiquarianism carried on the tradition of the eighteenth-century virtuoso: it was moderate in spirit, however enthusiastic, it could laugh at its own zeal and at the passions of the specialists. The Scott who as a young man tramped the Borders in search of ballads for the *Minstrelsy of the Scottish Border* was carrying on the work of Percy in England, of Burns in Scotland, and of many more whose fame was lesser: a work both antiquarian and creative, widening knowledge of the past and changing the poetry of the present and future.

All these elements meet in his first creative work of any note, the narrative poems which begin with *The Lay of the Last Minstrel* in 1805. Their themes are of balladry and Border warfare, of 'Gothick' medievalism, and of the feud between Highland and Lowland, Gael and Saxon. Their material is, in fact, the same as that which later – when he had found his proper form – enabled him to achieve his finest work. G. M. Young has pointed out the historical insight behind the speech of Roderick Dhu in the *Lady of the Lake*, which expounds the Highlands' case against the Lowlands: the sort of insight that was to inform the Scottish novels. But verse-narrative was not his proper form. With the best will in the world, one cannot say much for these poems. They have historical interest; they were perhaps the first best-sellers in verse – precursors, in that, of Byron's tales – creating the sort of excitement which, later, only novels could provoke. But now they seem irredeemably faded and fustian. Their manner is a versifying of the Horace Walpole–Mrs Radcliffe melo-dramatic-Gothick: burning tears flow from flashing eyes, breasts heave beneath corselets obviously filched from museums. Scott was always (as he often laments himself) an immensely careless and rapid writer, too diffuse to achieve the concentration of poetry and too indiscriminate about words. He was handicapped, too, when he wrote in verse, by the late Augustan canons of propriety in poetic diction, reinforced by the 'delicacy' epidemic in the age of the blue-stockings; these forbade him to use the resources of dialect and low life, so that all the characters in his poems talk the same language, stilted and theatrical. The immense popularity of these poems may be ascribed to three causes: they do have a certain story-telling power; they brought into contemporary verse the materials of the Gothick and the exotic; and they appeared at a very dead season of English verse – for although the work of Wordsworth and Coleridge had begun, its impact was small and uncertain and it was still a minority-cult.

Scott's real achievement came later, in the first group – the Scottish group – of the Waverley Novels, which begins with *Waverley* in 1814 and ends with *The Legend of Montrose* in 1819.[2] The greatness of these novels – and taken as a group, they *do* form a great achievement – lies in two things. Their material was such as engaged the deepest parts of Scott's mind: Scottish history and Scottish character, and both set in fairly recent times, so that living memories or living human protagonists had still existed in his childhood; and the form now suited his genius, his careless, quick-moving, genial, and digressive mind. The novel, as he wrote it, imposed on him no restrictions, whether of form, or of language, or of material. Though the extreme looseness of structure prevents any one of the Waverley Novels from being an absolute success, judged by the highest stand-ards, it was only by a helter-skelter shapelessness that Scott could create anything at all. He knew it himself. 'I am sensible,' he wrote in his Journal for 16 June 1826, 'that if there be anything good about my poetry or prose either, it is a hurried frankness of com-position . . .'

These novels gave something genuinely new: no earlier work had vitalized history in quite their way or with their effectiveness. Cock-burn's *Memoirs* testify to the effect of *Waverley*, the first of them:

Except the start of the *Edinburgh Review*, no work that has appeared in my time made such an instant and universal impression. The unexpected newness of the thing, the profusion of original characters, the Scotch language, Scotch scenery, Scotch men and women, the simplicity of the writing, and the graphic force of the descriptions – all struck us with a shock of delight.

The precursors that literary historians can point to, such as the works of Horace Walpole or Mrs Radcliffe, are feeble and unreal compared with them. The only possible parallels in English are Shakespeare's historical plays; even when the obvious Shakespearean advantages are discounted – a much tenser form and a deeper vision of human life, an audience much more intelligent and homogeneous than the huge amorphous public which Scott wrote for – still there remain similarities. Both Scott and Shakespeare aim at rendering the totality of a society at a given moment by showing the great events on levels of high and low in the community (Claverhouse and the Headriggs in *Old Mortality*, 1816, Jeanie Deans and the Duke of Argyll in *The Heart of Midlothian*, 1818). Both men were recreating ages not too remote in time and life from their own societies; the roots of the Middle Ages were still alive in Shakespeare's time as those of the Covenant and the Forty-five in Scott's. Both men could rise above their personal prejudices; Shakespeare's veneration for legitimate monarchy did not prevent him from doing justice to his self-made usurpers, and Scott's Augustan dislike of the Covenanting tribe, the sectaries and 'enthusiasts' of Scotland, did not blind him either to their heroism or to their importance in Scottish history. Scott was sometimes compared, in his lifetime, with Shakespeare, to which flattery his modest commonsense gave a blunt answer: 'The blockheads talk of my being like Shakespeare – not fit to tie his brogues.' Yet Scott was, in fact, as his journal and letters make clear, soaked in Shakespeare: Shakespeare and Burns were the writers to whom his mind most readily turned, with a confidence that always in them he would find what he wanted, some character or some comment on life which would speak his own conclusions.

In those poets, it was the human and the colloquial that most appealed to Scott, and these are what make the greatness of the Scottish novels. Released by prose from the inhibitions which his kind of verse imposed on him, Scott could now draw on the rich stock of Scottish character through all levels and on vernacular Scots to express it, and he uses both to immense effect. The vernacular is not, one has to admit, entirely integrated with the work as a whole; there are passages where the Scots dialogue has so much greater vigour and eloquence than the English narrative in which it is embedded, that one has an odd feeling as of two authors writing alternately. For Scott's everyday English prose is a tired and undistinguished medium; it is filleted Johnson, long boneless sentences whose heavy polysyllables have forgotten their Latin precision. Admittedly, when he is at his best and the book is going well, the story can drive one through these entanglements of bad writing: yet the handicap remains, this heavy English which contrasts so badly with the lively Scots.

In various ways that contrast has always haunted Scottish writing: it is there between Dunbar colloquial and Dunbar of 'aureate' and courtly poetic diction, and between the Burns of the vernacular and the Burns of literary English. Scott lived just at the time when the Scots dialect was ceasing to be spoken by the educated. 'And yet Scotch was a language,' he wrote to Constable in 1822,

which we have heard spoken by the learned and the wise and witty and the accomplished, and which had not a trace of vulgarity in it but on the contrary sounded rather graceful and genteel ... But that is all gone and the remembrance will be drowned with us the elders of this existing generation ...

Cockburn's *Memoirs* confirm and widen what Scott observes: he describes his own time, and Scott's, as 'the last purely Scotch age that Scotland was destined to see'. Both men saw the cause in the same phenomena: greater speed and ease of communications, which led to increasing centralization and a steady strengthening of the magnet of London. The effect is visible even in those of Scott's novels which deal with the Scottish past; his upper-class characters (Henry Morton in *Old Mortality*, for instance) always talk English English, only the servants and the rustics talk Scots. That this was unhistorical he must have known, as his remark to Constable proves; he did it, presumably, in obedience to that convention of novel-writing which insists that sympathetic heroes (and heroines) must talk genteelly. Dickens' Oliver Twist, the workhouse foundling, talks the most impeccable English; only his delinquent associates are allowed to be ungrammatical.

Of all these novels based on episodes of comparatively recent

Scottish history, the finest is perhaps *The Heart of Midlothian*. The incident round which the novel is constructed was in itself almost trivial – the lynching by the Edinburgh mob of one Captain Porteous, commander of the city guard, who had incurred their anger by firing on a crowd which had protested against a popular criminal's execution. Trivial in itself – but it occurred in 1736, between the Act of Union which had extinguished the Scottish Parliament and the Forty-five, in a period when Scottish nationalistic feelings were sore and touchy. The mob's behaviour was exceedingly offensive to the Government in London, which visited or threatened to visit dire penalties on the city. Hence the incident formed a perfect microcosm of the new situation to which Scotland henceforth must get itself accustomed, the situation of a not very important (because poor) province of England, governed from London or even from Hanover – since the king was George II, who was in fact (as normally) in his native land when all this was happening, leaving his Queen, Caroline, as Regent. By linking this incident with another – equally true, but unrelated historically – of a girl condemned to be hanged for murdering her baby, Scott achieves a double picture of this situation – for the girl's sister has to go to London to win the reprieve, and she (this is the heroine, Jeanie Deans) achieves it by a personal interview with Queen Caroline in London. This interview is the climax of the novel; it is one of Scott's finest achievements, and it fuses to perfection the personal and the general, on the one hand the simple country-girl pleading with another woman for her sister's life, and on the other hand the basic alienation and humiliation implied in the fact that the plea has to be made to a monarch of foreign blood, in what had been till recently a different country's capital some 400 miles away. This is surely what historical fiction has to achieve if it is to succeed – a convincing reconstruction of what a general historical situation may have meant to ordinary individuals at the time.

When the vein of recent Scottish history was exhausted, and Scott turned to themes more remote in time and place (from *Ivanhoe* in 1819), there is on the whole a decline in quality. Not that the later novels do not contain some very good things – the portrait of Louis XI in *Quentin Durward* (1823), for instance – but there do appear a more obtrusive historical pedantry, a greater staginess in dialogue and scene-painting, and a narrative more and more shapeless and careless under the pressure of incessant over-writing. Scott was the victim not only of a demon within himself, which drove him – and not only for the money he could make by it – to enormous productiveness, but also of an avid and uncritical public. He is, perhaps, the first lifelong and repeated best-seller in literature. As his publisher Constable (pioneer of publishing as big business) wrote to him in 1822: 'A new novel from the Author of Waverley puts aside, in other words puts down for the time, every other literary performance'; and Cadell, Constable's partner, wrote to the latter in terms which show how these gentry regarded 'their' author: 'Our most productive culture is the Author of Waverley – let us stick to him, let us dig on and dig on at that extraordinary quarry – and as sure as I now write to you all will be well.' All, of course, was not well, all went down in ruin; and the strain on the 'quarry' – the other sense of the word would not be inappropriate – was terrible, as his Journal very movingly shows. Yet it cannot be said that it harmed his character, for his humour and modesty were alike invulnerable. And if it did harm his work, he had, none the less, always written hastily, carelessly, and voluminously, and he had always looked on his public's enthusiasm with amused contempt. 'I thank God I can write ill enough for the present taste' he wrote in a letter to C. K. Sharpe (18 January 1809); one may enjoy the honesty that can make such a confession, but regret that a writer so immensely gifted did not have a public more capable of forcing him to do his best.

That Scott's true achievement lay in his novels is of course undeniable, and his verse cannot be seriously defended. But there is another area of his immense productiveness which deserves to be much better known and more admired than it is: his work as letter-writer, diarist, critic and editor – in short, as man of letters, and as commentator on the social and moral scene of his time. In this, he has much of the Johnsonian quality – a willingness to turn his hand to anything and to speak his mind on anything, a sort of cheerful professionalism. (Johnson, as one might expect, was one of his favourites, and the noble elegy on Levet was one of the poems he cited most often and with deepest understanding, for its blend of Christian and Stoic feeling was exactly his.) As diarist, he kept a journal from 1825 to 1832 (with intervals), which is fascinating reading from a variety of viewpoints, but in particular for its revelations of a side of his personality which his published writings, unfortunately perhaps, completely fail to represent – an acute, troubled, almost morbid sensibility. For example:

> I was sorely worried by the black dog this morning, that vile palpitation of the heart – that *tremor cordis* – that hysterical passion which forces un-bidden sighs and tears, and falls upon a contented life like a drop of ink on white paper, which is not less a stain because it conveys no meaning. (18 March 1828)

He did not indulge this, nor was he at all proud of it in the romantic way; on the contrary, he was ashamed of it, as a later entry confesses:

> About a year ago, I took the pet at my Diary, chiefly because I thought it made me abominably selfish; and that by recording my gloomy fits I encouraged their recurrence, whereas out of sight out of mind, is the best way to get rid of them ... (23 May 1830)

For precisely that reason, Johnson had abandoned an autobiography he had started.

As for his quality in the roles of social commentator and literary critic, probably the only way of demonstrating this (pending the appearance of a good selection from his letters, editions and journal) is by quotation. Here are a few, with the assurance that they are a very small sample from a very rich stock. First, two comments on the socio-political scene, which may serve to demonstrate that Scott, in spite of moments of frightened reaction, was an observer of that 'warlike and tragical age' more balanced and humane than most.

> *On the economic state of the country after Waterloo.* I think the temporary ague-fit will on the whole be advantageous to the country. It will check that inordinate and unbecoming spirit of expense or rather extravagance which was poisoning all classes and bring us back to the sober virtues of our ancestors. It will also have the effect of teaching the landed interest that their connection with their farmers should be of a nature more intimate than that of mere payment and receipt of rent and that the largest offerer for a farm is often the person least fit to be preferred as a tenant. (21 August 1816)

> *On the rack-renting Highland lairds of the 'Clearances'.* Some of the Ross-shire lairds have contrived to raise an insurrection among their tenants – I say *contrived* for it positively requires a wonderful degree of oppression

to turn these poor things against their landlords. They will manage it at last however and make us as bad as the South of Ireland. Non-Residence is a horrid business.

And here are a few of his comments on literature:

On Webster's 'Duchess of Malfi'. An odd and in some degree a terrific mixture of what is wild and extravagant with the simple, pathetic, and even childish turn of other places. I have not, I believe, a very good head for criticism, for it certainly is not *selon les règles* to be more affected by this sort of patch-work, than by regular scenes where every thing mean and trifling is completely excluded, and the mind visited by nothing but what is meant to be in unison with tragic feeling ... I feel terribly inclined to be hard hearted in the latter case, whereas I often light upon passages in these old neglected dramatists which, from the very strange and unexpected manner in which they are introduced, make the very blood tingle. (11 September 1811)

On the medieval Latin hymns. To my Gothic ear, indeed, the *Stabat Mater,* the *Dies Irae,* and some of the other hymns of the Catholic Church, are more solemn and affecting than the fine classical poetry of Buchanan; the one has the gloomy dignity of a Gothic church, and reminds us instantly of the worship to which it is dedicated; the other is more like a Pagan temple, recalling to our memories the classical and fabulous deities. (January 1813)

On a proposal to modernize the old rhymed psalmody of the Church of Scotland. I had peculiar views adverse to such an undertaking. In the first place, it would be highly unpopular with the lower and more ignorant rank, many of whom have no idea of the change which those spiritual poems have suffered in translation, but consider their old translations as the very songs which David composed ... Even the best informed, who think on the subject, must be of opinion that even the somewhat bald and rude language and versification of the Psalmody gives them an antique and venerable air, and their want of the popular graces of modish poetry shows they belong to a style where ornaments were not required. They contain, besides, the very words which were spoken and sung by the fathers of the Reformation, sometimes in the wilderness, sometimes in fetters, sometimes at the stake. (28 May 1829)

It is one of the ironies of literature that Scott should have been taken for a pioneer of romanticism – indeed, should have actually been one, on the Continent especially. For touch his mind at any point and set it against any of the basic trends of true romanticism, and the two will at once appear to be in flat opposition. The cult of wild Nature? – he said himself that he had no eye for the picturesque in scenery. Human beings came first for him; rocks, mountains, trees, and waterfalls were very bad seconds. The cult of the ego? –

he despised the autobiographical, what he called the age's 'desire, or rather rage, for literary anecdote and private history'; and though he liked Byron and admired his verse, he deplored and hated the Byronic exhibitionism. The cult of the unconscious? – he was a man of commonsense, of the conscious and controlling will. The cult of sentiment, of the Man of Feeling? – 'of all sorts of parade', he wrote to Maria Edgeworth, 'I think the parade of feeling and sentiment most disgusting'. The cult of the individualist genius, the law unto himself? – again and again he asserts that the writer should be and live like other men, accept their responsibilities and live by their standards. He was no Romantic; he was an Augustan, who brought to bear on romantic materials a mind humorous and worldly-wise, extrovert and sane.[3]

NOTES

1. This is recorded in the autobiographical fragment printed by Lockhart in the first chapter of his *Life* of Scott.

2. Many of his later novels have Scottish themes. But in most of them the periods are more remote, and the antiquarian element more obtrusive than the Scottishness.

3. Donald Davie, in his *Heyday of Sir Walter Scott* (1961), disagrees with the conclusions expressed in this paragraph, and sees Scott as a Romantic in spite of them. His book deserves to be read, though the present writer retains his opinion. On the other hand, Edgar Johnson, in his *Walter Scott* (1970), agrees with my conclusion.

THE ENGLISH LANGUAGE:
TRADITION AND INNOVATION

NORMAN PAGE

As a user of language every writer, like everyone else, both possesses a unique individuality and operates within the linguistic resources of his own period. He makes, that is to say, his own choices (and his complex combination of choices is what we call style); but everything is not equally possible in every age. (I am not concerned here with those who, usually for quite specific purposes, revive or invent a language not of their own time – Chatterton in the Rowley poems, say, or Thackeray in *Henry Esmond*.) Not all ages offer uniformly wide ranges of options to writers; but in a given period it is usually possible to establish a spectrum running from the most conservative, traditional and stable styles to those most innovative and open to change. The late eighteenth and early nineteenth century was a period of rapid linguistic development; but this does not mean that every writer reflected this to the same degree in his use of language.

It is important to remember that, in the period under discussion, English had not yet become a world language on the scale we now take for granted. As Barbara Strang has said:

> Looking back two hundred years we find ... an English-speaking community amounting to less than one-twentieth of its present size, less extensive in geographical range, at once more focused on a single centre of standardization and less open to intercourse with it; virtually stripped of its present international roles, but already in contact with a great number of other speech-communities.

English, especially in its written form, possessed a relative uniformity that contrasts strikingly with its present-day proliferation of varieties. Yet the period also saw the beginning of a process (still continuing) whereby the rate of linguistic change began to be vastly accelerated, and Professor Strang has pointed out that

> In the history of the sense of community-identity a period beginning around 1770 may be taken as a watershed, a division unique in history between before

and after. Before, movement between groups was limited to the range and speed of horse or human foot by land, and of sail by sea; ...After ... the mobile man [became] the norm ...[1]

The development of the steam-ship (effectively from 1790) and of the railway (1825), which roughly mark the limits of our period, represent major stages in an increased mobility that was to have, and is still having, profound effects on language, including the language of literature.

We think of literature as consisting of 'texts' (and students have been known, deplorably, to refer to *King Lear* as 'a book'); but it is as well to remember that the written language is only one of the forms of language, and because it is (or until very recently was) the easiest to preserve and study we should not suppose that it can be examined in isolation from the various kinds of spoken language. Moreover, literary English – the language of poems, novels, essays and so forth – is only one of a large number of varieties of written English. If, then, we ask the question: what kinds of evidence do we have for the state of the English language during this period, and the changes that were occurring during that time? part of the answer must be that, as in any period, the evidence is very diverse and can be found in letters, diaries, newspapers and journals, transcripts of court proceedings, and other sources apart from formal works of literature. If such masterpieces of high art as *The Prelude*, Keats's odes, and *Mansfield Park* are documents of the period, so for this purpose are Cobbett's *Rural Rides*, the memoirs of Harriette Wilson, the latter portions of Parson Woodforde's diary, the Creevey and Greville papers, and such near-forgotten plays as Thomas Holcroft's *The Road to Ruin*. Here is part of an account of a conversation overheard on the London to Oxford stage-coach in about 1810 by Harriette Wilson, the famous Regency courtesan:

'Lord! Mr Shuffle, how do you do? Who would a thort of our meeting *you* in the coach?' inquired Mr and Mrs Hodson ...

'Delighted to see you both,' said Shuffle ...

'And now pray, Mr Shuffle, if I may be so bold, what might have brought you up to London? What antics might you be up to, hey? Are you stage-struck as usual, or struck mad by mere accident?'

'Thereby hangs a tale,' said Shuffle.

'What! a pig-tail? I suppose you're thinking of the shop?'

'Not I, indeed,' Shuffle observed; 'I've done with wig-making these two years; for really it is not in the nature of a man of parts to stick to the same plodding trade all his life as you have done, Hodson.' . . .

'Aprepo!' said Mrs Hodson, 'by the bye, Mr Shuffle, you forgot to settle for that there pair of boots before you left Cheltenham six months ago.'

'Very true, my dear lady,' answered Shuffle, 'all very true: everything shall be settled. I have two irons in the fire at this time, and very great prospects, I assure you, only do pray cut the shop just now and indulge me with a little genteel conversation.'[2]

The accuracy of this transcription of semi-educated speech is open to argument; but, as James Sutherland claims, it certainly sounds authentic. The blending of genteel expressions with non-standard usages and proverbial phrases (a surprising number of them still in daily use) is a plausible indicator of the speakers' social class. There was no doubt a little judicious retouching on the writer's part; but Harriette Wilson was bound, as a novelist is not, by her recollection of an actual dialogue. A full consideration of this topic, far beyond the scope of the present chapter, would need to examine and compare evidence from a great variety of sources, not overlooking the fact that, since different generations live and use language at the same time, there is never a single 'contemporary' mode of expression. If, for instance, we look at the letters written by Wordsworth and Keats in or around the year 1820, we find marked differences of style that can be partly accounted for by differences in the writers' personalities and their relationship with their correspondents, and partly reflect differences of social, educational and perhaps regional background, but also partly derive from the fact that the two poets belong to different generations.

Since language reflects social, intellectual and other kinds of change, we should expect the rapid and profound changes in English society after about 1790 to have left their mark on the English language; and such is indeed the case. Upheavals in political ideology, scientific discovery, aesthetic doctrines, social attitudes and individual sensibility required different linguistic means to express their newly found or newly popularized tenets. One of the most striking as well as one of the most convenient ways of gauging and illustrating this is by considering the expansion of the English vocabulary during these years. To take a single outstanding area of expansion: Asa Briggs has shown how the *concept* of social class that took hold of men's consciousness in the late eighteenth century demanded a new *terminology* of social class that quickly established itself. The expression 'higher classes' seems to have been used for the first time by Burke in his *Thoughts on French Affairs* (1791), while 'working classes' appears in 1813 in Robert Owen's *Essays on the Formation of Character* (later retitled *A New View of Society*): and by about 1815 the phrase 'middle classes' was replacing 'middle ranks', though the latter remained current – such changes not occurring overnight. In *Persuasion*, written in 1815–16, Jane Austen uses *rank* rather than *class*, appropriately enough, in connection with the arch-conservative Sir Walter Elliot; indeed, Professor Briggs enters the timely caveat that it was a long time before 'the language of "ranks", "orders", and "degrees" was finally cast into limbo', traditionalists continuing to use the older terminology as late as the mid century.[3]

If we consider some of the words that entered the language or became widely current during this period, we can see clearly exposed some of the major movements of the age. *Aristocrat* appears, significantly and ominously, in 1789; *democrat* arrived in the following year; *revolutionize* belongs to 1797; and *terrorize* came somewhat later (1823). Others that owed their introduction to the ferment of political discussion in the years following the French Revolution are *democratize* (1798), *ideology* (1796), *radical* (noun, 1802), *capitalist* (1792), *Utilitarian* (1802), *industrialism* (1831), *socialist* (1833) and *doctrinaire* (noun, 1831; adjective, 1834). *Oxygen* (1790), *hydrogen* (1791), *nitrogen* (1794), *molecule* (1794), *galvanism* (1797) and others point to the rapid growth of science. *Anachronism* (1816), *medieval* (1827), *Elizabethan* (1817) and *baroque* (1818) suggest a heightened sense of historical change and the differences between epochs; *romance* (in the sense 'a romantic novel or narrative', 1831) and *myth* (1830) indicate changes in literary aesthetics (the word *aesthetic* itself had appeared in 1798); and the introduction by Southey of *autobiography* (1809) is a symptom of the growth of interest in the individual.

In many early instances of the use of such words, there is a distinct sense of the gloss of newness – as when the conservative Scott and the democratic Cobbett both use the noun *Radical*, the former remarking that 'Radical is a word in very bad odour here, being used to denote a set of blackguards' (1819), the latter that 'Love is a great leveller, a perfect Radical' (1822).[4] Some of the linguistic novelties of the period were revivals of old words. Scott, for instance, preferred *leechcraft* to *medicine*, anticipating the somewhat eccentric Saxon purism of William Barnes and others later in the century. More importantly, he was instrumental, together with Coleridge and Keats, in recruiting many archaic words to the service of romantic medievalism. Not all of the revivals gained a place in the standard language: Keats's *beldame* and *espial* (both used in *The Eve of St Agnes*) remain curiosities. But a few of these words succeeded in re-establishing themselves – sometimes, as Logan Pearsall Smith pointed out, with a significant shift of meaning that tended to idealize the commonplace:

> The earlier attitude of the x v i i ith Century towards the Middle Ages, which is expressed in phrases like *Dark Ages*, and *barbarous* or *Gothic*, to describe everything medieval, was not long after succeeded by the Romantic movement, and its revival ... of old and half-forgotten words. But these words of the Romantic revival – *chivalry*, *chivalrous*, *minstrel*, *bard*, etc., have now taken on a romantic glamour they by no means originally possessed.[5]

Minstrel could originally mean buffoon or juggler but is glamorized in the title of Scott's *Lay of the Last Minstrel*; a little earlier his *Border Minstrelsy* (1802–3) had revived, with a shift of meaning, a related word. *Chivalry* had been revived by Burke ('The age of chivalry is gone', 1765); *chivalrous* had become obsolete before 1600 but was resuscitated in the later eighteenth century and in the modern sense of 'gallant' or 'courteous' appears in 1818. Later in the century, Tennyson, Swinburne, Morris and others continued the fashion for linguistic revivalism.

Not only the individual words used in any period but the *kinds* of words used may be significant. Josephine Miles has shown in her statistical analyses of the vocabulary of Romantic poetry not only that (for example) Wordsworth uses *bright*, Shelley uses *dark*, and Wordsworth, Coleridge and Shelley all use *deep* with a markedly higher frequency than earlier poets, but also, more generally, that in the poetry of Wordsworth the proportion of descriptive adjectives increases, whereas the 'numericals' such as *all* and *every* decrease – the opposite of what is to be found in, say, the poetry of Donne.[6] With Keats, compound adjectives of some descriptive complexity are especially notable: in the first twenty lines of the *Ode to a Nightingale*, for instance, we find *light-winged*, *full-throated*, *deep-delved* and *purple-stained*.

Changes in syntax seem to have been less marked during this period than changes in vocabulary. F. E. Halliday has gone so far as to state that 'by 1800 the syntax of Wordsworth, Coleridge and Jane Austen was little different from that of today',[7] but this probably both over-states and oversimplifies the case. It is true that much of the prose of the period has a more modern flavour than that of, say, Fielding or Dr Johnson. Here is a passage that bequeathed to the language an expression used by millions who have never heard of its author:

> If you choose to represent the various parts in life by holes upon a table, of different shapes, – some circular, some triangular, some square, some oblong, – and the persons acting these parts by bits of wood of similar shapes, we shall generally find that the triangular person has got into the square hole, the oblong into the triangular, and a square person has squeezed himself into the round hole.

That is from Sydney Smith's lecture 'On the Conduct of the Under-standing', and although it is rather a long sentence it is no longer than many a sentence in a modern lecture and certainly does not possess the architectural elaboration of the Johnsonian sentence. But it was, after all, written to be spoken aloud, and is thus not a com-pletely typical sample of the prose of the period. If we look at the periodicals of the age – especially the heavyweights such as the *Edin-burgh Review* (founded 1802) or the *Quarterly* (founded 1809) – we find a stiffer, more ponderous syntax, closer to the *Rambler* than to this week's *The Times Literary Supplement*. Here are a couple of sentences from Scott's review of Jane Austen's *Emma*, published in 1816:

> Who is it, that in his youth has felt a virtuous attachment, however romantic or however unfortunate, but can trace back to its influence much that his character may possess of what is honourable, dignified, and disinterested? If he recollects hours wasted in unavailing hope, or saddened by doubt and disappointment; he may also dwell on many which have been snatched from folly or libertinism, and dedicated to studies which might render him worthy of the object of his affection, or pave the way perhaps to that distinction necessary to raise him to an equality with her.

Not only the abstract vocabulary but the formal and patterned syntax make this very different from modern prose. Regency prose, like Regency architecture, was often stately, elegant and based on classical models; and, as P. N. Furbank and K. C. Phillipps have argued, it survived well into the Victorian age.[8]

An important way in which the language was changing, and a good example of a development initially in the spoken language that came to have literary effects, was in its tolerance of, and even hospitality towards, slang. The term does not appear in Johnson's Dictionary, and in the modern sense dates only from 1802. It is true that the earliest compilations of slang belong to the sixteenth century, but before about 1800 the word, when used, generally referred to the specialized or 'secret' vocabulary of a particular group – the 'cant' of thieves, vagabonds and others. Francis Grose's *Classical Dictionary of the Vulgar Tongue* (1785; revised and expanded in subsequent editions) remained the most important work of its kind for a hundred years; racy and often obscene, its contents evoke a vigorous low-life indifference to the proprieties of the standard language. But the nature of slang was changing, and it was soon to become, if not respectable, at any rate fashionable in the upper reaches of society. No longer the language of a specialized group, it came to signify a colloquial vocabulary available to all who were uninhibited by notions of correctness, and especially attractive to those who wanted their speech, like their dress, to have an up-to-the-minute freshness.

A sign of the times was Samuel Pegge's *Anecdotes of the English Language* (1803), which gives considerable attention to colloquialisms and vulgarisms; and new editions of the aptly-named Grose continued to be published, including one (1823) by Pierce Egan, whose *Life in London* (1821), describing the manners and speech of the man-about-town, was popular and influential.[9] All these are evidence of the upgrading of slang as part of the general relaxation of linguistic decorum during the Regency period.

Slang, then, had risen in society and come to refer to the colloquial or sub-standard language currently in vogue at any social level, not necessarily the lowest. An early example of genteel slang, surprising in its anticipation of Victorian verbal coyness, is 'inexpressibles' for breeches or trousers, which dates from 1790 and was neatly ridiculed in the same year by 'Peter Pindar' (John Wolcot):

> I've heard that breeches, petticoats and smock,
> Give to thy modest mind a grievous shock;
> And that thy brain (so lucky its device)
> Christ'neth them *inexpressibles* so nice.

At the same time low-life slang was discovered to be a rich source of colour and variety, especially in fiction. According to Eric Partridge, Scott 'ransacked' Grose for *The Fortunes of Nigel* (1822); Bulwer-Lytton used slang terms in *Paul Clifford* (1830), as did Harrison Ainsworth in *Rookwood* (1834); and these two examples of the 'Newgate novel' influenced Dickens shortly afterwards in *Oliver Twist*, just as *Pickwick Papers* owes something (as contemporary reviewers were quick to point out) to Pierce Egan. The fashion can be seen as part of the democratization of the novel in the early nine-teenth century – a tendency exemplified in another direction by Scott's use of dialect not only for comic or low-life characters (the eighteenth-century tradition of Fielding, Smollett and others, partly deriving from Shakespeare) but for those who, like Jeanie Deans in *The Heart of Midlothian* (1818), lay claim to heroic status and moral grandeur.

In the remainder of this chapter I want to look more closely at two writers, a poet and a novelist, who are of particular interest in the relationship of their language to the language of the day and are at the same time representative of the opposing tendencies of the period: the conservative and the innovative, an impulse to preserve and defend linguistic stability, and an openness to linguistic novelty and change.

It has often been pointed out that Jane Austen's ethical and linguistic roots are in the later eighteenth century, the age of Johnson and Cowper; but she was aware of change, though usually good-humouredly critical of it. Only at the end of her life does the barely completed and posthumously published *Persuasion* suggest that the Romantic movement – in, for example, its response to landscape – had touched her in a serious way. More characteristic of her is a resistance to changes in sensibility and language. In *Sense and Sensibility*, the very title of which identifies the contrast between traditional and modern modes of feeling and style, notions of 'the picturesque' are satirized (see ch. 18) – notions that were new and disconcerting when the novel was written, for the word *picturesque* dates only from 1794 and the novel's earliest version was written no later than 1796. Jane Austen is also intent upon defending the language against the incursions of colloquialisms and the kind of foreign expressions that might be bandied about in fashionable society; she evidently saw the integrity of the English language and its usefulness as a precision instrument for serious discourse as threatened by such innovations. Characters who are fond of slang, such as the Steele sisters in *Sense and Sensibility* and Mary Crawford in *Mansfield Park*, are also branded as defective in taste or morals. The solecism is symptomatic of more profound deficiencies; and in *Emma* Mrs Elton's would-be smart use of foreign words and phrases only signals her incurable vulgarity. Even the heroine of *Northanger Abbey*, Catherine Morland, is taken to task by the hero-mentor Henry Tilney for her careless use of the word *nice* (see ch. 14).

C. S. Lewis has drawn attention to 'the hardness – at least the firmness – of Jane Austen's thought', and adds that in her writings 'the great abstract nouns of the classical English moralists are unblushingly and uncompromisingly used ... These are the concepts by which Jane Austen grasps the world'.[10] This vocabulary of moral discourse (some characteristic terms are *benevolence, principle, resolution, elegance, temper, openness*) is based on the values of a stable society, or at least one holding tightly on to its traditional values during a period of rapid change. Jane Austen was still a girl at the time of the French Revolution, and only thirty when the Battle of Trafalgar was fought; but, belonging as she did to the rural gentry of southern England, she was less touched by the changes of her time than many others, though she was certainly not unaware of these changes. (It is instructive to compare her with Wordsworth, who belonged to the same generation, but whose sex gave him a mobility and a range of experience that never came her way.) She represents, in the art of the novel, a tendency widespread in the period towards the maintenance of linguistic authority – the natural rearguard action against innovation. 'Purity' and 'propriety', key-words and even battle-cries for the traditionalists, are thus defined by the celebrated Dr Hugh Blair, whose *Lectures on Rhetoric* (1783) Jane Austen had no doubt perused (in *Northanger Abbey* she makes Henry Tilney's sister protest at being 'overpowered with Johnson and Blair'):

Purity, is the use of such words, and such constructions, as belong to the idiom of the language which we speak; in opposition to words and phrases that are imported from other languages, or that are obsolete, or new-coined, or used without proper authority. Propriety, is the selection of such words in the language, as the best and most established usage has appropriated to those ideas which we intend to express by them. It implies the correct and happy application of them, according to that usage, in opposition to vulgarisms, or low expressions.

Another manifestation of the stabilizing or standardizing tendency in the period was the appearance of numerous grammars, of which the most famous, long used as a text-book, was that of Lindley Murray (1795).

In *Emma* the romantic temperament again comes under fire – less obviously than in the high-spirited parody of *Northanger Abbey* or the somewhat schematic *Sense and Sensibility*, but none the less surely. Emma herself is an 'imaginist' (a word Jane Austen seems to have invented for the occasion) who romanticizes the commonplace Harriet; but by the end of the novel she has exchanged delusion for reality, the urgings of fancy for the dictates of common sense. A dialogue in chapter 42 between Mrs Elton and Mr Knightley catches beautifully the contrast between the folly of romantic primitivism and the sober rationality of eighteenth-century country-house civilization: Mrs Elton plans a picnic (the word, like *alfresco*, had made its appearance in the mid-eighteenth century) and promises that she will

'... wear a large bonnet, and bring one of my little baskets hanging on my arm ... Nothing can be more simple, you see ... There is to be no form or parade – a sort of gipsy party – We are to walk about your gardens, and gather the strawberries ourselves, and sit under trees: ... it is to be all out of doors – a table spread in the shade, you know. Every thing as natural and simple as possible. Is not that your idea?'

'Not quite. My idea of the simple and the natural will be to have the table spread in the dining-room. The nature and simplicity of gentlemen and ladies, with their servants and furniture, I think is best observed by meals within doors ...'

As so often, Jane Austen brings specific words and concepts – here, 'naturalness' and 'simplicity', those watchwords of the Romantic poets – under the scrutiny of her critical and sceptical intelligence. Only in her last novel, *Persuasion*, does she show a degree of sympathy with the new sensibility and an awareness that, for better or worse, society was changing very rapidly:

The Musgroves, like their houses, were in a state of alteration, perhaps of improvement. The father and mother were in the old English style, and the young people in the new. Mr and Mrs Musgrove were a very good sort of people; friendly and hospitable, not much educated, and not at all elegant. Their children had more modern minds and manners. (ch. 5)

'Improvement', for Jane Austen's contemporaries, had associations with new fashions in landscape gardening as well as in agricultural methods; 'modern' is in this context a distinctly modern epithet and gives the reader the sense that the nineteenth century has invaded Jane Austen's world; 'perhaps' suggests a limited enthusiasm on the author's part for the 'state of alteration' that is producing, in Auden's phrases, both new styles of architecture and a change of heart.

The late, unfinished *Sanditon* evinces, as Brian Southam has shown, a 'new style ... that Jane Austen was working for consciously' to correspond with her new subject-matter: a seaside village in the process of being transformed to a fashionable and rather raffish resort (as had, of course, happened to the Prince Regent's Brighton), thus representing

the spirit of change, of 'improvement' in Regency England, a process which Jane Austen catches here in all its ambiguities: its freshness and attractiveness and dynamic energy alongside its trampling of the past; its unrootedness; its restless, exploitative appetite; its Romanticism both solid and tawdry, idealistic and silly.[11]

That spirit of change, transforming the social order, manners and morals, finds its necessary counterpart in Jane Austen's use of language.

During her creative lifetime then – that is, during the generation that extended from about 1790 to 1817, or from the French Revolution to the Battle of Waterloo – we find evidence of response to changing conditions. But her main commitment after all is to preserve, defend and celebrate what is valuable in the traditional order; and that includes a strenuous effort to maintain, by practice and precept, the precision of words and to repel, with the weapons of satire and irony, the forces making for accelerated linguistic change. Finding the precision of the epithet *nice* threatened by a looser, more accommodating usage, she could see this only as a deterioration with moral as well as semantic dimensions. Byron, thirteen years younger than Jane Austen, published his earliest work in 1807; and his creative life, shorter than hers, extended until his death in 1824. Since he was at the same time a prolific poet, a brilliant conversationalist, a letter-writer of the first rank, and an assiduous journal-keeper, Byron offers a particularly rich and valuable case-study in the language of his period and in the relationship of the spoken to the written language and to forms (such as the letter and the diary) intermediate between them. The connection between Byron's practice of different literary media has often been made. John Jump, for instance, suggests that as we read Byron's letters 'we seem almost to be in the presence of the living and speaking man', and notes that the letters employ 'a kind of prose that is the equivalent of what we value in *Don Juan*', while C. M. Bowra says of the same poem that 'in it Byron speaks not in a slack version of the grand manner, but with the rich ebullience of his conversation and his incomparable letters'.[12] Byron's contemporaries, indeed, were quick to spot the connection: Thomas Moore said that Byron's habit of answering letters immediately gave his replies 'all the aptitude and freshness of replies in conversation'; and Francis Jeffrey, reviewing *Beppo* in the *Edinburgh Review* (February 1818), commented that 'the great charm is in the simplicity and naturalness of the language' – shades of Mrs Elton!– 'the free but guarded use of all polite idioms, and even of all phrases of temporary currency that have the stamp of good company on them'. Jeffrey's hierarchy of 'polite idioms' and 'phrases of temporary currency' (roughly and respectively corresponding, perhaps, to what we might designate by the terms 'colloquialisms' and 'slang') indicates an awareness of new developments in the literary language.

Byron was probably the first major writer to display a strong interest in the expressive potentiality of this area of vocabulary, just as Dickens (whose childhood belongs to the latter part of Byron's lifetime) was to do in the novel a few years later. We know from contemporary records that the language of Byron's spontaneous talk ranged over a wide lexical field: 'His conversation,' according to Colonel Leicester Stanhope, 'resembled a stream, sometimes smooth, sometimes rapid, and sometimes rushing down in cataracts; it was a mixture of philosophy and slang – of every thing – like his "Don Juan"'; and William Parry recalled that 'he had the greatest stock of quaint sayings and phrases of any man I ever met with; of the different languages and terms used by soldiers, sailors, tradesmen, and other classes of men, or of what is called *slang*, he was quite a master'.[13] An example of Byron's responsiveness to non-standard expressions is his comment on Edmund Kean's visit to America: 'I *guess* he could not have staid long enough to be spoiled; though I *calculate* no actor is improved by their stage. How do you *reckon*?'[14] (Again, Dickens was to record a similar response a generation later.)

This oral delight in a language that was rapidly expanding in unexpected and sometimes bizarre directions has its counterpart in Byron's poetry, and most notably in *Don Juan* (published in 1819–24), where the conversational style and wide range of topics accommodate an exceptional range of vocabulary – in Stanhope's phrase, 'philosophy and slang'. This emerges most clearly if we compare the language of *Don Juan* with that of other long poems of the same period: *The Prelude* (1805), for instance, or *Endymion* (1818), or *Prometheus Unbound* (1820), or such once-celebrated but now almost forgotten works as Rogers's *Pleasures of Memory* (1792). W. H. Auden has gone so far as to argue that this element in Byron's poetic style – the capacity to exploit the resources of the contemporary language as fully in a poem as in a familiar letter or a conversation – constitutes one of his main strengths: 'the more closely his poetic *persona* comes to resemble the epistolary *persona* of his letters to his male friends – his love letters are another matter – the more authentic his poetry seems'.[15] As Byron says of himself in *Don Juan*:

> And never straining hard to versify,
> I rattle on exactly as I talk
> With anybody in a ride or walk.

In the vocabulary and syntax of many other passages we seem to catch the flavour of the spoken English of the Regency period: consider, for example,

> The coast – I think it was the coast that I
> Was just describing – Yes, it *was* the coast – ...

and

> The illusion's gone for ever, and thou art
> Insensible, I trust, but *none the worse*,
> And in thy stead I've got *a deal of* judgment,
> Though *Heaven knows how* it ever found a lodgment.   (my italics)

A few examples of words used in *Don Juan* with the dates of their first appearance in the written language (according to the indispensable though not infallible *OED*) will demonstrate the up-to-date quality of Byron's language: *quiz* ('to make fun of', 'to regard mockingly', 1796); *dish'd* ('cheated', 'done for', 1798); *income-tax* (1799); *tact* (1804); *diddled* (1806); *swell* (noun, 1811); *riddled* (1817); *bagg'd* (1818); *longueur* (1821, and evidently first used in *Don Juan*). Not all of these words belong to the category of slang; but we must remember that even terms so tediously familiar in our generation as *income-tax*, or so quaintly old-fashioned as *galvanism* (also used in *Don Juan*), would have had for Byron's contemporaries something of the gloss of newness still upon them. The work of Byron – not only his verse, but his prose and the records of his conversation – illustrates very clearly the expansion of the English vocabulary and the recognition of the literary possibilities of colloquial modes during his creative lifetime. Some of his neatest effects (as, later, Auden's in his *Letter to Lord Byron*) derive from the juxtaposition of formal and colloquial diction:

> You're shabby fellows – true – but poets still,
> And duly seated on the Immortal Hill.

But slang too has its class-system; and Jeffrey's cautious formulation already quoted ('all phrases of temporary currency that have the stamp of good company on them') reminds us that there is upper-class as well as lower-class slang and that Byron would have had readier access to the former than to the latter, though Parry's reference to the slang of 'soldiers, sailors, tradesmen, and other classes of men' suggests that Lord Byron was not above a certain amount of linguistic slum-visiting. It was the author of *Sketches by Boz* in the decade after Byron's death – a man of very different social origins and experiences – who was to earn from one contemporary reviewer the title of 'regius professor of slang'. At the same time, slang was not excluded from the upward mobility characteristic of the age, and J. P. Thomas remarked in 1825 that it was 'painful to admit that the low verbiage which was but lately engrossed by thieves and vagabonds, is now adopted by those who would be highly affronted if you were to express a doubt whether they were gentlemen'.[16] The rich verbal resources of this period range all the way from the eighteenth-century abstractions of Jane Austen to the 'flash' language of smart society and its imitators; and the literature of the period gains accordingly in vigour, variety and originality.

NOTES

1. Barbara M. H. Strang, *A History of English* (London, 1970), 77, 75.

2. *The Oxford Book of English Talk*, ed. James Sutherland (Oxford, 1953), 283–4.

3. Asa Briggs, 'The Language of "Class" in Early Nineteenth-Century England', in *Essays in Labour History*, ed. A. Briggs and J. Saville (London, 1967), 73.

4. Quoted by Raymond Williams in *Keywords* (London, 1976), to which I am also indebted for several of my other examples.

5. Logan Pearsall Smith, *The English Language* (London, 1912), 229.

6. Josephine Miles, *Major Adjectives in English Poetry from Wyatt to Auden* (Berkeley, 1946).

7. F. E. Halliday, *The Excellency of the English Tongue* (London, 1975), 91–2.

8. See P. N. Furbank's introduction to the Penguin English Library edition of Dickens's *Martin Chuzzlewit* (Harmondsworth, 1968), 27; K. C. Phillipps, *The Language of Thackeray* (London, 1978), ch. 2.

9. See Eric Partridge, *Slang To-day and Yesterday*, 4th edn (London, 1970), especially Part II, ch. 5.

10. C. S. Lewis, 'A Note on Jane Austen', *Essays in Criticism*, 4 (1954), 363. See also Norman Page, *The Language of Jane Austen* (Oxford, 1972), especially ch. 2; and K. C. Phillipps, *Jane Austen's English* (London, 1970).

11. B. C. Southam, introduction to facsimile reproduction of the manuscript of *Sanditon* (Oxford, 1975), xi–xii.

12. John D. Jump, 'Byron's Letters', *Essays and Studies* (London, 1968), 62, 76; C. M. Bowra, *The Romantic Imagination* (London, 1950), 154.

13. E. J. Lovell, Jr. (ed.), *His Very Self and Voice: Collected Conversations of Lord Byron* (New York, 1954), 547, 574.

14. E. J. Lovell, Jr. (ed.), *Medwin's Conversations of Lord Byron* (Princeton, 1966), 134.

15. W. H. Auden, *The Dyer's Hand* (London, 1963), 401.

16. Quoted in Partridge, *Slang To-day and Yesterday*, 84.

JANE AUSTEN: *MANSFIELD PARK*
LIONEL TRILLING

Sooner or later, when we speak of Jane Austen (1775–1817), we speak of her irony, and it is better to speak of it sooner rather than later because nothing can so far mislead us about her work as a wrong understanding of this one aspect of it. Most people either value irony too much or fear it too much. This is true of their response to irony in its first simple meaning, that of a device of rhetoric by which we say one thing and intend its opposite, or intend more, or less, than we say. It is equally true of their response to irony in its derived meaning, the loose generalized sense in which we speak of irony as a quality of someone's mind, Montaigne's for example. Both the excessive valuation and the excessive fear of irony lead us to misconceive the part it can play in the intellectual and moral life. To Jane Austen irony does not mean, as it means to many, a moral detachment or the tone of superiority that goes with moral detachment. Upon irony so conceived she has made her own judgement in the figure of Mr Bennet of *Pride and Prejudice* (pub. 1813), whose irony of moral detachment is shown to be the cause of his becoming a moral nonentity.

Jane Austen's irony is only secondarily a matter of tone. Primarily it is a method of comprehension. It perceives the world through an awareness of its contradictions, paradoxes, and anomalies. It is by no means detached. It is partisan with generosity of spirit – it is on the side of 'life', of 'affirmation'. But it is preoccupied not only with the charm of the expansive virtues but also with the cost at which they are to be gained and exercised. This cost is regarded as being at once ridiculously high and perfectly fair. What we may call Jane Austen's first or basic irony is the recognition of the fact that spirit is not free, that it is conditioned, that it is limited by circumstance. This, as everyone knows from childhood on, is indeed an anomaly. Her next

154

and consequent irony has reference to the fact that only by reason of this anomaly does spirit have virtue and meaning.

In irony, even in the large derived sense of the word, there is a kind of malice. The ironist has the intention of practising upon the misplaced confidence of the literal mind, of disappointing comfortable expectation. Jane Austen's malice of irony is directed not only upon certain of the characters of her novels but also upon the reader himself. We are quick, too quick, to understand that *Northanger Abbey* (pub. 1818) invites us into a snug conspiracy to disabuse the little heroine of the errors of her corrupted fancy – Catherine Morland, having become addicted to novels of terror, has accepted their inadmissible premise, she believes that life is violent and unpredictable. And this is exactly what life is shown to be by the events of the story: it is we who must be disabused of our belief that life is sane and orderly. The shock of our surprise at the disappointment of our settled views is of course the more startling because we believe that we have settled our views in conformity with the author's own. Just when we have concluded in *Sense and Sensibility* (pub. 1811) that we ought to prefer Elinor Dashwood's sense to Marianne Dashwood's sensibility, Elinor herself yearns towards the anarchic passionateness of sensibility. In *Emma* (pub. 1815) the heroine is made to stand at bay to our adverse judgement through virtually the whole novel, but we are never permitted to close in for the kill – some unnamed quality in the girl, some strait of vivacity or will, erects itself into a moral principle, or at least a vital principle, and frustrates our moral blood-lust.

This interference with our moral and intellectual comfort constitutes, as I say, a malice on the part of the author. And when we respond to Jane Austen with pleasure, we are likely to do so in part because we recognize in her work an analogue with the malice of the experienced universe, with the irony of circumstance, which is always disclosing more than we bargained for.

But there is one novel of Jane Austen's, *Mansfield Park* (pub. 1814), in which the characteristic irony seems not to be at work. Indeed, one might say of this novel that it undertakes to discredit irony and to affirm literalness, that it demonstrates that there are no two ways about anything. And *Mansfield Park* is for this reason held by many to be the novel that is least representative of Jane Austen's peculiar attractiveness. For those who admire her it is likely to make an occasion for embarrassment. By the same token, it is the novel which the depreciators of Jane Austen may cite most tellingly in justification of their antagonism.

About this antagonism a word must be said. Few writers have been the object of an admiration so fervent as that which is given to Jane Austen. At the same time, she has been the object of great dislike. Lord David Cecil has said that the people who do not like Jane Austen are the kind of people 'who do not like sunshine and unselfishness', and Dr Chapman, the distinguished editor of Jane Austen's novels and letters, although he dissents from Lord David's opinion, has speculated that perhaps 'a certain lack of charity' plays a part in the dislike. But Mark Twain, to take but one example, manifestly did not lack charity or dislike sunshine and unselfishness, and Mark Twain said of Jane Austen that she inspired in him an 'animal repugnance'. The personal intensity of both parties to the dispute will serve to suggest how momentous, how elemental, is the issue that Jane Austen presents.

The *animality* of Mark Twain's repugnance is probably to be taken as the male's revulsion from a society in which women seem to be at the centre of interest and power, as a man's panic fear at a fictional world in which the masculine principle, although represented as admirable and necessary, is prescribed and controlled by a female mind. Professor Garrod, whose essay, 'Jane Austen, A Depreciation', is a *summa* of all the reasons for disliking Jane Austen, expresses a repugnance which is very nearly as feral as Mark Twain's; he implies that a direct sexual insult is being offered to men by a woman author who 'describes everything in the youth of women which does not matter' in such a way as to appeal to 'that age in men when they have begun to ask themselves whether anything matters'. The sexual protest is not only masculine – Charlotte Brontë despised Jane Austen for representing men and women as nothing but ladies and gentlemen.

The sexual objection to Jane Austen, which I believe is not valid, is a very common one, even when it is not made explicit. But then there is Emerson with his characteristic sexual indifference, his striking lack of animality, and Emerson's objection to Jane Austen is quick and entire, is instinctual. He says that she is 'sterile' and goes on to call her 'vulgar'. Emerson held this opinion out of his passion of concern for the liberty of the self and the autonomy of spirit, and his holding it must make us see that the sexual reason for disliking Jane Austen must be subsumed under another reason which is larger and, actually, even more elemental: the fear of imposed constraint. Dr Chapman says something of this sort when he speaks of 'political prejudice' and 'impatient idealism' as perhaps having something to do with the dislike of Jane Austen. But these phrases, apart from the fact that they prejudge the case, do not suggest the biological force of the resistance which certain temperaments offer to the idea of society as a limiting condition of the individual spirit.

Such temperaments are not likely to take Jane Austen's irony as a melioration of her particular idea of society. On the contrary, they are likely to suppose that irony is but the engaging manner by which she masks society's crude coercive power. And they can point to *Mansfield Park* to show what the social coercion is in all its literal truth, before irony has beglamoured us about it and induced us to be comfortable with it – here it is in all its negation, in all the force of its repressiveness. Perhaps no other work of genius has ever spoken, or seemed to speak, so insistently for cautiousness and constraint, even for dullness. No other great novel has so anxiously asserted the need to find security, to establish, in fixity and enclosure, a refuge from the dangers of openness and chance.

There is scarcely one of our modern pieties that it does not offend. Despite our natural tendency to permit costume and manners to separate her world from ours, most readers have no great difficulty in realizing that all the other novels of Jane Austen are, in essential ways, of our modern time. This is the opinion of the many students with whom I have read the novels; not only do the young men controvert by their enthusiasm the judgement of Professor Garrod that Jane Austen appeals only to men of middle age, but they easily and naturally assume her to have a great deal to say to them about the modern personality. But *Mansfield Park* is the exception, and it is bitterly resented. It scandalizes the modern assumptions about social relations, about virtue, about religion, sex, and art. Most troubling of all is its preference for rest over motion. To deal with the world by condemning it, by withdrawing from it and shutting it out, by making oneself and one's mode and principles of life the very centre of existence and to live the round of one's days in the stasis and peace thus contrived – this, in an earlier age, was one of the recognized strategies of life, but to us it seems not merely impracticable but almost wicked.

Yet *Mansfield Park* is a great novel, its greatness being commensurate with its power to offend.

Mansfield Park was published in 1814, only one year after the publication of *Pride and Prejudice*, and no small part of its interest derives from the fact that it seems to controvert everything that its predecessor tells us about life. One of the striking things about *Pride and Prejudice* is that it achieves a quality of transcendence through comedy. The comic mode typically insists upon the fact of human limitation, even of human littleness, but *Pride and Prejudice* makes comedy reverse itself and yield the implication of a divine enlargement. The novel celebrates the traits of spiritedness, vivacity, celerity, and lightness, and associates them with happiness and virtue. Its social doctrine is a generous one, asserting the right of at least the *good* individual to define himself according to his own essence. It is animated by an impulse to forgiveness. One understands very easily why many readers are moved to explain their pleasure in the book by reference to Mozart, especially *The Marriage of Figaro*.

Almost the opposite can be said of *Mansfield Park*. Its impulse is not to forgive but to condemn. Its praise is not for social freedom but for social stasis. It takes full notice of spiritedness, vivacity, celerity, and lightness, but only to reject them as having nothing to do with virtue and happiness, as being, indeed, deterrents to the good life.

Nobody, I believe, has ever found it possible to like the heroine of *Mansfield Park*. Fanny Price is overtly virtuous and consciously virtuous. Our modern literary feeling is very strong against people who, when they mean to be virtuous, believe they know how to reach their goal and do reach it. We think that virtue is not interesting, even that it is not really virtue, unless it manifests itself as a product of 'grace' operating through a strong inclination to sin. Our favourite saint is likely to be Augustine; he is sweetened for us by his early transgressions. We cannot understand how any age could have been interested in Patient Griselda. We admire Milton only if we believe with Blake that he was of the Devil's party, of which we are fellow-travellers; the paradox of the *felix culpa* and the 'fortunate fall' appeals to us for other than theological reasons and serves to validate all sins and all falls, which we take to be the signs of life.

It does not reconcile us to the virtue of Fanny Price that it is rewarded by more than itself. The shade of Pamela hovers over her career. We take failure to be the mark of true virtue, and we do not like it that, by reason of her virtue, the terrified little stranger in Mansfield Park grows up to be virtually its mistress.

Even more alienating is the state of the heroine's health. Fanny is in a debilitated condition through the greater part of the novel. At a certain point the author retrieves this situation, and sees to it that Fanny becomes taller, prettier, and more energetic. But the first impression remains of a heroine who cannot cut a basket of roses without fatigue and headache.

Fanny's debility becomes the more striking when we consider that no quality of the heroine of *Pride and Prejudice* is more appealing than her physical energy. We think of Elizabeth Bennet as in physical movement; her love of dancing confirms our belief that she moves gracefully. It is characteristic of her to smile; she likes to tease; she loves to talk. She is remarkably responsive to all attractive men. And to outward seeming, Mary Crawford of *Mansfield Park* is another version of Elizabeth Bennet, and Mary Crawford is the antithesis of Fanny Price. The boldness with which the antithesis is contrived is typical of the uncompromising honesty of *Mansfield Park*. Mary Crawford is conceived – is calculated – to win the charmed admiration of almost any reader. She is all pungency and wit. Her mind is as lively and competent as her body; she can bring not only a horse but a conversation to the gallop. She is downright, open, intelligent, impatient. Irony is her natural mode, and we are drawn to think of her voice as being as nearly the author's own as Elizabeth Bennet's is. Yet in the end we are asked to believe that she is not to be admired, that her lively mind compounds, by very reason of its liveliness, with the world, the flesh, and the devil.

This strange, this almost perverse, rejection of Mary Crawford's vitality in favour of Fanny's debility lies at the very heart of the novel's intention. 'The divine,' said T. E. Hulme in *Speculations*, 'is not life at its intensest. It contains in a way an almost anti-vital element.' Perhaps it cannot quite be said that 'the divine' is the object of

Fanny's soul, yet she is a Christian heroine. Hulme expresses with an air of discovery what was once taken for granted in Christian feeling. Fanny is one of the poor in spirit. It is not a condition of the soul to which we are nowadays sympathetic. We are likely to suppose that it masks hostility – many modern readers respond to Fanny by suspecting her. This is perhaps not unjustified, but as we try to understand what Jane Austen meant by the creation of such a heroine, we must have in mind the tradition which affirmed the peculiar sanctity of the sick, the weak, and the dying. The tradition perhaps came to an end for literature with the death of Milly Theale, the heroine of Henry James's *The Wings of the Dove*, but Dickens exemplifies its continuing appeal in the nineteenth century, and it was especially strong in the eighteenth century. Clarissa's sickness and death confirm her Christian virtue, and in Fielding's *Amelia*, the novel which may be said to bear the same relation to *Tom Jones* that *Mansfield Park* bears to *Pride and Prejudice*, the sign of the heroine's Christian authority is her loss of health and beauty.

Fanny is a Christian heroine: it is therefore not inappropriate that the issue between her and Mary Crawford should be concentrated in the debate over whether or not Edmund Bertram shall become a clergyman. We are not, however, from our reading of the novel, inclined to say more than that the debate is 'not inappropriate' – it startles us to discover that ordination was what Jane Austen said her novel was to be 'about'. In the letter in which she tells of having received the first copies of *Pride and Prejudice*, and while she is still in high spirits over her achievement, she says, 'Now I will try and write something else, and it shall be a complete change of subject – ordination'. A novelist, of course, presents a new subject to himself, or to his friends, in all sorts of ways that are inadequate to his real intention as it eventually will disclose itself – the most unsympathetic reader of *Mansfield Park* would scarcely describe it as being about ordination. Yet the question of ordination is of essential importance to the novel.

It is not really a religious question, but, rather, a cultural question, having to do with the meaning and effect of a *profession*. Two senses of that word are in point here, the open avowal of principles and beliefs as well as a man's commitment to a particular kind of life-work. It is the latter sense that engages us first. The argument between Fanny and Mary is over what will happen to Edmund as a person, as a *man*, if he chooses to become a clergyman. To Mary, every clergyman is the Mr Collins of *Pride and Prejudice*; she thinks of ordination as a surrender of manhood. But Fanny sees the Church as a career that claims a man's best manly energies; her expressed view of the Churchman's function is that which was to develop through the century, exemplified in, say, Thomas Arnold, who found the Church to be an adequate field for what he called his talent for command.

The matter of a man's profession was of peculiar importance to Jane Austen. It weighs heavily against Mr Bennet that, his estate being entailed, he has made no effort to secure his family against his death, and by reason of his otiosity he is impotent to protect his family's good name from the consequences of Lydia's sexual escapade. He is represented as being not only less a man but also as less a gentleman than his brother-in-law Gardiner, who is in trade in London. Jane Austen's feelings about men in relation to their profession reach their highest intensity in *Persuasion*, in the great comic scene in which Sir Walter Elliot is flattered by Mrs Clay's telling him that every profession puts its mark upon a man's face, and that a true gentleman will avoid this vulgar injury to his complexion. And in the same novel much is made of the professional pride of the Navy and the good effect it has upon the personal character.

In nineteenth-century England the ideal of professional commitment inherits a large part of the moral prestige of the ideal of the gentleman. Such figures as the engineer Daniel Doyce of *Little Dorrit* or Dr Lydgate of *Middlemarch* represent the developing belief that a man's moral life is bound up with his loyalty to the discipline of his calling. The concern with the profession was an aspect of the ethical concept which was prepotent in the spiritual life of England in the nineteenth century, the concept of duty. The Church, in its dominant form and characteristic virtue, was here quite at one with the tendency of secular feeling; its preoccupation may be said to have been less with the achievement of salvation than with the performance of duty.

The word grates upon our moral ear. We do what we should do, but we shrink from giving it the name of duty. 'Co-operation', 'social mindedness', the 'sense of the group', 'class solidarity' – these locutions do not mean what duty means. They have been invented precisely for the purpose of describing right conduct in such a way as *not* to imply what duty implies – a self whose impulses and desires are very strong, and a willingness to subordinate these impulses and desires to the claim of some external non-personal good. The new locutions are meant to suggest that right action is typically to be performed without any pain to the self.

The men of the nineteenth century did not imagine this possibility. They thought that morality was terribly hard to achieve, at the cost of renunciation and sacrifice. We of our time often wonder what could have made the difficulty. We wonder, for example, why a man like Matthew Arnold felt it necessary to remind himself almost daily of duty, why he believed that the impulses must be 'bridled' and 'chained down', why he insisted on the 'strain and labour and suffering' of the moral life. We are as much puzzled as touched by the tone in which F. W. H. Myers, in his autobiography, tells of walking with George Eliot in the Fellows' Garden at Trinity 'on an evening of rainy May', and she, speaking of God, Immortality, and Duty, said how inconceivable was the first, how unbelievable the second, 'yet how peremptory and absolute the third'. 'Never, perhaps, have sterner accents affirmed the sovereignty of impersonal and unrecompensing Law. I listened, and night fell; her grave majestic countenance turned towards me like a sybil's in the gloom; it was as though she withdrew from my grasp, one by one, the two scrolls of promise, and left me the third scroll only, awful with inevitable fate.'

The diminution of faith in the promise of religion accounts for much but not for all the concern with duty in nineteenth-century England. It was not a crisis of religion that made Wordsworth the laureate of duty. What Wordsworth asks in his great poem *Resolution and Independence* is how the self, in its highest manifestation, in the Poet, can preserve itself from its own nature, from the very sensibility and volatility that define it, from its own potentiality of what Wordsworth calls with superb explicitness 'despondency and madness'. Something has attenuated the faith in the self of four years before, of *Tintern Abbey*, the certitude that 'Nature never did betray/The heart that loved her': a new Paraclete is needed, and he comes in the shape of the Old Leech Gatherer, a man rock-like in endurance, rock-like in insensibility, annealed by a simple, rigorous religion, preserved in life and in virtue by the 'anti-vital element' and transfigured by that element.

That the self may destroy the self by the very energies that define its being, that the self may be preserved by the negation of its own energies – this, whether or not we agree, makes a paradox, makes an irony, that catches our imagination. Much of the nineteenth-century preoccupation with duty was not a love of Law for its own sake, but rather a concern with the hygiene of the self. If we are aware of this, we are prepared to take seriously an incident in *Mansfield Park* that on its face is perfectly absurd.

The great fuss that is made over the amateur theatricals can seem to us a mere travesty on virtue. And the more so because it is never made clear why it is so very wrong for young people in a dull country house to put on a play. The mystery deepens, as does our sense that *Mansfield Park* represents an unusual state of the author's mind, when we know that amateur theatricals were a favourite amusement in Jane Austen's home. The play is Kotzebue's *Lovers' Vows*, and it deals with illicit love and a bastard; but Jane Austen, as her letters and novels clearly show, was not a prude. Some of the scenes of the play permit Maria Bertram and Henry Crawford to make love in public, but this is not said to be decisively objectionable. What is decisive is a traditional, almost primitive, feeling about dramatic impersonation. We know of this, of course, from Plato, and it is one of the points on which almost everyone feels superior to Plato, but it may have more basis in actuality than we commonly allow. It is the fear that the impersonation of a bad or inferior character will have a harmful effect upon the impersonator; that, indeed, the impersonation of any other self will diminish the integrity of the real self.

A right understanding of the seemingly absurd episode of the play must dispel any doubt of the largeness of the cultural significance of *Mansfield Park*. The American philosopher George Mead has observed that the 'assumption of roles' was one of the most important elements of romanticism. Mead conceived of impersonation as a new mode of thought appropriate to that new sense of the self which was romanticism's characteristic achievement. It was, he said further, the self's method of defining itself. Involved as we all are in this mode of thought and in this method of self-definition, we are not likely to respond sympathetically to Jane Austen when she puts it under attack as being dangerous to the integrity of the self as a moral agent. Yet the testimony of John Keats stands in her support – in one of his most notable letters Keats says of the poet that, as poet, he cannot be a moral agent; he has no 'character', no 'self', no 'identity'; he is concerned not with moral judgement but with 'gusto', subordinating his own being to that of the objects of his creative regard. Wordsworth implies something of a related sort when he contrasts the poet's volatility of mood with the bulking permanence of identity of the old leech gatherer. And of course not only the poet but the reader may be said to be involved in the problems of identity and of (in the literal sense) integrity. Literature offers the experience of the diversification of the self, and Jane Austen puts the question of literature at the moral centre of her novel.

The massive ado that is organized about the amateur theatricals and the dangers of impersonation thus has a direct bearing upon the matter of Edmund Bertram's profession. The election of a profession is of course in a way the assumption of a role, but it is a permanent impersonation which makes virtually impossible the choice of another. It is a commitment which fixes the nature of the self.

The ado about the play extends its significance still further. It points, as it were, to a great and curious triumph of Jane Austen's art. The triumph consists in this – that although on a first reading of *Mansfield Park* Mary Crawford's speeches are all delightful, they diminish in charm as we read the novel a second time. We begin to hear something disagreeable in their intonation; it is the peculiarly modern bad quality which Jane Austen was the first to represent – insincerity. This is a trait very different from the *hypocrisy* of the earlier novelists. Mary Crawford's intention is not to deceive the world but to comfort herself; she impersonates the woman she thinks she ought to be. And as we become inured to the charm of her performance, we see through the moral impersonation and are troubled that it should have been thought necessary. In Mary Crawford we have the first brilliant example of a distinctively modern type, the person who cultivates the *style* of sensitivity, virtue, and intelligence.

Henry Crawford has more sincerity than his sister, and the adverse judgement which the novel makes on him is therefore arrived at with greater difficulty. He is conscious of his charm, of the winningness of his personal style, which has in it – as he knows – a large element of *natural* goodness and generosity. He is no less conscious of his lack of weight and solidity; his intense courtship of Fanny is, we may say, his effort to add the gravity of principle to his merely natural goodness. He becomes, however, the prey to his own charm, and in his cold flirtation with Maria Bertram he is trapped by his impersonation of passion – his role requires that he carry Maria off from a dull marriage to a life of boring concupiscence. It is his sister's refusal to attach any moral importance to this event that is the final proof of her deficiency in seriousness. Our modern impulse to resist the condemnation of sexuality and of sexual liberty cannot properly come into play here, as at first we think it should. For it is not sexuality that is being condemned, but precisely that form of a-sexuality that incurred D. H. Lawrence's greatest scorn – that is, sexuality as a game, or as a drama, sexuality as an expression of mere will or mere personality, as a sign of power, or prestige, or autonomy; as, in short, an impersonation and an insincerity.

A passage in one of her letters of 1814, written while *Mansfield Park* was in composition, enforces upon us how personally Jane Austen was involved in the question of principle as against personality, of character as against style. A young man has been paying court to her niece, Fanny Knight, and the girl is troubled by, exactly, the effect of his principledness on his style. Her aunt's comment is especially interesting because it contains an avowal of sympathy with Evangelism, an opinion which is the reverse of that which she had expressed in a letter of 1809 and had represented in *Pride and Prejudice*, but the religious opinion is but incidental to the affirmation that is being made of the moral advantage of the profession of principle, whatever may be its effect on the personal style.

Mr J. P. – has advantages which do not often meet in one person. His only fault indeed seems Modesty. If he were less modest, he would be more agreeable, speak louder & look Impudenter; and is it not a fine Character of which Modesty is the only defect? – I have no doubt that he will get more lively & more like yourselves as he is more with you; – he will catch your ways if he belongs to you. And as to there being any objection from his *Goodness*, from the danger of his becoming even Evangelical, I cannot admit *that*. I am by no means convinced that we ought not all to be Evangelicals, & am at least persuaded that they who are so from Reason and Feeling, must be happiest & safest. Do not be frightened from the connexion by your Brothers having most wit. Wisdom is better than Wit, & in the long run will certainly have the laugh on her side; & don't be frightened by the idea of his acting more strictly up to the precepts of the New Testament than others.

The great charm, the charming greatness, of *Pride and Prejudice* is that it permits us to conceive of morality as style. The relation of Elizabeth Bennet to Darcy is real, is intense, but it expresses itself as a conflict and reconciliation of styles: a formal rhetoric, traditional and rigorous, must find a way to accommodate a female vivacity, which in turn must recognize the principled demands of the strict male syntax. The high moral import of the novel lies in the fact that the union of styles is accomplished without injury to either lover.

Jane Austen knew that *Pride and Prejudice* was a unique success, and she triumphed in it. Yet as she listens to her mother reading aloud from the printed book she becomes conscious of her dissatisfaction with one element of the work. It is the element that is likely to delight us most, the purity and absoluteness of its particular style:

> The work [she writes in a letter to her sister Cassandra] is rather too light, and bright, and sparkling; it wants to be stretched out here and there with a long chapter of sense, if it could be had; if not, of solemn spacious nonsense, about something unconnected with the story; an essay on writing, a critique on Walter Scott, or the history of Buonaparté, or anything that would form a contrast, and bring the reader with increased delight to the playfulness and epigrammatism of the general style.

Her overt concern, of course, is for the increase of the effect of the 'general style' itself, which she believes would have been heightened by contrast. But she has in mind something beyond this technical improvement – her sense that the novel is a genre that must not try for the shining outward perfection of style, that it must maintain a degree of roughness of texture, a certain hard literalness, that, for the sake of its moral life, it must violate its own beauty by incorporating some of the irreducible prosy actuality of the world. It is as if she were saying of *Pride and Prejudice* what Henry James says of one of the characters of his story, *Crapy Cornelia*: 'Her grace of ease was perfect, but it was all grace of ease, not a single shred of it grace of uncertainty or of difficulty.'

Mansfield Park, we may conceive, was the effort to encompass the grace of uncertainty and difficulty. The idea of morality as achieved style, as grace of ease, is not likely ever to be relinquished, not merely because some writers will always assert it anew, but also because morality itself will always insist on it – at a certain point in its development, morality seeks to express its independence of the grinding necessity by which it is engendered, and to claim for itself the autonomy and gratuitousness of art. Yet the idea is one that may easily deteriorate or be perverted. Style, which expresses the innermost truth of any creation or action, can also hide the truth; it is in this sense of the word that we speak of 'mere style'. *Mansfield Park* proposes to us the possibility of this deception. If we perceive this, we cannot say that the novel is without irony – we must say, indeed, that its irony is more profound than that of any of Jane Austen's novels.

In the investigation of the question of character as against personality, of principle as against style and grace of ease as against grace of difficulty, it is an important consideration that the Crawfords are of London. Their manner is the London manner, their style is the *chic* of the metropolis. The city bears the brunt of our modern uneasiness about our life. We think of it as being the scene and the cause of the loss of the simple integrity of the spirit – in our dreams of our right true selves we live in the country. This common mode of criticism of our culture is likely to express not merely our dissatisfaction with our particular cultural situation but our dislike of culture itself, or of any culture that is not a folk culture, that is marked by the conflict of interests and the proliferation and conflict of ideas. Yet the revulsion from the metropolis cannot be regarded merely with scepticism; it plays too large and serious a part in our literature to be thought of as nothing but a sentimentality.

To the style of London Sir Thomas Bertram is the principled antagonist. The real reason for not giving the play, as everyone knows, is that Sir Thomas would not permit it were he at home; everyone knows that a sin is being committed against the absent father. And Sir Thomas, when he returns before his expected time, confirms their consciousness of sin. It is he who identifies the objection to the theatricals as being specifically that of impersonation. His own self is an integer, and he instinctively resists the diversification of the self that is implied by the assumption of roles. It is he, in his entire identification with his status and tradition, who makes of Mansfield Park the citadel it is – it exists to front life and to repel life's mutabilities, like the Peele Castle of Wordsworth's *Elegiac Verses*, of which it is said that it is 'cased in the unfeeling armour of old time'. In this phrase Wordsworth figures in a very precise way the Stoic doctrine of *apatheia*, the principled refusal to experience more emotion than is forced upon one, the rejection of sensibility as a danger to the integrity of the self.

Mansfield stands not only against London but also against what is implied by Portsmouth on Fanny's visit to her family there. Fanny's mother, Lady Bertram's sister, had made an unprosperous marriage, and the Bertrams' minimal effort to assist her with the burdens of a large family had been the occasion of Fanny's coming to live at Mansfield nine years before. Her return to take her place in a home not of actual poverty but of respectable sordidness makes one of the most engaging episodes of the novel, despite our impulse to feel that it ought to seem the most objectionable. We think we ought not to be sympathetic with Fanny as, to her slow dismay, she understands that she cannot be happy with her own, her natural, family. She is made miserable by the lack of cleanliness and quiet, of civility and order. We jib at this, we remind ourselves that for the seemliness that does indeed sustain the soul, men too often sell their souls, that warmth and simplicity of feeling may go with indifference to disorder. But if we have the most elementary honesty, we feel with Fanny the genuine pain not merely of the half-clean and the scarcely tidy, of confusion and intrusion, but also of the vulgarity that thrives in these surroundings. It is beyond human ingenuity to define what we mean by vulgarity, but in Jane Austen's novels vulgarity has these elements: smallness of mind, insufficiency of awareness, assertive self-esteem, the wish to devalue, especially to devalue the human worth of other people. That Fanny's family should have forgotten her during her long absence was perhaps inevitable; it is a vulgarity that they have no curiosity about her and no desire to revive the connection, and this indifference is represented as being of a piece with the general indecorum of their lives. We do not blame Fanny when she remembers that in her foster-father's house there are many rooms, that hers, although for years it had been small and cold, had always been clean and private, that now, although she had once been snubbed and slighted at Mansfield, she is the daughter of Sir Thomas's stern heart.

Of all the fathers of Jane Austen's novels, Sir Thomas is the only one to whom admiration is given. Fanny's real father, Lieutenant Price of the Marines, is shallow and vulgar. The fathers of the heroines of *Pride and Prejudice*, *Emma*, and *Persuasion* (pub. 1818), all lack principle and fortitude; they are corrupted by their belief in their delicate vulnerability – they lack *apatheia*. Yet Sir Thomas is a father, and a father is as little safe from Jane Austen's judgement as he is from Shelley's. Jane Austen's masculine ideal is exemplified by husbands, by Darcy, Knightley, and Wentworth, in whom principle and duty consort with a ready and tender understanding. Sir Thomas's faults are dealt with explicitly – if he learns to cherish Fanny as the daughter of his heart, he betrays the daughters of his blood. Maria's sin and her sister Julia's bad disposition are blamed directly upon his lack of intelligence and sensibility. His principled submission to convention had issued in mere worldliness – he had not seen to it that 'principle, active principle' should have its place in the rearing of his daughters, had not given them that 'sense of duty which alone can suffice' to govern inclination and temper. He knew of no other way to counteract the low worldly flattery of their Aunt Norris than by the show of that sternness which had alienated them from him. He has allowed Mrs Norris, the corrupter of his daughters and the persecutor of Fanny, to establish herself in the governance of his home; 'she seemed part of himself'.

So that Mansfield is governed by an authority all too fallible. Yet Fanny thinks of all that comes 'within the view and patronage of Mansfield Park' as 'dear to her heart and thoroughly perfect in her eyes'. The judgement is not ironical. For the author as well as for the heroine, Mansfield Park is the good place – it is The Great Good Place. It is the house 'where all's accustomed, ceremonious', of Yeats's *Prayer For His Daughter* –

> How but in custom and ceremony
> Are innocence and beauty born?

Yet Fanny's loving praise of Mansfield, which makes the novel's last word, does glance at ironies and encompasses ironies. Of these ironies the chief is that Lady Bertram is part of the perfection. All of Mansfield's life makes reference and obeisance to Sir Thomas's wife, who is gentle and without spite, but mindless and moveless, concerned with nothing but the indulgence of her mild, inexorable wants. Middle-aged, stupid, maternal persons are favourite butts for Jane Austen, but although Lady Bertram is teased, she is loved. Sir Thomas's authority must be qualified and tutored by the principled intelligence, the religious intelligence – Fanny's, in effect – but Lady

Bertram is permitted to live unregenerate her life of cushioned ease.

I am never quite able to resist the notion that in her attitude to Lady Bertram Jane Austen is teasing herself, that she is turning her irony upon her own fantasy of ideal existence as it presented itself to her at this time. It is scarcely possible to observe how *Mansfield Park* differs from her work that had gone before and from her work that was to come after without supposing that the difference points to a crisis in the author's spiritual life. In that crisis fatigue plays a great part – we are drawn to believe that for the moment she wants to withdraw from the exigent energies of her actual self, that she claims in fancy the right to be rich and fat and smooth and dull like Lady Bertram, to sit on a cushion, to be a creature of habit and an object of ritual deference, not to be conscious, especially not to be conscious of herself. Lady Bertram is, we may imagine, her mocking representation of her wish to escape from the requirements of personality.

It was Jane Austen who first represented the specifically modern personality and the culture in which it had its being. Never before had the moral life been shown as she shows it to be, never before had it been conceived to be so complex and difficult and exhausting. Hegel speaks of the 'secularization of spirituality' as a prime characteristic of the modern epoch, and Jane Austen is the first to tell us what this involves. She is the first novelist to represent society, the general culture, as playing a part in the moral life, generating the concepts of 'sincerity' and 'vulgarity' which no earlier time would have understood the meaning of, and which for us are so subtle that they defy definition, and so powerful that none can escape their sovereignty. She is the first to be aware of the Terror which rules our moral situation, the ubiquitous anonymous judgement to which we respond, the necessity we feel to demonstrate the purity of our secular spirituality, whose dark and dubious places are more numerous and obscure than those of religious spirituality, to put our lives and styles to the question, making sure that not only in deeds but in *décor* they exhibit the signs of our belonging to the number of the secular-spiritual elect.

She herself is an agent of the Terror – we learn from her what our lives should be and by what subtle and fierce criteria they will be judged, and how to pass judgement upon the lives of our friends and fellows. Once we have comprehended her mode of judgement, the moral and spiritual lessons of contemporary literature are easy – the metaphysics of 'sincerity' and 'vulgarity' once mastered, the modern teachers, Lawrence and Joyce, Yeats and Eliot, Proust and Gide, have but little to add save in the way of abstruse contemporary examples.

Jane Austen's primacy in representing this large mutation in the life of the spirit constitutes a large part of her claim to greatness. But in her representation of the modern situation *Mansfield Park* has a special place. It imagines the self safe from the Terror of secularized spirituality. In the person of Lady Bertram it affirms, with all due irony, the bliss of being able to remain unconscious of the demands of personality (it is a bliss which is a kind of virtue, for one way of being solid, simple, and sincere is to be a vegetable). It shuts out the world and the judgement of the world. The sanctions upon which it relies are not those of culture, of quality of being, of personality, but precisely those which the new conception of the moral life minimizes, the sanctions of principle, and it discovers in principle the path to the wholeness of the self which is peace. When we have exhausted our anger at the offence which *Mansfield Park* offers to our conscious pieties, we find it possible to perceive how intimately it speaks to our secret inexpressible hopes.

JANE AUSTEN: *EMMA*

MALCOLM BRADBURY

'Jane Austen,' said Henry James, in one of the few large misjudge-
ments we can lay at his door, 'was instinctive and charming ... For
signal examples of what composition, distribution, arrangement can
do, of how they intensify the life of a work of art, we have to go
elsewhere.' We do not, of course; and the purpose of this essay is
to suggest something of the managed complexity of structure that
Jane Austen creates in probably her best novel, *Emma* (1816), and the
way it is used to compose and elaborate a pattern of perceptions and
values – an enterprise of, in fact, a very Jamesian kind. 'I am going
to take a heroine whom no-one but myself will much like', said Jane
Austen of the novel, in a comment worth setting against her observation about a later heroine, Anne Elliot in *Persuasion* (1818), the book
that rivals *Emma* in its distinction, that Anne Elliot was almost too
good for her. In other words, here are two books, not unalike, that
nonetheless require very different tasks of persuasion, two different
dispositions of design, two different patterns of relation between
author and characters and author and reader, two different processes
of composing, distributing and arranging her social and moral world.
Moral issues are much at stake, for it is presumably a moral objection
that the author expects to be brought about Emma; it will therefore
be by resolving that situation, by accommodating her sense of the
interest of such a heroine so as to amend a probable and in some sense
desired disapproval, that her book will work. The book, in short,
is going to be an education, in which certain qualities that are liked,
and are likely to make Emma seem attractive to the reader, above
all her quality of self-will, are appropriately amended in directions
which neither totally constrain them nor let them survive quite as
they are. Emma's story is a learning, to be conducted through reason
and emotion, in which what is potential in her is developed and what
is excessive in her amended, not towards social convention but to-

wards social possibility, not towards doctrine but towards experienced awareness of human decency.

As a novelist, Jane Austen is always concerned with two kinds of
world, the social world and the moral world, and with the possibilities of their interaction, which are not given but have to be made
or discovered. It is often complained of her that she measured life from
the conventional social standards and values of the upper middle class
about which she writes and to which she belonged; this is sometimes
said to limit her wider relevance, to confine her historical awareness,
and to 'exclude' her from the larger creative enterprise of the modern
novel, which draws much of its complexity from its social range,
its multiplicity of viewpoint, its elaborate refractions of value. It is,
it seems, in this sense that Henry James found her 'charming' rather
than intense, 'instinctive' rather than artistically complex. 'Why
shouldn't it be argued against her that where her testimony com-
placently ends, the pressure of our appetite presumes exactly to
begin?' he asked, in a complaint that is clearly about both social and
aesthetic provincialism. It is therefore worth stressing at once that
it is in the capacity which the careful reader will always find in her
work to dissipate or sceptically to test her own apparent predilections
that a good deal of her force resides – a force we will better see if
we consider that, like any novelist, Jane Austen does not simply
mirror a society but subtly composes it into existence. She is indeed
that kind of novelist who depends on the guarantee of society – on
her and our recognition of its substantial existence, its deceits, its follies, but also its capacity to generate standards of life worthy enough
to measure lives by – to bring her fictional world into being; of course
at the same time her fictional creation brings that society into being.
The society is a world carefully ordered, narrow in social spread,
hierarchical, formal and conventionalized, more so perhaps in fiction
than in life; it is a world of classes and hierarchies constituted for us
on the basis that such things do exist in life. Yet it is visibly
constructed into existence as we read, and constructed not simply for
its social substance but for the way in which, from such substance,
moral judgement and force may be elicited.

What, therefore, Jane Austen must do in the composition of *Emma*
is to create and interconnect a social world and a moral world, leading
us from the former to the higher level of action and judgement in

the latter. And this social world is carefully and precisely given, a world elaborate in detail and range, though not in its disposition of classes. The action of *Emma* takes place in Highbury, a 'large and populous village, almost amounting to a town', sixteen miles out of London, at a time which is effectively the time of writing (*Emma* was written in 1814–15). The landscape of Highbury is a landscape of property: its main landmarks are Hartfield, the home of the Wood-houses, who are 'the first in consequence in Highbury'; Randalls, home of Mr Weston, 'a little estate'; and Donwell Abbey, 'in the parish adjoining, the seat of Mr Knightley'. London is not far off, and Emma's sister lives there, in Brunswick Square, but that is only relatively accessible; Highbury is a more or less self-contained social unit, and it contains almost all of the action. And most of the significant characters are its upper-middle-class citizens – landowners with tenant farmers, persons of private income – who form a small society held together by links of kinship and common social duty; it is from their perception and their level that we see the society at large of the novel. There are persons of higher rank – in particular the Churchills, the great Yorkshire family – but we feel them to be high; there are characters clearly 'below' the social balance of the book, like the tenant-farmer Robert Martin and the former Miss Taylor and Mrs Goddard and Miss Bates, who come from the depressed 'professional' middle class. And then there are the socially indeterminate characters, who function so importantly in the action: Miss Harriet Smith, illegitimate, of obscure origins, and so unattached by clear kinships or duties; Frank Churchill, split between families; and Jane Fairfax. These figures, who come from outside the dominant locale and exist in uncertain relation to it, are the disturbing forces, so that it is their presence that promotes most of the action. Of course these people are related to the life at the centre by kinships or credentials; nearly all the characters in the novel exist in some kind of established relationship to the heroine or her immediate friends. But it is they, and especially Harriet Smith, who disorder the order, and become tests of people's observations of innate qualities. For Miss Smith can fit in at any of a number of class levels; indeed, she can claim her class by her own merits, and is thus in the singular position of being mobile within a largely stable society. Stable, but at its maximum point of mobility; for the book is concerned with the stage just prior to marriage, the institution that re-sets the marriageable young at a deserved level within the class structure.

Thus, as Jane Austen forms and relates the community of the novel, she establishes her own possibility of generating action and development. Her essential society is small, concentrated in houses and families, having few points of reference outside Highbury. The limits of the world are determined from the centre – the opposite method to that of picaresque fiction, where the relationships with the hero are regularly those of casual encounter, a structure consonant with an open, pragmatic view of the world, and contingency offers significance and valuable change. Here, though, there is a homogeneous community, taking its standards essentially from within itself and from what works for the best in its own relationships, needs, and duties. In this world of chosen probabilities, no real violation of rank is likely. The Highbury equals are capable of intimacy; but there are places to be known and kept in. Rank governs as the relationship to the Woodhouses grows more distant (the vicar is not close, the schoolmistress is received, the poor are visited), and characters in mobile situations pose essential problems – like the rising Coles, who, like other pleasant and intelligent characters in Austen's novels, function as a serious test to Emma's judgement ('The Coles were very respectable in their way, but they ought to be taught that it was not for them to arrange the terms on which superior families would visit them'). So the constraints of a fixed society are firmly felt, and in this novel Jane Austen does not – as she does in *Persuasion* – test the values that arise in this world beyond the milieu in which they are recognized as proper and significant. There is, indeed, no need to; for in this agrarian and hierarchical world, where individuals subscribe by intelligent assent to a stylized pattern of properties and duties, she finds a context in which those values can be put to the necessary tests.

The society which generates and supports the book's moral action, then, is a local, limited, self-consistent world. It has its own operative values and occasions, provincial and unelaborate. People meet over dinner, or at balls, or in Ford's shop; encounters occur by formal arrangement; there are few accidental meetings, and so precise are the circumstances of this life that when these occur (as when Harriet meets Robert Martin in the shop) they are deeply disturbing. People stand large, families stand whole, conventions acquire universality. Our own sense of propriety as réaders is demanded and engaged, so that when Jane Fairfax and Frank Churchill are, by a conjunction of accidents, left alone with the sleeping Miss Bates and this 'breach' goes unobserved, we alone are called on to observe it and reflect on its significance. The degree of social stability, the preciseness of social expectations, the limitations on eccentric behaviour or concealments or violent action, reinforce and make significant the moral order. They enable a concentration on the quality of the individual life. They create a high degree of consensus about behaviour – about what constitutes decent action. They provide a relatively closed and rounded world in which, once a level of adequate living has been acquired, it can be reinforced from without, for the future will be reasonably like the present.

Within these limits, though, the society throws up a broad range of values, out of which the tensions of the novel arise. The characters think about similar things, but they think differently about them. They think differently about the importance of rank, about the relative value of taste or courtesy or honour, and about the importance of reason or emotion in conduct. Certain things are commonly approved or frowned upon – frivolity is disliked and goodwill valued – while on other matters different characters take different stands. And this is the way in which we are coerced, by the novelist, into perceiving and adopting a measure, for, either through direct authorial intervention or more commonly by the relative elevation and demotion of various characters, this latter done by a complex strategy and tone, we perceive a pattern. The public values are placed according to a private and interestingly pragmatic view. People define themselves by their actions, and as they act we perceive that there are in the novel superior and inferior people in moral as well as social terms. The social order yields to the moral. The morally inferior people tend in fact to be socially high, to considerable dramatic effect; Emma herself, at the beginning, is one of them and Frank Churchill another, while people of lower rank, like the Martins and the Coles, elevate themselves by their actions.

In this fashion certain values emerge as positive – particularly values having to do with care and respect for others, the decent discharge of one's duties, and the scrupulous improvement of oneself.

They are values associated with, but by no means intrinsic to, an upper-middle-class social position. So frivolity may be despised, but accomplishments count high, since they evidence self-discipline and self-enlargement and please others – the fact that Mr Martin reads is highly in his favour in this emergent scale, while Harriet Smith's taking a long time to choose materials at Ford's is not in hers. A friendly and social disposition is valued, but not *too* highly, since Emma's criticism of Jane Fairfax's reserve comes to tell more against Emma than it does against Jane and, what is more, it blinds her to some of the excellence of Mr Knightley. Goodwill and a contented temper are valued, but have their associated failures – Mr Weston is too easy-going for reasonable living, and Emma at once too indulgent over moral matters and not indulgent enough over social ones. To be 'open, straight-forward and well judging', like Martin, is important, but not as important as the rewarding side of Mr Knightley's more closed and critical temper. All this is the central area of the action, for it is what is at issue between Knightley and Emma; and yet we do come to value Emma's warmth and openness, only wanting it placed and ordered.

Birth and good manners are important, but only when there is something behind them. Elegance is admired, highly by Emma, less so by others. Mr Elton is 'self-important, presuming, familiar, ignorant and ill-bred'; the observations are Emma's, and have to be mediated by us carefully, for they show up Mr Elton *and* Emma. This picking up of tone is most important for the book, and we are helped by alternative views – for instance, Jane Fairfax is more tolerant of Mr Elton. Mr Weston is a little too open-hearted for Emma – 'General benevolence, and not general friendship, make a man what he ought to be. She could fancy such a man.' To Harriet she commends 'the habit of self-command', but responds to Harriet's 'tenderness of heart': 'There is nothing to be compared to it. Warmth and tenderness of heart, with an affectionate, open manner, will beat all clearness of head in the world for attraction.' But Mr Knightley, in one of the debates in which the education of Emma – and to a lesser extent of Knightley himself – is conducted and in which a permissible range of *difference* of value is reconciled, offers a more rational and mature view; he states the case for a plan of life strictly adhered to, a sense of duty and of courtesy, and a right realization of what one owes to one's social situation and therefore one's function. This competition of values between Knightley and Emma, which is one of our main guides to the direction of the book, touches on other issues and other people, of course – an interesting example of its method being the way in which Knightley reappraises Emma's description of Churchill as 'amiable':

'... No, Emma; your amiable young man can be amiable only in French, not in English. He may be very "amiable", have very good manners, and be very agreeable; but he can have no English delicacy towards the feelings of other people – nothing really amiable about him.'

Other issues come into these debates, to add to the dense moral atmosphere. Thus Churchill is criticized early for being above his connections, later for being too exuberant; while he himself criticizes 'civil falsehoods', but employs them. Emma admires elegance highly; she has a practical, advantage-seeking view of attractive qualities in people; she criticizes Mr Knightley for inventing lines of conduct that are not practical. Mr Knightley reverses this case, condemns Emma's fancy and whim, and recommends 'judging by nature'. In consequence, the moral life is in the front of the characters' minds throughout; it is *linked* with class – as in the description of the estate at Donwell Abbey as belonging to 'a family of such true gentility, untainted in blood *and understanding*' – but understanding is insistently prior to blood as the notion of gentility begins to take a kind of ideal shape.

And so from the very first page of the book we are conscious of a disparity between the moral and the social scale. Emma's situation is, from the start, shown to be happy:

Emma Woodhouse, handsome, clever, and rich, with a comfortable home and a happy disposition, seemed to unite some of the best blessings of existence, and had lived nearly twenty-one years in the world with little to distress or vex her.

But the complexities of the handling are already present. There is the hint, offered through nuances of diction, that the 'best blessings of existence' only *seem* to be hers; there is the point, further taken up and insisted on, that she has not been vexed but rather over-indulged. Her father is 'affectionate, indulgent'; her governess has 'a mildness of temper' that 'had hardly allowed her to impose any restraint', and presently by an explicit statement Jane Austen converts the hints into a direct moral observation: 'The real evils, indeed, of Emma's situation were the power of having rather too much of her own way, and a disposition to think a little too well of herself.'

A distinction is to be made between social and moral 'success', then; and this is reinforced when we are told, for instance, of the history of Mr Weston's previous marriage into a family of high rank, which

was an unsuitable connection, and did not produce much happiness. Mrs Weston ought to have found more in it, for she had a husband whose warm heart and sweet temper made him think everything due to her in return for the great goodness of being in love with him; but though she had one sort of spirit, she had not the best. She had resolution enough to pursue her own will in spite of her brother, but not enough to refrain from unreasonable regrets ...

The moral scale is centred rather particularly, throughout, upon what is reasonable and desirable in a social life whose basic unit is the family, what makes for good and open dealing between people, prospers and opens their relationships and makes them dutiful and considerate in all their public actions. Jane Austen's novels are domestic novels, novels centred on marriage; most of the commentary and moral discussion is in fact directed towards defining the conditions for a good marriage, and preparing the one good marriage which contrasts with all others in the novel and so dominates it. But marriage is a social pact and so must answer to the public dimension. The general expectations of this book are that people will make the marriages they deserve, and that the climax will be Emma's marriage, made when she has answered to her faults and resolved her dilemmas.

Whom, then, will Emma marry? This is the question on which the plot turns. This plot, simply summarized, is concerned with a girl of many fine qualities but of certain considerable errors deriving from the misuse of her own powers, who realizes these errors, perceives that they have made her make false attributions of worth to the people in her circle and, repenting, marries the man who can instruct her in an accurate reaction to the world. The first part of the plot, the compositioned 'beginning', takes us to chapter 17. In this section Emma is a detached agent in someone else's destiny; this is that part of the novel concerned with Emma's attempt to intervene in the life of Harriet Smith by marrying her to Mr Elton, and its function is to demonstrate the nature of Emma's mistakes about the world, and the dangers of detached and desultory action. By the time we reach chapters 16 and 17, where we are presented with Emma's regrets, we have all we need in the way of moral direction for the rest of the book. Mr Knightley's interpretation of character and event has been shown to be better than Emma's, and we have a clear sense of Emma's tendency to misread what is before her, as well as of the faults, particularly snobbery and whimsy, which make her do this. The use of Harriet Smith as a device to expose the two different versions of the world espoused by Emma and Mr Knightley is singularly skilful. For Harriet's illegitimacy means that she can be judged very differently by different people; and all of them associate her with a rank that indicates the nature of their judgement. The uncertainty about Harriet's background thus becomes a dramatic delaying device, and much depends on the discovery of her true station, for then we shall see who is correct about her. The point is, as I have indicated, that her statement of herself, unlike that of any other characters in the book, depends entirely upon her *own* attributes; she is not reinforced by any class position. And so the question that arises is – is it Emma who is snobbish about Mr Martin, and damaging to Harriet in seeking to link her with Mr Elton; or is it Mr Knightley who is snobbish in his assumption that she deserves no better than Mr Martin, and that she is harmful company for Emma? The matter goes further – for to Emma Harriet has the virtues which commend a woman to men (beauty and good nature) and with these she has all she needs to win affection. But Mr Knightley sees the marriage connection as involving larger issues:

'Men of sense, whatever you may choose to say, do not want silly wives. Men of family would not be very fond of connecting themselves with a girl of such obscurity . . .'

The beautifully managed scene where Knightley puts this to Emma, and dissipates any feeling we may have of *his* snobbery by talking of Robert Martin's 'sense, sincerity and good humour' and his 'true gentility' of mind, is quickly supported by his being proved right about Mr Elton:

'Depend upon it. Elton will not do ... Elton may talk sentimentally, but he will act rationally. He is as well acquainted with his own claims as you can be with Harriet's.'

Indeed, Knightley's criticism of Emma's behaviour has a precise moral tenor; he points to a specific fault:

'If you were as much guided by nature in your estimate of men and women, and as little under the power of fancy and whim in your dealings with them as you are where these children were concerned, we might always think alike.'

That Emma *is* guided by fancy and whim we begin to see the more when, after a succession of delightfully handled comic scenes founded on the ambiguity of Mr Elton's supposed wooing of Harriet, Mr John Knightley points out to Emma that Mr Elton seems to have an interest in her. Emma's response is clearly self-deluding:

She walked on, amusing herself in the consideration of the blunders which often arise from a partial knowledge of circumstances, of the mistakes which people of high pretensions to judgement are for ever falling into, and not very well pleased with her brother for imagining her blind and ignorant, and in want of counsel.

The irony is turned directly against her; and her ignorance on the matter, her failure to perceive that it is *she* who is being courted by Mr Elton, takes on a dimension beyond the comic – takes on the status of a moral fault.

The second part of the novel, the 'middle', is that concerned with Emma's mistakes about the nature of Frank Churchill's and Jane's characters, and her inability to infer the truth here because of her pre-judgements. The situations are now more complicated, but Emma repeats her errors without real improvement, inventing a romance before she has even met her between Jane and Mr Dixon, and another between Churchill and herself. Here the purpose of the action is to show how she behaves in events which increasingly come to involve not a protégé's but her own destiny, to show how she is capable of misusing herself. This part of the plot ends with a significant and crucial discovery, Emma's discovery that she is in love.

The 'end' of the novel beautifully enforces the weight and meaning of the book; the waters clear, and all the significances are laid bare in a simple delaying action which enables Jane Austen to make plain all the inadequacies of her characters and the moral lesson to be learned from them. Repentance in Emma is delayed to the last and therefore most effective moment, and it comes after a train of thought in which we see Emma affected, involved, pressed into realization of her follies. On top of understanding comes marriage, a right resolution to the plot in that it enforces the significance of true understanding. The preparation is over and by extending the novel indefinitely by a closing sentence referring to 'the perfect happiness of the union' Jane Austen assures us that it is an effective understanding that Emma has come to.

These final effects are so precisely controlled and placed that it is evident that we *do* have a plot in which 'composition, distribution and arrangement' are handled with the greatest finesse. It is reached through such indirect methods that one cannot but wonder at the vast number of threads that need to be woven into the resolution. The most complex strategy of the novel is the device of filtering it through the eyes of a character of whom Jane Austen doesn't wholly approve, yet with whom she is strongly in sympathy. There is no unsureness about the moments of understanding and improvement that must (despite her position as heroine) come to her. The device is handled particularly by the use of Mr Knightley as a 'corrective'; but that is by no means the whole of the effect, for Mr Knightley is not always right either. Another force exists to handle this; it resides in the values that emerge when we have taken away the irony from the treatment of events seen through Emma's eyes. For we must be careful to see that Emma is right sometimes; we must know, however, precisely when she is wrong, and how well this is managed. Emma judges excessively by elegance; but though her criticism of Mrs Elton is that she lacks elegance, she perceives most of her faults. Indeed Emma is by no means consistently in error; she is clever enough to be right on nearly all the occasions where she is not giving rein to her snobbery and her prejudice – or prejudgement. It is Mrs Elton's snobbery that makes Emma's seem mild; and we need the scene where the two talk together to place Emma in that good light. The point then is that if Emma were judged by Jane Austen from 'outside', she would be unlikeable and highly criticized. In fact she is a violator of Jane Austen's moral scale to such a degree that it is hard at first to understand how she could have been made a heroine by her. And the fact that she *is* the heroine is the most remarkable thing about her – *Emma* is Jane Austen's *Tom Jones* in which the most devout expectation roused in the reader is the expectation that she will in some way come to grief; but we demand that her grief, like Tom Jones's, will not be too painful, that repentance will occur, redemption be won and all the blessings of the prodigal son be given to her. This is what happens. The artistic problem of the book is then to make us care for Emma in such a way that we care about her fate, and like her, but that we in no way subdue our moral feelings about her faults.

And here another aspect of the tone is involved. For *Emma* is a comic novel, a novel concerned with comedy of manners in such a way as to make this the comedy of morals. There is comedy in various veins. There is the straightforward humorous treatment of Mr Woodhouse and Miss Bates as 'comic characters'. This, of course, does function in the moral dimension of the book – Mr Woodhouse's affectations are based on an indulgence to himself and it is an indulgence of the same order that has harmed Emma, while Miss Bates's absurdities make her a kind of test-case for Emma's power of responding to other people. But the significant action of the comedy in the management of the plot is to be found, for example, in the comic flavour of the scenes at the beginning where Emma, Harriet and Mr Elton are playing at picture-making and with riddles. These scenes are treated lightly, and they are designedly about trivial events; but they are organized to show us one thing above all, that Emma is capable of misreading radically the significance of these situations. What makes them most comic to the reader is his sense of a completely different possible explanation for Mr Elton's actions. The operative principle is, in short, an irony that works against the heroine.

This irony dominates the novel. It is contrived through the device of an omniscient narrator who is able to offer an alternative set of values, and it concerns almost always the difference between what the character sees and comes to judgement about, and other potential readings of the incident. It refers then particularly to Emma's habit of prejudging situations. It is offered by a variety of methods, such as the changes in point of view that – for example – let us, at the beginning of chapter 20, see Jane Fairfax independently of Emma's judging eye. Its effect is not simply to set up another set of *facts* against which Emma's foolish interpretations are judged; we have to wait a while for *those*. What, at the time, we are invited to realize is not that Emma is wrong, but that she might be – that she has pre-judged. In short, then, we are drawn away from a determined interpretation or prejudice about people and events, and towards a sense of possible variety. The irony is thus in favour of empiricism; and the pattern of the book is one in which the events presented before us are capable of more complex interpretation. And because we commonly see through Emma's eyes, and because Emma doesn't see this further interpretation, it is dramatically delayed and becomes the centre of our sustained interest. The devices which assure us that it is there are, among other things, the insistent and critical presence of Mr Knightley, the occasional movements to other points of view, and the revelation of the first part that Emma has been wrong about Harriet Smith and so can be wrong again. This tension between events as they seem and events as they might be – between the pleasing Frank Churchill that Emma sees, and the temporizing and cunning Churchill that Mr Knightley sees – is the dynamic of the book. When Churchill comes to Randalls and talks so pleasantly, pleasing everyone, we wonder, we have been prepared to wonder, whether this is because he is deeply amiable or simply cunning. Events will bear at least two interpretations. But it should be said that Emma suspects this, that her views put to Mr Knightley are views she doubts, and that to some extent she has learned from the Harriet incident. As readers, however, skilled in plots, we are put into the position of being encouraged to entertain our suspicions longer; there is a devised relationship between reader and heroine, inherent in the ironic note.

The novel closes on a final irony. One of Emma's faults has been her external view of persons, and her willingness to interfere in the destinies of others without being prepared to involve herself. Marriages are to be made only for others. In being forced into true feelings of love, she is released and opened out; love is the final testimony, in fact, of her redemption. She concludes the book by involving herself in the essential commitment of the Austen universe, which is marriage; so she has opened out into tenderness of heart, a tenderness without weakness or sentimentality. If she has still some faults to recant, these will come in time, for the fundamental liberation has taken place; she is no longer the Sleeping Beauty.

And in this way the shape of the novel is fulfilled. It has begun by delineating a variety of contesting moral viewpoints; it ends by clarification, by offering to the reader a way through the variety. We have learned this particularly through our understanding of Emma's faults, and by learning above all how significant, how *fundamental*, they are. For Emma's aloof relation to others, her willingness to treat them as toys or counters, her over-practical view of the good quality, which she sees simply as ensuring for its possessor a good match – these become significant betrayals of human possibility.

> With insufferable vanity she had believed herself in the secret of everybody's feelings; with unpardonable arrogance proposed to arrange everybody's destiny. She was proved to have been universally mistaken; and she had not quite done nothing – for she had done mischief. She had brought evil on Harriet, on herself, and, she too much feared, on Mr Knightley . . .

The social and moral universe I described at the beginning of these comments takes on all the weight of its significance here, for it provides a context in which Emma's faults are not peccadilloes to be regarded with indulgence, but total violations of a whole worthwhile universe. Jane Austen's method is to rouse our expectations and draw on our moral stringency to such an extent that this insight becomes absolutely essential, and retribution is demanded. The agents of retribution here are Mr Knightley and Jane Austen herself, and the retribution, once understanding has come, is genial – the lesson learned by Emma is that of how to commit herself fully and properly in the moral and social act of marriage, an act whose validity she has begun by denying and with which she begins her mature life.

What is rendered for us, then, is the moral horror of values we are awfully apt to associate with Jane Austen herself – snobbery, an excessive regard for the elegant and smart, a practical regard for goodness because it is such a *marriageable* trait. These are the values that are purged. We have been turned another way; we have learned of the duty of the individual to immerse himself in the events about him and to accept his obligations to his acquaintance finely and squarely; we have learned of the value of 'the serious spirit', involved and totally responsible. We have been persuaded in fact of the importance of true regard for self and others, persuaded to see the full human being as full, fine, morally serious, totally responsible, entirely involved, and to consider every human action as a crucial, committing act of self-definition. If literary artists construct not only their work but their reader, Jane Austen, a great artist working in a small compass, has constructed one who, however remote from her social and moral world, is capable of recognizing and recovering an experience of life as serious and intense as even Henry James could have wished for.

THE SPIRIT OF THE AGE IN PROSE

G. D. KLINGOPULOS

That heightening of feeling which is distinctively Romantic was caused by stresses at several levels of human affairs, from the practical and political to the philosophic and 'religious'. Though poetry, with its concentration and finality, is, at its finest, more deeply representative of its age than most prose, we should expect the prose to reveal affinities of subject and feeling with the poetry. In both the prose and poetry of the Romantic period we find attempts to express unfamiliar experience, frequently in the form of autobiography, reminiscence and confession. There is a willingness in both to experiment with language. The prose writers, like the poets, look back on history with greater humility and insight than the writers of the previous age had usually shown. 'Empiricism' had seemed at times a means of disowning the past, and it gave to much eighteenth-century writing – to Gibbon, for example – a shallow urbanity not really worthy of the name of scepticism. Prose writers share in the common effort to establish less unstable notions of history and of human nature. They share, too, in the task of critical assessment which was especially important at such a time. We should hope, in turning to four prose writers, Peacock, De Quincey, Lamb and Hazlitt, to see Romanticism in better perspective.

Thomas Love Peacock (1785–1866) may be said to have made critical assessment the main purpose of all his writings. He has a place in the history of the novel, but it would be misleading to describe his books as novels. The modern reader could not take them up as he takes up *Pride and Prejudice*, and enjoy them as self-explaining presentations of human relationships. His books are all satirical in varying degrees, and are composed mainly of conversation. The perfunctoriness of the scene-setting and scene-changing is part of the impression of casualness which Peacock is concerned to maintain. We are reminded of *Candide* or of Fielding's burlesque play *Tom Thumb* rather than of Jane Austen. It is no injustice to Peacock to describe him as essentially a humorous social satirist and critic.

The main influence on Peacock's early life was not that of his father, the London glass merchant who died when Peacock was three, but that of his mother, whose favourite reading was Gibbon, and of his grandfather Thomas Love, a retired master in the Royal Navy who had lost a leg in that service. In Peacock's upbringing there was very little tincture of religion, to which he referred, in Gibbonian fashion, as 'superstition', and he did not go to a university. It is important to mention these items of biography, as they seem to be clues to the sturdy independence of Peacock's outlook and to its limitations. He is one of several self-made men of the period, normal to the point of eccentricity. He is in some ways a Cobbett at a different social level, with the same combination of hard sense and lyricism; very proud of his practical abilities and his self-acquired knowledge, especially of Greek. His Hellenism is obtrusive. In his case, it was not allied to any academic ambition or to an interest in philosophy or religion. He uses Greek as a source of elaborate jokes, such as the derivation of the name of Moley Mystic Esquire from the moly of Hermes; or as an alternative to things he dislikes; or as an elegant source of drinking songs. But much more interesting is its use in his last book, *Gryll Grange* (1860), which came after an enormous silence of thirty years. Greek had become his tap-root into human history, enabling him to view, with apparent detachment, some of the manifestations of spiritual loneliness in his time.

Late in life, Peacock contributed to *Fraser's Magazine* three important articles entitled *Memoirs of Shelley*, in which he gave an account of his own relations with the poet between 1812 and 1822. It was the contrast in the temperaments of the two men, as well as their common interest in Greek, which made the friendship possible. The *Memoirs*, being written in the first person, give a clear impression of Peacock's views; these can only be guessed at in the 'novels', where his tendency is to satirize all viewpoints. The disapproving detachment of the following reminiscence suggests clearly enough how it was that Peacock came to write *Nightmare Abbey* (1818), in which the Romantic temperament is the main target.

His vegetable diet entered for something into his restlessness. When he was fixed in a place he adhered to this diet consistently and conscientiously, but it certainly did not agree with him; it made him weak and nervous, and exaggerated the sensitiveness of his imagination. Then arose those thick-coming fancies which almost invariably preceded his change of place. While he was living from inn to inn he was obliged to live, as he said, 'on what he could get'; that is to say, like other people. When he got well under this process he gave all the credit to locomotion, and held himself to have thus benefited, not in consequence of his change of regimen, but in spite of it.

The *Memoirs* are not remarkable for their comments on Shelley's poetry, and it would be inappropriate to make claims for Peacock as a literary critic, though many of his travesties of Byron, Shelley and Scott have the force of serious appraisal. His essay *The Four Ages of Poetry* (1820) was probably meant to be chiefly provocative, but there is ample evidence in it that Peacock found the poetry of his day uncongenial. By describing Wordsworth as 'a morbid dreamer', and by stating briefly that 'Mr Wordsworth picks up village legends from old women and sextons', Peacock acts the philistine with great energy. The essay is an unsatisfactory performance. A comprehensive criticism of Romantic poetry would have been worth having, but it would have been a criticism of much more than the poetry and of much that came before the Romantics. It is on the 'novels' that we must base our judgement of the scope and adequacy of Peacock's satire.

Of the seven 'novels', *Maid Marian* (1822) and *The Misfortunes of Elphin* (1829) are considerably different from the others in aim and form. They are romantic narratives based on Robin Hood legends in the one case and on Celtic legends in the other. Peacock had married a Welsh girl and knew a little of the language. The mixture of pastoral, satire and song in these stories makes it more difficult to generalize about Peacock's range of interests and temperament; but they are plainly from the same pen that produced the other five books. It is a burlesque Romanticism that we are offered, in which Peacock takes care to deflate his own bardic prowess – the songs are quite brilliant examples of their kind, which is that of comic opera. Amongst many amusing passages is the parody of Tory arguments against parliamentary reform in *The Misfortunes of Elphin*. Prince Elphin visits Prince Seithenyn the Lord High Commissioner of Royal Embankment to complain of the state of the sea walls.

'Prince Seithenyn,' said Elphin, 'I have visited you on a subject of deep moment. Reports have been brought to me, that the embankment, which has been so long entrusted to your care, is in a state of dangerous decay.'

'Decay,' said Seithenyn, 'is one thing, and danger is another. Everything that is old must decay. That the embankment is old, I am free to confess; that it is somewhat rotten in parts, I will not altogether deny; that it is any the worse for that, I do most sturdily gainsay. It does its business well: it works well: it keeps out the water from the land, and it lets in the wine upon the High Commission of Embankment. Cupbearer, fill ... I say, the parts that are rotten give elasticity to those that are sound ... If it were all sound, it would break by its own obstinate stiffness; the soundness is checked by the rottenness, and the stiffness is balanced by the elasticity.'

(ch. ii)

For all their charm, however, these tales do not make the same sharp impression as the five 'novels' of talk, which give the sting of a contemporary reaction to literature, to philosophic movements, to politics, and to crotchets and crotcheteers of all kinds. Peacock shared Cobbett's abhorrence of paper money, and of what Cobbett called 'the beastly Scotch feelosofers', and he had a large number of equivalents, from Malthusians to boroughmongers, for Cobbett's much-abused Methodists. Especially useful to the modern reader are the reminders everywhere in his work of the real scorn aroused by certain aspects of the careers of the chief Romantics, aspects which are sometimes too easily discounted. It is true, of course, that, viewed from a distance, the retractions of Wordsworth, Coleridge and Southey appear deeply human and even endearing; the Romantics would not have been interesting had they remained sensibly impassive at such a time. We can be grateful to Peacock for stating the case against them so amusingly, if not persuasively. The exaggeration and unfairness in, for example, the episode at Mainchance Villa in *Melincourt* (1817), counteract a good deal of the venom. Mainchance Villa was the 'new residence of Peter Paypaul Paperstamp, Esquire' (Wordsworth), with whom Mr Feathernest (Southey), Mr Vamp and Mr Killthedead (Tory reviewers), and Mr Anyside Antijack (Canning), discuss a letter received by Antijack from Mr Mystic of Cimmerian Lodge, warning him of 'an approaching period of public light'. They consider 'the best means to be adopted for finally and totally extinguishing the light of the human understanding'. The discussion is turned into a debate by the arrival of Mr Forester (Shelley?) and Mr Fax (Malthus or 'the champion of calm reason'). We are told that

> Mr Paperstamp did not much like Mr Forester's modes of thinking; indeed he disliked them the more, from their having once been his own; but a man of large landed property was well worth a little civility, as there was no knowing what turn affairs might take, what party might come into place, and who might have the cutting up of the Christmas pie.

It is not long before Paperstamp and Feathernest raise the alarm 'The Church is in danger! The Church is in danger!' – an appeal to close ranks much favoured by the *Quarterly Review*. Mr Vamp applauds: 'Keep up that. It is an infallible tocsin for rallying all the old women in the country about us when everything else fails.' Mr Feathernest recalls the opinion of his friend Mr Mystic that it is a very bad thing for the people to read, and sighs for 'the happy ignorance of former ages'. Paperstamp feels that his side has a strong case:

> But you must not forget to call the present public distress an awful dispensation; a little pious cant goes a great way towards turning the thoughts of men from the dangerous and jacobinical propensity of looking into moral and political causes for moral and political effects.

(ch. xxxix)

One would need to be serious indeed not to enjoy these 'novels'. Peacock is extremely successful in exploiting some of the more obvious affectations of Romantic poets and the more hideous propensities of political economists. Both threatened to undermine the independent way of life that Peacock, like Cobbett, preferred. Though he was friendly with both the Mills and dined regularly with Jeremy Bentham, he was as little of a 'philosophical' Radical as Cobbett himself; but he was certainly not made in the heroic mould of that 'pattern John Bull'. His comic observation of the social scene never builds up to anything of Dickensian proportions, though occasionally the resemblance to Dickens is strong; as here, in the description of the foggy atmosphere surrounding Mr Mystic of Cimmerian Lodge:

> The fog had penetrated into all the apartments: there was fog in the hall, fog in the parlour, fog on the staircase, fog in the bedrooms;

PART THREE

The fog was here, the fog was there,
The fog was all around.

It was a little rarefied in the kitchen, by virtue of the enormous fire; so far, at least, that the red face of the cook shone through it, as they passed the kitchen door, like the disk of the rising moon through the vapours of an autumnal river: but to make amends for this, it was condensed almost into solidity in the library, where the voice of their invisible guide bade them welcome to the adytum of the LUMINOUS OBSCURE.

(Melincourt, ch. xxxi)

The point, of course, is not that Dickens copied the opening of *Bleak House* from Peacock, but that there is a comic tradition, a matter of tone, degree of exaggeration, and mock-heroic visual imagery that goes back beyond Fielding and links novel with stage. Peacock took the epigraph to *Nightmare Abbey* from Jonson's *Every Man in his Humour*, in which play Dickens acted Captain Bobadil.

Coleridge is the butt of a great deal of Peacock's humour in other books, as Mr Flosky, Mr Skionar, or Mr Panscope. In time one's sense of Peacock's limitations defines itself around his treatment of Coleridge. For in his repeated caricatures Peacock seems to be drawing on a caricaturist's set of over-simplified impressions. This does not matter when he is satirizing Byron, who went in for a good deal of over-simplification in his own poetry. That he made so little of Wordsworth and Coleridge, and put so great a distance between himself and them, suggests an inadequacy in his judgements as a whole. How different was Peacock's attitude from that of his exact contemporary De Quincey who, as a young man, sought out the two poets in admiration and gratitude, yet was by no means blind to their selfishness and conceit. At best, Peacock's attitude resembles that of his own Mr Crotchet, who perceives a division taking place in his time, a bifurcation of English culture. Mr Crotchet tells Mr Skionar and Mr Mac Quedy (Mac Q.E.D. son of a demonstration):

'The sentimental against the rational, the intuitive against the inductive, the ornamental against the useful, the intense against the tranquil, the romantic against the classical; these are great and interesting controversies, which I should like, before I die, to see satisfactorily settled.'

(Crotchet Castle, ch. ii)

There is some penetration in this; we think of similar perceptions in Hazlitt and, later, in John Stuart Mill. But there is no feeling of the importance of what has been perceived. The 'settling' desired by Mr Crotchet is far removed from the constant striving of Hazlitt to think beyond this opposition of the 'rational' and 'inductive' to the 'sentimental' and 'intuitive'. Peacock's granddaughter tells us 'He would not be worried'. Fastidiously, Peacock turned from Romantic attempts to interpret a lucid Hellenistic religion with the help of German metaphysics, and collected epigraphs that seemed to make his kind of rationalism historically respectable.

Gryll Grange is a delightful book, written well after the Romantic sense of crisis, which had always been a state of individual minds, had subsided into contagious Victorian gloom. Aristophanes is frequently mentioned, but the hard-hitting contemporary quality of the humour in the earlier books which justified such a comparison is now almost entirely absent. There are general reflections on the trend of modern life and its restlessness – 'going for the sake of going'. The reflections are extensive, but they usually come to some brief conclusion, such as the Rev. Dr Opimian's: 'I almost think it is the ultimate destiny of science to exterminate the human race'. There are contemptuous references to the new craze for schools for all, for competitive examinations, for lectures by lords, especially for lectures on Education or Pantopragmatics, 'a real art of talking about an imaginary art of teaching every man his own business'. The book is a less satirical, more ample working of the underlying theme of *Nightmare Abbey*; the 'Shelleyan' idealist in love and unable to act. The idealist Mr Falconer is contrasted with the 'epicurean' Dr Opimian and the hard-headed Mr MacBorrowdale the Utilitarian. He lives in a tower, worships chastity, and is waited on by seven beautiful girls who are sisters. There is nothing harshly unsympathetic in Peacock's presentation of him and his distresses, especially of his reverence for Saint Catherine of Alexandria and Mount Sinai, and his longing for ritual, history, and art, whilst keeping 'very carefully in view that Saint Catherine is a saint of the English Church Calendar'.

Mr Falconer: 'I think I can clearly distinguish devotion to ideal beauty from superstitious belief. I feel the necessity of some such devotion, to fill up the void which the world, as it is, leaves in my mind. I wish to believe in the presence of some local spiritual influence; genius or nymph; linking us by a medium of something like human feeling, but more pure and more exalted, to the all-pervading, creative, and preservative spirit of the universe; but I cannot realize it from things as they are. Everything is too deeply tinged with sordid vulgarity. There can be no intellectual power resident in a wood, where the only inscription is not "Genio loci", but "Trespassers will be prosecuted"; ... No; the intellectual life of the material world is dead. Imagination cannot replace it. But the intercession of saints still forms a link between the visible and invisible. In their symbols I can imagine their presence. Each in the recess of our own thought we may preserve their symbols from the intrusion of the world. And the saint, whom I have chosen, presents to my mind the most perfect ideality of physical, moral, and intellectual beauty.'

The Rev. Dr Opimian: 'I should be sorry to find you far gone in hagiolatry. I hope you will acquiesce in Martin, keeping equally clear of Peter and Jack.'

(ch. ix)

The humour is of some complexity, especially when, in self-defence, Falconer goes on to quote, quite fairly, the grotesquely apologetic yearning for religious symbols in Wordsworth's sonnet *The Virgin*.[1] A good deal of the effect depends on our noticing the identity of the speaker, so that we catch the succession of tones. For example, a sympathetic observation that 'the forms of the old Catholic worship are received with increasing favour' is given to the old physician who has only this speech in the book; his name is Dr Anodyne. *Gryll Grange* is the work of a humorist rather than of a satirist; and all the 'novels' lack the intensity of satire. Peacock reviews the possibilities, satirizing many kinds of mind but never taking any kind of mind quite seriously. He often seems a special sort of philistine. Yet his convivial epigraphs are often utterly sad. Judgements of any finality require an affirmative quality lacking in Peacock.

Critics tend to stress the elusiveness of Peacock's work and mentality. Even more elusive is his contemporary De Quincey (1785–1859). De Quincey's work was almost entirely composed of contributions to magazines, and was collected only a few years before his death. His most recent biographer, at the end of a long book, makes no assumptions concerning Thomas De Quincey's 'ultimate literary importance. That is still hanging in the balance.' This seems excessively cautious; perhaps what is meant is that there is a disproportion between the extent of De Quincey's work in fourteen volumes and the small amount of it which is widely read at the present time. His reputation must always rest on the autobiographical writings, but the whole of his work, despite its prolixity, reveals an alert though wayward intelligence, and a keen interest in the contemporary world which is rather unexpected in a drug addict. After being absurdly generous to Coleridge and John Wilson out of a small patrimony, De Quincey was obliged in middle life to turn author and to pour out a stream of autobiographical, critical, philosophic and historical articles, to interpret Kant, and to translate Lessing and novels from the German. He even wrote a stylish Gothic novel, *Klosterheim* (1832). There must have been an extraordinary resilience under De Quincey's frail appearance. No doubt his sense of responsibility for the simple Westmorland girl he had involved in his fate, and for their eight children, spurred him on, but it cost him great pain to write.

His career has always invited a moralistic approach. What could be more 'decadent' than an opium eater? In vain De Quincey pleaded that he could not even have begun to write without the stimulus of opium. Even Baudelaire, who admired, borrowed from, and summarized[2] De Quincey, expressed disapproval of his justification of the use of drugs for certain purposes. One would not speak of De Quincey's life, any more than of Kafka's, as a 'success'. Yet the fourteen volumes, after allowing for what Leslie Stephen calls 'a good deal of respectable padding for magazines', contain rather more than 'a few pages which revealed new capacities in the language'. There was much, of course, in De Quincey besides the opium eating, which would understandably displease Leslie Stephen. 'De Quincey', he notes, 'is a Christian on Epicurean principles.' De Quincey did, in fact, have a simple piety rather than faith, which, though it was occasionally responsible for some Paterish rhetoric, counted for much in his sensibility, in his understanding of history, and in his life. In one of his autobiographical articles, he thanks Providence that he and his brothers and sisters 'were dutiful and loving members of a pure, holy, and magnificent church' (Vol. I, 32). Stephen comments sarcastically on the unusual sequence of epithets – 'the last epithet should be emphasized'. De Quincey certainly invited sarcasm by risking an impression of parody. It suggests an underestimate to say with Stephen that 'De Quincey's prejudices are chiefly the reflection of those of the Coleridge school in general'. De Quincey's personal experience had its own quality. The early experience of a finality in death was not the invention of the retrospective adult. The loss of a second dearly loved sister had made an indelible mark on his mind, inflicted a sorrow which had for him an absolute significance, and implied a judgement on life that life itself only deepened.

About the close of my sixth year, suddenly the first chapter of my life came to a violent termination ... *Life is Finished!* was the secret misgiving of my heart; for the heart of infancy is as apprehensive as that of maturest wisdom in relation to any capital wound inflicted on the happiness. *Life is Finished! Finished it is!* was the hidden meaning that, half-unconsciously to myself, lurked within my sights. The peace, the rest, the central security which belong to love that is past all understanding – these could return no more.

(Vol. I, 28–9)

Childish grief found comfort in church music. Through the chants 'it was that the sorrow which laid waste my infancy, and the devotion which nature had made a necessity of my being, were profoundly interfused'. That last word brings in Wordsworth – the Wordsworth of the *Lines Composed a Few Miles Above Tintern Abbey*. How different are the two contexts! There is little affirmative 'joy' in De Quincey. His sensibility stands in a peculiar relationship to Wordsworth's, often, one feels, a dependent relationship. He speaks of 'the deep deep magnet' that Wordsworth was to him as a schoolboy. But the assumption of interest in the record of his personal sufferings was not as presumptuous as it may seem. De Quincey could be confident that his prose would contain at least as much first-hand experience as, say, the poetry of *Childe Harold*. In his way he had been an explorer. Though he lacked the moral concentration and ability to simplify that go to make a novelist, he was interested in the power of language to express modes of consciousness which not even poetry could adequately render; the experience of dreams and of music, the impressions of childhood, the arrest of time under the influence of laudanum, the sense of multitude and tumult and of fear; and he had the confidence of genius in the originality of his mode of autobiography, his vision of his own life. His nature was that of a lifelong younger brother, too unassertive, rather feminine, sensual, but with its own integrity. His running away from school and university, where he was a brilliant pupil, might even be interpreted as attempts to preserve this integrity, this 'self'. It was a too sensitive, too generous, and withdrawing self, to which money was disturbing and incomprehensible and the world was always 'the world of strife'. He tended to project into his love of children his own sense of precariousness; it was not only their innocence but also their utter dependence that attached him to them. This is quite different from anything to be found in Blake or Wordsworth.

De Quincey was without family when Catherine Wordsworth died in June 1812 at the age of three. A sense of contrast between the record left by the father and the extremity of De Quincey's grief at the loss of his little friend is forced upon us if we happen to remember Wordsworth's beautiful sonnet 'Surprised by joy – impatient as the wind' when we come to De Quincey's account of 'The Death of Little Kate Wordsworth' (Vol. II, 440–45). The completeness of the sonnet creates a detachment, as if the meaning of the suffering had been found. De Quincey, though he had lost two sons of his own by the time he wrote his account (1840), cannot make even a semblance of meaning for the love or the death. The deaths of children were the most incomprehensible form of pain.

De Quincey's earliest memories were of the deaths of sisters and the brutality of a nurse. 'The feeling which fell upon me was a shuddering horror, as upon a first glimpse of the truth that I was in a world of evil and strife.' If Wordsworth's influence has some part in De Quincey's preference for autobiographical prose and in his perception of the importance of childhood, there remains a considerable originality in the use to which De Quincey puts his very different early experience. Concerning the impression of 'dark sublime' left upon him as a child by the story of Aladdin, he wrote:

Unable to explain my own impressions in Aladdin, I did not the less obstinately persist in believing a sublimity which I could not understand. It was, in fact, one of those many important cases which elsewhere I have called *involutes* of human sensibility; combinations in which the materials of future thought or feeling are carried as imperceptibly into the mind as vegetable seeds are carried variously combined through the atmosphere, or by means of rivers, by birds, by winds, by waters, into remote countries.

(Vol. I, 128)

De Quincey first made his mark with his *Confessions of an English Opium Eater*, which appeared originally in two successive parts in the

London Magazine for September and October 1821, and was later much enlarged for the edition of 1856. His theorizing came later as he tried, in article after article, to put into words the psychological quality of various periods of his life. At its best his prose rises above the contrivance of a deliberate rhetoric and becomes poetic in the same sense that *Kubla Khan* and *The Pains of Sleep* are poetic; but it can be strained and pretentious, rhetorical in a bad sense, without any sustaining impulse, a fault which even his models, Sir Thomas Browne, Milton and Jeremy Taylor, did not escape. The familiar passages describing the pains of opium tend to create misconceptions concerning the main content of the *Confessions* and the staple of their style. The book is written in an extraordinarily engaging and loquacious English which modulates easily from intimacy to the high stylization of prose-poetry, from colloquial humour to pathos. Though the originality of De Quincey's rendering of opium dreams is beyond doubt, a certain resemblance to Coleridge's poems can be distinguished. He writes, for example:

I seemed every night to descend ... into chasms and sunless abysses, depths below depths, from which it seemed hopeless that I could ever reascend.

The drug seemingly made bearable, and also widely significant, an impression of suffering at the centre of De Quincey's experience:

Then came sudden alarms, hurryings to and fro; trepidation of innumerable fugitives ... and at last, with the sense that all was lost, female forms; and the features that were worth all the world to me; and but a moment allowed – and clasped hands, with heart-breaking partings, and then – everlasting farewells!

The significance of this and similar passages is that they concentrate a sense of unhappiness, anxiety and alarm (or 'trepidation') dispersed throughout De Quincey's work. He would have sympathized with Henry James's admission: 'But I have the imagination of disaster – and see life as ferocious and sinister.' The autobiographical writings are extraordinarily successful in depicting the feelings of adolescence, and the confused misery of not having the purposeful outlook and competitive zest required for practical living. The experience would be much less interesting if it could be simply described as 'abnormal'.

Two very different pieces of writing, his *Knocking at the Gate in*

Macbeth (1823) and the two essays on *Murder Considered as One of the Fine Arts* (1827), derive much of their effectiveness from De Quincey's ability to exploit the tendency towards trepidation and alarm in his own feelings. He reports that from his 'boyish days' the Knocking at the Gate produced an effect on his feelings for which he could never account. 'It reflected back upon the murderer a peculiar awfulness and a depth of solemnity.' This is by far the most useful piece of literary interpretation in De Quincey, and it derives from his hypersensitiveness to what is violent and sinister. The 'humour' of the other two essays has often troubled critics; the usual word for it is 'sardonic'. But its power, which might seem to be accounted for by the aesthetic treatment of murder, derives ultimately from De Quincey's horror at the Williams murders. It is not a 'moral' reaction, but a recognition in them of something ferocious in life itself. In the *Suspiria de Profundis* (1845), he wrote:

> Upon me, as upon others scattered thinly by tens and twenties over every thousand years, fell too powerfully and too early the vision of life. The horror of life mixed itself already in earliest youth with the heavenly sweetness of life. (Vol. XIII, 350)

The two remarkable articles on *The Glory of Motion* and *The Vision of Sudden Death*, which make up *The English Mail Coach* (1849), had their origin in the experience many years earlier of a narrowly averted collision between a heavy mail coach on which De Quincey was riding and a gig.

> A movement of horror, and of spontaneous recoil from this dreadful scene, naturally carried the whole of that scene, raised and idealized, into my dreams, and very soon into a rolling succession of dreams.

The excitement of coach travel is vividly described, so that we think of Tolstoy's descriptions of troikas in the Russian snow. De Quincey was expert in creating feelings of suspense and of tumultuous movement, and although he was not a traveller, he could maintain a thrilling narrative speed in re-describing a contemporary event such as *The Revolution of Greece* or in a historical panorama such as *The Revolt of the Tartars*.

De Quincey has a place in the history of criticism, but he was not a great critic. A gifted Hellenist, he was often perverse in his appraisal of Greek literature. Though quick to admire Wordsworth, he was not good at describing what he admired. The promising fragment on *Macbeth* was not followed by an important contribution to Shakespeare criticism. His observations on contemporary writers lacked balance. He accuses Keats of 'the most shocking abuse of his mother tongue'. His remarks on Shelley are mainly a pompous condemnation of the poet's attitude to Christianity. His Tory prejudices are least attractive in his treatment of Hazlitt. 'He hated, with all his heart, every institution of man ... He loathed his relation to the human race ... This inveterate misanthropy was constitutional.' De Quincey is always interesting in his reminiscences of Wordsworth, Coleridge, Lamb and Wilson.

De Quincey's writings on Kant, Lessing and Richter, and his numerous skilful translations of German tales, give him some importance as an early propagandist on behalf of German studies, a work in which he was followed by Carlyle. He produced articles explaining Ricardo's economics which earned him the praise of John Stuart Mill, and his articles on ancient history are substantial pieces of work. A good example of De Quincey's historical insight and style is his review of the first volume of Finlay's *Greece under the Romans* (1844), in which he presents a highly original view of Byzantium and its historical mission which subsequent scholarship has thoroughly substantiated and for which De Quincey has never received any credit. He finds Finlay timid and lacking in understanding of the historic concentration and transmission of power and culture. He asks why Byzantine history should have a relevance to 'the greatest of modern interests'. Byzantium was first of all important 'as the earliest among the kingdoms of our planet which connected itself with Christianity'.

Secondly, as the great aegis of Western Christendom, nay the barrier which made it possible that any Christendom should ever exist, this Byzantine Empire is entitled to a very different station in the enlightened gratitude of us Western Europeans from any which it has yet held. I do not scruple to say that, by comparison with the services of the Byzantine people to Europe, no nation on record has ever stood in the same relation to any other single nation, much less to a whole family of nations, whether as regards the opportunity and means of conferring benefits, or as regards the astonishing perseverance in supporting the succession of these benefits, or as regards the ultimate event of these benefits. A great wrong has been done for ages; for we have all been accustomed to speak of the Byzantine Empire with scorn, as chiefly known by its effeminacy; and the greater is the call for a fervent palinode.

(Vol. VII, 263)

He develops this criticism of parochial versions of history with scholarly feeling. The consensus of modern scholarship was stated recently in Professor Baynes's words: 'It is hardly an exaggeration to say that the civilization of western Europe is a by-product of the Byzantine Empire's will to survive.'[3] It was a real achievement for De Quincey to have seen, at so early a date, such an un-Gibbonian meaning in European history. Perhaps because his view of human nature was neither 'romantic' nor 'classical', and because, though a disinterested recluse, he was always extremely sensitive to the role of power in human affairs, De Quincey saw history as dynamic and full of living issues. If De Quincey's miscellaneous writings do not entitle him to rank as an historian, they do, nevertheless, provide an important example of the deepening sense of history which is part of the Romantic achievement.

De Quincey's work has not, of course, those positive qualities that distinguish major creative writing. There was more endurance than mastery in his attitude to life. But his work is quite free from that suggestion of valetudinarianism which pervades the work of his friend, Charles Lamb (1775–1834). 'My belief,' wrote Augustine Birrell, 'is that Lamb, feeling his own mental infirmity, and aware of the fearful life-long strain to which he was subjected, took refuge in trifles seriously, and played the fool in order to remain sane.'[4] This is a probably explanation of the impression of slightness and intangibleness in Lamb's work. Pater's description is, 'a casual writer for dreamy readers'. The frightful tragedy in Lamb's life has always attracted sentimental treatment. Pater's essay is an example of such self-indulgent 'appreciation'. Critical comments about Lamb often become inventive or evasive, primarily because there is a disproportion between the legend and the actual literary achievement. One reason for this disproportion is the exceptional richness of Lamb's friendships with the principal writers of his time. Lamb's omnipresence establishes a presumption of his own literary importance. The publication of the letters also added to the pathos surrounding the lives of Charles and Mary Lamb, and made it still easier for readers to invent their own Charles Lamb, the loyal brother and friend.

There is much, of course, in Lamb's work to encourage such inventiveness. His most considerable work, the *Essays of Elia* (1823–33) relies heavily on the reader's willingness to be charmed by Lamb's self-idealization. As De Quincey put it: 'You must sympathize with this *personality* in the author ... To appreciate Lamb it is requisite that his character and temperament should be understood in their coyest and most wayward features.' Some of the Essays are indeed, amusing, though they tend to seem rather thin fare even in the schoolroom. There are superficial resemblances to Addison and Steele; for example, in the mode of humour of *Mrs Battle's Opinions on Whist*. The conception of Elia as an author's mouthpiece might also seem to be in the *Spectator* tradition. Here are a few sentences from Addison's essay on *The Royal Exchange*:

> There is no Place in the Town which I so much love to frequent as the Royal Exchange. It gives me a secret Satisfaction, and, in some measure, gratifies my Vanity, as I am an Englishman, to see so rich an Assembly of Countrymen and Foreigners consulting together upon the private Business of Mankind, and making this Metropolis a kind of Emporium for the whole Earth. I must confess I look upon High-Change to be a great Council, in which all considerable Nations have their Representatives.

And here is Elia in *Oxford in the Vacation*:

> I can here play the gentleman, enact the student. To such a one as myself, who has been defrauded in his young years of the sweet food of academic institution, nowhere is so pleasant, to while away a few idle weeks at, as one or other of the Universities ... I can rise at the chapel-bell, and dream that it rings for *me*. In moods of humility I can be a Sizar, or a Servitor. When the peacock vein rises, I strut a Gentleman Commoner ... Only in Christ Church reverend quadrangle I can be content to pass for nothing short of a Seraphic Doctor.

The difference is not merely that the ease of the first passage makes the second appear wordy; there is a more important difference of intention and of manners. Addison, though a little ingenuous, is making what he hopes will be interesting, objective conversation. Lamb is self-consciously ingratiating; in Birrell's phrase, he 'plays the fool'. The manner reminds us embarrassingly of the talk of an Elizabethan coxcomb. We can imagine Ben Jonson putting into the mouth of one of his gulls the sentence from Lamb's essay *On Books and Reading*: 'I bless my stars for a taste so catholic, so unexcluding.' We should not, of course, look for the decorum of the *Spectator* in the *London Magazine*, which first published the *Confessions of an English Opium Eater* as well as *Elia*. Yet De Quincey has a certain proud integrity which is part of our interest. Hazlitt, who wrote before the legend of Charles Lamb had had time to develop, described quite adequately though not unkindly the quality of Lamb's mind:

> Mr Lamb has a distaste to new faces, to new books, to new buildings, to new customs ... He evades the present, he mocks the future. His affections revert to, and settle on the past, but then, even this must have something personal and local in it to interest him deeply and thoroughly; he pitches his tent in the suburbs of existing manners ... No one makes the tour of our southern metropolis, or describes the manners of the last age, so well as Mr Lamb – with so fine, and yet so formal an air – with such vivid obscurity, with such arch piquancy, such picturesque quaintness, such smiling pathos ... His taste in ʀʀench and German literature is somewhat defective; nor has he made much progress in the science of Political Economy or other abstruse studies, though he has read vast folios of controversial divinity, merely for the sake of the intricacy of style, and to save himself the pain of thinking.
>
> (*The Spirit of the Age*)

Claims have been made from time to time for Lamb's importance as a literary critic. It would be easier to sustain his right to consideration as a propagandist on behalf of sixteenth- and seventeenth-century literature, more particularly of Elizabethan drama. His *Specimens of English Dramatic Poets who lived about the Time of Shakespeare* (1808), with its notes, certainly helped to bring about a better understanding of Elizabethan drama, which had been underestimated since the time of Dryden. The choices and omissions of scenes from various plays are often puzzling, but some of the comments are happy – 'Heywood is a sort of *prose* Shakespeare'. Of Sir Epicure Mammon's speeches he writes: 'If there be no one image which rises to the height of the sublime, yet the confluence and assemblage of them all produces a result equal to the grandest poetry.' In his *Autobiographical Sketch* (1827) Lamb claimed that 'he was the first to draw the Public attention to the old English Dramatists', and the claim was perhaps too easily accepted. Several warnings[5] have been given of late against exaggerating the pioneer quality of Lamb's work; editions and collections such as Dodsley's *Select Collection of Old Plays* (1744) had kept interest alive throughout the eighteenth century. Lamb's work was part of a gradual revival of interest in the national past.

Although Lamb is too much a part of the literary history of this period ever to suffer neglect, it is possible that many readers will remember him not for his more deliberate work but for his letters. These often contain interesting passages of criticism, such as the description of Defoe's narrative manner (Letter 285), which is so much more alive than the *Estimate of De Foe's Secondary Novels*. It is not one of the great collections of letters such as that of Keats. But it gives a clear impression of a fairly simple, friendly man – simple, that is, compared with Peacock, De Quincey, or Hazlitt.

Lamb and Hazlitt are fated always to be paired in literary history, as 'essayists'. Hazlitt (1778–1830) is much the more important figure, and the more gifted and better-equipped mind. Much of his writing – there are twenty-one volumes in the standard edition – was ephemeral, but there remains a nucleus of literary and social criticism which holds an important place in our understanding of the Romantic period and in the history of English criticism. He was the exact opposite of a valetudinarian or office-holder. Hazlitt is significant because he was so completely exposed to the intellectual stresses of his time. He earned the right to be critical of Wordsworth and Coleridge, for no contemporary surpassed him in understanding and praise of their work, and he was utterly disinterested. He had the moral energy that surveys the whole field. Of the various attitudes to life revealed by the writers considered in this chapter, Hazlitt's seems the most responsible. He was interested in painting, in literature, in philosophy and in politics, all of which he studied in an affirmative spirit, and he had the independence of judgement of the dissenter.

He was trained to follow his father into the Unitarian ministry, but, becoming deeply involved at an early age in philosophic difficulties, he was driven to change his plans. For a time he remained at home, reading widely and attempting at intervals to carry on with the writing of an essay significantly entitled *On the Principles of Human Action* (1805). What Hazlitt called 'the modern or material philosophy' never ceased to preoccupy him, and he lacked the gift of poetry which afforded a Wordsworth or a Coleridge a creative outlet for their intellectual distress. The later developments in the philosophies of these two poets he had no wish to copy. But he had the luck to meet them both in 1798, and his admiration went out to them. Though his beautiful essay *My First Acquaintance with Poets* (1823) was a distant retrospect, it still conveys the delight and encouragement which Hazlitt derived from the meeting. This attachment did not last, but Hazlitt never ceased to find in the poetry of Wordsworth his own kind of primary conviction of 'the disinterestedness of human action'. It was the personal need to justify this conviction theoretically against the insistence on egotism and self-interest in English philosophy since Hobbes that tied Hazlitt for years to a philosophic undertaking for which he was not qualified. But the task was at least a good preparation for a career of literary and social criticism at a time of ideological revolution and counter-revolution. His characteristic poise is suggested by his remarks on Southey's political recantation:

When his chimeras and golden dreams of human perfectibility vanished from him, he turned suddenly round, and maintained that 'whatever *is*, is right'. Mr Southey has not fortitude of mind, has not patience to think that evil is inseparable from the nature of things.

The last sentence, meditating between extremes, owes more to a religious upbringing than to Burke or Coleridge. Hazlitt's hatred of minimal accounts of human nature, and his perception of the individual's dependence on society, institutions, and tradition, seem to have been qualified by a religious sense of the human condition; so that he cannot readily be classified as a disciple of this or that thinker. There is no suggestion of worldliness in his appreciation of the relevance of different points of view, his recognition of complexities. He had the restlessness and uncertain temper of the man who could find no 'prejudices' to trust as completely as Burke recommended.[6]

Much of his writing must have been threadbare even when it was composed. The best of his essays are those, such as *My First Acquaintance with Poets* or *The Indian Jugglers*, which gave his direct, forceful style an adequate subject-matter. But it is as a critic that Hazlitt has a claim to something more than Lamb's importance. Hazlitt did not have that poet's insight into the creative process which distinguishes Coleridge. The best of Coleridge's observations on Shakespeare's genius or on the effects of metre could not have been made by Hazlitt. Yet the latter's *Characters of Shakespeare's Plays* (1817) suggests an appreciation not inferior to Coleridge's of the scope of Shakespeare's achievement, and of the way in which Shakespeare's poetry works.

To describe the impression made on us by 'characters' is not the best way of doing justice to the cululative significance of Shakespeare's poetry. But the modern reader, who has read modern criticism of Shakespeare, would not feel that his knowledge of more extensive analyses of, say, *Macbeth* had given him a necessarily closer grasp of the complex movement of that play than is suggested by Hazlitt's chapter.

> It is a huddling together of fierce extremes, a war of opposite natures which of them shall destroy the other ... Every passion brings in its fellow-contrary, and the thoughts pitch and jostle against each other in the dark. The whole play is an unruly chaos of strange and forbidden things, where the ground rocks under our feet.

This reads like a summary of a detailed analysis. Hazlitt had obviously responded to the poetry and had experienced the play as more than a collection of parts or of 'characters'. He is not hampered by eighteenth-century reading habits. He notices the

> abruptness and violent antitheses of the style, the throes, and labour which run through the expression, 'So foul and fair a day I have not seen', 'Such welcome and unwelcome news together', 'Look like the innocent flower, but be the serpent under it'.

The attitude to words revealed here is a personal endowment; it is not an eighteenth-century attitude with its prejudice in favour of clear statements and explicit moral conclusions, and against verbal complexity and implicitness of theme. Though modern criticism has given a greater historical depth to our reading of Shakespeare than Hazlitt's reveals, his is not a simplified nor a conspicuously 'romantic' Shakespeare. About *Henry V*, for example, where we should expect a romantic simplification like that of the Olivier film, Hazlitt is critical: 'Henry V, it is true, was a hero, a King of England, and the conqueror of the King of France. Yet we feel little love or admiration for him.' His remarks are not sufficiently related to the play, yet the resistance to any idealizing of Henry is in great part a sensitiveness to Shakespearean complexity. There is the same resistance to romantic paraphrase in his accounts of Othello and of Cleopatra. As we should expect, *Coriolanus* touched on some of Hazlitt's principles, but we are left in no doubt that the play is extraordinarily alive and that Shakespeare is not to be fitted into some political scheme. It is the fresh and alert judgement of Hazlitt's response to Shakespeare that still gives his book a more than historical interest. Even where Hazlitt is most diffuse and superficial, as he often is in the lecture courses, he does not lose sight of the fact that reading implies judging. He divagates, but he does not fill his pages with factitious, all-trivializing praise. At a time when knowledge of past literature was increasing, Hazlitt tried to maintain consistency of judgement over a wide and uncharted area. His sense of comparative worth derived its vigour from his deep interest in the literature of his own day. Literature mattered, and therefore criticism also.

Few works of criticism illustrate as vividly as does *The Spirit of the Age* (1825) those extra-literary considerations which should help to form a critic's awareness of his own times. Hazlitt is concerned to show that rationalists such as Bentham and Godwin had much to learn about induction from the intuitive poets. It was the poets who were concrete, the rationalists who were abstract. The articles are summary, but they are all pointed and they cannot be ignored. Together they give the impression of an alert, responsive mind establishing its relationship to the main influences in the contemporary world. The writers and their writings are considered together, with an effect of portraiture. The description of Wordsworth's appearance and voice is especially beautiful. Avoiding all caricature, Hazlitt's appraisals help to define an important level of English thought and tradition.

NOTES

1. *Ecclesiastical Sonnets*, Part II, Sonnet 25.

2. *Paradis Artificiels* (1860). See G. T. Clapton's *Baudelaire et De Quincey* (Paris, 1931).

3. *Byzantium*, ed. Norman H. Baynes and H. St L. B. Moss, 1948, xxxi.

4. Introduction to *Essays of Elia*, Everyman edn., xvi.

5. *Antiquarian Interest in Elizabethan Drama before Lamb*, Robert D. Williams, Publications of the Modern Language Association of America, Vol. LIII,

No. 2, June 1938, 434–44. Also *Charles Lamb and the Elizabethan Dramatists*, F. S. Boas, Essays and Studies by Members of the English Association, Vol. XXIX, 1943, 62–81.

6. See Burke's *Reflections on the French Revolution*, 1790.

THE EUROPEAN BACKGROUND
TO ROMANTICISM

GEOFFREY STRICKLAND and CHRISTOPHER THACKER

While allowing a welter of exceptions, variations and contradictions, it remains true that Romanticism at the end of the eighteenth century – whether simply in England, or in Western Europe as a whole – had arisen as a reaction to Classicism, as represented by different aspects of French culture and society in the age of Louis XIV. Not only in politics, but in religion and in aesthetics, Louis' régime had been authoritarian, indeed absolutist in its insistence that French government, the French form of Roman Catholic Christianity, and the French interpretation of architectural, artistic and literary forms possessed unique and indisputable rightness over all other alternatives.

Reaction against French absolutism – against what might be termed 'the aesthetic of Versailles' – began most firmly, and in a variety of ways, in England, and it was from the initial English impetus that Romanticism on the Continent began. The influence of Shaftesbury and Addison was the most important. Shaftesbury had claimed that God's perfection might be perceived more readily in the untouched natural world than in the works of man, and that the poet, the creative artist, was uniquely able to seize and describe this Divine perfection through the contemplation of Nature's works, in a trance-like state of inspiration (*The Moralists*, 1709, and *Characteristics*, 1711); Addison applied Shaftesbury's view of the superiority of untouched nature to the practice of gardening, and attacked the dominant, French-inspired fashion of formal, clipped hedges outlining a geometrical plan, contrasting this unnatural practice with the attraction of the unspoiled surrounding countryside (*Spectator*, Nos. 414, 477). In another direction, Addison expressed a common British view that while France under Louis XIV was a tyranny, the most cherished right of the British was their liberty (e.g. *Tatler*, No. 161). Looking back over nearly three centuries, it is easy to exaggerate Addison's claim, which was in its essence the belief that Britons should be entitled to proceed (in political, religious and artistic matters) independently of French authority. To these alternatives to French domination should be added an architectural style – the gothic, or 'Saxon' as it was also called (as in Batty Langley's *Gothic Architecture Improved*, 1742). While the château and gardens of Versailles employed wholly 'classical' forms of architecture, it was possible to see the many surviving examples of pre-Renaissance architecture in Britain as a 'national' style derived from the – supposedly free – Anglo-Saxon inhabitants before the Norman Conquest. A notable politico-architectural monument to this belief is James Gibbs's *Gothic Temple* in the grounds at Stowe (*c*. 1741). Built in an uncompromisingly jagged 'gothic' style, and containing the busts of Anglo-Saxon kings of England, it was at first called the *Temple of Liberty*.

Two further British divergences from French absolutism should be noted, related to the impetus given by Shaftesbury and Addison. In the theatre, British critics continued to admire the native exuberance of Shakespeare, which they contrasted (as Dryden had already done) with the controlled *froideur* of French tragedy – and this, in spite of the paradoxical attempt by Addison himself in his tragedy *Cato* (1713) to establish the French drama as a genre on the British stage. In the general sphere of poetics, while prevailing standards were the reasoned control and orderly expression of Pope and Jonson, approval came gradually to be given to poets of a primitive and untutored, rather than of a sophisticated and highly educated kind. In the long Dispute of the Ancients and the Moderns, Richard Bentley's rediscovery of the digamma at the turn of the century led to a re-evaluation of Homer's verse, which was now seen to scan perfectly, and was therefore not technically inferior to that of Virgil. In 1735, Thomas Blackwell's *Enquiry into the Life and Writings of Homer* claimed unequivocally that Homer's excellence was in large part due to his simple and uneducated way of life – he had the unparalleled advantage of being 'a blind strolling Bard'. In his *Conjectures on Original Composition* (1759) Edward Young transferred admiration for Homer and his primitive existence to all poets whose life and work could be seen as 'original' (in Young's view, Milton and Shakespeare in particular) as opposed to those – such as Virgil or Alexander Pope – whose work suffered from the constricting influences of academic learning and literary 'rules'. In 1760, James Macpherson brought the veneration of the 'Bard' to a climax. In his *Fragments of Ancient Poetry*, followed by *Fingal* in 1762, and *Temora* in 1763, he produced the supposed 'translations' into measured English prose of the work of a Highland bard, the blind, uneducated poet Ossian, thought to have lived in the ninth century. Britain could now boast two great 'bards' to rival other countries and ages – Ossian, the northern Homer, and Shakespeare, the dramatist superior to France's Corneille and Racine.

These attitudes and these examples were directly or indirectly transmitted to the Continent, especially to France and Germany, and, whether they were properly or only imperfectly appreciated, provided the principal pretext for devising alternatives to the absolutist aesthetic of Louis XIV and Versailles. At the political level, French critics professed to admire the British love of liberty. After a brief exile in England in the 1720s, Voltaire described the British way of life as one in which religious, political, commercial and aesthetic toleration was successfully maintained. In contrast to the French king, the British monarch ruled under a constitution which left him solely 'the power to do good'. In Britain, government was the affair of Parliament, not the king – while in France the equivalent to the British Parliament, the États Généraux, had not met since 1615, and was not to be summoned again until 1789, the year of the French Revolution.

Elsewhere in the *Lettres philosophiques* Voltaire described his experience of the London theatre; discussing tragedy, he admired Addison's *Cato* as 'the greatest Character that was ever brought upon any stage'; but his main fascination was with Shakespeare, who both attracted and repelled him by his vitality and 'genius', and by his apparent lack of discipline and 'good taste'. Voltaire was no romantic, yet his recommendation of British liberty and his introduction of Shakespeare to the French helped, willy-nilly, to further different apsects of Romanticism – the French Revolution, which was itself in some respects the culmination of early Romantic aspirations, and Romantic drama, inconceivable without Shakespeare as example and excuse.

Though Voltaire turned away from Shakespeare (in part because of Shakespeare's growing vogue, which he had himself started, and because of the declining favour of French classical tragedy, of which he believed himself to be the greatest living exponent), others in France were attracted to the thought that 'serious' plays did not necessarily have to be written in Alexandrines, nor need they conform precisely to the unities of time, place and action. By mid-century Diderot was formulating his theory on the 'genre sérieux', a genre midway between comedy and tragedy, avoiding both the extremes of farce and of high tragedy, and embracing the 'naturalness' of ordinary speech and everyday situations. The plays which Diderot wrote to illustrate his theory – Le Fils naturel (1757) and Le Père de famille (1758) – were not especially daring, but accompanying essays – Entretiens avec Dorval and Discours sur la poésie dramatique – were remarkable for their emphasis on the moral seriousness of the theatre, and for their presentation of the poet as hero, genius and passionate individual. Diderot's views here come mainly from Shaftesbury (he had translated Shaftesbury's Inquiry concerning Virtue into French in 1745) and, at this point, to a lesser extent from Rousseau, with whom he was then friendly.

Although Diderot's dramatic theory had slight effect in France, his plays and his dramatic criticism were all quickly translated into German by Lessing (Das Theater des Herrn Diderot, 1760), and became important as theatrical documents for the writers struggling to create a new and genuine German theatre. Lessing valued Diderot for his recommendations in favour of a serious bourgeois drama – in German, the bürgerliches Trauerspiel; but for those younger writers who were to become known as the Sturm und Drang or 'Storm and Stress' (after Klinger's play of this name in 1776), Diderot's worth lay in his praise of the genius, the creative artist who draws his creative inspiration from nature (and from nature's wilder aspects), scorning the artificial and debilitating conventions of society. For the writers of the Sturm und Drang, from Gerstenberg in the 1760s to Herder, Goethe and Lenz in the 1770s and Schiller in the early 1780s, Diderot's influence was united with that of Shakespeare himself and of Young, writing on the nature of the 'bard'; of Macpherson's Ossianic poetry, quickly translated and imitated in France and Germany; and with the influence of Rousseau.

In the 1750s and 60s, Rousseau had denounced the corruption of most towns and cities, with the exception of his native Calvinist Geneva in which, as he pointed out in his Lettre à d'Alembert of 1758, there were no theatres and hence no opportunity for the public ridicule of an honest and virtuous man such as the hero of Molière's Misan-

thrope. Rousseau's work and personality contain many extraordinary contradictions and he himself was continually misunderstood in his own lifetime and, as he saw it, unjustly persecuted. Any brief account of his influence is therefore bound to be over-simple. Despite his affirmation in *Emile* (1762) of a divine moral intuition in man (and in woman too, taking a distinctly feminine form) distinguishing him from brute creation, and despite the care he believed that the perfect upbringing of a boy and girl such as his Emile and Sophie required,[1] he could be seen also as the apologist for spontaneous instincts such as those of the 'noble savage' postulated in his *Discours sur l'origine de l'inégalité* of 1755 or his own boldly confessed if not exactly shameless urge to expose himself in the streets of Turin, memorably recorded in his *Confessions.* Despite the passionate and erotic love of Saint-Preux for Julie in *La Nouvelle Héloïse* (1761), this epistolary novel also contains reasoned arguments for marriage based on mutual convenience and esteem. And the paradoxical nature of Rousseau's thought is never more obvious than when we consider his influence on the politics of modern Europe. In *Le Contrat Social* (1762), he raises the question of how, if at all, the assertion of authority by one man over another can be justified, and having (unlike Voltaire and Montesquieu) condemned the English Parliamentary system he concludes that it is in the 'general will' of the people (not the will of the majority or even 'the will of all') that sovereignty resides and that this will is indivisible. This appealing, though intellectually extremely difficult, notion of a collective will which is inalienable and even morally infallible can be taken to justify the exercise of power in the name of 'the people' by any allegedly representative group. It was on good Rousseauistic principles, for example, that all successive governments during the Revolution and Empire in France forbade trade unions (Pitt's Combination Acts were urged on less idealistic grounds) as constituting 'factions' within the state.

Few 'movements' are uniformly consistent in their interests and ideals – even less than individuals such as Diderot or Rousseau. The writers of the *Sturm und Drang* are no exception. But from a distance they can all be seen to be sharing that distrust of French absolutism which was known in Britain near the beginning of the eighteenth century, and to be admiring with Shaftesbury and Young and Diderot the alternative of the unspoiled natural world, and the unconstrained, spontaneous enthusiasm of the individual in response to nature. Already in the 1720s and 1730s the Swiss J. J. Bodmer had helped to make the *Spectator* known to German readers, and had translated Milton. In 1732 von Haller's long poem *Die Alpen* was published, enlarging the appreciation of Alpine scenery by thoughtful praise of the peasants' simple life in the mountains. In 1745 Brockes had included a translation of Thomson's *Seasons* in a volume of his own poems in praise of the natural world. These and a score of lesser writers lay behind the attitudes of the *Sturm und Drang*. Nature, and even nature's wildness, were seen to be good, while society was a corrupting force, harming those who submitted to its rules. Those who turned to nature, to live 'naturally' and spontaneously – like the 'bard' and the 'genius' – might well be at war with society. Therein lay their glory, and their tragedy.

With the supposed 'freedom' of Shakespeare's plays as an example to be followed, and the three unities of French classical tragedy as rules rather to be broken, the writers of the *Sturm und Drang* produced many plays which are moving – at least in part – though they are often shapeless and confused. It is characteristic that Klinger's play *Sturm und Drang*, which gave its name to the movement as a whole, was first intended to be called *Wirrwarr* or 'Turmoil'. The plays often present characters who are violent, rebellious and in conflict – despairingly so – with the complacency of society, authority and tradition; and the themes are often taken from past ages, when violence might be imagined to be more possible than in the weak and divided Germany of the 1770s. Gerstenberg's *Ugolino* (1768) is taken from Dante, telling of the death by starvation of Ugolino and his sons in the Tower of Famine. The stage is in effect a prison, where the characters all die, as if in one of Piranesi's *Carceri*. Goethe's *Götz von Berlichingen* (first version, 1771) follows Shakespeare's history plays with its panorama of nobles, clergy, townspeople, peasants and soldiers, but the hero Götz is distinctively of the *Sturm und Drang*, being in continual rebellion and dying with the words 'Freedom! Freedom!' on his lips. Schiller's *Die Raüber* (1781) is set nearer the present, but his hero Karl Moor is a bandit, in rebellion against society and his (aristocratic) family; and Goethe's earliest version of *Faust*, the 'Urfaust' sketched out in 1773-5, has as its hero a scholar who is so dissatisfied with all that he has achieved that he turns to the super-natural for help, and obtains the infernal support of Mephistopheles. The Faust theme was known to others of the *Sturm und Drang*, Klinger in particular, and a version of the story became known to M. G. Lewis, whose Gothic novel *The Monk* (1796) depends for its super-natural framework on a pact between the monk Ambrosio and the devil. Not all the heroes of the *Sturm und Drang* are as brave, and these are shown as oppressed by the constricting forces of society. Echoing Rousseau's *Nouvelle Héloïse*, Lenz's play *Der Hofmeister* (1774) condemns the uncompromising snobbery of the petty nobil-ity, and presents the sad and long-drawn-out results of a middle-class private tutor's *amour* with his aristocratic pupil. Goethe's novel *Die Leiden des jungen Werthers* (1774) sums up this feeling of impotent dissatisfaction with society. Young Werther, the hero, is – unlike Faust – irremediably set in the Germany of the 1770s; unlike Faust, he has no help from the supernatural to relieve his yearnings, and, unlike Faust or Götz or Ugolino or Karl Moor, he is weak, vacil-lating, alternately elated and cast down by his experiences. He loves a woman who is already engaged, and lacks the determination either to declare or to stifle his passion. He takes to reading the wistful, hopeless poetry of Ossian, and his suicide at last declares his utter inability to endure either the force of his own desires, or the intrac-tability of the world in which he must live.

Though largely inspired by British examples, these movements towards Romanticism in France and Germany were only partially known and appreciated in Britain, and rarely in a simple and direct manner. While the writings of the major French authors were read in French by the educated in the British Isles, not many were translated apart from novels such as the *Nouvelle Héloïse*, while the exciting, tumultuous writings of the *Sturm und Drang* in Germany remained virtually unread, untranslated and unknown in Britain (apart from Goethe's *Werther*) until the nineteenth century. Brockes and Haller, the writers in German who most reflect the British rediscovery of nature, are to this day known in Britain only to those who can read them in the original.

It is curious that the individual who did most to transmit the spirit and the themes of the *Sturm und Drang* to Britain was a painter –

Heinrich Füssli or Fuseli (1741–1825).* Born in Switzerland, he travelled widely in Italy, England, France and Germany before settling in
England in 1779. Though he was not attracted to Landscape, his work
ranges through the widest choice of human themes, from the Bible,
Homer, Dante, the *Nibelungenlied* (recently rediscovered in Germany), Shakespeare and Milton, from lesser sources and from others
invented by himself; and almost all his paintings and drawings run
parallel to the themes of the *Sturm und Drang*, which are, by Fuseli,
transmitted to England. There is hardly a placid picture in his entire
oeuvre – all are tense, vibrant with expectation of the unknown, of
violence, of death or disaster, coming from God or the Devil, from
a jealous husband or wife, from the Erinnye or from the turbulent
depths of the artist's own mind.

Certainly, Romanticism in Britain was influenced by Europe, yet
it was not just individual Europeans who provided the influence, but
also the scenery, the *mountains* of Europe, and a European *event* – the
French Revolution – which were important. While Haller's *Die
Alpen* remained unknown, English delight in mountain scenery had
begun with Addison's tentative approval of the Alps in 1705, followed by the ecstatic comments of Gray and Walpole on the scenery
of the Grande Chartreuse in 1739. In the eighteenth-century rediscovery of nature, Rousseau's part is far more to do with the new
alliance of the individual with nature (and his dissociation from
society) than with the reassessment of man's opinion of this or that
natural phenomenon. Rousseau's own taste was generally timid, pre-
ferring a 'smiling countryside' of a rural nature to any more
barren or forbidding scene. Though readers of the *Nouvelle Héloïse*,
with its subtitle 'the story of two lovers living in a little town at the
foot of the Alps', thrilled to the idea that Julie and Saint-Preux were –
and could only be – happy in the bosom of nature, Rousseau never
takes his characters, or his readers, above the foothills. His importance
lies in the persuasiveness of his statement that nature is 'good' while
society is 'bad', and of the corollary that 'natural' behaviour (unreflecting, and impulsive) is good, in contrast to behaviour which is
governed by reason, and by the rules and customs of society. These
statements, embodied in the *Discours sur . . . l'inégalité* (1755), praising

---

* See the account of Fuseli in Geoffrey Grigson's chapter on English painting,
pp. 358–72.

the 'noble savage', and, in the *Nouvelle Héloïse*, praising the innocence
of unreflecting 'love at first sight', are completed in Rousseau's
Rêveries du promeneur solitaire, published in 1782, four years after his
death. In these ten 'promenades', Rousseau recalls his repeated rejection by society and his profound and incomparable delight in solitary,
instinctive communion with nature. So deep and so sublime were his
emotions, alone by the shores of an Alpine lake, that at times he
would 'feel with pleasure' his 'existence', '*sans prendre la peine de
penser*', 'without taking the trouble to think' (Fifth promenade). This
is an intuition it is impossible to imagine being expressed by any of
the contemporary *philosophes* in France and one which brings out his
deep affinity in certain ways with the English Romantic poets, especially Wordsworth, but also Byron writing in 1816 in Canto iii of
Childe Harold: 'High mountains are a feeling, but the hum/Of human
cities torture'.

Yet, while Rousseau would have understood and agreed with
Byron's way of separating and valuing nature and the city, he would
not have shared Byron's ecstatic admiration of the higher Alps, nor
his belief that God was especially immanent in the Alpine ice and
snow, being nature's purest form, nor Byron's wish to be annihilated
and united with God in the fall of the avalanche. Such love of the
wildest Alpine scenery was a gradual development of appreciation
which took place mainly in the British Isles, in the Lake District, the
Pennines, in Snowdonia and in Scotland in the second half of the
eighteenth century.

To say that the French Revolution was a 'romantic' phenomenon
would be grotesque; it had far too many causes, elements and aspects
to be so labelled. No more could it be attributed principally to the
propaganda of the rationalist *philosophes*, going back to Montesquieu,
Voltaire and Diderot. But it did have an aspect which was Romantic –
– the Rousseauan belief of many of its leaders, especially Robespierre,
that the Revolution marked a rebirth of humanity, in which the old
society must be destroyed to enable regenerated man to live without
corruption in natural innocence and happiness. The joy of many
British observers of the Revolution and their sanguine expectations
are well known, and, whether it was Blake, Mary Wollstonecraft,
Wordsworth, Coleridge, Southey or Byron, they all rejoiced at the
prospect of such a Rousseauan rebirth of mankind. Attempts to

define 'Romanticism', as we know, rarely meet with unqualified success. One distinguished modern historian of the subject has, however, claimed that the Romanticism of England, if nowhere else, lay precisely in the enthusiasms and disillusionments inspired by the revolutionary movement in Europe and North America. Even in the *Lyrical Ballads*, he quotes Hazlitt as saying that Wordsworth's 'Muse' was 'a levelling one'.[2] In the interests of historical accuracy, there is a great deal to be said for such a comprehensive view and there is a danger, if we try to define Romanticism more rigorously, of our seeing differences where these are only negligible and of failing to note the signs of genuine originality. The revolutionary movement in politics and the Romantic in literature were both inspired by a notion of human nature which is at variance with the Christian doctrine of the Fall. As Tocqueville wrote in the 1850s of the generation of his grandparents:

> If the Frenchmen who made the revolution were more prone to religious incredulity than ourselves, they possessed one admirable belief which we lack: they believed in themselves. They had no doubt of the power and perfectibility of man ... [or] ... that they had been called upon to transform society and regenerate our species.[3]

This is nowhere more evident than in Germany, where Romanticism is part of the history of philosophy just as much as of literature. During the Romantic period there were, of course, many Germanies and the necessarily provincial nature of German culture[4] proved incompatible with the development of anything like French urban civilization, with its deep historical roots, its educated public and unassuming formality. German self-consciousness tends always towards the explicitly critical and German insecurity towards the need for absolute certainty. The classic instance is that of Kant, whose daily walk through Königsberg was delayed because he had started to read Rousseau's *Emile* and was unable to put it down and whose relentless consistency contrasts with Rousseau's inspired insights and simple rhetoric. One of the many things that made Rousseau remarkable for Kant was his bold refusal to follow the leading French and English thinkers of his day in accepting Locke's theory, expressed in *The Essay Concerning Human Understanding* (1690), of the primacy of the senses in the formation of ideas and standards of behaviour. And one of the lessons of *Emile* is that 'conscience' is innate and not the product of social circumstances and animal needs satisfied in certain habitual ways. This belief, developed systematically in Kant's *Critique of Practical Reason* of 1788, is crucial to subsequent philosophical and critical debate.

The rejection of the Lockean theory has its parallel, as we know, in England. For Blake, 'imagination' is the light of truth and the 'five senses' (in the *Marriage of Heaven and Hell*) an 'abyss'. Wordsworth earnestly followed the Lockean theory of what, through the writings of Hartley, became known as 'associationism', rearranging his collected poems, for example, to correspond to a Hartleian scheme and thereby illustrate the growth of the mind. His failure to produce in *The Prelude* a great Hartleian poem and his success (as F. R. Leavis has argued) in creating something deeper and finer testify to the inadequacy of his guiding principles. It was Coleridge who, in the *Bibliographia Literaria*, claimed that Hartley's system was 'neither tenable in theory nor founded in fact' and who was assisted in the process of saying why by his study of Kant, Fichte and Schelling.

These names, of course, stand for widely divergent points of view, even if for Coleridge their combined influence served to justify his allegiance to the 'metaphysics' of which the Lockean appeal to experience had appeared to dispose for all time. Kant's own rejection of metaphysics, in the sense of an attempt to understand the nature of 'things in themselves', was contested by the German thinkers who followed him, though they argued from Kantian and not from Lockean premises when examining the scope and nature of the mind. It is impossible to characterize briefly what is known as German philosophical 'idealism' or to underestimate its influence on the thought of our own time: that of Hegel on modern notions of history or of Herder and Schelling on the study of language and symbolism. One can, however, point to a single crucial factor when trying to say why such developments took place in Germany rather than any other European country. This is that the interminable philosophical debates which were to have such a momentous outcome took place between university professors, with an audience of future pastors, lawyers and administrators, at a time when theological and constitutional innovations were calling for a constant re-examination of first principles. Fichte, Schelling and Hegel all lectured at the University of Jena, which at the turn of the century enjoyed an unrivalled and, outside Germany, unsuspected intellectual pre-eminence. A. W. Schlegel's history of world drama, in which the French classics are relegated to the status of a mere national drama in a world whose giants remain Euripides and Shakespeare, is the text of his course of lectures of 1808 at nearby Weimar; while it was in Berlin in the same year that Fichte in his 'Address to the German nation' added a political dimension to the self-conscious national feeling and the reaction against French supremacy.

The popularity of the public lecturer and preacher is not sufficient, however, to explain the vitality and originality of German literature and philosophy at this time. Corresponding to the student audience, there was no reliable reading public; and apart from the royalties from *Werther*, Goethe made little from sales of his work. His freedom from material cares which enabled him to devote his life to literature and science was due to the patronage of his high-spirited friend, that princely Squire Headlong, the Duke of Saxe-Weimar, to whom he was to become a conscientious and indispensable first minister. The absence of a demanding public may itself, however, have contributed to the freedom German writers display, as it did with Blake, and it could be argued that this is as true in the theatre as in the novel or poetry.

If the original German answer to French classicism is to be found in the essays of Lessing and the kind of heroic melodrama which takes its name from Klinger's *Sturm und Drang*, this does not mean that a professional theatre comparable to that of Paris or London was there to sustain it. Professional actors were, till the end of the century, usually members of travelling companies, like that in which Klinger performed himself (before becoming a general in the Russian army) and bearing some resemblance, presumably, to Goethe's in his picaresque if also unreal and idyllic first book of *Wilhelm Meister*.[5] Many, especially the Italian opera companies, came from abroad, and in Vienna established the conventions exploited by Mozart; though Mozart was considered inferior to the Italians by the Empress who called *La Clemenza di Tito* 'German muck'. Court patronage in the German theatre was essential for its elevation to the level of serious art (far more than in the Paris of Molière and Racine who had made their names in the predominantly middle-class Paris theatre before receiving the summons to Versailles) and it was under the protection of the providential Duke of Saxe-Weimar that the German theatre produced some of its finest masterpieces: Schiller's *Maria Stuart* (1800) and *Wilhelm Tell* (1804). Goethe himself was clearly less concerned than his friend Schiller with the demands of the actual stage, and the *Faust* to which he devoted almost a lifetime is the work of a man who could do without ordinary dramatic success. There is in fact a similarity, remote but real, between Goethe's own theatrical career and that of Wagner in the Munich and Bayreuth of Ludwig II. The triumph of Bayreuth is in many ways an apotheosis of earlier German Romanticism.

Court patronage is not enough, however, to explain the originality of German Romanticism or the uninhibited freedom with which exalted states of feeling were cultivated in poetry and fiction together with a dream-world, anticipating that of Wagner, an imaginary medieval Germany inhabited by spirits of the ethnic past. Of significance here is the influence of Herder whose investigations into the origins of language and philosophy of history led to a reverent study of the German past and whose collection of *Volkslieder* (1779), itself prompted by Bishop Percy's *Reliques of Ancient English Poetry* (1765), stimulated both the study of folklore and the writing of lyrical poetry. This too, however, is insufficient to explain the freedom, audacity and above all innocence of the German Romantic mind: in *Wilhelm Meister*, for example, in which the hermaphrodite young dancer Mignon and the 'man-woman' Natalie manifest poignantly (as in the occult authors whom Goethe, like his Faust, had keenly studied) a kind of human perfection; or in the writings of the young genius Novalis in which the hermaphrodite theme is dwelled on with special fervour.[6] Abnormal sexuality, it is true, is described with increasing candour not only in Germany but in France in the period following the publication of Rousseau's *Confessions*. One need only think of Sade and Rétif de la Bretonne. In Goethe and Novalis, however, the eroticism is not defiant, as in Sade, but almost devout in its exaltation and if we are to seek a precedent here, it may be found in the so-called Herrnhut Pietism in which many German protestants had been schooled and which, no less than the cult of 'feeling' in Rousseau and Diderot, may explain some of German Romanticism. Its encouragement of a 'heart religion' among those who would look upon themselves as the future leaders of society lent itself to what in a more orthodox age would have seemed like the extremes of personal heresy and presumption. The reaction against this and against the extremes of 'enlightened' optimism (in, for example, the essays of Novalis himself who makes the case for a return to old-fashioned catholicism) has many parallels throughout the subsequent history of what has become our own Romantic age.

In France the movement that came to call itself 'Romantic' in the 1820s and 1830s drew its inspiration partly from Germany, following the publication of Mme de Staël's De l'Allemagne (1810), but also from the widespread European reaction against the spirit that had made the revolution. It is usually agreed that the French middle classes who, after 1789, put an end to the economic privileges of the nobility and the church, found, when the revolution had been saved by Bonaparte, a useful ally in the latter; and that where the literature of the eighteenth century had been free-thinking and irreverent, from 1802 onwards it was devout and prudish, in manner at least, whatever the private beliefs and behaviour of the writers themselves. As well as Bonaparte's Concordat with the Vatican, the year 1802 saw the publication of Le Génie du christianisme by the returned Breton émigré Chateaubriand, and no book did more to establish the beliefs and the style of French Romanticism. It is a defence of Christian 'civilization', using arguments that will appeal to the religious sceptic as well as to the devout believer. It describes the usefulness as well as the beauty of religion. From it, as from Herder and later from Scott, derives the nostalgia for an idealized feudal past, as well as that distinctive romantic trait, the cultivation of religious sentiment as distinct from religious belief. There is a striking contrast, in this respect, beneath the language and assumptions of Lamartine, Vigny and the young Hugo in France and those of Shelley, Peacock and Hazlitt; and it was Byron's Childe Harold and not his Don Juan which established his reputation in France and to which Lamartine added a 'last canto'.

No survey as brief as this could escape the charge of over-simplification. And among the obvious omissions so far is any reference to the countries which meant so much to Goethe and Byron, Greece and Italy. Greece, of course, during this period scarcely belongs to Europe, unjust though this may be to the memory of Koraïs, the disciple of the European enlightenment and architect of the modern 'purified' Greek language or of the poet Rhigas whose version of the *Marseillaise* was paraphrased by Byron as 'Sons of the Greeks, arise'. The cause of Greek independence was inspired by classical pieties and idyllic travelogues rather than by a sense of intellectual or artistic kinship with the victims of Ottoman rule and it was one in which Tories could join with political radicals. There are statues in Athens today of both Byron and Canning. No such alliance was possible with regard to Italy which, in the north especially, with the return of Austrian rule, was even more than France the victim of the Congress of Vienna; this despite the fact that Italian thinkers and poets were regarded, as they regarded themselves, as enlightened modern Europeans using a language with a far more illustrious past than the German of Vienna.

The legacy of Dante and Petrarch was, however, a liability as much as an asset to many Italian writers, and even today the dialects of the regions differ markedly from the Italian of grammars and dictionaries. Alfieri, in his remarkable autobiography published in 1803, records how, for a Piedmontese, learning to write in Italian meant quite literally mastering a foreign tongue. This 'Tuscan' Italian lends itself to formal declamation and hence to the expression of the political passions which inspire so much of the writing of the period: Alfieri's own heroic verse and the essays in which he expresses his angry republican (if also distinctly patrician) view of tyranny; Foscolo's patriotic *Sepolcri* (1807) and his novel of personal and political disillusionment, *The Last Letters of Jacopo Ortis* (1802); the poems of Monti, that Vicar of Bray of Italy during her many changes of régime; and those of the other contributors to Silvio Pellico's *Conciliatore* until its suppression by the Austrian police and Pellico's imprisonment in the atrocious prison conditions described in his classical *Le mie prigioni*. The Milanese circle of writers was visited by Byron during the autumn of 1816 and an engaging though almost entirely fictitious account of their adventures during his stay has been left by another member of the circle, the French writer Stendhal, who won Byron's attention by passing himself off as a former aide-de-camp to Napoleon.[7] Stendhal's unique blend of fact and fiction makes him an unreliable chronicler but in his *Rome,*

Naples et Florence en 1817 he describes what many Italians seem to have felt was the mood of the divided nation after 1815: 'Music alone remains alive in Italy; the other pleasures of the soul have all been frustrated; and one can die poisoned by melancholy to the extent that one feels any vestige of public spirit ...' This description is borne out certainly by the inspiration and success of Leopardi.

What is usually omitted, of course, from any account of literary or political history during the Romantic period is the fate of the great majority of Europeans, the uneducated poor. In France these, it would now appear, almost certainly grew poorer after the revolutionary governments' condemnation of private and ecclesiastical charity and their inability to replace this by practical measures of their own.[8] The return of the church brought some measure of relief but also of spiritual terror and hierarchical control. Catechisms, during Napoleon's reign, included fidelity to the Emperor among the duties of the Christian, failure to comply with which could be punished in the life to come. The increasing scepticism of the educated with regard to the doctrine of damnation was to take over a hundred years to pervade society as a whole.

NOTES

1. 'The prefectibility of which man?', D. H. Lawrence asks in his essay on Franklin in *Studies in Classic American Literature*: 'I am many men ... which do you propose to suppress?' This essay is highly relevant to the study of Rousseau as is Lawrence's remarkable essay on the cult of benevolence in Diderot and Rousseau, 'The good man' in *Phoenix I*. Among other things, it helps dispose of the idea of Rousseau as an eighteenth-century D. H. Lawrence.

2. See Hazlitt's essay, 'The Spirit of the Age' and the essay by M. H. Abrams in *Romanticism Reconsidered*, ed. Northrop Frye (New York, 1963).

3. *L'Ancien régime*, ed. J. P. Mayer (Paris, 1952), Vol. I, 176.

4. The prestige of French in eighteenth-century Germany and slow emergence of German as a language considered fit for literary and philosophical use are described by E. A. Blackall in *The Emergence of German as a Literary Language* (Cambridge, 1959).

5. See W. H. Bruford, *Theatre, Drama and Audience in Goethe's Germany* (London, 1950).

6. The best-known source of the notion that perfect love consists of the

reuniting of male and female in the original perfect hermaphrodite form is to be found in Plato's *Symposium*.

7. See Stendhal's reminiscences of Byron in *Mélanges de Littérature*, Vol. 3 (Paris, 1933) and Doris Langley Moore, *The Late Lord Byron* (London, 1961).

8. See Alan Forrest, *The French Revolution and the Poor* (Oxford, 1980).

JOHN CLARE, WILLIAM COBBETT
AND THE CHANGING LANDSCAPE

JOHN BARRELL

In 1700, something like half the arable land of England lay in 'open' or 'common' field, that system whereby the arable land of a parish was divided into three or four large fields arranged around a nuclear village, those fields in turn being subdivided into 'furlongs', within each of which several different proprietors often held strips of one or more 'lands', or ploughed ridges. The area where most of the common fields were to be found stretched north-eastwards from Dorset, its southern boundary passing just north of London to reach the Norfolk coast around Great Yarmouth, its northern edge running through the south-west midlands to reach the North Sea at Holder-ness. Outside this area, common fields were the exception rather than the rule, and within it there were, in 1700, wide variations from parish to parish in the amount of arable land which had already been enclosed by agreement or coercion. The enclosure of what remained was largely effected by a host of private acts of enclosure: from the 1750s onwards the number of these steadily in-creased, so that between 1760 and 1800 nearly five hundred were passed, providing for the enclosure of some two and a half million acres of arable land; and in the following forty years or so there were about another thousand acts, enclosing a further one and a half million acres.

In the area of the south-east midlands where the open-field system had been particularly tenacious of life, the change in the appearance of the land, and so also in the consciousness of place and space of many of those who lived there, must have been very great. In an open-field parish only the contours of the land, the occasional pieces of arable or pasture enclosed by 'agreement', a patch of wood-land, or the houses and trees of the village itself, obstructed a view of the fields to a horizon more distant than we could find in such a parish now. The 'whole' was 'spread under the eye, at once', as one observer commented; or in the words of another, 'the husbandman sees at a glance all that is happening on the parcels he possesses in a single furlong, or even over the whole field'. The same parish, enclosed by act of Parliament, its hedges well-established and planted with trees, might give the impression to those walking or riding along its roads that they were passing through a wood: behind the roadside-hedges were visible only the trees in the next hedgerow – an effect often noticed by writers on agriculture as they travelled through the landscape of those parts of England which had never been in open field, and where each field had been separately cleared from the original woodland. The change in the visual character of an open-field parish, to something like that of a landscape which had been enclosed from woodland, would have been completed within the space of one generation.

The characteristic sense of space which the topography and organization of an open-field parish created could be described as circular. In the first place, the village was usually established more or less at its centre, where the three or four fields of the parish came together. They formed around the settlement a rough circle: the crops rotated about the village, and it is fair to say that the fields, too, rotated about the hub of the village, as for example one year the wheat-field might be to the north of the village, then to the east, then to the south, and so on. The roads that led out of the village were not primarily thought of as leading out of the parish, towards the neighbouring villages or market towns. They were originally laid out to facilitate the circulation of cattle *around* the parish, as they grazed the different areas of land that, through the year, became available to them: the fallows, the commons, the meadows, the stubble, the fallows again. No doubt, in many open-field parishes, this self-centred sense of space, even among those inhabitants with least reason to travel regularly outside the parish boundary, had been by 1750 to an extent overprinted by a more linear sense of space: an awareness, for example, of the village as existing on a road between two major towns, or as now situated in relation to a new turnpike-road. But as long as the layout of the open-field parish survived, the old, circular sense of space could not have been entirely effaced from the consciousness even of the most substantial, the most mobile of the farmers of the parish, for it remained inscribed in the daily and seasonal agricultural practice of the village.

The new landscape formed by the commissioners appointed by acts of enclosure, who were usually drawn from the rural professional class of land-agents, surveyors and valuers, attempted to replace this circular organization of space by a linear one, most clearly expressed in the grid-like pattern of rectangular fields they designed, and in the straight roads by which they attempted to connect the village itself with the neighbouring villages, towns, and trunk roads.[1] It is a landscape which expresses what it was designed to facilitate, the replacement of communal farming practices – which had long been weakened in many open-field parishes by other means than enclosure by agreement, but which could not be much altered as long as the arable land remained largely in open-field; and these it replaced by a landscape expressive of an individualism in farming practice, whereby farms were consolidated into integrated holdings, no longer scattered among the various fields and furlongs. Large farmers no longer found it convenient to live in the village at the centre of the field-system, but in farmhouses built on their newly consolidated holdings. It is a landscape, too, which expresses the importance of a facility of movement from place to place, no longer largely within the parish but from the parish outwards, and thus it replaced a landscape which, as an image and expression of a self-centred sense of place, was probably most representative of the consciousness of the smallholder and the labourer, by a landscape more expressive of the interests of the great landowner, the substantial farmer, and the wholesale trader in agricultural produce.

To those members of open-field village society who had least reason to travel regularly, and to whom all other landscapes but their own were more or less unfamiliar, an enclosure of their parish may have been a disorienting experience. Many of the landmarks by which places in the parish were known and identified would have ceased to exist. Old roads disappeared, to be replaced by others running to places which, to them, may hardly have been 'places' at all, but abstract notions of the unknown; fields over which they had been formerly free to walk at will were now closed to them, or open only by permission of their owners. If an area of waste land had been included in the enclosure, then that area too suddenly became private property – and this in the part of the parish where even some of those who owned no land may formerly have enjoyed the right to graze a cow, keep geese or gather fuel. The sense of locality, of belonging to this parish and not another, which may formerly have been reinforced mainly by an involvement in communal agricultural practices, was now reinforced largely, in the minds of the local poor, by their entitlement to be maintained out of the poor-rates levied by the parish.

John Clare (1793–1864) was the son of an agricultural labourer of Helpston, a parish situated about half-way between Peterborough and Stamford. In 1809 an act was passed for the enclosure of Helpston and of several neighbouring parishes, and four or five years later the new landscape had probably been laid out. At about the same time as the act was being passed, Clare began writing the poems which were collected in his first publication, *Poems Descriptive of Rural Life and Scenery*, which appeared in 1820; the following year he produced *The Village Minstrel*, a long poem in the stanza of Spenser. These two books of poems are remarkable in various ways: they contain moving elegies to the old landscape of Helpston; they communicate with great immediacy Clare's sense of the oppression of the rural poor; and they include passages of descriptive verse equal to the best writing of the poets who were, at this time, Clare's principal models, in particular Thomson, Goldsmith and James Beattie. But after the publication of *The Village Minstrel*, it was the sense that his poems were challenging comparison with models inappropriate to him that seems to have persuaded Clare to seek a different mode of expression. He wrote to John Taylor, his publisher, of *The Village Minstrel* that 'the reason why I dislike it is that it does not describe the feelings of a rhyming peasant strongly or *locally* enough' (my italics). Clare's subsequent attempt to write more 'locally' found expression in his two remaining published collections, *The Shepherd's Calendar* (1827) and *The Rural Muse* (1835), and in *The Midsummer Cushion*, a manuscript collection made by Clare of his poems from the mid-1820s to the early 1830s, which was not published in full until 1979.

The decision to write more locally seems to have involved Clare in an attempt to recognize what it was – what sort of knowledge, of place, and of nature – that he did not share with the poets who had influenced him: what they knew and he did not, by virtue of the greater freedom they had enjoyed to move, in space across a range of landscapes in Britain and abroad, in time through a tradition of past literature that he had access to only in a more piecemeal, less coherent way; and what, also, *he* could know and *they* could not, by virtue of the fact that, except for a few journeys into Lincolnshire, to London, and so on, he had never had much reason or opportunity to travel outside a radius of some ten miles from Helpston. Such journeys as he did make, he regarded as being excursions 'out of his knowledge' – whatever he knew, he knew as it were only in Helpston; and it seems that this recognition led him increasingly to resist generalizing his experience into statements which would ask to be recognized as true everywhere, in the manner of the eighteenth-century poets he had sought to emulate; and in his more mature work, his poems much less often conclude with general statement, or with a movement outward from description or narrative to reflective moralizing. Such notions as 'Nature' or 'landscape' he seems to have come to see as foreign to him, deriving as they do from that ability to generalize from a range of diverse experiences; so that, for example, he came to make less and less use of the methods by which eighteenth-century poets represented landscape as 'composed' in a manner analogous to the way in which it was composed in contemporary landscape-painting; for principles of pictorial composition became established by being applied to a range of different landscapes, and Clare had experience of no such range.

What, on the other hand, Clare enjoyed which his models had not, was a vastly more intimate knowledge of one place than they could ever have arrived at: an extraordinarily full knowledge, for example, of the habits and habitats of the flora and fauna of Helpston, though not of elsewhere; of the processes of seasonal change there; and of what changes occurred, almost from day to day, in the aspect of Helpston, and in the occupations of villagers through the year. This knowledge did not come to him piecemeal – it was not easily analysable, in the sense of being broken up, categorized, and ascribed to one body of knowledge or another – but it existed for him as a complex manifold, in which every fact or experience suggested another, and was understood in connection with the whole body of knowledge which was Helpston. The preservation and ex-

pression of this knowledge, and of this mode of knowing, he seems
to have undertaken because his sense of locality was threatened not
only by an alien poetic tradition but also by the enclosure of Helpston and the attempt to attach the place, by the formulaic layout
of the new landscape and its new straight roads, to a wider region,
and to impose upon its inhabitants a sense of being a part of some
wider whole, so that they would come to understand their knowledge, also, as an instance only of general knowledge, or as true
by reference only to some more abstract general truth. The undertaking involved, as we shall see, the construction by Clare of a
language of poetry quite different from what he had found in
Goldsmith or Thomson, one which corresponded, perhaps, more
nearly with the conversational language of the villagers of Helpston,
and whose function was entirely misunderstood by his London
publisher and by his admirers (Charles Lamb, for example) in
London.

    We may take as an example of Clare's mature style the opening
of *The Pewit's Nest* from *The Midsummer Cushion*:

> Accross the fallow clods at early morn
> I took a random track where scant & spare
> The grass & nibbled leaves all closely shorn
> Leaves a burnt flat all bleaching brown & bare
> Where hungry sheep in freedom range forlorn
> & neath the leaning willow & odd thorn
> & molehill large that vagrant shade supplies
> They batter round to shun the teazing flies
> Trampling smooth places hard as cottage floors
> Where the time-killing lonly shepherd boys
> Whose summer homes are ever out of doors
> Their chockholes form & chalk their marble ring
> & make their clay taws at the bubbling spring
> & in their rangling sport & gambling joys
> They straine* their clocklike shadows – when it cloys
> To guess the hour that slowly runs away
> & shorten sultry turmoil with their play[2]

The tense of the first main verb of this sentence, 'I took', seems to
refer to a past before the enclosure; for to be able to take a
'random track' across the 'fallow clods' suggests that the site of this

---

* Robinson and Summerfield (*Selected Poems and Prose of John Clare*, London, 1967)
read 'strime' = stride, or measure the length of by the length of one's stride.

poem is an extended tract of land larger than that of a single enclosure; and that the sheep are in the care of a number of shepherd boys seems to suggest a period of communal farming practice abolished by the enclosure. A large number of Clare's poems about Helpston written ten and more years after the new enclosed land-scape had been laid out seem to represent the landscape as still un-enclosed, as though a part of Clare's attempt to write more 'locally' involved disregarding what it was that had particularly threatened his 'local' consciousness. That disregard is reinforced by the movement, in the following clauses, into a present tense, one which suggests habitual action – 'this is how it always is', 'this is what always happens' – which in this poem and numerous others represents Helpston as a place where nothing has changed and nothing changes. I do not intend by that observation to suggest that Clare habitually chose to ignore the enclosure: his work is full of denunciations of it, many of them at once movingly elegiac and politically acute; but in other parts of his work he is more concerned to criticize the enclosure and its effects by an evocation of the parish when it still lay in open field.

The present tense in these lines, however, also performs another function: in referring to a generalized, unchanging, habitual present instead of one particular moment of present time, Clare indicates that the objects and actions represented do not find their way into the poem because, on the occasion when he took this walk, he observed them, and is now describing what he observed, but because they are part of a complex manifold of *knowledge*, elements of which are engaged and released into utterance when he turns his attention to the topic 'fallows in summer' – this is what the sheep and the boys do, at that place and time, whether Clare happens to be observing them or not. This present tense thus tells us a great deal about the nature of Clare's poetry, which is often not descriptive at all in the sense in which we use that term of much eighteenth-century landscape-poetry. It does not suggest that the truth of his descriptions is dependent on his having been at a particular place at a particular time when he saw such-and-such to be the case; but, on the contrary, that his knowledge of what goes on in his parish is so full and so intimate as itself to guarantee the truth of what he represents, independently of whether he represents himself as observing it. For that reason, his descriptions of objects and actions are rarely detailed, though they have often been praised for being so; instead of a minuteness which guarantees that he has the object under his eye, we find a habit of qualifying things often by single adjectives or participles, or by a single active verb – 'nibbled leaves', 'bubbling spring', 'they batter round' – which indicate instead that he knows what these things are and do and are like, without having to look at them again.

Nor is there *time* in Clare's writing for detailed, poly-adjectival description: objects are hardly named before they are replaced by others; and that hurry and plenitude are at once made possible, and enacted, by the characteristic structure of his sentences. These often begin with a simple main clause – in this poem taking up the first line-and-a-half of the poem – and then continue in a host of subordinate clauses qualifying the noun that immediately precedes them: 'a random track where ...', 'a burnt flat ... where ...', 'molehill large that ...', 'smooth places ... where ...', and so on. Such clauses, almost always adjectival, do not suggest a sequence of separate observations through time – they offer instead a sense of place as a manifold of knowledge, recalled at once, necessarily written down bit by bit, but all simultaneously present in Clare's mind, so that the function of the syntax is not to *make* relations between different events, but to represent a pre-existent inseparability of all the events attached to the notion 'fallows in summer'. It is in the expression, particularly by syntax, of this intimate and indivisible local knowledge, reinforced by a diction hospitable to dialect words and informal reference ('hard as cottage floors'), that Clare's attempt to write more 'locally' makes itself most apparent. And it is an important measure of Clare's achievement as a poet that this was not a 'natural' language for him; it was one that he had to discover, or recover, by the deliberate attempt to question, as Wordsworth did, what it was in the language of eighteenth-century verse that was falsifying his own experience and knowledge.

It may be that the particularly indivisible nature of what Clare knew about Helpston can be related to the mode of knowing available in an open-field landscape, where, as we have seen, a great deal more was visible at once, at a glance, than in the more occluded landscape of enclosure. This certainly is suggested by such a sentence as this, from 'June', in *The Shepherd's Calendar*:

> The wheat swells into ear and leaves below
> The may month wild flowers and their gaudy show
> Bright carlock bluecap and corn poppy red
> Which in such clouds of colors widly spread
> That at the sun rise might to fancys eye
> Seem to reflect the many colord sky
> And leverets seat and lark and partridge nest
> It leaves a schoolboys height in snugger rest
> And oer the weeders labour overgrows
> Who now in merry groups each morning goes
> To willow skirted meads wi fork and rake
> The scented hay cocks in long rows to make
> Where their old visitors in russet brown
> The haytime butterflies dance up and down
> And gads that teaze like whasps the timid maid
> And drive the herdboys cows to pond and shade
> Who when his dogs assistance fails to stop
> Is forced his half made oaten pipes to drop
> And start and halloo thro the dancing heat
> To keep their gadding tumult from the wheat
> Who in their rage will dangers overlook
> And leap like hunters oer the pasture brook
> Brushing thro blossomed beans in maddening haste
> And 'stroying corn they scarce can stop to taste[3]

There is no space in this chapter for the extended analysis this astonishing sentence deserves – in particular of what it owes to the conventions and methods of eighteenth-century poetry, as well as of where it departs from them. I am thinking, for example, of the conventionally pastoral image of the herdboy making 'oaten pipes' which is recalled from being 'merely' conventional by the fact that his work requires him to 'drop' them 'half made'; or of the use of a line-structure from Pope to close the sentence – compare the last line above with Pope's 'Affrights the beggar whom he longs to eat', or 'Now sweep those allies they were born to shade', in the same position of emphatic closure.[4] This sentence has a structure similar to the first sentence of *The Pewit's Nest*: after the repetition of the verb 'leaves', the sentence is continued by a series of adjectival clauses, which here, however, have the function not only of revealing the events they represent as indissolubly bound together within the same manifold of knowledge, but as comprising together an account of what is happening, or rather of what happens, over something like the whole area of the parish in June. The mention of the 'weeders', whose labour is overgrown by the growing wheat, allows the reflection that those who in spring were weeders, in early summer are haymakers, and so we move from the wheat-field to the meadows. The 'gads' we find there are to be found also in the pasture, where the cows, enraged by them, will unless restrained leap over the brook and into the bean-field, and thence into the wheat-field to which, therefore, our attention is returned at the end of the sentence. Wheat-field, meadow, pasture, bean-field and wheat-field again are thus linked not only as inseparable parts of a unitary knowledge, but in a circular structure which may be related to what I argued was the circular sense of space encouraged by the landscape of open field; and, as I have argued elsewhere, this circular structure is a common feature of Clare's mature work.

What we may discover about Clare's sense of place, and about the language by which he learned to represent it, has become clear only recently, when Clare's poems have begun to be republished from his original manuscripts. It was obviously a condition of their being published at all in Clare's lifetime that they be punctuated by his publisher and made to look as if written in something like standard English; but the poems as edited by Taylor look and read entirely differently from what Clare wrote. Here, for example, are the opening lines of a sonnet by Clare, *Beans in Blossom*, from *The Midsummer Cushion*:

> The southwest wind how pleasant in the face
> It breaths while sauntering in a musing pace
> I roam these new ploughed fields & by the side
> Of this old wood where happy birds abide
> & the rich blackbird through his golden bill
> Utters* wild music when the rest are still
> Now luscious comes the scent of blossomed beans
> That oer the path in rich disorder leans
> Mid which the bees in busy songs & toils
> Load home luxuriantly their yellow spoils

(p. 401)

And here is the poem as it appeared in *The Rural Muse*:

* Robinson and Summerfield read 'litters'.

> The south-west wind! how pleasant in the face
> It breathes! while, sauntering in a musing pace,
> I roam these new-ploughed fields; or by the side
> Of this old wood, where happy birds abide,
> And the rich blackbird, through his golden bill,
> Utters wild music when the rest are still.
> Luscious the scent comes of the blossomed bean,
> As o'er the path in rich disorder lean
> Its stalks; whence bees, in busy rows and toils,
> Load home luxuriantly their yellow spoils.

It is evident from this comparison not only that the punctuation conceals the indivisibility of the events described by Clare, but that Taylor has, in other ways, imposed upon the poem a sense of place alien to Clare's own. The punctuation divides as it regulates – by the attempt to determine who or what is doing the 'sauntering' in line 2, and by the separation into phrases of lines 4 and 5, whereby the fact that 'happy birds abide' in the 'old wood' becomes a matter of additional information about the identity of the wood, no longer something constitutive of that identity. But more happens than this: the change from '&' to 'or' in line 3 divides, into alternative locations for the experience, what Clare represents as one; the removal of ambiguities from Clare's grammar – he often uses, and it is a normal eastern-counties dialect use, the form of the third person singular for the third person plural – so as to determine what it is that leans 'o'er the path', the beans or their scent, cramps Taylor's style in line 9, so that instead of the bees appearing 'mid' the 'rich disorder' of the beans, we now read 'whence', and are required to imagine the bees not as inextricably a part of the bean-field, but as separating themselves from it. Clare's space has no internal divisions, there are no separate parts in its whole; for Taylor, space is divided into, and consists of, separate spaces.

In 1832, Clare was offered a cottage in Northborough, a village some three miles to the north-east of Helpston, but in a landscape more entirely fenny than Helpston's, and without the area of lime-stone heath that lay to the south of Helpston, which was common land before the enclosure and of which Clare wrote that it 'made up my being'. Disoriented again in this new landscape, he wrote some moving accounts of his deracination, but the bulk of his poetry changed utterly: his sonnets became discontinuous collections of discrete couplets, which often seem able to be arranged in any order, and which announce the loss of that intimate and indivisible knowledge of place. From the late 1830s until his death in 1864 he spent all but a few months in asylums at Epping and Northampton. He seems to have recognized his illness as a loss of 'self-identity'; and it seems reasonable to believe that the successive disorientations brought about by the enclosure, by the move to Northborough, and by being incarcerated miles from either, contributed to and exacerbated his condition. For Clare, the open fields and commons of Helpston were his knowledge and his identity: he describes in his *Autobiography* an occasion when, as a child, he wandered beyond the parish boundary, until he got, as he says, 'out of my knowledge': the sun seemed to shine in 'a different quarter of the sky', and 'the very wild flowers seemed to forget me'.[5] That notion, not only that he could not know what lay 'out of his knowledge', but that what was there did not recognize him, suggests more clearly than anything else the effect that the enclosure and the move to a different landscape were likely to have on one who regarded as inseparable the place he lived in, his knowledge, and his identity as a person.

On 2 September 1826, the year before the publication of *The Shepherd's Calendar*, William Cobbett (1762–1835) arrived in Devizes on one of his 'rural rides'. 'When I got to Devizes,' he recorded, two days later,

and came to look out of the inn-window into the street, I perceived that I had seen that place before, and always having thought that I should like to *see* Devizes, of which I had heard so much talk as a famous corn-market, I was very much surprised to find that it was not new to me. Presently a stage-coach came up to the door with 'Bath and London' upon its panels; and then I recollected that I had been at this place on my way to Bristol last year. (*4 September 1826*)[6]

The experience was strange enough to Cobbett for him to think it worth recounting, but still nothing could indicate more clearly than this passage the vast difference between his own experience of places and of travelling and Clare's. It is impossible to imagine Clare forgetting any of the handful of towns he had visited: to see a new one was for him an epoch in his life. Cobbett's experience at Devizes, on the other hand, is that of an habitually *itinerant* man: it is only when he sees the street through an inn-window that he recognizes the town; it is only when he sees a stage-coach that he can recall the occasion of his previous visit. For Cobbett had been a traveller almost all his life: first as a soldier, and then as a journalist, he had lived (or been obliged to live to escape prosecution) in Canada, in Philadelphia, in France, on Long Island and in London, as well as on the farm he had bought himself at Botley in Hampshire.

The difference between the sense of space he had developed as an itinerant journalist, and the sense he found among many of the people he met on his rural rides, was perfectly evident to Cobbett. It is a waste of time, he remarks, to ask for directions in remote parts of the country, 'unless you meet some one at every half mile; for the answer is, *keep right on*; aye, but in ten minutes, perhaps, you come to a Y, or to a T, or to a +'. Near Winchester he asked the way to Stoke Charity, and was told that to get there he must go '*right over the down*'. ' "Aye," said I, "but what do you mean by *right over the down?*" "Why," said he, "*right* on to Stoke, to be sure, Zur." '[7] Those with a complete and intimate knowledge of the one place they do know cannot grasp the implications of the fact that what they know is not common knowledge, is not knowledge elsewhere.

Like Clare's father, Cobbett's grandfather had been a journeyman-labourer, but his father had risen to be a small farmer in the prosperous area around Farnham in Surrey. He was modestly well-educated, and was a competent land surveyor; and Cobbett himself, throughout his life, retained the attitudes to land and landscape characteristic of the farming interest, and of the new rural professional class. In many ways, the journeys he made through England in the 1820s and wrote up as his *Rural Rides* show him as sharing the interests of such men as the professional surveyors and land-agents and farmers, interests expressed in the landscapes they created and in the articles, reports and books they contributed to the growing literature concerned with agricultural improvement. He is interested in seeing Devizes particularly because it was 'a famous corn-market'; he was a passionate spokesman for new strains of corn and of root-crops, for drilling seed instead of sowing it broadcast, for anything indeed that would increase the productivity of the land. He was a firm advocate of the enclosure of 'those very ugly things, common-fields'; he describes wastelands, so barren and yet often so important to the standard of living of the rural poor, as 'rascally commons', 'villainous heaths', 'ugly tracts'. For the most part his enjoyment of land as landscape is inseparable from his delight in its productivity: when he writes of a landscaped park that 'everywhere utility and convenience is combined with beauty' it is hard to imagine what sort of beauty, for him, might not be combined with convenience and utility.

Thus, of the landscape around Hurstbourn Tarrant in Hampshire he writes:

> This, to my fancy, is a very nice country. It is continual hill and dell. Now and then a *chain* of hills higher than the rest, and these are downs or woods ... The undulations are endless, and the great variety in the height, breadth, length, and form of the little hills, has a very delightful effect. – The soil, which, to look *on* it, appears to be more than half flint stones, is very good in quality, and, in general, better on the tops of the lesser hills than in the valleys. (*4 November 1821*)

And he says, of a landscape in Surrey,

> Lea is situated on the edge of that immense heath which sweeps down from the summit of Hind-Head, across to the north over innumerable hills of minor altitude, and of an infinite variety of shapes towards Farnham, to the north-east, towards the Hog's Back ... and to the east, or nearly so, towards Godalming. Nevertheless, the inclosed lands at Lea are very good and singularly beautiful. The timber of all sorts grows well; the land is light, and being free from stones, very pleasant to work. (*26 September 1822*)

One might imagine, on reading the first passage, that Cobbett is simply endorsing a notion of beauty common in contemporary writings on aesthetics, that it arises from the experience of a smooth and easy transition among elements of variety – an experience, like that described in Burke's famous remark, of 'being swiftly drawn in an easy coach, on the smooth turf, with gradual ascents and declivities'. Yet, as we compare the two passages, it seems that this notion of beauty has to be combined with the evidence of productivity for the landscape to be truly delightful. Thus, as the dash in the first passage indicates, the smoothness of the downs is in contrast with, is scuffed up a little by the flint stones on their surface, which do not however affect adversely the properties of their soil, or apparently, therefore, the beauty of the view; and though the landscape around Hind-Head and the Hog's Back is described as no less undulating, no less various than the other, it is only when Cobbett turns his attention to the enclosures that he can discover anything of beauty there, a beauty which is not itself *described*, however, unless it is to be found in the profitable growth of the timber, and the ease with which the soil may be worked.

But whereas many other writers of agriculture were happy to assume that a delightful tract of productive agricultural land was of itself a guarantee of the prosperity of a district, and of a prosperity enjoyed by landowner, farmer and labourer alike, Cobbett is continually struck by the contrast between the smiling landscapes that greet him, and the depressed condition of those who worked to make the landscape smile. The reasons for that contrast, as Cobbett understood them, have been usefully summarized by James Sambrook:

Farmers could not afford to pay a living wage to their labourers, because they were so heavily taxed to support the 'dead-weight' of pensioners, sinecurists, fundholders and a thundering standing army in time of peace. Loanmongers and stock-jobbers became rich and with their financial power propped up a corrupt government which ruled in their interest and retained perpetual power by its control of rotten boroughs. The once independent landed gentry had enough political power to check all this, but, in order to share the places and pensions, they had cravenly thrown in their lot with the moneyed men. However, they would soon find that the moneyed men had eaten them all up; the gentry would follow the farmers and the labourers in a total ruin of what had once been 'the landed interest'.[8]

It is for evidence of the truth of this analysis that Cobbett looks in the landscapes he rides over, and it is this analysis he finds always confirmed, even when, for example, in Suffolk, he finds landscape and labourers in an equally healthy condition; for Suffolk and Essex have had 'millions upon millions of money' poured into them 'from Wiltshire and other inland counties', to support the standing army of 'not less than sixty thousand men' until recently quartered there; and 'the increase of London', 'the swelling of the immortal Wen', where the system he attacks, the 'THING' as he calls it, has concentrated the money of England and its moneyed men, has assisted also 'to heap wealth upon these counties'.[9]

Thus Cobbett is never content simply to record and to exult in the sight of 'views that a painter might crave': the abundance of the crops, the fine condition of the livestock, the neatness of habitations. He is always *reading* the landscape and discovering that good and bad husbandry, that evidence of an increasing population here, a declining one there, disclose much the same thing in the condition of England as a whole. He continually remarks on the size of the medieval churches, for example, in agricultural parishes where now the entire population could be accommodated within the church-porch: evidence, he insists, that several hundred years ago England had once been far more populous than now. What has happened to the millions of missing people, who could still now be supported by the agricultural wealth of the country? They have emigrated, been killed in imperial wars, or they have, most of them, simply been starved. The complete inadequacy of wages and of poor relief, and the consequent temptation to poach and steal, reduce the 'liberty' of the English poor to a ' "liberty" to choose between death by starvation (quick or slow) and death by the halter'.[10]

This concern for the condition of the labouring poor, and for what it confirmed about the economic and political organization of Britain, works continually to qualify the pleasure that earlier writers on agriculture had taken in 'improvements' in the countryside that did not tend directly to increase the productivity of the soil. Cobbett is alarmed, for example, at the engrossing of small farms into large estates, and therefore at the eviction of small tenant-farmers and of the labourers who are no longer employed where economies of scale are possible: a farmer in the 'North of Hampshire', he discovers, 'has nearly eight thousand acres of land in his hands' and 'occupies what was formerly 40 farms! Is it any wonder that *paupers increase?*' He is not impressed by the new turnpike roads paid for out of taxes levied directly or indirectly on the poor; as far as possible he avoids them, travelling along by-roads where 'we see the people without any disguise or affectation'; and he regards the '*facilities* which now exist of *moving human bodies from place to place*' as 'amongst the *curses* of the country, the destroyers of industry, of morals, and, of course, of happiness'. Among such facilities he includes the canals that, in the course of the previous century, had been constructed 'to convey away the wheat and all the good food to the tax-eaters and their attendants in the Wen!'[11]

The growth of watering-places, and of the suburbs of the 'Wen', the erection of new barracks and gaols, and other, such 'vast improvements' in the aspect of the country, Cobbett reads only as evidence of the increasing gap between the rich and poor, between London and the countryside, and of the increasing need to defend privilege by force and violence. Though nothing delights his eye more than the sight of an extended tract of rich, enclosed corn-fields, he deplores the futility of the attempts to raise corn, in the period of high agricultural prices during the Napoleonic Wars, on tracts of barren soil which were formerly wasteland and common and which, however 'rascally' and 'villainous', had once enabled the poor to keep geese or to collect firing upon them. On more than one occasion he notes of woodlands that the labourers there are in-variably better off than in arable districts, for it is 'absolutely im-possible' to reduce the poor in woodland areas 'to that state of starvation in which they are in the corn-growing part of the kingdom' because they have abundance of fuel at all times of the year, and, in corn-country, 'where the mighty grasper has *all under his eye*', they can get little of the necessaries of life, without attracting the attention of their employers to the possibility of lowering their wages still further.[12]

At the end of September 1826, Cobbett spent a night at Stanford Park in Worcestershire at the invitation of Sir Thomas Winnington. He was delighted by the estate – 'the park is everything that is beautiful'; but in this landscape, though far from a wilderness, Cobbett was tempted by 'the devil of laziness': 'could you not be contented to live here all the rest of your life; and never again pester yourself with the cursed politics?' Cobbett imagined himself replying:

'Why, I think I have laboured enough. Let others work now. And such a pretty place for coursing and for hare-hunting and woodcock shooting, I dare say: and then those pretty wild ducks in the water, and the flowers and the grass and the trees and all the birds in spring and the fresh air, and never, never again to be stifled with the smoke that from the infernal Wen ascendeth for ever more and that every easterly wind brings to choke me at Kensington!'

But 'the *last word* of this soliloquy carried me back, slap, to my own study', and made him think of the 'complete triumph' he was yet to enjoy over his enemies by the fulfilment of his prophecies of woe and by the consequent destruction of the 'THING'; and though, in due form, the devil tempted him twice more, he was easily and more easily resisted. 'Tell them to saddle the horses', ordered Cobbett – 'for it seemed to me I had been meditating some crime'.[13] That anecdote contains the key to Cobbett's attitudes to the changing landscapes of Britain; for, in looking forward so persistently to the destruction of the 'THING', the *Rural Rides* look forward also to a time when it might once again be possible to contemplate the view of an orderly and productive landscape with an unguilty pleasure.

NOTES

1. For a brief but informative account of the landscape of Parliamentary enclosure, see W. G. Hoskins, *The Making of the English Landscape* (London, 1955), ch. vi.

2. Anne Tibble (ed.) *The Midsummer Cushion* (Ashington, Northumberland, and Manchester, 1979), 211.

3. Eric Robinson and Geoffrey Summerfield (eds), *The Shepherd's Calendar* (London, 1964), 64.

4. 'Epistle to Bathurst', line 198; 'Epistle to Burlington', line 98.

5. J. W. and Anne Tibble (eds), *The Prose of John Clare* (London, 1951), 13, 28.

6. The *Rural Rides* were first collected in 1830; quotations in this chapter are from the enlarged edition, ed. James Paul Cobbett (London, 1853, repr. 1957).

7. *Rural Rides*, 2 October 1826.

8. J. Sambrook, *William Cobbett* (London, 1973), 144–5.

9. *Rural Rides*, 22 March 1830.

10. *Rural Rides*, 4 September 1826.

11. *Rural Rides*, 14 November 1821; 23 October 1825; 27 August 1826; 11 September 1826.

12. *Rural Rides*, 13 November 1825; 30 August 1823.

13. *Rural Rides*, 27 September 1826.

WORDSWORTH'S POETRY

R. O. C. WINKLER

It is not uncommon for readers of poetry to feel a special kind of difficulty when they approach Wordsworth (1770–1850). He is a 'great' poet – even, it is sometimes said, one of the greatest. Yet there are aspects of his verse which, in the light of this placing, are unexpected; and, even before the verse itself is attempted, there are features of the reputation which can cause uneasiness.

Everyone knows that Wordsworth was (to use his own phrase) a 'worshipper of nature', and the suspicion arises that a taste for his verse may have less to do with the appreciation of poetry as such than with a sentimental interest in his characteristic subject-matter and a fellow-feeling for his attitude towards it. There is, moreover, a general understanding that Wordsworth has, in some sense, a moral lesson to teach us; and most of us, like Keats, are uneasy about 'poetry that has a palpable design upon us'.

These misgivings are not automatically dispelled when we turn to the verse itself. We find not only that a self-conscious attitude towards nature is very much one of Wordsworth's preoccupations, but that there is a readiness to moralize about – to draw moral conclusions from – this attitude, and to press them upon the reader. Didacticism did not, of course, enter poetry with Wordsworth or leave it with him, but in his verse there seems sometimes to be a disturbing willingness to achieve the moral purpose at the expense of the poetry itself. Complaints can be made of strained simplicity, banality, or rhetoric; and even when these positive vices are absent, there is often felt to be a deficiency of concreteness conveyed by the play of imagery of the kind associated with, say, Shakespeare, Donne, or Keats.

The climate of opinion in which, during the last generation or so, renewed importance has been attached to the element of 'wit' in poetry has, perhaps, been especially unfavourable to the appreciation of Wordsworth. But misgivings about his verse are of much longer standing than that. Keats's remark, quoted above, was thrown out in reference to Wordsworth himself. Jeffrey's famous tirade ('This will never do! ...') and Shelley's satirical parody in *Peter Bell the Third* are only the most extreme expressions of an attitude that was common. Hazlitt, a sympathetic critic, summarized the general opinion of Wordsworth's poems in these terms in 1825: 'The vulgar do not read them; the learned ... do not understand them, the great despise, the fashionable ... ridicule them.'

Much of this criticism went beyond the bounds of what was valid or valuable; but it would be a disservice to the appreciation of Wordsworth to pretend that, widespread and persistent as it has been, it is entirely without foundation. Coleridge himself, the most perceptive of Wordsworth's contemporary admirers, thought it necessary to devote a chapter of *Biographia Literaria* to 'The characteristic defects of Wordsworth's poetry'. Some consideration of the basis for an unfavourable reaction to Wordsworth's verse does, in fact, throw light upon the nature of his achievement.

The themes he adopted in his poetry, and his manner of expressing them, were not, of course, fortuitous. The *Lyrical Ballads* which he and Coleridge published in 1798, and which embodied his first major achievements in poetry, were the product of a deliberate programme, set out in later editions in the famous *Preface*:

> The principal object ... proposed in these poems was to choose incidents and situations from common life, and to relate or describe them, throughout, as far as was possible in a selection of language really used by men ... and ... to make these incidents and situations interesting by tracing in them ... primary laws of our nature ... Humble and rustic life was generally chosen, because, in that condition, the essential passions of the heart find a better soil in which they can attain their maturity, are less under restraint, and speak a plainer and more emphatic language; because in that condition of life our elementary feelings co-exist in a state of greater simplicity ...; because the manners of rural life germinate from those elementary feelings, ... are more easily comprehended, and are more durable; and ... because in that condition the passions of men are incorporated with the beautiful and permanent forms of Nature.

To propose a thoroughgoing application of this point of view to the writing of poetry was a new and controversial thing. But, in the general outlook which it reflected, Wordsworth was a child of his time. The preference for humble and rustic life followed naturally from the conception, associated with Rousseau's name, of the 'noble savage', with its implication that men are better when closer to their 'natural' state, uncorrupted by the artificialities of civilization. The rustic idyll was an accepted theme for painting and architecture; and the taste for natural scenery advocated by writers like Uvedale Price and Gilpin had, by the time *Lyrical Ballads* was published, already established the vogue of the Lake District among English tourists. In the field of poetry itself, Akenside was (as Professor Nichol Smith has pointed out) writing of natural scenery in terms scarcely distinguishable from Wordsworth's before Wordsworth was born; and readers of Burns were familiar enough with the use in poetry of the language of 'humble and rustic' men.

Born and brought up in the Lake District, Wordsworth found in his childhood experiences a source of material very much in keeping with this tendency in the temper of the age, and his introduction of autobiography into poetry as a central theme was much more of a new departure than most of the points on which he laid stress in the *Preface*. *The Prelude*, written between 1799 and 1805, was explicitly and consistently autobiographical on a scale quite unfamiliar to readers of English poetry, and Wordsworth himself remarked that it was 'a thing unprecedented in literary history that a man should talk so much about himself'.

But the importance to Wordsworth of contemporary trends in taste was not that he was able, by securing their orientation to poetry, to serve them. It was rather that they provided a climate of ideas in which experiences which were of a particular significance and value to him could form material for poetry. For every poet his own experience is, of course, the raw material of the creative process. But in Wordsworth's case it was something more than this: it was his characteristic subject-matter, so that much of his best verse, even outside *The Prelude*, constitutes a kind of diary; and when his verse is least effective, it will often be found that he has, in some way, withdrawn to a distance from his experience, that the immediacy of the personal record is absent.

One way in which this withdrawal commonly occurs stems from his desire to generalize his experience, to draw the moral from it, to ensure that the reader has not missed the point. Wordsworth made no secret of his desire to instruct. 'Every great poet is a teacher: I wish either to be considered as a teacher, or as nothing', he wrote to Sir George Beaumont; and to Lady Beaumont: 'There is scarcely one of my poems which does not aim to direct the attention to some moral sentiment, or to some general principle, or law of thought, or of our intellectual constitution.' 'Each of them,' he wrote of his poems in *Lyrical Ballads*, 'has a purpose.'

The words that follow this assertion, though, indicate that he has his own conception of how the purpose should be communicated:

> Not that I always begin to write with a distinct purpose formally conceived: but habits of meditation have, I trust, so prompted and regulated my feelings, that my descriptions of such objects as strongly excite those feelings will be found to carry along with them a purpose.

The purpose is not, it appears, something to be stated, in general terms: it is to be 'carried along' by descriptions of objects which strongly excite the poet's feelings. Now, although Wordsworth is here giving a fair account of his own best practice, it often turns out, on examination of particular poems, to be less than the whole story. The poem *Influence of Natural Objects* may serve as an illustration. Written in 1799, this was eventually printed as part of *The Prelude*, but first appeared separately in Coleridge's periodical *The Friend*.

The full title of the poem is *Influence of Natural Objects in Calling Forth and Strengthening the Imagination in Boyhood and Early Youth*, and the initial apostrophe, down to 'A grandeur in the beatings of the heart', is a rhetorical elaboration of this title.* It is a statement, an assertion, that the spirit of the universe achieves certain things (purification of thought and feeling, etc.) through certain agencies ('with enduring things, with life and nature'). Some of it we are likely to find obscure: what is 'the Eternity of thought' and what is the 'discipline' referred to, for example? We may guess or be told, but we ought not to have to ask. We are prompted to ask by the controversial presentation ('the mean and vulgar works of Man'), and by the provocative pulpit tone ('soul', 'everlasting', 'purifying', 'sanctifying', etc.), but there is no argument or demonstration here that

---

* It is impossible to do justice to Wordsworth in brief quotations, and to print in full all the passages referred to in this essay would more than double its length. It has therefore been assumed throughout that the reader will find it convenient to refer to a copy of Wordsworth's poems.

will convince us if we are not already convinced. We are still waiting for the evidence to be produced.

With the words 'In November days', however, the autobiographical account begins, the oratorical tone is abandoned, and the movement of the verse immediately becomes more subtle and flexible. The effect of the words from this point onwards is at one and the same time to describe the scene as it appeared to Wordsworth as a boy, and to create, in the reader's mind, the effect that it had on the boy's mind; not, that is, the effect as it then appeared to the boy himself, but rather the effect which it was having on him without his being aware of it. This overall result is achieved by recreating for the reader, step by step, the boy's experiences, and hence enabling him to share them; so that it is not simply the boy, but the reader, who feels the 'influence of natural objects'.

The opening lines of the section build up the atmospheric setting. The adjectives used to describe the scene – 'lonely', 'lonesome', 'calm', 'trembling', 'gloomy' – could be used equally well to describe a state of mind as to describe a scene; so that they serve to establish the intimacy of the boy's relationship with his surroundings without describing anything but those surroundings. Hence, by the time Wordsworth says 'such intercourse was mine', the intercourse has already been established for the reader.

Then with a rising note of excitement in

It was a time of rapture!

the strokes of the village clock break in –

Clear and loud
The village clock tolled six.

After the meditative tone of the earlier lines, the verse itself is suddenly 'clear and loud'. From the earlier atmospheric intimacy there is a swift transition to ebullient animal spirits –

I wheeled about,
Proud and exulting like an untired horse

– and the verse itself bounds forward. The boy is immersed in the pleasure of physical sensation, and we with him, sharing the speed and smoothness of skates –

> All shod with steel
> We hissed along the polished ice

– the sense of movement through the sharp air –

> So through the darkness and the cold we flew,

and the echoes ringing from the cliff –

> ... with the din
> Smitten, the precipices rang aloud;
> The leafless trees and every icy crag
> Tinkled like iron.

The brittle and abrupt consonantal movement of the verse, with two heavy stresses on 'smitten' and 'tinkled', when linked with 'iron', suggest the clamour of the blacksmith's forge without its heat.

Then the more distant hills intrude themselves again by sending back a different kind of echo, and the mood of the poem changes once more. The sense of solitude of the earlier lines is recovered, but the sense of movement of the later ones is retained. The boy retired

> Into a silent bay, or sportively
> Glanced sideway

on a pursuit of his own:

> To cut across the reflex of a star;
> Image that, flying before me, gleamed
> Upon the glassy plain.

The verse repeats the earlier swift skimming movement, but this time the experience is more complex than that of mere physical sensation. The boy is following the image of a star reflected in the ice. He tries to cut across it, because a star should be stationary, but the star in the ice moves with him, so that the boy, the ice, the star, and its reflection are all bound up together in a single experience, which the verse re-enacts for us. The 'intercourse' with nature has been established in another way.

The experience of the star reflected in the ice is followed in *Influence of Natural Objects* by an account of another experience which explores the same point again, but in a different way still. The verse, with a swinging, accelerating movement, builds up a sense of speed –

> ... and oftentimes,
> When we had given our bodies to the wind,
> And all the shadowy banks on either side
> Came sweeping through the darkness, spinning still
> The rapid line of motion

– then pulls up suddenly:

> ... then at once
> Have I, reclining back upon my heels,
> Stopped short.

The two sharp monosyllables at the beginning of the line stop the verse momentarily dead at this point. But it continues to unwind itself as it describes the illusion created by giddiness:

> ... yet still the solitary cliffs
> Wheeled by me – even as if the earth had rolled
> With visible motion her diurnal round!

The slow turning movement of 'diurnal' is only a local instance of the effect of the movement as a whole. Gradually the dizziness wears off, and the effect fades away to the complete calm of the last line:

> Behind me did they stretch in solemn train,
> Feebler and feebler, and I stood and watched
> Till all was tranquill as a summer sea.

Thus, once more, natural objects – this time the cliffs – are made part of the boy's consciousness in a peculiarly intimate way: by having to his senses a movement which is not their own, but is imparted to them by his own movement. First they move past him as he moves, then still more startlingly they move past him as he stands still. But here again the experience is not one of which we are simply told; it is one which we are enabled to share. By rehearsing with the reader these varieties of direct experience of natural objects, Wordsworth contrives to induce something of the almost traumatic awareness of their intimate presence and its coherence with other modes of awareness which is the fruit of the boy's experience.

Another famous passage from the *Preface* to *Lyrical Ballads* can be used to throw some light on the process of communication as we have followed it in this poem:

I have said that poetry is the spontaneous overflow of powerful feelings: it takes its origin from emotion recollected in tranquillity: the emotion is contemplated till, by a species of re-action, the tranquillity gradually disappears, and an emotion, kindred to that which was before the subject of contemplation, is gradually produced, and does itself actually exist in the mind.

Wordsworth – it is plain from the context – is describing part of the process of poetic creation as it appears to the poet. But the creation, to be effective, must involve communication: communication is essentially creation for the reader. It is not surprising, therefore, that Wordsworth's account tallies closely with the process we have been tracing. Wordsworth so describes the boy's experiences as to recreate in the reader sensations and feelings, the 'emotion', experienced by the boy. But the action on the reader of this sequence of feelings is to generate a new emotion, akin to but different from that consciously felt by the boy. It is this complex emotion which, experienced by the reader, constitutes the poet's communication of the 'influence of natural objects'. It does indeed 'itself actually exist in the mind' – in, in this context, the reader's mind.

The difference, in terms of effectiveness of communication and richness of experience, between this part of the poem and that of the rhetorical prolegomena need hardly be emphasized. It achieves by *creation* something of what the prolegomena merely assert. In itself, however, it hardly goes all the way to validating the large cheque drawn by the prolegomena. It is not easy to see, for example, how 'pain' and 'fear' are 'sanctified' as a consequence of experiences such as these. In this respect the poem falls short of the level achieved in some other poems we shall be considering. But we should bear in mind that, although Wordsworth chose to publish the poem separately, he regarded *The Prelude* as its proper context: and in that context it may be regarded as making its own small contribution to a total effect which is a much more complex matter.

Read, indeed, in its proper place in *The Prelude*, the reference to fear has an obvious relevance, as this has been the theme of the section of the poem that immediately precedes this one (lines 357–400). There Wordsworth describes how one summer evening he took a boat out without permission. He set a course by the 'summit of a craggy ridge', and rowed towards it.

>   ... lustily
> I dipped my oars into the silent lake,

> And, as I rose upon the stroke, my boat
> Went heaving through the water like a swan.

Once more the reader shares with the boy Wordsworth immediate sensations – this time the sensation of rowing. The movement of the verse enacts the sense of physical effort, and preoccupied as we are with this, what follows is as unexpected to us as it was to the boy:

> When from behind that craggy steep till then
> The horizon's bound, a huge peak, black and huge,
> As if with voluntary power instinct
> Upreared its head.

Unlike the 'craggy ridge', the peak has no definite contour: its vague but profound menace is established in the boyish adjectives 'black' and 'huge', the menace and the vagueness both insisted on by the repetition of 'huge'. The next line, with its tortuous syllables, coils itself up like a snake – to be released in 'Upreared' at the beginning of the next line, so that the word towers, as it were, above us. The boy's panic is reflected in the changed movement –

> I struck and struck again

– but the inexorable beat of the next lines carries the peak steadily and relentlessly upward to the final awful climax of the last three words:

> And growing still in stature the grim shape
> Towered up between me and the stars, and still,
> For so it seemed, with purpose of its own
> And measured motion like a living thing,
> Strode after me.

The boy is chastened by his experience and, to the extent that we have shared it, so are we. But this is not simply a moral tale of a naughty boy being frightened by a mountain. It demonstrates also, by its careful account of a single fragment of experience, something of the way in which natural objects came to play a significant part in Wordsworth's emotional life – the same sort of part that men and women might play in another man's life. Just because natural objects could be a source of terror, they could also be a source – it elsewhere becomes apparent – of strength, delight, or comfort. Fear itself was the less terrible because related to what in other contexts were objects of familiar pleasure, though at the same time awesome enough to give a dignity even to terror.

This sort of gloss, however, outruns what the verse itself has to tell us here, and is something to be derived from *The Prelude* as a whole, rather than from any particular part of it. Just as, in the passages we have considered, there is an overall effect which is built up from a series of local effects but is more than just the sum of them, so these various sections in turn make their contribution to the total effect of the poem, which is our experience of the 'Growth of the Poet's Mind'. The central theme is the development of Wordsworth's sense of the intimacy of natural objects, an intimacy that was – as in the passage last considered – more than just physical: so that they were able to provide a stable background to his emotional life, a necessary source of strength. By sharing his particular experiences at first hand, we share also, as they accumulate, the sense of growth which is the poet's theme. In the resultant complex emotional pattern which is created, seen as relating Wordsworth to natural objects, fear is only a single strand, qualified, as it were, by the many other strands.[1]

The success of *The Prelude* depends upon genuine personal experience being available to validate, by its work upon the reader, what otherwise would be a series of empty assertions. Where such experience is not available, assertion is apt to become the staple of the verse; and it then sometimes declines into the declamatory or even strident, as though to make up by emphasis what is lacking in evidence. A particularly painful case of the kind is the Ode, *Intimations of Immortality from Recollections of Early Childhood* (1807), where the actual theme of the poem is the failure of his experience of natural objects to renew itself on its old terms, his explanation of this, and the counting of his compensations for the loss. In the first two stanzas he achieves a wistfulness that is poignant. For all the clarity with which Wordsworth evokes them, the experiences of natural objects appealed to here are all generalized; the subtle and sensitive detail of the intimate personal encounter we have earlier considered is absent. The main force lies in the twelve evenly-stressed monosyllables of the last line of the first stanza. Their knell-like flatness of tone, after the two short, feverish lines which precede, achieves a sense of desolation too empty even to imply resignation:

> Turn wheresoe'er I may,
>   By night or day,
> The things which I have seen I now can see no more.

The rest of the poem, in which Wordsworth attempts to discount his loss, never again achieves this kind of force. He develops his thesis – that a small child, being nearer to its divine origins, enjoys an insight into the nature of things that is denied the grown man – in verse which attracted Coleridge's censure in a well-known passage in *Biographia Literaria*.[2] In the absence of evidence to support this view, Wordsworth relies upon force of assertion to carry his point, and by the use of sonorous phrases like

> Haunted for ever by the eternal mind

he seems to seek to distract our attention away from the tenuous significance of the words. But as the account proceeds, we become increasingly conscious of his failure to enlarge our imaginative grasp of the infant's communion with the eternal, and, in the absence of this, all that is developed is a sense of incongruity; so that when Wordsworth draws a picture of what is implied by his earlier account –

> Hence in a season of calm weather
> Though inland far we be,
> Our souls have sight of that immortal sea
> Which brought us hither,
> Can in a moment travel thither,
> And see the Children sport upon the shore,
> And hear the mighty waters rolling evermore.

– it is difficult, despite the sonority, to elude altogether the suggestion of a fast coach to a sort of celestial Brighton.

Despite the implied self-reassurance the poet remains preoccupied with the irrecoverable losses; and there is a marked contrast between the impact of the lines recording these:

> Though nothing can bring back the hour
> Of splendour in the grass, of glory in the flower;

– with the two abrupt bursts of words like flames going up from a collapsing fire – and the lines that flatly and unconvincingly record the consolations that remain:

> We will grieve not, rather find
> Strength in what remains behind.

The tone is simply assertive –

> Which having been must ever be

– and the thought is abridged to a sentientiousness that approaches the unfeeling:

> In the soothing thoughts that spring
> Out of human suffering.

In this poem Wordsworth is, as it were, providing his own case-book. He recognizes that natural objects no longer have the same significance in his emotional life, and claims that the loss is compensated for by gains of other kinds. He convinces us of the loss, but the gains are merely asserted, not created for the reader to share. They derive, indeed, from theory rather than from experience. Wordsworth's failure to establish as part of the reader's experience of the poem the gains which he claims is itself evidence of the loss he so poignantly records.

It is apparent from the examples so far considered that Wordsworth's successful verse differs in technique, not only from his own less successful work, but also, in some important ways, from that of what can conveniently be regarded as the Shakespearean tradition. The most obvious feature of any representative passage of Shakespeare is the highly figurative character of the language:

> ... for the harlot king
> Is quite beyond my arm, out of the blank
> And level of my brain, plot-proof; but she
> I can hook to me.

Apart from the words needed to give the passage its grammatical structure, the only word used here in its literal sense is 'king'. The technique is not, of course, peculiar to Shakespeare, and passages from many other poets – Donne, Marvell, Pope, Keats, Hopkins, Eliot – would serve as well to illustrate the point.

Wordsworth is far from eschewing figurative language, but the staple of his verse presents a sharp contrast in directness of statement and comparative freedom from imagery. Whereas in the Shakespeare passage the emotional impact and colouring are obtained by referring away from the immediate given situation to import the overtones of quite other realms of experience, Wordsworth proceeds rather by extracting from the given situation its own intrinsic emotional content, choosing the language which records most literally and exactly the quality of the experience described; and thus enabling

the reader to re-live it. In the stolen boat passage, for example, 'Strode
after me' is not a metaphor: it is, in the given context, an exact
description and recreation of the boy's illusion.

In some passages – usually of crucial significance – Wordsworth
goes farther still, and leaves behind not only figurative but even
evocative language: relying upon the bare significance of what is said
to create the required effect, and choosing his words so as to convey
his meaning with the minimum of distraction, stripping them down
to just so much as is necessary to communicate the sense alone. We
have seen an example of this in the *Ode*, in the line

> The things which I have seen I now can see no more.

There is a more extended example in the short poem, *A Slumber Did
My Spirit Seal* (1799):

> A slumber did my spirit seal;
>   I had no human fears:
> She seemed a thing that could not feel
>   The touch of earthly years.
>
> No motion has she now, no force;
>   She neither hears nor sees;
> Rolled round in earth's diurnal course,
>   With rocks, and stones, and trees.

The emotional force generated by this poem depends upon the
apparent similarity, but profound disparity, between the two stanzas.
The first creates a sense of security and reassurance by its quiet, even,
almost soporific, movement. But the figurative language used gives
this sense a trance-like unreality. The second stanza proceeds in the
same quiet, even tone, but saying things which imply the total
destruction of the dream-world created by the first. These statements
are by no means either generalized or figurative. Each of them is a
statement of bald fact, couched in what are practically clinical terms,
and containing a terrible ironic contrast with those of the first stanza.
Now the trite figure of the girl not feeling 'the touch of earthly
years', untrue when it was believed, has been validated by the inescapably literal fact of death, which puts her securely beyond the
reach of time. The calmness of this stanza is the calmness of death.
Yet the tone of the poem is not, in total, simply one of bitterness or
desolation, but rather of a sort of desperate consolation, derived from

this same fact that the dead girl is now at last secure beyond question, in inanimate community with the earth's natural fixtures. Wordsworth has deliberately exploited here the contrast between the effect of a generalized, figurative manner and of bare particularization.

In the examples so far quoted, Wordsworth's concern was to re-create experience, but his point of departure was events in the external world. In *Tintern Abbey* (1798), however, his central datum is itself subjective, the contents of his own consciousness. His method, nevertheless, is the same.

He starts with a description of the scene that is the occasion for the poem, but keeps it at a distance and does not involve the reader in it. It is framed and remote, orchards reduced to tufts, and hedgerows to 'little lines of sportive wood run wild'. His concern is, it immediately appears, not with the scene as such, but with recollections of it that he has carried with him since a previous visit; and not even with those as such, but rather with sensations they have generated.

> But oft, in lonely rooms, and mid the din
> Of towns and cities, I have owed to them,
> In hours of weariness, sensations sweet,
> Felt in the blood, and felt along the heart;
> And passing even into my purer mind,
> With tranquil restoration.

At this stage the experience is a comparatively simple one, an infusion of a sense of well-being, conveyed to us by the sense of release and relief that comes with the words 'sensations sweet' after the broken, disharmonious movement of the earlier lines. This, however, is only the preparation for a more far-reaching effect:

> ... that blessed mood,
> in which the burthen of the mystery,
> In which the heavy and the weary weight
> Of all this unintelligible world,
> Is lightened: – that serene and blessed mood
> In which the affections gently lead us on, –
> Until, the breath of this corporeal frame
> And even the motion of our human blood
> Almost suspended, we are laid asleep
> In body, and become a living soul:
> While with an eye made quiet by the power
> Of harmony, and the deep power of joy,
> We see into the life of things.

The three lines which follow the introductory half-line build up the sense of a crushing burden with their slow movement, their ponderous repetition of the awkward phrase 'In which' and the dragging, encumbering effect of words like 'weary weight' and 'unintelligible'. With the beginning of the new line, the burden is removed and the verse moves more freely – still slowly, but gently and without effort. Then, with the word 'Until', we are required, as it were, to hold our breath while the long interposed clause which follows slowly unwinds itself, slowing the verse down gradually to a virtual standstill at 'suspended'; so that 'we are laid asleep in body' simply records the trance-like state which the verse itself has achieved. With the imprisoning body spellbound, the sudden vigour of 'and become a living soul' announces the release of the non-corporeal faculties to the state of perceptive clarity recorded in:

> We see into the life of things.

We are not, as we might have been in a different context, provoked into asking what Wordsworth means by 'seeing into the life of things'. Through the medium of the verse itself, Wordsworth has re-enacted for us the sequence of experience which has brought him to this state, so that we know, by demonstration, what that state is. We are not concerned to know *what* he sees; the point of the verse is to enable us to follow the process which makes the state possible. Wordsworth himself, indeed, is disarmingly frank in expressing his doubts about what he actually sees, for the line continues:

> If this
> Be but a vain belief, yet, oh! *etc.*

He goes on to tell us that, on his previous visit, his interest in nature was passionate, unintellectual, an 'appetite'. But this state he has left behind, as he might have (and, indeed, did) an early love affair.

> That time is past,
> And all its aching joys are now no more,
> And all its dizzy raptures.

The sense of deprivation in these lines is not lessened, but underlined by what follows:

> Not for this
> Faint I, nor mourn nor murmur; other gifts
> Have followed; for such loss, I would believe,

> Abundant recompense. For I have learned
> To look on nature, not as in the hour
> Of thoughtless youth; but hearing oftentimes
> The still, sad music of humanity,
> Nor harsh nor grating, though of ample power
> To chasten and subdue.

The opening lines of this passage belie what they say, since the stress falls not on 'Not' but on 'Faint', 'mourn', and 'murmur' (to which the two 'nors' are assimilated by assonance); and the 'I would believe' emphasizes the difficulty of believing. Thus the sense of Wordsworth's own loss is carried forward into the lines that follow and gives them a special poignancy. The 'still, sad music of humanity' is the sadder because we are conscious of Wordsworth's own cause for sadness: that it has cost him so much to have learnt to know it. The reader's sympathetic involvement contrasts with the detachment, or even repulsion, with which, in *Intimations of Immortality*, he hears of 'the soothing thoughts that spring Out of human suffering'.

Tintern Abbey forms a kind of bridge which links the purely autobiographical poems with those that concern themselves with the 'still, sad music of humanity' in a wider sense. 'Nature' is to embrace not only inanimate nature but (in the true eighteenth-century tradition) human nature also. The connection between the two he expresses in the lines that follow those considered above:

> And I have felt
> A presence that disturbs me with the joy
> Of elevated thoughts; a sense sublime
> Of something far more deeply interfused,
> Whose dwelling is the light of setting suns,
> And the round ocean and the living air,
> And the blue sky, and in the mind of man:
> A motion and a spirit, that impels
> All thinking things, all objects of all thought,
> And rolls through all things.

The dichotomy between the mental and material worlds which philosophers had increasingly taken for granted since the seventeenth century was to Wordsworth (as to Kant) wholly antipathetic, and he frequently in his verse attempts a general statement of the basis of their unity. Nowhere does he do so more impressively or more successfully than here. But even here the success is equivocal. Despite

Wordsworth's obvious striving to be as specific as he can, the sonor-ity of the verse distracts attention from the meaning rather than en-forces it. Clarity of vision concentrates upon the separate fragments – 'the light of setting suns', 'the round ocean', 'the living air', 'the blue sky', 'the mind of man' – rather than on what it is that unites them. Hence the various references to this latter read like a series of attempts rather than a cumulative description: 'a presence', 'a scene', 'some-thing', 'a motion', 'a spirit'; and the two verbs predicated of this thing, 'impels' and 'rolls through', contradict rather than reinforce each other. The attempt to convey its universality by repeating four times in two lines the word 'all' is heroic rather than successful.

This is not to say that the passage is not impressive: only that the claim Wordsworth makes in it is not, to use his own phrase, 'carried alive into the heart by passion'. We have seen that that is achieved when Wordsworth is able to recreate for the reader the feelings he has derived from 'natural objects', thereby making those feelings part of the common stock of human experience and hence capable of being brought to bear on other modes of experience.

But for the full exploitation of this capability, we have to look to those poems in which the poet's own feelings are not the sole subject-matter, and the experiences of others, particularly their sufferings, are explicitly dealt with. It is in this context that three major poems must be considered: *Resolution and Independence*, *Margaret*, and *Michael*.

In *Resolution and Independence* (1802) Wordsworth meets on a moor an old leech-gatherer who is not only himself a natural object, so closely is he assimilated to his surroundings, but at the same time mediates between the natural world and Wordsworth in such a way as to bring home to him the qualities of mind and character which are the fruit of the influence of natural objects, and which, in the immediacy of his personal melancholy, he has temporarily lost sight of.

For several stanzas the poet remains preoccupied with his own thoughts, feeding on his own melancholy and taking the reader farther and farther away from the external scene.

> And fears and fancies thick upon me came;
> Dim sadness – and blind thoughts, I knew not, nor
> could name.

Then in the eighth stanza the outside world breaks in again in the shape of the leech-gatherer.

> Beside a pool bare to the eye of heaven
> I saw a Man before me unawares:
> The oldest man he seemed that ever wore grey hairs.

From the first the conception of the old man as himself a natural object is insinuated: 'Beside a pool' – the pool comes first, and the old man is seen as an adjunct to it, 'unawares'. In contrast with the restlessness of the preceding stanzas, the verse describing him moves forward with an impressive deliberation, creating a sense of primitive strength and reliability, a rock in the turmoil of the poet's thoughts:

> As a huge stone is sometimes seen to lie
> Couched on the bald top of an eminence;
> Wonder to all who do the same espy,
> By what means it could thither come, and whence;
> So that it seems a thing endued with sense:
> Like a sea-beast crawled forth, that on a shelf
> Of rock or sand reposeth, there to sun itself;

> Such seemed this Man, not all alive nor dead,
> Nor all asleep – in his extreme old age.

This is one of Wordsworth's comparatively rare similes, and he develops it at length so that it takes on a life of its own in which the original subject is submerged. Its independent force is, indeed, considerable enough to make possible an internal simile: 'Like a sea-beast . . .' The slow, almost laboured, building up of the image gives an effect of timelessness and permanence which contrasts with the feverish state of the poet's mind. 'Eminence' and 'wonder' suggest the impact made on that mind. The internal simile serves to reinforce the permanence of inanimate objects with the strength of beasts: of the sort of beast that might belong to another element as old and permanent as rock – the sea. The verse drags itself along heavily and slowly as the beast emerges from the sea –

> Like a sea-beast crawled forth, that on a shelf
> Of rock or sand reposeth, there to sun itself

– as though it were itself a sort of manifestation of the sea. So the three primeval elements – rock, sea, and sun – are all associated in the image, and at the same time related to the strength of beasts. Even in reality the old man seems half-way to being an inanimate object:

> . . . not all alive nor dead,
> Nor all asleep.

Wordsworth himself endorses this sort of account in one of his rare pieces of analysis, in the *Preface* to the 1815 edition of *Lyrical Ballads*:

> The stone is endowed with something of the power of life to approximate it to the sea-beast; and the sea-beast stripped of some of its vital qualities to assimilate it to the stone: which intermediate image is thus treated for the purpose of bringing the original image, that of the stone, to a nearer resemblance to the figure and condition of the old Man; who is divested of so much of the indications of life and motion as to bring him to the point where the two objects unite and coalesce in just comparison.

The effect is reinforced – as Wordsworth goes on to imply – by the further image in the next stanza:

> Motionless as a cloud the old Man stood,
> That heareth not the loud winds when they call,
> And moveth all together, if it move at all.

It is a reminder – if one is needed – of how remote Wordsworth is from the Victorian vocabulary of romantic images that he can so appropriately find in a cloud a simile for immobility and coherence.

Up to this point the old man has been apprehended only at the periphery of the poet's consciousness – in strong contrast to his own state of mind, but external to it. The succeeding stanzas trace the gradual penetration into the poet's mind of the old man's significance: that he is old, poor, and decrepit, but has a strength of mind, a dignity and poise which the poet, in his present state, cannot claim. At first the old man's words fail to make a full impact on the poet, who still sees him as something more or less inanimate:

> But now his voice to me was like a stream
> Scarce heard; nor word from word could I divide.

The stream of words, that is, becomes, in the poet's mind, literally a stream. His earlier state of depression returns, but, dimly perceiving the significance for him of the old man, he tries to break the grip of his melancholia by renewing his questions. The reassurance he is

offered is felt in the measured simplicity of the verse, its unemotional
and unruffled acceptance of the bleakest of realities:

> He with a smile did then his words repeat:
> And said that, gathering leeches, far and wide
> He travelled; stirring thus about his feet
> The waters of the pools where they abide.
> 'Once I could meet with them on every side;
> But they have dwindled long by slow decay;
> Yet still I persevere, and find them where I may.'

His life, in fact, is identified with that of the leeches: where they
'abide', he abides. As they 'have dwindled long by slow decay', so has
he. We were prepared for this by the earlier simile: he was 'like a sea-
beast crawled forth' – or, on a smaller scale, a leech from a pond: the
ultimate of humility, but with its strength.

As this dawns on the poet, the leech-gatherer emerges in his mind
as a symbol, a talisman:

> While he was talking thus, the lonely place,
> The old Man's shape, and speech – all troubled me:
> In my mind's eye I seemed to see him pace
> About the weary moors continually,
> Wandering about alone and silently.

Into these last two lines is compressed the whole force of the poet's
realization of the implications of what he has seen and heard. The
long syllables drag after one another, so that the end of the word
'continually' is reached with effort only for the same wearying pace
to continue relentlessly in the new line; relentlessly, but persistently –
the pace never flags, the old man plods on. And he plods on uncom-
plainingly, as we are reminded by the final 'silently'. The point has at
last come home to the poet, and the verse brings it home to the
reader.

Such weakness as there is in the poem derives mainly from the
drawing of the old man's character. The impression that he makes on
the poet is very tellingly conveyed, but the reality which is the basis
for this impression is less substantial. The evidence for the 'resolution and independence' on which the poem turns appears to consist
in no more than that the leech-gatherer pursues – perhaps without
much choice – 'employment hazardous and wearisome', and is prepared to discuss it courteously and eloquently. The verse in which

is evoked the old man's character, as distinct from the impression it made on the poet, includes some of the least effective lines in the poem –

> a stately speech;
> Such as grave Livers do in Scotland use,
> Religious men, who give to God and man their dues

– tending, as it does, to lead the reader away from the old man himself into a comparison which smacks of special pleading. Such passages appear the more colourless when measured against those – such as that of the stone and the sea-beast – in which the poet's subjective impression is evoked; and when the comparison is made, the image of the sea-beast seems rather out of scale, since the reality to which it corresponds is so faintly drawn. If, indeed, the image of the huge stone and the sea-beast relates only to the old man's physical appearance, it seems more than out of scale, it seems incongruous; and yet at the point in the poem at which it occurs, the poet has learnt nothing of the leech-gatherer's character.

This kind of difficulty is one which does not arise in poems like *Influence of Natural Objects* or the passage about the illicit row on the lake. In these the significant point is the effect on the boy's imagination: it is sufficient that the mountain *seemed* to stride after him, and, in fact, the seeming is the point. But when it comes to moral values, the case is different. It clearly is not sufficient that the old man should merely *seem* to the poet to signify resolution and independence if in reality he does nothing of the kind. Then the poet would merely be rescuing himself from his melancholia by means of an illusion, and playing off one failure of the mind against another. It is therefore important for the poem's success that it should adequately establish the old man's strength of character independently of the poet's impression of it; and to the extent that it does not, the poem has a weakness.

The weakness is, indeed, one that flows from Wordsworth's own too great strength in certain directions. We have seen how successfully he can recreate for the reader his own subjective experiences. It is, therefore, natural for him to recreate the leech-gatherer primarily in these terms also, though to achieve the moral point it is no less important to establish him objectively also. He has, in fact, in this poem come some distance from autobiography towards a moral tale, but without making the whole of the technical adjustment that is necessary. In *Margaret* and *Michael* he goes much farther towards making this adjustment.

Margaret; or the Ruined Cottage is another 'moral tale', but this time it is not, in terms, autobiographical; though, as the story of a woman and her children deserted by their father, it has obvious parallels with what little we know of Wordsworth's relationship with Annette Vallon, whom he had left in France at the end of 1792, less than three years before he began the poem in 1795.[3] Something of the place occupied in Wordsworth's mind by the theme of the wronged, betrayed, or deserted woman is indicated by its recurrence in his output between 1793 and 1799. In addition to *Margaret*, *Guilt and Sorrow*, *The Borderers*, *The Thorn*, *Her Eyes Are Wild*, *The Complaint of a Forsaken Indian Woman*, and *Ruth* all deal with it in one form or another. But although all these poems are, like *Margaret*, variations on the theme of human suffering and sorrow, in none of them does he bring this theme into the relationship of imaginative unity with the world of inanimate nature that he achieves in *Margaret*.[4]

Wordsworth himself appears in the poem in two separate roles: explicitly as the 'I' of the poem, for whom the story is almost unrelievedly tragic; and in an idealized form, as the Wanderer,[5] who tells the story and suggests the sort of consolation to be derived from nature. It is as though Wordsworth were able to achieve a reconciliation of the suffering of humanity with the tranquillity of nature only by separating the two aspects of his sympathies for the purpose of the poem. Without the Wanderer, the 'I' would find no support for the burden of sorrow; without the 'I', the burden might seem too easily borne.

As in *Resolution and Independence*, the poem opens by setting the scene, but here the canvas is larger, and the stress is on the stability of nature rather than on its activity, a background against which can be seen to perfection the particular case of human tribulation which is to follow. This is introduced, not as something distinct from the natural background, but in terms of one inanimate object among others:

> amid the gloom
> Spread by a brotherhood of lofty elms,
> Appeared a roofless Hut; four naked walls
> That stared upon each other . . .

It is the absence of man that is implied by the activity of nature:

> It was a plot
> Of garden ground run wild, its matted weeds
> Marked with the steps of those, whom, as they passed,
> The gooseberry trees that shot in long lank slips,
> Or currants, hanging from their leafless stems,
> In scanty strings, had tempted to o'erleap
> The broken wall.

The activity of 'run wild' and 'shot' results only in the confusion and disorder of 'matted weeds', 'long lank slips', 'leafless stems', and 'scanty strings'. The Wanderer introduces Margaret by reference to a broken wooden bowl which she had used for giving water to travellers, and now almost reassimilated to nature:

> Green with the moss of years, and subject only
> To the soft handling of the elements.

Nature's 'soft handling' has taken the place of Margaret's, and in the lines that follow an unusual concentration of imagery links nature with Margaret's kindness and gentleness. Water connotes charity and

> they whose hearts are dry as summer dust
> Burn to the socket.

Margaret's own taper of life has been prematurely extinguished, and her death is followed by the decay of her surroundings, of which she is herself now only a part:

> She is dead,
> The light extinguished of her lonely hut,
> The hut itself abandoned to decay,
> And she forgotten in the quiet grave.

Margaret's husband, unlike the leech-gatherer, or the old shepherd in *Michael*, is not a very positive personality. He is not actually seen or described. He at once symbolizes and holds together the orderly natural background which is the essential condition for Margaret's happiness.

After her husband's desertion, the order of Margaret's life gradually goes to pieces, and the decline is reflected in her garden:

> The honeysuckle, crowding round the porch,
> Hung down in heavier tufts: and that bright weed
> The yellow stonecrop, suffered to take root
> Along the window's edge, profusely grew,
> Blinding the lower panes ...

Later, the decline has gone farther:

> ... weeds defaced
> The hardened soil, and knots of withered grass:
> No ridges there appeared of clear black mold,
> No winter greenness; of her herbs and flowers,
> It seemed the better part were gnawed away
> Or trampled into earth; a chain of straw,
> Which had been twined about the slender stem
> Of a young apple-tree, lay at its root;
> The bark was nibbled round by truant sheep.

The ravages now go beyond mere debility and disorder. The words are stronger: 'defaced', 'hardened', 'gnawed away', 'trampled'. Earlier symbols of order – the chain of straw – have now become the reverse. Margaret herself connects in thought the decline of her world of ordered nature with the source of her sorrow –

> noting that my eye was on the tree,
> She said 'I fear it will be dead and gone
> Ere Robert come again.'

– though at the same time implying her expectation that Robert will come again. Her sorrow is not despair. The survival of her hope, in the absence of anything to sustain it, is poignantly evoked.

> I have heard, my Friend,
> That in yon arbour oftentimes she sate
> Alone, through half the vacant sabbath day;
> And, if a dog passed by, she still would quit
> The shade, and look abroad. On this old bench
> For hours she sate; and evermore her eye
> Was busy in the distance, shaping things
> That made her heart beat quick.

The pathos is real because it is not asserted, but felt. It lies in the quickening of the movement with the words 'Was busy in the distance', the breathless pause before 'shaping things', followed by the rapid pulses of 'That made her heart beat quick'. Again:

> And by yon gate,
> That bars the traveller's road, she often stood,
> And when a stranger horseman came, the latch
> Would lift, and in his face look wistfully:
> Most happy if, from aught discovered there
> Of tender feeling, she might dare repeat
> The same sad question.

So reduced is she in her sorrow that eventually it is a happiness to her even to see enough sympathy in a traveller's face, when she has lifted the latch for him, to dare ask him if he has seen her husband. But the hopelessness of the situation is tolled out for the reader in the words:

> The same sad question.

The two themes, of Margaret's wretchedness sustained by a vain hope and its physical counterpart in the cottage's decline into ruin, come together in the lines which conclude the Wanderer's story:

> Meanwhile her poor Hut
> Sank to decay; for he was gone, whose hand,
> At the first nipping of October frost,
> Closed up each chink, and with fresh bands of straw
> Chequered the green-grown thatch. And so she lived
> Through the long winter, reckless and alone;
> Until her house, by frost, and thaw, and rain,
> Was sapped; and while she slept, the nightly damps
> Did chill her breast; and in the stormy day
> Her tattered clothes were ruffled by the wind,
> Even at the side of her own fire. Yet still
> She loved this wretched spot, nor would for worlds
> Have parted hence; and still that length of road,
> And this rude bench, one torturing hope endeared.
> Fast rooted at her heart: and here, my Friend, –
> In sickness she remained; and here she died;
> Last human tenant of these ruined walls!

The backward glance at the lost order and efficiency of her husband's régime, told in brisk, crisp verse, serves as a foil for the final debacle, in which Margaret's ruin and the cottage's are so identified that the wind blows through the walls and her clothes indifferently. But the cottage and her hope are tied inexorably together, and both go down together, so completely identified that 'ruined', linked by assonance to 'human', applies equally to the hut and to its tenant.

The poet – the 'I' of the poem – turns to the cottage and traces in the wilderness the still surviving signs of human occupation:

> Then towards the cottage I returned; and traced
> Fondly, though with an interest more mild,
> That secret spirit of humanity
> Which 'mid the calm oblivious tendencies
> Of nature, 'mid her plants, and weeds, and flowers,
> And silent overgrowings, still survived.

To the poet nature seems indifferent, apathetic, perhaps almost stealthily hostile, in its 'oblivious tendencies' and 'silent overgrowings', to the human spirit and its sufferings. But the Wanderer thinks the signs should be read differently:

> ... no longer read
> The forms of things with an unworthy eye.
> She sleeps in the calm earth, and peace is here.
> I well remember that those very plumes,
> Those weeds, and the high spear-grass on that wall,
> By mist and silent rain-drops silvered o'er,
> As once I passed, did to my mind convey
> So still an image of tranquillity,
> So calm and still, and looked so beautiful
> Amid the uneasy thoughts which filled my mind;
> That what we feel of sorrow and despair
> From ruin, and from change, and all the grief
> The passing shows of Being leave behind,
> Appeared an idle dream, that could not live
> Where meditation was.

For the Wanderer, the symbols of Margaret's desolation, the weeds and overgrown grass, are images of peace and tranquillity, with which Margaret is now identified; and the gentle, measured movement of the verse enforces the point. If, however, he were doing no more than claiming that death is a form of sleep, the conclusion would be too facile to sustain the weight of what has gone before. The Wanderer is not arguing that Margaret's sufferings were unreal. He is concerned with what we should do about the legacy of sorrow, despair, and grief that we inherit when we contemplate such suffering, and his conclusion is that we should not yield to it, but recognize that the tranquillity represented by nature has a permanence which survives the individual human tragedy, and remains available to us.

The poignancy and pathos of Margaret's story is movingly

established; the lines on the tranquillity of nature are among the most effective that Wordsworth wrote in communicating directly to the reader the state of mind described. But does the poem as a whole truly resolve the suffering of the story in the calm of the conclusion? This poem is so delicate that even a limited failure of attention on the reader's part can affect it; dogmatism, therefore, is unwise. But there are, interspersed in the poem, passages of commentary by the Wanderer which seem to betray too great a readiness to retreat from compassion, too lively an awareness of the possible consequences of personal involvement. For example:

> Why should we thus, with an untoward mind,
> And in the weakness of humanity,
> From natural wisdom turn our hearts away,
> To natural comfort shut our eyes and ears,
> And, feeding on disquiet, thus disturb
> The calm of nature with our restless thoughts?

Such passages seem to demonstrate a need on Wordsworth's part to avoid the risks of over-indulgence in compassion – risks that were represented, perhaps, by the melancholia of *Resolution and Independence*. This leads to an over-ready dismissal of 'the passing shows of Being' as 'an idle dream'. Despite the potency of the verse which conveys the Wanderer's final explanation, there seems more than a trace of insensibility in his concluding remark:

> I turned away
> And walked along my road in happiness.

Elsewhere in Book I of *The Excursion*, Wordsworth says of the Wanderer,

> He could *afford* to suffer
> With those whom he saw suffer.

(The italics are his own.) The implication is that Wordsworth himself, in his proper person, could not; and this could account for a certain eagerness to pass from the contemplation of suffering to the consolations of nature. But this, of course, in no way implies an insensitivity on Wordsworth's part to the sufferings of others. On the contrary, the force with which Margaret's suffering is conveyed makes it plain that his danger is of being overborne by too powerful a sympathy, and thrown into the melancholia which was rarely, during the early creative years, altogether out of sight.

Several years passed between the completion of *Margaret* (in its original form) and the writing of Wordsworth's next great narrative poem, *Michael*. In 1799, Wordsworth wrote the last of his poems about deserted women, *Ruth*, and in 1800 *Michael* followed. In this he leaves the autobiographical framework almost completely behind, and concerns himself, as he says at the beginning of the poem, with 'passions that were not my own'. He is concerned with the 'influence of natural objects' in the aspect in which it led him to 'feel for' these passions, rather than as a consolation for the effect of sympathies more directly stimulated. It is for this reason, perhaps, that the characters in the story, particularly Michael himself, are so completely fused with their natural surroundings, and that Wordsworth's control of the emotional implications of their history never falters.

The old shepherd is drawn as a man with all the strength and reliability of a tree or a rock:

> An old man, stout of heart, and strong of limb.
> His bodily frame had been from youth to age
> Of an unusual strength ...
>   ... he had been alone
> Amid the heart of many thousand mists,
> That came to him, and left him, on the heights.

The description is illustrative of Wordsworth's emotional distance from his subject. The ready phrases 'stout of heart' and 'strong of limb' are saved from being clichés only by the lines that follow, which effectively maintain the 'hearts of oak' suggestion and enlarge upon it. The last line particularly is, in all its simplicity, remarkably suggestive of the drifting to and fro of a mist, leaving the old man as unaffected as a rooted tree. His natural affinity was with the hills and fields in which he lived and worked.

But the birth of a son, late in his life, generates a feeling of a different order. He looks after the baby

> with patient mind enforced
> To acts of tenderness

– patience and tenderness are the key features of the old man's character, strength 'enforced' to sensibility. When Michael hears that he may be forced to sell some of his fields, so that they will not be passed on to his son, all the life is drained out of the verse as it is drained out of the old man:

> This unlooked-for claim,
> At the first hearing, for a moment took
> More hope out of his life than he supposed
> That any old man ever could have lost.

The simplicity of that last line is the simplicity of exhaustion, and the comparison of himself with 'any old man' suggests the momentary extinction of personality that comes with loss of hope.

The verse of *Michael* approaches this starkness whenever the underlying emotional intensity increases. Thus when, at the moment of enforced parting from Luke, Michael asks him to lay a stone of the sheep-fold they were going to build together, he epitomizes the whole situation in the words:

> 'This was a work for us; and now, my Son,
> It is a work for me.'

The whole bleak prospect, and the strength of mind with which the old man regards it, is contained in these few words; and at the same time they establish the building of the sheep-fold as a symbol of the link between the old man and his son.

Michael's reception of the news of Luke's disgrace and flight does not break him physically – there is no escape that way. Wordsworth reminds us of his capacity for physical endurance by repeating the words he has used already:

> His bodily frame had been from youth to age
> Of an unusual strength. Among the rocks
> He went, and still looked up to sun and cloud,
> And listened to the wind.

The repetition approaches the ironic. The strength which had once been Michael's mainstay now becomes a burden to him. The potency of his love was earlier suggested by its power to 'enforce' his 'patient mind' to 'acts of tenderness'; now the potency of his grief is implied by its capacity to render his physical strength pointless.

> And to that hollow dell from time to time
> Did he repair, to build the Fold of which
> His flock had need . . .

> ... and 'tis believed by all
> That many and many a day he thither went,
> And never lifted up a single stone.

The futility of his efforts is suggested by the repetition without progress of 'many and many' (reminiscent of 'Tomorrow and tomorrow and tomorrow'), and the pointlessness of his life is combined with the ruin of his hopes in the bare statement of the last line: symbolic, but effective on the plane of reality too, because it so exactly expresses Michael's state of mind.

Wordsworth points no moral. The poem ends where it began, with the straggling heap of unhewn stones by the brook:

> ... the remains
> Of the unfinished Sheep-fold may be seen
> Beside the boisterous brook of Greenhead Ghyll.

There is a suggestion here, perhaps, of the idea Tennyson later took up, of the brook continuing boisterously without regard to the vicissitudes of man. But there is no appeal to nature as a source of redress or consolation, as there is at the end of *Margaret*. In *Michael*, nature is not something outside the human situation. Michael is part of the natural world himself, and the strength of his body and mind, the birth, growth, and bereavement of his love for Luke, are all enforced in terms of his work among the things of nature; so that the old man's feelings are shown as working themselves out with the power and simplicity appropriate to the forces of nature themselves. Because of this identification of Michael's feelings with the natural world around him, there is no scope for turning to nature for consolation. The natural world – the rocks, the trees, the hills – simply endures, and the only support that Michael has for his suffering is endurance. But that endurance, in its silent undemonstrativeness, is made to seem even more terrible than the wasting and extinction of Margaret.

The narration of a simple tale of human suffering, with a sparing use of imagery and an unelaborate vocabulary, is not a common mode of expression for English poetry; not, at any rate, for successful poetry. To find adequate parallels for *Margaret* and *Michael* we need to turn to *Adam Bede* and *The Mill on the Floss* rather than to another poet. (When Wordsworth was supposed to be preparing for his Tripos examination, he was reading *Clarissa Harlowe* instead.) But poetry, with its greater scope for tautness and economy, enables the

273

simple or fragmentary experience to be dealt with in a way which would – in Wordsworth's day, at any rate – scarcely support a novel. Wordsworth did, in fact, devise for himself the mode best fitted to communicate the sort of experience he had to communicate. This is the ultimate justification of his theories of poetry. Applied simply as theories, when he had nothing of significance to communicate, simplicity (to borrow Coleridge's terms) declined into simpleness, and the banality of poems like *Rural Architecture* or *Alice Fell* are the result; or assertion becomes the sort of rhetoric exhibited *passim* in the *Ecclesiastical Sonnets*. But when he had a valid experience to communicate, whether slight, as in *Animal Tranquillity and Decay* or *Strange Fits of Passion Have I Known*, or considerable, as in *Michael* or *Margaret*, it is clear that the means do much more than justify the end.

The story of Wordsworth's decline as a poet is well known and sometimes overstated. Though *The Prelude* underwent over forty years of revision before it was published, comparison of the text published in 1850 with the original one of 1805 shows that it did not by any means always lose by the changes made. Nevertheless, the published output of the intervening years included much of his poorest work, and rarely reached the high peaks of the earlier years. Although experience of nature had supplied him with a reservoir from which to draw strength to deal with human suffering, he was not confident that this would never fail him, and longed for

a repose that ever is the same.

That was something that the delicate, almost precarious balance of sympathies represented by, for example, *Margaret* could never be. That sort of battle needed to be fought afresh whenever occasion demanded. The permanence of repose was achieved at the expense of sensitivity of feeling, and the poetry suffered accordingly.

But the extent of the achievement of the fruitful years – far from wholly accounted for in this essay – makes out of place any complaint that it was not more extensive. The faults of Wordsworth's verse were not, in any case, confined to any particular period of his life; and if they were the price paid for his achievements, it was not, in the light of those achievements, an excessive one.

NOTES

1. While every part of the poem has its own relevance to the total effect, there are passages in which (as in those already quoted) the particular local effect is to some degree isolable. See, for example, Book I, 301–39, 499–543; Book V, 370–469; Book XII, 208–69, 287–335; and Book XIII, 11–62. (The references are to the 1850 edition, but the 1805 version should also be consulted. E. de Selincourt's 1928 edition prints the two versions side by side.)

2. Wordsworth omitted from later editions four of the lines to which Coleridge objected.

3. Wordsworth might, in an oblique way, be establishing the connection himself in a passage in one of the Prefaces to *The Excursion*: '. . . that state in which I represent Robert's [Margaret's husband's] mind to be I had frequent opportunities of observing at the commencement of our rupture with France in '93'. He adds that he used those opportunities in *Guilt and Sorrow* also.

4. The choice of text is not a simple matter. There were several versions before publication (see the notes to the 1949 Oxford edition of *The Excursion* and Miss Darbishire's contribution to *Essays Presented to Sir Humphrey Milford*), and several revisions of the published text. No one version is unequivocally the best. On the whole, Matthew Arnold's version of 1879 in the Golden Treasury edition of the poems is the most convenient, but it does not correspond exactly to any single version authorized by Wordsworth himself.

5. 'I am here called upon freely to acknowledge that the character I have represented in his person is chiefly an idea of what I fancied my own character might have been in his circumstances.' – Preface to *The Excursion*.

COLERIDGE: POET AND PHILOSOPHER

LEO SALINGAR

Coleridge (1772–1834) was a poet and philosopher by calling and, largely by circumstance, a journalist, preacher, lecturer, and playwright. His main work was to transform the mechanistic psychology of the eighteenth century and to initiate a reaction against it. He revived the older tradition of Platonism and introduced to England the new idealism of Germany. He set out to explore the unconscious workings of the mind – 'the *terra incognita* of our nature' – for poetry. He completed the revolution of taste which has enthroned Shakespeare as a genius no less remarkable for his judgement than his inventiveness. More than any other of the English Romantics, he brought about the revolution in literary thought that consists in regarding the imagination as the sovereign creative power, expressing the growth of a whole personality. Besides all this, he wrote and talked incessantly about politics and religion, biology and language and education. And, in addition, his career was a chain of unfinishable Utopian projects, from his scheme with Southey in 1794 for Pantisocracy (which was to provide a model for social regeneration in the founding of a communal farm beside the Susquehanna) to the all-embracing prose epic or 'Logosophia' he was compiling at the end of his life, which was to ensure the reconciliation of religion and philosophy. All the published prose of the second half of his life, including *Biographia Literaria* (1817), consists of fragments and digressions wrenched from him by the occasion, but intended as preparatives for this vast undertaking, which Coleridge thought of as his counterpart to Wordsworth's *Prelude*.

It is hardly surprising, then, that Coleridge – aided here by his self-comparison to Hamlet and his reputation as a victim of opium – should have earned the name of a subtle but aimless and irreclaimable dreamer. 'There is no subject on which he has not touched,' said Hazlitt, 'none on which he has rested'; and René Wellek today calls him a random eclectic. Nevertheless, a contrary and probably more adequate impression of Coleridge is the sense of his intellectual determination. 'He was most wonderful,' said Wordsworth, the best placed of authorities, 'in the power he possessed of throwing out in profusion grand central truths from which might be resolved the most comprehensive systems.' And Keats criticized Coleridge precisely for lacking the 'Negative Capability' of suspending judgement in the midst of mysteries and doubts; he was 'incapable of remaining content with half-knowledge'.

The central truths that Coleridge was after were always to be drawn from 'facts of mind', whether under the guise of perfectionistic enlightenment or of disenchanted self-knowledge. Through all his shifts of topic and doctrine his attention was fixed on the 'increase of consciousness', the causes favouring or hindering it, and its effects. For Coleridge, as Keats and Wordsworth imply, the increase of consciousness should never willingly stop short of the whole. His ideal poet, as he is described in his main statement in *Biographia* (ch. XIV), is not a dreamer at all, but a man of rounded character: 'The poet, described in *ideal* perfection, brings the whole soul of man into activity, with the subordination of its faculties to each other, according to their relative worth and dignity.' Nor was wholeness of mind possible, in Coleridge's view, for a self-contained individual; on the contrary, it entailed the individual's perception, his consenting recognition, of the 'absolute oneness' of the whole universe: 'The dim intellect,' he wrote in 1803, 'sees an absolute oneness, the perfectly clear intellect *knowingly perceives* it. Distinction and plurality lie in the betwixt.' Again: '*All* is an endless fleeting abstraction; *the whole* is reality.' Although Coleridge never proclaimed the poet as such to be a healer, a prophet or an unacknowledged legislator, he came very near to doing so; and clearly a doctrine requiring the intuition of wholeness entrusts or saddles the poetic imagination with a heavy metaphysical burden.

The burden was not altogether of Coleridge's seeking. Dr Johnson (who died while Coleridge was a schoolboy) had always rejoiced 'to concur with the common reader' in applauding a poet's expression of generally accepted truths. But for Coleridge there was no 'common reader'; only, in London and the new manufacturing districts, a huge miscellaneous 'reading public', uninformed but exacting, pressing for excitement and receptive to revelation. And in a lifetime of public upheavals – an 'age of anxiety', in Coleridge's phrase – there could be no sentiments that found an echo in every bosom unless, as Wordsworth contended, the poet could first put them there. There were strong social motives, then, in Coleridge's insistence on wholeness. Strong personal motives, too; for Coleridge lacked the local roots and local pieties, besides the strength of temperament, that helped Wordsworth to recover from the stresses of the 1790s. He was an orphan who got on badly with his elder brothers, a keenly affectionate but often sick and frustrated man, who was constantly haunted by self-pity or remorse, by his yearning for family happiness and his impulse to run away. In a sense, the '*ideal* perfection' of the poet in *Biographia* is Coleridge's ideal for himself in his struggle for self-mastery.

The prevailing attitude of Coleridge's formative years – not without fluctuations – was an emotional pantheism. He declared later that pantheism had only appealed to his head; but in 1802 he wrote that 'strong feeling and an active intellect conjoined' will at first lead a philosopher almost inevitably to Spinoza, and as late as 1826 he noted that he required a deliberate effort to resist his old pantheistic 'habit of feeling'.[1] In the 1790s a nature-worship like Wordsworth's appealed to his heart as well as his head. It seconded his political creed, which might be described as a compound of Milton, Godwin, and Rousseau; it supported him emotionally after 1798, when his hopes in the French Revolution broke down; and it held together his favourite themes of speculation. He was both a student of 'facts of mind' in the Neoplatonic mystics and a disciple of the enlightenment descended from Locke and Hartley, believing with them that the contents of the mind are formed from sense-impressions combined by association, and even maintaining 'the corporeality of *thought* – namely that it is motion'. Coleridge's pantheism gave house-room to these unlikely partners. For his associationism (or 'necessitarianism') meant for Coleridge the Pantisocrat that evil was the product of civilization and private property; while his Neoplatonic faith was a faith that 'fraternized' by revealing that all men were 'Parts and proportions of one wonderous whole'. His first ambitious poem, *Religious Musings* (1794–6), is a philanthropic hymn wherein he nominates Hartley and Newton to the Elect, together with Milton and the Unitarian Priestley. And Coleridge's pantheism was ultimately to lead him to his central problem as a critic. In a letter to Sotheby of 10 September 1802, after asserting that 'a Poet's *Heart & Intellect* should be *combined, intimately* combined & *unified*, with the great appearances in Nature', Coleridge claims that Greek religious poetry at best exhibits Fancy, for to the Greeks 'all natural Objects were *dead*'; whereas the Psalms show Imagination, for 'in the Hebrew Poets each Thing has a Life of its own, & yet they are all one Life'. This argument contains Coleridge's first reference to his distinction between imagination and fancy; he brings it forward as 'a most compleat answer to those, who state the Jehovah of the Jews, as a personal & national God'.

From 1801 to 1803, however, Coleridge was engaged on an intensive re-thinking of his philosophy, which was at the same time a prolonged effort to recover the 'self-impelling, self-directing Principle' in his personal life.[2] His new outlook, though yet to undergo many, and sometimes bewildering, changes of detail, was in essentials a reversal of the old. In 1803, with the renewal of the Napoleonic War, Coleridge emerged as a nationalist and a disciple of Burke, holding that government must be founded on property and inequality. At the same time, he returned to Anglican orthodoxy – or, rather, to a prolonged reinterpretation of Protestantism in the light of Plato and of Kant. By the end of 1803, similarly, he was repudiating Wordsworth's nature-worship and rejecting Hartley's theory of the mind, or severely limiting its application, mainly because he had now come to locate the source of moral evil in submission to the senses, in 'the streamy nature of the associative faculty', especially with people like himself, 'who are most reverie-ish and streamy'. His cardinal doctrine now was the freedom and initiative of the moral will – the divine spark in each of us, 'the *"I"* of every rational Being', the ultimate source alike of religious faith and of genuine perception. And the moral or rational will is now outside the chain of natural causes and effects altogether; it is apparently the same as the 'primary Imagination' of a famous and oracular passage in *Biographia*, namely 'a repetition in the finite mind of the eternal act of creation in the infinite I AM' (ch. XIII). While he was preparing *Biographia*, Coleridge wrote to Wordsworth that the aims of *The Prelude* should have been to refute the school of Locke, to show how man's senses are evolved from his mind or spirit and to show how the doctrine of redemption rescues mankind 'from this enmity with Nature'. The corner-stone of 'Logosophia' was to be the idea that 'Life begins in detachment from Nature and ends in unition with God'.[3]

Coleridge still seeks the Whole as urgently as before. But the Bible now is emphatically not a pantheist document. It still reveals, as Coleridge writes in *The Statesman's Manual* (1816), that 'every agent' (if not 'each Thing') has 'a life of its own, and yet all are one life'. But now, 'the elements of necessity and free-will are reconciled in the higher power of an omnipresent Providence, that predestinates the whole in the moral freedom of the integral parts'. And, since now God is not in Nature but omnipresent outside it, the poet's sense of wholeness cannot be a single decisive revelation (as the letter of 1802 to Sotheby implies), but must be a progressive development or a perpetual re-creation. In the passage in *Biographia* defining the act of perception, or 'primary Imagination', as a form of the creative will, Coleridge goes on to define the poetic (or 'secondary') imagination as one of its derivatives. As everywhere in Coleridge's critical writings, the poetic imagination imposes unity on its material; but here, on very different terms from those of the letter of 1802:

> The secondary Imagination ... dissolves, diffuses, dissipates, in order to re-create; or where this process is rendered impossible, yet still at all events it struggles to idealize and to unify. It is essentially *vital*, even as all objects (*as* objects) are essentially fixed and dead.

Although the intention of this passage and of *Biographia* as a whole is to bring out a contrast between Fancy and Imagination, it is noticeable that Imagination now stands where the Greek Fancy had stood in 1802; for the Greeks, 'all natural Objects were *dead*'.

Evidently, then, Coleridge held two different theories about poetic creation. According to the first, it springs from self-identification with Nature; for the second, it is a product of the autonomous will. Both theories involve the co-operation of the poet's whole personality. But the main problem before the first is to account for Mind in the process; that of the second, to account for Nature.

Many of Coleridge's favourite images in his poems and notebooks are related closely to his interests in Hartley and in the mystics. They are images of illumination – moonlight suffusing the sky, or the Neoplatonic symbol of the sun dispersing mists of ignorance and super-stition. Or they are images of natural motion – studies of waterfalls ('the continual *change* of the *Matter*, the perpetual *Sameness* of the *Form*'), studies of a ship's foam, of clouds or the leaves of a tree in the wind, of the flight of insects or of birds. He delights in noting how individuals or particles of matter seem to combine in spontaneous motion; or how the mind itself appears to move in sympathy (or empathy) during the act of observation:

One travels along the lines of a mountain. Years ago I wanted to make Wordsworth sensible of this ...

And in *The Eolian Harp* (1795) Coleridge presses the wind-harp into service as a symbol both of spontaneous inspiration and of the life-force as a whole:

> What if all of animated nature
> Be but organic harps diversely framed,
> That tremble into thought, as o'er them sweeps
> Plastic and vast, one intellectual breeze,
> At once the Soul of each, and God of all?

Here he struggles to reconcile associationism with the concept of a 'plastic', 'organic' World-Soul that he may have borrowed from the Cambridge Platonists of Milton's day. For the moment he recoils from such 'idle flitting phantasies', 'shapings of the unregenerate mind'; but the appeal of an ecstatic communion with Nature was too strong to be repelled. For example, in *France: an Ode* (or *The Recantation*, 1798), he turns away from men to the elements to find true Liberty ('The guide of homeless winds, and playmate of the waves'). And as Liberty means the sensation of projecting his spirit into nature, 'Possessing all things with intensest love', so, in *The Nightingale; a Conversation Poem* (addressed, a few weeks later, to William and Dorothy Wordsworth), happiness means 'surrendering his whole spirit', to 'the influxes/Of shapes and sounds and shifting elements'. A letter to Thomas Wedgwood early in 1803 relates how, as he climbs a mountain, away from men and animals, he feels a conviction of universal life rush in on him in 'a wild activity, of thoughts, imaginations, feelings, and impulses of motion', so that his spirit 'courses, drives, and eddies, like a Leaf in Autumn'. There is a striking anticipation of Shelley in this account of inspiration.

The trouble with most of this spontaneous, 'involuntary' inspiration in Coleridge is that he wants it to teach a doctrine and has clearly come by it in obedience to a doctrine. The strongest influences behind his poetry are Milton and the semi-Miltonic tradition of sublimity and pathos represented by Gray and Collins; and many of his poems, either in Miltonic blank verse or the form of odes, are philosophical declamations, somewhat like the contemporary prophetic writings of Blake, descended, like them, from the strains of Gray's *Bard*, with its echoes of Milton, Pindar, and the Bible, and its background of mountain torrents and primitive liberty. What Coleridge aimed at was 'that impetuosity of transition, and that precipitation of fancy and feeling, which are the *essential* excellencies of the sublimer Ode' (1796); and this tradition of bardic sublimity was very much in his thoughts when he wrote his letter about imagination to Sotheby in 1802. But impetuosity to order is difficult to sustain.

Coleridge was more at home in his personal verse, which begins with sentimental 'effusions' and continues with 'conversation poems' like *The Eolian Harp* and *The Nightingale*, and finally with the long series of miscellaneous lyrics springing from his love for Sara Hutchinson, Wordsworth's sister-in-law. In the blank-verse 'conversation poems' written during the productive months that led on to *Lyrical Ballads* (1798) – and especially in the fine *Frost at Midnight* – Coleridge finds a distinctive manner of his own. They are sensitive descriptive pieces within the framework of a verse-letter or domestic monologue. They owe something to 'the divine Chit chat of Cowper' and something, no doubt, to Wordsworth's friendship and his theory of plain speech. But Coleridge's landscape is no longer that of Cowper or of Bowles, with their 'perpetual trick of *moralizing* every thing'; nor is it Wordsworth's landscape, with its haunting presences and solitary encounters. It is intimate, tender, and animated. His conversation poems have the same qualities of keen, extemporized analysis and affectionate communication as the best of his letters. Nevertheless, Coleridge could not remain satisfied with intimacy in poetry unless he could infuse it with the sublime.

Coleridge could only reach his goal of unselfconscious communion with nature, therefore, by evading (or repressing) the demands of his rational will – or else by finding a new synthesis of mind and feelings altogether. The triumph of *Kubla Khan* and *The Ancient*

Mariner represents the first of these alternatives. In the autumn of 1797, when he was about to begin work on *The Ancient Mariner* and – it seems likely – had just composed *Kubla Khan*, Coleridge wrote to Thelwall that he could often wish to sleep or die, or 'like the Indian Vishnu, to float about along an infinite ocean cradled in the flower of the Lotos, & wake once in a million years for a few minutes'.[4] The complete transmutation of the bardic ode in *Kubla Khan*, so that scattered memories from Coleridge's immense reading and conflicting feelings and sensations seem to find their own order in his mind, without effort and without question, seems due to some such moment of inner release. And there is a similar exhilaration, in spite of all the horror, in the voyage of the Ancient Mariner, from the 'free' movement of the ship in the wind at the outset to the release of the roaring wind and cascade of rain that bring his sufferings to an end. Whatever part opium may have taken in the process, Coleridge maintained that in both poems his rational mind was somehow held in abeyance. He said *Kubla Khan* was composed in a 'dream' (when he published it in 1816) or a 'reverie' (according to an earlier manuscript which has recently come to light). And although there is no question of dreaming in the actual writing of the other poem, which was planned deliberately and then revised and improved (1797, 1800, 1817), Coleridge called *The Ancient Mariner* also 'A Poet's Reverie', until Lamb made him drop the title. Presumably 'a poet's' reverie indicates some degree of rational control – but still imperfect control; for by 'reverie' Coleridge meant expressly a state 'akin to somnambulism, during which the understanding and moral sense are awake, though more or less confused'.

Moreover, Coleridge classed nightmare with reverie, and published *The Pains of Sleep* (1803) together with *Kubla Khan* as if to point the connection. He found it difficult to square *Kubla Khan* and even, to some extent, *The Ancient Mariner*, with his doctrinal leanings and his increasing moral anxiety. As for *Kubla Khan*, it was not a 'poem' at all, but a 'fragment', a 'psychological curiosity'. As for *The Ancient Mariner*, he found two ways of accounting for it, neither of them wholly satisfying. One was to deny that it contained any moral at all and to class it, by implication, with literature of escape such as the 'Gothic' novels of the 1790s, the *Arabian Nights* and Coleridge's favourite 'happy nightmare', *Robinson Crusoe*.[5] The

other was to link it with Coleridge's intended essay on the preternatural in poetry – the essay which would have discussed 'that willing
suspension of disbelief for the moment, which constitutes poetic
faith' and would no doubt have embodied Coleridge's life-long
interest in occult 'facts of mind' and his belief that an open-minded
psychologist could find at least a 'poetic faith', a vital if garbled
revelation, by attending to popular superstitions and such abnormal
psychic events as obsessions, presentiments and the hallucinations of
mystics.[6] On this reading, the Ancient Mariner may resemble Macbeth, who, as Coleridge says, is forced into 'a preternatural state' because he 'tears himself live-asunder from nature'. But as a text for his
essay Coleridge preferred his unfinished *Christabel* (1797–1801), in
which he seems to have meant to include a more explicit religious
teaching. And yet it is precisely the presence of a still undefined moral
or sentimental purpose in *Christabel* that makes it a much slighter
achievement than *The Ancient Mariner*.

There are haunting echoes of a moral struggle in *The Ancient
Mariner*, but, as Wordsworth complained, Coleridge withholds from
reducing them to a daylight morality. The tale is consistently
irrational, with none of that effort of resistance typical of a nightmare
allegory by Kafka. Although the Mariner speaks of his saint and his
cross, the effective agents in his story are the nature-spirits from
Coleridge's Neoplatonic reading; and the effective morality, or
binding-force, is an involuntary, spontaneous contact with nature.
Symbolically, the Mariner may resemble Macbeth; but he does not
speak as a moral agent. He is passive, in guilt and remorse. He acts
when he shoots the albatross, bites his arm, or blesses the water-
snakes; but he acts blindly, under compulsion, like Robinson Crusoe
(as Coleridge interpreted him) or like Coleridge himself in *The Pains
of Sleep*, where

> all confused I could not know
> Whether I suffered or I did.

He invokes the nightmare of life-in-death blindly when he kills the
albatross and dispels it passively when he blesses the water-snakes
'unaware'. From this paralysis of his conscience, terrifying and yet
refreshing, the Mariner has gained his mesmeric authority, though he
pays for it by remaining in the condition of an outcast. Coleridge

makes him spectator as well as actor in the drama, so that he can re-count even his worst terrors with a calm after-thrill of lucid retro-spection; and the crown of the poet's achievement is his steadiness in preserving – even sharpening – the sensations of nightmare (or 'happy nightmare') for their own sake, in spite of the emotional conflicts they involve.

Only one of Coleridge's poems, however, *Dejection: an Ode* – in its original form a verse-letter to Sara Hutchinson – answers fully to the ideal of poetical completeness that Coleridge came to define in *Biographia* as a condition of 'judgement ever awake and steady self-possession' as well as 'enthusiasm and feeling profound or vehement'; and, paradoxically, *Dejection* is one of the outstanding records of that *ennui*, that loss of enthusiasm, which was the tragic malady of the Romantics. When he wrote it, in April 1802, Coleridge knew that his marriage was near collapse and he was also afraid, like Wordsworth, that 'the poet in him' was 'dying'. It was partly a response to Wordsworth's Ode on childhood and was echoed in turn in *Resolution and Independence*, so that the three poems together form a kind of dialogue. The published version of *Dejection* has less hope but also less self-pity than the private letter;[7] it contains a remarkable effort at self-therapy.

In the first stanza of *Dejection* Coleridge is in the situation he often describes, looking at the sky and trying to find 'a symbolical language' there for something in himself. But his usual sources of inspiration seem to fail him, and he is only dispirited by the noise of the wind-harp outside his room. Then, however, in the second stanza, he begins to reach his symbolical language as he approaches what is at once a self-judgement and a rounded ideal of poetry:

> A grief without a pang, void, dark, and drear,
>   A stifled, drowsy, unimpassioned grief,
>   Which finds no natural outlet, no relief,
>   In word, or sigh, or tear –
> O Lady! in this wan and heartless mood,
> To other thoughts by yonder throstle wooed,
>   All this long eve, so balmy and serene,
> Have I been gazing on the western sky,
>   And its peculiar tint of yellow green:
> And still I gaze – and with how blank an eye!
> And those thin clouds above, in flakes and bars,

> That give away their motion to the stars;
> Those stars, that glide behind them or between,
> Now sparkling, now bedimmed, but always seen:
> Yon crescent Moon, as fixed as if it grew
> In its own cloudless, starless lake of blue,
> I see them all, so excellently fair,
> I see, not feel, how beautiful they are!

'I see, not feel' is like Wordsworth's regret for vanishing glory or the Mariner's apathy before he blesses the water-snakes. But here Coleridge is searching for relief within himself, and he finds it in the rhythm of his stanza as he rises through images of solemn calm and friendly movement to contemplate the perfect self-centredness and self-illumination of the lotus-like moon. More continuously than any other writer, Coleridge had admired Milton, the poet whose 'self-possession' enabled him to 'attract all forms and things to himself';[8] and this whole stanza, with its emphasis on *seeing*, is a tribute to the great invocation in Book III of *Paradise Lost*, where Milton in his blindness prays for a 'Celestial light' that may

> Shine inward, and the mind through all her powers
> Irradiate ...

With Milton behind him, Coleridge can resist his own despair. The first words of the next stanza are the words of *Samson Agonistes* but the rhythm is the triumphant rhythm of the *Nativity* hymn:

> My genial spirits fail;
> And what can these avail
> To lift the smothering weight from off my breast?
> It were a vain endeavour
> Though I should gaze for ever
> On that green light that lingers in the west:
> I may not hope from outward forms to win
> The passion and the life, whose fountains are within.

These lines imply a positive statement within their negation; in the published version of the poem, Coleridge builds on this at once:

> O Lady! we receive but what we give
> And in our life alone does Nature live:
> Ours is her wedding garment, ours her shroud!
> And would we aught behold, of higher worth,
> Than that inanimate cold world allowed
> To the poor loveless ever-anxious crowd,

> Ah! from the soul itself must issue forth
> A light, a glory, a fair luminous cloud
>> Enveloping the Earth
> And from the soul itself must there be sent
>> A sweet and potent voice, of its own birth,
> Of all sweet sounds the life and element!

The inner glory is 'Joy', given only to those, like Sara Hutchinson, who are 'pure of heart'. For the poet himself, distress and the research he has resorted to for anodyne have 'suspended' his birthright, his 'shaping spirit of Imagination'. Yet he can now turn his thoughts again to the Eolian harp and that 'mighty Poet', the wind.

Admittedly, this later, bardic stanza about the wind is rather forced; and none of Coleridge's many subsequent poems have the same ease and power as the first parts of *Dejection*. But it was no less important that he had gained a new insight into the Imagination, which he identifies here for the first time with the creative and governing spirit of poetry. In an earlier poem, Coleridge had claimed 'Energic Reason and a shaping mind'; but the muse he invokes before 1802 is neither Reason nor Imagination but Fancy, a 'wild' or an 'idle' Fancy in the manner of Collins.[9] In *Dejection* he took a long stride forward towards a new view of poetry, as he began to consider the imagination as both a state of inner harmony in the poet and the power that shapes the whole world of his poetry from within.

Before composing *Dejection*, Coleridge had written of the imagination in conventional eighteenth-century terms, as the faculty by which we enjoy, recall, or combine images (typically visual images), or else as the faculty at work in 'the fairy way of writing' and responsible for delusions and preternatural visions. In either case, it was subject to the laws of association; it was a 'law of our nature', he wrote in 1797, by which we 'gradually represent as wholly like' whatever is 'partially like'. In the last analysis, it was part of the automatic nervous system.

But while he was writing *Dejection*, Coleridge was coming to revise his theories about associationism completely. The mind, he writes in 1801, is not 'always passive – a lazy Looker-on on an external World'. Nor does it always meet with separate atoms of experience, as Locke and his successors assumed. It is always active as well as passive, always contains the current of the past and an impulse towards continuity. Even memory, the stronghold of associationism, is not an automatic linkage of 'ideas',* but the result of a 'state of general feeling' (or a 'state of affection or bodily Feeling') which resembles the past; and if so, he asserts towards the end of 1803, 'Hartley's system totters':

I almost think that Ideas *never* recall Ideas – any more than Leaves in a forest create each other's motion – The Breeze it is that runs thro' them/it is the Soul, the state of Feeling . . .

Similarly, Coleridge finds a potential continuity even in the sensation of the here-and-now:

How opposite to nature and the fact to talk of the 'one moment' of Hume, of our whole being an aggregate of successive single sensations! Who ever felt a single sensation? Is not every one at the same moment conscious that there co-exist a thousand others, a darker shade, or less light . . . ?

More and more, after 1803, Coleridge tends to emphasize wholeness and 'continuity in . . . self-consciousness' as the ground of all mental experience and to absorb it all into a single dynamic source, the '"I" of every rational Being', the will.[10] This solution raises new problems, for it becomes difficult to distinguish between the will as a separate act of volition, a resolution of conflicting impulses, and the will as focus or expression of a unified personality. Coleridge tends to merge the first of these into the second. What are 'motives', he asks, 'but my impelling thoughts – and what is a Thought but another word for "I thinking"?' At the same time, however, Coleridge does not deny that the mind is inclined to be passive and is subject in some ways to external laws of association; indeed, it is just this passivity that he now, from about 1803 onwards, wishes above all to resist. Just as we counteract the force of gravity in order to jump, he says, so does the 'I' (which is synonymous with the moral will) counteract the force of association in order to perceive or think. Association of ideas, 'idle flitting phantasies', indolence of will, are now very close to the roots of evil; there is a latent imperative in

---

* Ideas here are images or traces of (separate) sense-impressions (i.e. Hume and Hartley's 'ideas', not Plato's).

Coleridge's new psychology. Hence its inconsistencies and his continuous effort to overcome them – an effort that both enriches and complicates his new insight into the imagination.

This 'shaping spirit' has already cast off the chains of the association theory in the writing of *Dejection*. It is no longer passive towards Nature, for 'in our life alone does Nature live'. And it is no longer merely a more or less trustworthy instrument of cognition (and hence of detached enjoyment), but a part of the poet's vital emotions; indeed, the image-combining faculty can only come into force, the poem suggests, as the result of a state of enthusiasm or 'Joy' that enables the poet to see *and* feel the beauty of Nature. This state reaches back, in turn, through the whole of his past life: 'To carry on the feelings of childhood into the powers of manhood,' Coleridge writes later (with Wordsworth's 'Homogeneity of character' in his mind, as it is in *Dejection*) – '. . . This is the character and privilege of genius.'[11] Imagination, then, gives the poet an undivided self in an undivided world. As Coleridge defines it in his important letter to Sotheby of 10 September 1802 (and again many times later), it is 'the *modifying* and *co-adunating* Faculty'. As such, moreover, it has no need of that external check by the judgement and rules of common assent so carefully provided by neoclassical theorists; in itself it is the 'shaping spirit' of poetry. Ultimately, then, the 'design' of a poem, its 'machinery', its 'ornament' – every part or aspect that matters for enjoyment and criticism – find their coherence in the poet's state of feeling. This insight of Coleridge has made a lasting difference to literary thought.

But the imagination is much more for Coleridge than a state of inner harmony; it is also a reaching towards the Whole – a worldview, a religious intuition – disguised as a psychological 'faculty'. This postulate of 'faculties' in the mind, while necessary for one part of Coleridge's outlook, is inconsistent with another; and, in addition, the relationship of Self and Whole changes as he rejects his original Nature-worship.

In his pantheist letter to Sotheby, the imagination, exemplified by the Psalms (and by English poetry), unifies the poet's heart with his mind, and both with God and Nature; 'we are all *one Life*'. For the Greeks, 'all natural Objects were *dead* – mere hollow Statues', unless there was 'a Godkin or Goddessling *included* in each'. 'In the Hebrew Poets' – on the other hand – 'each Thing has a Life of its own, & yet they are all one Life'; moreover:

In God they move & live & *have* their Being – not *had* as the cold System of Newtonian Theology represents/but *have* ...

Taking this letter and *Dejection* together, then, the imagination is opposed to 'that inanimate cold world' of 'the poor loveless everanxious crowd' who regulate their lives by the ruling mechanistic theology of eighteenth-century society and its self-centred, utilitarian ethics; and at the same time it is opposed to Greek mythology – the stale reservoir of eighteenth-century poetic diction. One is the product of the creative faculty which at least 'struggles' to reach the Whole, 'modifies' and 'co-adunates'; the other is at best 'but Fancy, or the aggregating Faculty of the mind', which (according to *Biographia*, ch. XIII) 'has no other counters to play with, but fixities and definites'. This opposition between two kinds of world-view, the vital and the mechanical, the universal and egocentric, becomes the central theme of Coleridge's later writing. After 1803, he even postulates another pair of mental faculties in order to explain it; he makes a division between Reason (which grasps eternal, absolute Ideas such as the definitions of mathematics and is identical, in its practical aspect, with the laws of the conscience) and Understanding, which can only record and classify the notices of the senses and is competent, at best, in matters of prudence. Coleridge's 'Understanding' is much the same as the 'reason' of eighteenth-century thinkers; but he holds that it can or should only operate under the control of the absolute Reason and by means of the Imagination which mediates between them.[12]

In Coleridge's original, pantheist scheme of Imagination and Fancy it is difficult to see, however, where Fancy comes in at all. For if we are, categorically, 'all *one Life*', why should we need a special faculty to recognize as much; and why should this faculty be shared by some races and not by others? Coleridge's later philosophy removes this objection to some extent (by making the imagination approach the Whole progressively, 'struggle' to reach it); but only to introduce another. For if, as *Biographia* argues (ch. XIII), the imagination (and the imagination alone) springs from the 'primary Imagination' or power of perceiving, where does Fancy derive from? Either it also uses perception, in which case the distinction between the faculties here breaks down; or it is carried along entirely by the stream of associations, in which case it can have no active role in poetry at all. Sometimes Coleridge uses the term in a traditional way (much as Johnson had said that Cowley yoked 'the most heterogeneous ideas' together 'by violence'): for example, he finds Fancy, too, in Cowley's poetry, finds 'fancy under the condition of imagination' in Spenser, and fancy in the images of Shakespeare's line, 'A lily prison'd in a gaol of snow'. At other times the term carries a distinct edge of moral disapproval, as when Coleridge attributes fancy, but not imagination, to the verse of Scott, whom he thought of as typifying the cold-hearted upper-class religion of the day.[13] Apparently Coleridge retains his separation of faculties in order to claim a distinct and higher origin for the vision that seeks unity; but having done this, he cannot find any consistent place for the minor faculty in his criticism.

Moreover, as Coleridge drives a wedge between the moral will and the sensory appearance of nature, so, in theory, he gives the imagination itself more and more labour with less and less material. For example, in 1802 Shakespeare is a 'metaphysician', but with the senses of 'a wild Arab' or 'a North American Indian'; by 1811, he works from observation, guided by self-knowledge; but by 1818 he is entirely 'self-sustained', working from meditation alone, having no contact with the environment or even the language of his time.[14] This bias towards the isolated consideration of the moral will is responsible for the one-sidedness of Coleridge's criticism in general. He is not interested at all in the plots or subject-matter of Shakespeare's plays; and, in spite of his reputation as a psychological analyst, he only considers with interest the characters he can idealize or those like Hamlet, Richard III, and Edmund, in whom he can trace an over-balance of intellect or meditation and a defect of the moral will.

On the other hand, with his bias goes a search for living principles of continuity in literature that makes Coleridge one of the greatest and most original of critics. Whereas at first he had paid more attention to the emotional, involuntary aspects of poetic creation – the wind in the wind-harp – he gives more emphasis later to character and education, so that imagination becomes almost synonymous with 'method'. In one of his finest essays, in *The Friend* (Section II, 4; 1818)[15], he praises the man of method as one who calls time 'into life and moral being'; this is essentially the quality of mind and character that he admires in Milton or in Wordsworth, the 'homogeneity of character' that enables Wordsworth to sustain his 'original gift' of imposing himself on his material, of 'spreading the tone, the *atmosphere* ... of the ideal world around ... situations, of which, for the common view, custom had bedimmed all the lustre'. And when Coleridge differs from Wordsworth over poetic diction (in *Biographia*, chs XVII–XVIII), he concentrates on method, ignoring the original question of vocabulary; educated speech and not rustic speech is the best for poetry, he says, because the rustic can only 'convey *insulated facts*', while the cultivated mind seeks '*connexions*', a prospective view of a subject, the subordination of its parts to 'an organized whole'. Similarly, Coleridge prefers the 'stately march and difficult evolutions' of seventeenth-century prose, with its 'cement of thought as well as of style', to the 'short and unconnected sentences' of his own day; just as he prefers the movement of Milton's verse to the movement of Pope's.

The most fruitful passages in Coleridge's criticism are those where he distinguishes method and internal inter-connectedness as signs of the imagination. A famous example, from his Shakespeare lectures of 1808, is his comment on two lines from *Venus and Adonis*:

> 'Look! how a bright star shooteth from the sky,
> So glides he in the night from Venus' eye.'

How many images and feelings are here brought together without effort and without discord – the beauty of Adonis – the rapidity of his flight – the yearning yet hopelessness of the enamoured gazer – and a shadowy ideal character thrown over the whole.

It is Coleridge rather than Shakespeare here who provides a 'shadowy ideal character'; but probably no other critic had so been able to demonstrate the instantaneous combination of qualities in a poet's lines. The essay on Method in *The Friend* provides a similar instance, this time of Coleridge's skill in analysing the sequence of Shakespeare's thought. Here he demonstrates Shakespeare's judgement by examining two passages of narrative, by Hamlet and by Mrs Quickly, both immethodical but for opposite reasons – 'Hamlet from the excess,

Mrs Quickly from the want, of reflection and generalization'. Mrs Quickly, he points out, has no pauses in her speech save those enforced by 'the necessity of taking breath, the efforts of recollection, and the abrupt rectification of its failures'; and no connectives, except 'in the fusion of passion'. On the other side, with Hamlet, who is 'meditative to excess', 'all the digressions . . . consist of reflections, . . . either directly expressed or disguised in playful satire'. From all this, Coleridge draws the moral that method consists in a due balance 'between our passive impressions and the mind's own reactions on the same'. The whole essay is complementary to his debate with Wordsworth over diction and the moral, clearly, has some reference to himself. But it is precisely this interest that gives Coleridge his grip on those surface details of a passage that lead directly to fundamentals; and it is here that the strength of his criticism lies, not in character-analysis.

As a third example of this strength, there is his discussion of the music of verse in *Biographia*. In chapter XVIII he suggests a biological explanation of the effects of metre in poetry. Metre, he says, is the natural accompaniment to 'language of excitement' because it arouses expectancy and surprise in a continuous, though barely perceptible, alternation; and because it is determined by the balance of two fundamental human tendencies, '*spontaneous* impulse' and '*voluntary* purpose'. Now this theory – a profoundly original one – is really an extension of Coleridge's thought at the time of the *Dejection* Ode, where he tries to derive the music of verse 'from the soul itself', from the imagination conceived as an attunement of the conscious mind to the spontaneous wholeness of Nature; and Coleridge shows how he applies it in his remarkable chapter on the first signs of genius in Shakespeare, where he begins by emphasizing the sense of musical delight (*Biographia*, ch. XV). Striking images and interesting thoughts, he says there, may be acquired by a writer of talent:

But the sense of musical delight, with the power of producing it, is a gift of imagination; and this together with the power of reducing multitude into unity of effect, and modifying a series of thoughts by some one predominant thought or feeling, may be cultivated and improved, but can never be learned.

Coleridge scrupulously refrains here from merging instinct into method; but he goes as far as he honestly can in bringing them together. Approaching poetry in this way, he gives a wholly new and far richer significance to the century-old praise of Shakespeare as the 'child of Nature'.

In developing these views, Coleridge took over from the German Romantics the theory that poetry is, or should be, an independent organic growth – organic growth, as opposed to mechanical construction.[16] Unlike a classical drama by Sophocles or Racine, he contends, a play by Shakespeare grows from within, as a tree does. In Shakespeare, contrasted this time with Beaumont and Fletcher, 'all is growth, evolution, *genesis* – each line, each word almost, begets the following – and the will of the writer is an interfusion, a continuous agency, no series of separate acts'; and in Shakespeare (as contrasted with Massinger), changes in the characters are prepared for, because each of his characters 'has indeed a life of its own ..., but yet an organ of the whole'. In opposition to previous English critics, therefore, Coleridge claims that Shakespeare's plays are highly organized unities. Further – and here Coleridge's metaphysics or metabiology comes into play – this organizing power in Shakespeare was no gift of instinct but the reward of deliberate meditation. Shakespeare discerns the universal Idea, the '*I* representative', within his own personality; and through the dialectical interchange between the two poles of his own self (the individual ego and the universal self), he evolves solid and natural characters, whereas the characters of other playwrights, who lack this dynamic self-knowledge, have no more reality than ventriloquists' dolls. A modern critic here might speak more barely of the impersonality of Shakespeare's art. Coleridge's description, whatever its defects, has the advantage of stressing the complex union of living forces in the mind.

Coleridge could only describe such an organic unity on a purely abstract plane, because the world of his later thought was essentially a divided world, which the imagination 'struggled' to unify. It was a world divided between 'civilization' (including the industrial revolution), which was the sphere of Understanding, and faith, ethical values and 'cultivation', the sphere of Reason. But how important the search for wholeness and the 'cement of thought' were to Coleridge can be seen from his last work, *Church and State* (1830), where he argues that part of the Idea of the English constitution is a permanent national endowment for the advancement of learning and the provision of a schoolmaster in every parish. Here the residual Pantisocrat in Coleridge passes over into the first of the Victorian social prophets.

NOTES

1. *Miscellaneous Criticism*, 253; *Biographia Literaria*, I, 134; see McFarland, *Coleridge and the Pantheist Tradition*, 165–90. Hanson, ch. X (see Part IV, Appendix, below), gives a good general account of Coleridge's early thought.

2. Coleridge to Godwin, 22 January 1802 (*Collected Letters*, No. 432; cp. Nos 381–3); see House, *Coleridge*, 52–5, 146–8.

3. Coleridge to Wordsworth, 30 May 1815 (*Collected Letters*, No. 969; extract in Potter, *Selected Poetry and Prose*, 66off.).

4. Coleridge to Thelwall, 16 October 1797 (*Collected Letters*, No. 209).

5. *Miscellaneous Criticism*, 193, 299, 370–73, 405.

6. *Biographia*, I, 202; II, 6 (ch. XIV); cp. *Poetical Works* (ed. Campbell), 499, 590; *Shakespearean Criticism*, I, 151; *Miscellaneous Criticism*, 191ff., 321; *Philosophical Lectures*, 44–7, 105, 239–40, 283; *Inquiring Spirit*, 14–17, 45–58, 404–7. Beer, *Coleridge's Poetic Intelligence*, examines the place of his psychological theories in his 'supernatural' poems.

7. House, 157ff., and Beer, ed., *Poems*, 272ff., print the verse-letter.

8. *Biographia*, I, 23; II, 20; cp. *Poetical Works* (ed. Campbell), 540; *Collected Letters*, No. 184. The early letters contain many more references to Milton than to Shakespeare.

9. See *Lines on a Friend*, lines 39–40; and e.g. *Lines on an Autumnal Evening*, *Songs of the Pixies*, *Monody on the Death of Chatterton* (both versions), *The Destiny of Nations*, lines 79–87.

10. Coleridge's psychological ideas: see *Inquiring Spirit*.

11. *The Friend* (ed. Rooke), I, 40, 109–10; *Biographia*, I, 59–60; cp. letters to Sotheby, 10 September 1802, and Sharp, 15 January 1804 (*Collected Letters*, Nos 459, 535).

12. Reason and Understanding: see letter to Thomas Clarkson, 13 October 1806 (*Collected Letters*, No. 634); *The Statesman's Manual* (in *Political Tracts*, ed. White); *Aids to Reflection* (Bohn's Library), 143–7 (extract in Potter, 456–8); *Table Talk*, 4 January 1823.

13. *Shakespearean Criticism*, I, 214–17; *Miscellaneous Criticism*, 38 (see Potter, 335), 323–35; *Biographia*, I, 15, 57–62, 202; II, 66–8.

14. Letter to Sotheby, 13 July 1802 (*Collected Letters*, No. 444); *Shakespearean Criticism*, II, 217 (Potter, 347), 312; cp. *Statesman's Manual* (in *Political Tracts*, ed. White), 53.

15. *The Friend* (ed. Rooke), I, 448ff.; (also in Potter, 439ff.; Richards, *Portable Coleridge*, 339ff.).

16. *Miscellaneous Criticism*, 44, 88, 95 (Potter, 348, 411). On the complex problem of Coleridge's debt to German thinkers, see e.g. McFarland and Fruman (Part IV below) for contrasting views – basic independence, or plagiarism.

SHELLEY'S POETRY

D. W. HARDING

Ever since its first appearance Shelley's poetry has met with sharply
conflicting judgements, and though from time to time one or the
other dominates critical opinion, both seem to survive. His life
(1792–1822) and personality have provoked endless interest and discussion, issuing (according to age and taste) in hero-worship, moral
condemnation or amateur psychiatric diagnosis. Much of his life-
history is irrelevant to the assessment of his work, but some aspects
of his personality have literary significance through the expression
they find in his poetry and the limiting effect they sometimes have on
its appeal for the adult reader. Mario Praz[1] has sufficiently shown
how fully Shelley responded to the attraction of the modish topic
of incest, how much he was influenced by Sadism, and with what
gusto he used the 'charnel' vocabulary and exploited the fascination
of physical decay. And F. R. Leavis,[2] dealing with the main literary
outcome of those traits, gave what I take to be a conclusive assessment of *The Cenci* (1819) with its banal Shakespearean imitations.

A feature of Shelley's personality that is possibly of more importance, because pervading more of his better work, is his self-
absorption or narcissism. Praz points out (what indeed Shelley
practically avowed) that in *Alastor* the poet's feminine ideal is a
projection of himself:

> He dreamed a veilèd maid
> Sate near him, talking in low solemn tones.
> Her voice was like the voice of his own soul
> Heard in the calm of thought . . .

And the picture of himself in *Adonais* (1821) (stanzas xxxi to xxxiv)
combines self-pity and self-delight in an embarrassing way.

Intellectually, Shelley could see the objections to self-absorption.
In *Alastor: or the Spirit of Solitude* (1816) his conscious intention

(explained in the Preface) is to show the deplorable fate of those who indulge in 'self-centred seclusion' and 'attempt to exist without human sympathy', or demand their own conception of perfection in any potential companion. What the poem actually conveys, none the less, is entranced self-absorption; and although the poet dies, beautifully worn out, it seems obvious that Shelley found it an intoxicatingly lovely death, enjoying in it a refined form of the ordinary deathbed fantasy of the self-preoccupied.

His narcissism makes it understandable that he should eagerly welcome the idea of finding his feelings mirrored in nature or induced by 'her'. He could rely on her sympathy in all his moods without disturbance or challenge or the disappointment of an unsympathetic response from another person:

> Away, away, from men and towns,
> To the wild wood and the downs –
> To the silent wilderness
> Where the soul need not repress
> Its music lest it should not find
> An echo in another's mind ...
> (*To Jane: the Invitation*)

True, this passage comes from an invitation to Jane to join him, but her presence evidently plays a negligible part in the anticipated perfection

> Where the earth and ocean meet,
> And all things seem only one
> In the universal sun.

Such bliss is undefined except as a state of universal harmony reflecting his own unchallenged values, in effect his own idealized self enlarged to universality.

Contentment with harmony of such thinness and emptiness is related to the strongly regressive yearnings that reveal themselves in Shelley's work. For diagnostic purposes a weak piece of occasional verse, *The Magnetic Lady*, demonstrates abundantly the longing for return to an infantile kind of bliss in union with a mother-figure. In the more serious work the empty states of peace represented by the 'poetic' ideas of sleep and death have a fascination for him:

> How wonderful is Death,
> Death and his brother Sleep!
> (*The Daemon of the World*, ll. 1–2)

or,

> She met me, Stranger, upon life's rough way,
> And lured me towards sweet Death ...
> *(Epipsychidion*, ll. 72–3)

The same regressive inclination tinges Shelley's concern with eternity and universality as he expresses it in the last stanza but one of *Adonais*, with its suggestion that birth interrupts a state of bliss which death will reinstate:

> That Light whose smile kindles the Universe,
> That Beauty in which all things work and move,
> That Benediction which the eclipsing Curse
> Of birth can quench not ...

Ancient and respectable as its alliances may be with some systems of philosophical and religious thought, this view of post-natal life as an interruption of bliss merges readily with the impulse to regress towards an early state of existence that seems in retrospect to have given perfect satisfaction without effort, problem, or conflict. Even the final chorus of *Hellas* (1821), in spite of triumph, ends on the note of longing for mere cessation:

> Oh cease! must hate and death return?
>   Cease! must men kill and die?
> Cease! drain not to its dregs the urn
>   Of bitter prophecy.
> The world is weary of the past –
> Oh, might it die or rest at last.

The millennium at the end of *Prometheus Unbound* (1819) is extremely abstract and nebulous, and such content as it has becomes remarkably diluted through the wearying length of verbal luxuriance. Where it deals with human experience (Act III, Scene IV) the effective part, as always with Shelley, is the negative part, the denunciation of what he hates in human relations. The positive satisfactions come from a vaguely conveyed oneness with the movements of large natural forces and spirits · representing the vaster features of the universe.

Shelley's weaker verse, unfortunately, is available in abundance, and a large proportion of his writing is totally unrewarding. Poem

after poem shows him putting himself into the habitual poetic pos-
tures, trying to work up the customary pressure of feeling, and filling
out facile lines with the limited range of poetic properties that he used
over and over again – the stars, the abyss, ocean, spirits of the air,
lightning, promontories, mountains, the whirlwind, et cetera. Often
enough both theme and emotional attitude are totally banal (as, for
instance, in the inflated *Ode to Liberty* or in such sub-Hollywood
exercises as *The Fugitives*). The damaging feature of his poetic
properties is that in the weak bulk of his verse they are utterly remote
from any experienced outer thing. His promontories, mountains, and
islands are unlike Wordsworth's: he can submit himself to no process
of learning or self-examination by contemplating them for, having
no life of their own beyond him, they are completely within the
power of his own manipulation. They act only as artificial stimulants
to the favourite emotional states that he was determined to stir in
himself.

This kind of writing, together with thinness of content in much of
even the best work, is partly responsible for the complaint that
Shelley was incapable of effective reasoning and the intellectual control of his emotional outpourings. But the impression of unreason
sometimes comes from the reader's failure to cope with the elliptical
structure of Shelley's sentences and the sheer difficulty of grasping his
sense, with the consequent temptation to suppose that he had none
and was content with mere incantation. This compression sometimes
causes difficulty with, for instance, *Ozymandias*, a fine poem, compact enough to be quoted in full:

> I met a traveller from an antique land
> Who said: Two vast and trunkless legs of stone
> Stand in the desert ... Near them, on the sand,
> Half sunk, a shattered visage lies, whose frown,
> And wrinkled lip, and sneer of cold command,
> Tell that its sculptor well those passions read
> Which yet survive, stamped on these lifeless things,
> The hand that mocked them, and the heart that fed:
> And on the pedestal these words appear:
> 'My name is Ozymandias, king of kings:
> Look on my works, ye Mighty, and despair!'
> Nothing beside remains. Round the decay
> Of that colossal wreck, boundless and bare
> The lone and level sands stretch far away.

In this context Shelley's feeling for immensity and emptiness, expressed in the last two lines, justifies itself; and none of his denunciatory prophecy against kings is more effective than the ironic double application of 'Look on my works, ye Mighty, and despair'. But the grammatical construction makes it difficult at first to see the meaning of lines 6 to 9: the sculptor well perceived those passions which have now (stamped in the stone record) outlived both the sculptor's hand that imitated them and the kingly heart that nourished them. ('Mock' is said to be commonly used for 'imitate' by Shelley, but here obviously carries an undertone of contempt, too.) The sentence is fairly complex and is compressed to the point of obscurity in line 8, but it remains entirely logical and asks to be intellectually understood, not accepted as merely emotional incantation.

The need for similar close attention can be illustrated – though the difficulties here are not grammatical – in the early stanzas of *Ode to the West Wind* (1819), Leavis's critical analysis of which should be read by anyone who wants to come to grips with the problem:

> Thou on whose stream, mid the steep sky's commotion,
> Loose clouds like earth's decaying leaves are shed,
> Shook from the tangled boughs of Heaven and Ocean,
>
> Angels of rain and lightning: there are spread
> On the blue surface of thine aëry surge,
> Like the bright hair uplifted from the head
>
> Of some fierce Maenad, even from the dim verge
> Of the horizon to the zenith's height,
> The locks of the approaching storm.

Shelley watched the windy sky from a wood beside the Arno, and in the preceding section he describes the actual dead leaves being swept along by the wind. Now he sees detached bits of cloud being similarly swept along and, behind them, streaming up from the horizon, streaks and trails of cloud which he later compares with locks of hair. Before using that simile, however, he suggests that the lines of cloud are the boughs from which the cloud leaves have been blown ('tangled boughs of Heaven and Ocean' because thought of – so the footnote indicates – as vapours drawn up from the sea). Then, with a shift from the horizontal stream of wind to the vault of the sky, he sees the clouds spread from the horizon upwards 'to the zenith's height' like hair *uplifted* from the head of the Maenad, who is still below the horizon at the centre of the coming storm (not, I think, as Leavis suggests, running before it).

The passage needs specially careful reading if only because it seems not to insist on it, but to offer ample, if muddled, emotional reward to slovenly gusto. The 'angels' of rain and lightning, for instance, could conceivably be mistaken for rain and lightning themselves, heightening the emotion and increasing the confusion in a blue sky: they are of course still the loose clouds, the 'bright' hair, 'angels' in the sense of 'messengers' of the rain and lightning that Shelley says will come at nightfall. The great value of Leavis's criticism here is its challenge to flabbily emotional *reading*, though we may differ from him in estimating how far Shelley wrote in the same slack way. The reader's job is to expect a disciplined use of language and to decide for himself how far Shelley achieves it.

On the other hand, the demand for discipline must not degenerate into a cross-examination of image and metaphor along mechanically literal lines that ignore the purposes to which Shelley was choosing to put language. Some of his writing can validly be assessed by ordinary Augustan standards of clarity and effectiveness in the 'expression' of a 'thought'. Consider, for instance, the last lines of *Prometheus Unbound*, the early stanzas of *The Mask of Anarchy*, or the denunciation of reluctant monogamy in *Epipsychidion* (1821):

> ... the beaten road
> Which those poor slaves with weary footsteps tread,
> Who travel to their home among the dead
> By the broad highway of the world, and so
> With one chained friend, perhaps a jealous foe,
> The dreariest and the longest journey go.
> (*Epipsychidion*, 154–9)

The same standards are not applicable to such writing as:

> ... the dead live there
> And move like winds of light on dark and stormy air.
> (*Adonais*, xliv)

In some of the most characteristic of Shelley's poetry what is primarily conveyed is an emotional quality of outlook towards rather vaguely outlined situations and ideas, the emotional quality defining itself more precisely than the object that aroused it. In the description of the Hours, for instance, the onrushing eagerness that was one aspect of Shelley receives convincing expression, partly through the rhythm, the vowel choice, the assonance, and other sound effects, partly through the ideas and visual imagery:

> The rocks are cloven, and through the purple night
> I see cars drawn by rainbow-wingèd steeds
> Which trample the dim winds: in each there stands
> A wild-eyed charioteer urging their flight.
> Some look behind, as fiends pursued them there,
> And yet I see no shapes but the keen stars:
> Others, with burning eyes, lean forth, and drink
> With eager lips the wind of their own speed,
> As if the thing they loved fled on before,
> And now, even now, they clasped it. Their bright locks
> Stream like a comet's flashing hair: they all
> Sweep onward.
>
> (*Prometheus Unbound*, II, iv)

What he contemplates with such intense eagerness is the stream of destined events. Nothing in the context of the drama makes it necessary that the hours of destiny, for one of which Prometheus has been waiting in long-drawn-out torment, should now be seen flying past at such breathless speed. But this burning anticipation and wondering excitement is a state of mind that Shelley valued, and the imagery of the Hours seems to have risen as part of the spontaneous occurrence of such feelings and to have stimulated ideas and language that would convey them effectively although without providing 'reasonable' causes for experiencing them.

For the emotional quality of language to reinforce the sense is familiar enough, but a passage like this description of the Hours goes much further towards the expression of emotion without support from a stated theme. In ordinary experience, and much literature, such direct generation of mood and emotion comes most commonly from the contemplation of natural things – storms, waves, sunlight, birdsong, and so forth. Nature consequently meant much more to the Romantics, who were eager to take emotional states seriously, from whatever source they rose, than it did to the Augustans, who were more concerned to relate their emotions to a reasoned structure of values. In many of his poems Shelley bases himself on the emotion induced in him by some natural event – a skylark's song or the rising west wind – and then finds some other feature of human life to which the emotion is fitting – the poet's role or the loss of youthful impetuosity and the yearning to be revivified in later life. When Shelley starts from his response to the natural event, we notice nothing strange in the emotion or in the introduction of analogous human experience. His method becomes rather less familiar when he provides his own fantasy images, as he does in the description of the Hours (and as we all do in dreams), and it then becomes clearer that he is starting out from an emotional state and finding images and ideas with which to bring it into the realm of thought.

Movement in this direction – from feeling states to images and ideas – may be usual, but in most people formulated thought and logical control establish themselves, for better or worse, at an earlier stage than they appear to in Shelley. He has only words with which to express mood, attitude, and emotional state, and the words cannot operate unless they are conveying ideas as well. The relatively greater emphasis that he places on the emotional states than on the more precise and checkable ideas in which they issue can lead to thinness and confusion, but can at times give lines of remarkable and satisfying complexity. Some of the stanzas towards the end of the long, high-pitched course of *Adonais* illustrate well how his mind worked. In stanzas xxxviii to xlvii he is expressing his belief in Keats's union through death with the universal and eternal spirit. There are fine lines here and there –

> From the contagion of the world's slow stain
> He is secure

– but the passage as a whole is a rather conventional effusion, a basically simple statement made with great emotional heightening.

Stanza xlviii nominally introduces a variant of the same theme, but in reality the five stanzas xlviii to lii hold much greater complexity than the preceding ten. It is when he restates the theme in terms of a concrete situation – 'Or go to Rome ...' – that a richer pattern of attitudes presents itself. Previously he was content to think in abstract terms of the poet (but not his reviewer) as a portion of the Eternal:

> Dust to the dust! but the pure spirit shall flow
> Back to the burning fountain whence it came,

and his death as something not to be lamented:

> He hath awakened from the dream of life –
> 'Tis we, who lost in stormy visions, keep
> With phantoms an unprofitable strife.

Beneath this simple view, however, lie conflicting attitudes, which begin to emerge as Shelley contemplates Rome and the Protestant cemetery. The first step is to leave the idea of Keats's union with the Eternal and affirm the earthly survival of his works among those of other

> kings of thought
> Who waged contention with their time's decay
> And of the past are all that cannot pass away.

But 'time's decay' turns him to its appearance in the Roman setting where it has aspects of immense appeal, and the next two stanzas depict the beauty that surrounds the dead amidst the wreckage of the city:

> Go thou to Rome – at once the Paradise,
> The grave, the city, and the wilderness;
> And where its wrecks like shattered mountains rise,
> And flowering weeds, and fragrant copses dress
> The bones of Desolation's nakedness
> Pass, till the spirit of the spot shall lead
> Thy footsteps to a slope of green access
> Where, like an infant's smile, over the dead
> A light of laughing flowers along the grass is spread.

The conflicting aspects of the city – simultaneously Paradise and grave – form a setting for the juxtaposition, in the last lines, of death with continuing, unregarding life. The 'infant's smile' which at first sounds sentimental conveys the irrelevant, uncomprehending gaiety of the flowers, a contrast reinforced in the next stanza by the picture of recent graves standing in cheerful sunlight:

> And gray walls moulder round, on which dull Time
> Feeds, like slow fire upon a hoary brand;
> And one keen pyramid with wedge sublime,
> Pavilioning the dust of him who planned
> This refuge for his memory, doth stand
> Like flame transformed to marble; and beneath,

A field is spread, on which a newer band
Have pitched in Heaven's smile their camp of death,
Welcoming him we lose with scarce extinguished breath.

That stanza also introduces, in the reference to the ancient tomb of Caius Cestius, the possibility of the long survival of a material memorial in great beauty, and so dissipates still further the earlier concentration on the Eternal alone.

Contrasting with the high-flown effort to rejoice in Keats's entry into the Eternal, stanza li voices the ordinary human sense of grief in bereavement, making it more personal by the reference to William Shelley's grave. And then Shelley breaks abruptly into his own sense of protest at the world, and sees death neither as a matter for grief nor positively as a reunion with the universal, but regressively as a refuge from the pains of living:

From the world's bitter wind
Seek shelter in the shadow of the tomb.

Immediately afterwards he recovers the nominal theme:

What Adonais is, why fear we to become?

But the recovery comes with an illogical jerk, for we have certainly not been asked previously to think of Adonais as seeking shelter in the tomb.

Some of the contrasting and at times inconsistent ideas in these stanzas seem to have reached expression partly through verbal associations that we could call 'accidental' were it not that they evidently gave openings for important variants of attitude to emerge. 'Time's decay' that the kings of thought defy leads to the physical evidence of it in Rome; the ancient monument, a 'refuge' for memory, later produces the 'shelter' of the tomb; the tears and 'gall' that await every one of us suggest the world's 'bitter' wind that immediately follows. In this way the manipulation of – the partial surrender to – language becomes a means by which ideas and attitudes are discovered and released – not a tool for 'expressing' them after previous sifting.

All through these stanzas there have been incompatibilities and partly concealed conflicts of attitude. The reaffirmation of the immortality theme is itself in the form of a question that admits the fear of death –

What Adonais is, why fear we to become?

– a question echoed a little later in the line

Why linger, why turn back, why shrink, my heart?

Shelley in these stanzas has been swinging in unstable equilibrium between his nominal welcoming of eternity (allied with a regressive longing for death as an escape from the bitterness of the world) and his keen appreciation of the beauty of life and earthly things despite their transience (allied with his grief in bereavement).

The opening of stanza lii attempts to recapture the convincingness of the immortality theme, but with much too explicit a statement –

> The One remains, the many change and pass;
> Heaven's light forever shines, Earth's shadows fly;

– lines that might belong to the poorer hymnody of the nineteenth century. But when, characteristically, he explores further among the possibilities of light and eternity, instead of a well-worn poeticism he produces the lines

> Life, like a dome of many-coloured glass,
> Stains the white radiance of Eternity,
> Until Death tramples it to fragments.

– lines that are not only vivid but extraordinarily concentrated and accurate in their expression of the cluster of attitudes and partly formed ideas, some mutually conflicting, that Shelley has been exploring. The crucial word is 'stains': on the one hand it suggests a stain blemishing the radiance of eternity ('the world's slow stain'), but on the other it refers to the colourful interest of life which makes Shelley compare it with a dome of stained glass (interposed between the pure spirit and the burning fountain whence it came). Lest the value of eternity should be overstated, the value of life is emphasized by the suggestion of brutal destruction in the way it ends and its vulnerability before the vastness of Death; instead of the colours of life recombining to find fulfilment in the white radiance (as the nominal theme would demand) life persists in its colourfulness

> Until Death tramples it to fragments.

The lines are so remarkably effective because they succeed – to use the concept developed by I. A. Richards – in achieving a momentary stable equilibrium among ideas and attitudes that usually conflict or alternate. In the preceding stanzas we can watch the conflicts and alternations actually occurring as Shelley, surrendered to his fluency, gives spontaneous expression to the contrasting aspects of his emotional state.

The whole passage illustrates the way he poured out emotionally-toned and sometimes only half-formulated ideas 'In profuse strains of unpremeditated art'. *To a Skylark* (1820) states revealingly his ideals as a poet. The profusion is a characteristic on which he could well have valued himself less. The unpremeditated outpouring of the full heart suggests the use of language for as direct as possible an expression of emotional states, dependent as little as possible upon intellectual analysis and ordering. Yet the notion is included of the 'Poet hidden/ In the light of thought', and *Adonais* puts Keats among 'the kings of thought'.

Shelley would obviously not have been content with emotional outpourings devoid of thought, but from his practice it seems equally obvious that for him thought is valid only as part of a more inclusive state of being and has to be judged by its truth to the matrix of mood and attitude from which it emerges. He stands remote from the important line of English poetry in which exact thinking interpenetrates emotion and seems to give it a structure it would otherwise have lacked. In Shelley's poetry, discursive thought does little or nothing to bring more order into his emotional states than they had already achieved in their pre-verbal existence.

NOTES

1. *The Romantic Agony* (London, 1933).
2. *Revaluation* (London, 1936).

JOHN KEATS

WILLIAM WALSH

'I am ambitious of doing the world some good:' Keats (1795–1821) wrote to Richard Woodhouse, 'if I should be spared that may be the work of maturer years – in the interval I will assay to reach to as high a summit in Poetry as the nerve bestowed upon me will suffer.'[1] 'The nerve bestowed' upon Keats was a poetic endowment of an exquisite and powerful kind. It would be hard to name anyone in the nineteenth century with natural gifts of genius and character superior to his. Secure in their possession, he could even hold as an axiom 'That if Poetry comes not as naturally as the Leaves to a tree it had better not come at all'.[2] But the truth was that Keats's best poetry did not come 'naturally' at all, it came only as the result of a sustained and deliberate effort of self-education. Indeed, an essential clue to the understanding of Keats's poetic life, that astonishing passage from Cockney to classic, is an educational one, since Keats's career is the most brilliant example in literature of the education of a sensibility.

For Keats began his poetic life with a corrupted sensibility. The career of most artists moves from simplicity to complexity, from uncertainty to assurance, or from illusion to reality. The direction of Keats's progress, in ironic contrast with that of his body, was from sickness to health. With tradition in decline, family ineffective, education inadequate, and contemporaries supine or uncomprehending, it requires gifts of genius and heroism of character, and both arduously and perseveringly developed, to arrive at that health and order which other poets in more fortunate times have started from.

The first works of a young poet are more frequently expressions of the intent to be a poet than exercises of a poet's powers. They are also, almost necessarily, derivative. In Keats's case the influence of Spenser is distinct – not the homely, English and moral Spenser,

but the cultivator of the enamelled and the musical, and in particular
Spenser as mediated by the eighteenth-century imitators Thomson
and Beattie. These early poems also exhibit, often with pitiless clarity,
the modes of sensibility current at the time. The character of those
of Keats's time may be inferred from a remark in a letter from
Haydon to Keats. (The remark was in fact made about *Endymion*,
1818.) 'I have read your delicious poem with exquisite enjoyment.'
The poems in Keats's first volume, *Poems*, published in 1817 by
C. and J. Ollier (although these publishers were rapidly to be replaced
by John Taylor and James Hessey when the book proved to be a
disastrous flop) are generally notable for their lack of organization
and internal complexity. Most of them are to some degree agitated
by the anxiety which deeply troubled Keats at this time, namely
the question as to whether or not he had the talent to become a
poet. Indeed, in Stillinger's view this is the true ordering principle
of the poems and the criterion by which Keats chose poems to be
included.[3] Of structure they have little more than the external verse
pattern and a single generalization or introductory remark followed
by a long catalogue of more or less pertinent examples. The characteristic mood is one of romantic pain, 'sweet desolation' – 'balmy pain';
the characteristic pose is one of indulgent relaxation:

> So when I am in a voluptuous vein
> I pillow my head on the sweets of the rose;

and the characteristic place:

> Some flowery spot sequester'd, wild, romantic; ...

Those moments of the past are significant which produced an intoxi-
cated retreat from the rough edges of reality:

> But many days have passed since last my heart
> Was warmed luxuriously by divine Mozart; ...

The staple of the idiom is composed of such phrases as warm desires,
coy muse, quaint jubilee, curious bending, luxuries bright, milky,
soft and rosy, luxurious wings, pleasant smotherings. The un-
expressed premise of these poems is that poetry is a drug, a more
refined form of alcohol. But art, says Santayana,

so long as it needs to be a dream, will never cease to prove a disappointment.
Its facile cruelty, its narcotic abstraction, can never sweeten the evils we return

to at home; it can liberate half the mind only by leaving the other half in abeyance.[4]

Undoubtedly a part of Keats's mind, the more critical and intelligent part, was in abeyance during the composition of many of these poems – but not wholly so. There are moments when the indolence gives way to a more energetic, a more keenly apprehensive grasp, when the fumes of indulgence are dispersed by a fresher air. At these moments the verse shows a more biting sense of reality, a firmer rhythm, a more particularized sort of imagery, and a use of language at once more strenuous and more controlled. Here is an example:

> A pigeon tumbling in clear summer air;
> A laughing schoolboy without grief or care
> Riding the springy branches of an elm.
>
> (*Sleep and Poetry*)

And here are other lines enlivened by an unpretentious gaiety and simplicity in the manner of Herrick:

> The stalks and blades
> Chequer my tablet with their quivering shades
> On one side is a field of drooping oats
> Through which the poppies show their scarlet coats,
> So pert and useless, that they bring to mind
> The scarlet coats that pester human kind.
>
> (*To My Brother George*)

There is also that more modest, objective and very successful poem, *On the Grasshopper and the Cricket*. The significance of these stirrings of a more complete, a more responsible mind, and a less partial response to experience is corroborated by evidence of a more explicit sort. Keats was becoming aware that a poet could not remain content to loll a prisoner of his own senses; his sensations must be filtered through a judging mind and be informed by deliberate thought:

> though no great ministering reason sorts
> Out the dark mysteries of human souls
> To clear conceiving: yet there ever rolls
> A vast idea before me, and I glean
> Therefrom my liberty; . . .
>
> (*Sleep and Poetry*)

(The trouble, of course, is that a due poetic relation of sensation to thought is not achieved by mulling over specific sensations in the light of a vast idea, as *Lamia* and *Hyperion* are later to show. A relationship more intimate and more informing is required, in which sensation and thought are not divided by the discrepancy implied in Keats's lines but exhibit what Coleridge called 'a coincidence of subject and object'.) Again, in the Preface to *Endymion* (1818) Keats confesses himself troubled by just the imperfections we have noted:

> the reader ... will soon perceive great inexperience, immaturity and every error denoting a feverish attempt, rather than a deed accomplished ... The imagination of a boy is healthy, and the mature imagination of a man is healthy; but there is a space of life between in which the soul is in a ferment, the character undecided, the way of life uncertain, the ambition thick-sighted: thence proceeds mawkishness ...

Mawkish is perhaps too severe an epithet to apply to *Endymion* but not to the *Poems*. It is no surprise indeed that Keats's own criticism of himself is so just and pointed. Keats, in Eliot's view, never once made an inaccurate or unwarranted judgement on poetry itself. In the comment just quoted Keats points unerringly to the profound weakness in *Poems*, the existence, by implication at least, of two Keatses. Arnold discerned this double character when he divided the man with flint and iron in him from the merely sensual one, John from Johnnie Keats. Leavis remarked in Keats's poems, on the one hand 'a wilful delimitation of the "true" or "real" in experience, a focussing of the vision so as to shut out the uncongenial' *and* an 'irresistible rush of joyous energy'. John Jones, the most ardent of Keatsean critics, discriminates between the romantic Keats and the unique Keats. He quotes from 'In drear-nighted December' the line 'The feel of not to feel it', to illustrate his distinction. The substance of this lies in the difference between 'feel' and 'feeling'. 'Feeling' is romantic, 'feel' is Keatsean. 'Feeling' is entangled with ideas, explanations, consequences, and connections; 'feel' is pure, absolute, sensational, that 'wrapping up of sense' which in John Jones's view is the essence of Keatsean achievement.

It will be clear that with Arnold and Leavis I also have been assuming this double Keats, or rather, this twofold strain in the personality and the art. It is indeed hard not to do so when one sees in the letters the intellectual and moral struggle of a brilliantly gifted mind and nature, and contrasts the profound maturity and the quality of humanity manifested there with such poems as 'Woman! when I behold Thee':

> Woman! when I behold thee flippant, vain,
>   Inconstant, childish, proud, and full of fancies;
>   Without that modest softening that enhances
> The downcast eye, repentant of the pain ...
>
> Light feet, dark violet eyes, and parted hair;
>   Soft dimpled hands, white neck, and creamy breast,
>   Are things on which the dazzled senses rest
> Till the fond, fixed eyes, forget they stare ...
>
> Ah! who can e'er forget so fair a being?
>   Who can forget her half-retiring sweets?
>   God! she is like a milk-white lamb that bleats
> For man's protection ...

in which pretentious Regency masculinity is combined with that sugar-plum sense of sex that Arnold discerned in Keats. Arnold and Leavis, then, see Keats's career as the history and friction of these two elements in his nature and they judge his higher achievement to be those poems in which one is quite ousted by the other. But there are those, John Bayley in his *Keats and Reality* and Christopher Ricks in *Keats and Embarrassment* are the most significant, who want to bring Keats's sensuousness into the centre of his seriousness (to use the pair of terms that Dr Leavis put into circulation):

Mr Bayley argued that Keats's genius was essentially 'unmisgiving' – the word was Leigh Hunt's, and Mr Bayley held that the influence of Hunt was truly benign; the central Keats is the rich poet of *Endymion* and 'The Eve of St Agnes', rather than the sombre mature poet (strained and against the grain) of, say, *The Fall of Hyperion*. Keats's art at its best risks vulgarity: 'It turns what might appear mean and embarrassing into what is rich and *disconcerting.*'

Christopher Ricks's modification of John Bayley's view is to want to extend it:

I think, then, that Mr Bayley was rather too eager to see the embarrassing in Keats give way to something nobler, whereas the nobility of Keats (the man and the poet) is very much a matter of his not flinching from embarrassment while at the same time thinking it always inextricably involved in important moral concerns ... The case for a great deal that is best in Keats is the case for that space of life, adolescence; or rather for a recognition and incorporation of those insights into life which may be more accessible to a perceptive adolescent than to others.[5]

In Ricks's view Keats was peculiarly sensitive to the nature of embarrassment and he insists that we cannot understand the shape of Keats's imagination or his special goodness as a man and a poet unless we see an ambivalence of feeling as characteristic of his truest imagination. 'For a particular strength of Keats is the implication that the youthful, the luxuriant, the immature, can be, not just excusable errors, but vantage-points.'

The presence of this adolescent Keats is certainly substantial in *Poems* and *Endymion*, which Keats worked on during visits to the Isle of Wight, Magdalen Hall, Oxford (with his friend Benjamin Bailey), and Burford Bridge near Box Hill. His original publishers having parted from him in considerable annoyance and distaste at the lack of success of *Poems*, *Endymion* was published by a more sympathetic publisher, Taylor and Hessey.

The most notable of Keats's biographical critics, Walter Jackson Bate, Robert Gittings and Aileen Ward, find the interest of *Endymion* primarily in that, having occupied eight months of Keats's short career and representing a large proportion of his poetry, it was bound to be of great significance in his development. Keats himself spoke of the poem in an ashamed way as mawkish, and contemporary critics were much harsher. 'The phrenzy of the *Poems*,' for example, wrote Lockhart in *Blackwood's Edinburgh Magazine*, 'was bad enough in its way; but it did not alarm us half so seriously as the calm, settled, imperturbable drivelling idiocy of *Endymion*.' George Santayana clearly voices in his own way the reaction of many unprejudiced contemporary readers:

Long passages in Shelley's *Revolt of Islam* and Keats's *Endymion* are poetical in this sense; the reader gathers, probably, no definite meaning, but is conscious of a poetic medium, of speech euphonious and measured, and redolent of a kind of objectless passion which is little more than the sensation of the movement and sensuous richness of the lines.[6]

John Jones, perhaps Keats's most sympathetic critic, writes:

Endymion is a rambling storehouse of pleasures, but of pleasures which claim a new gravity by doting on their own fair features and murmuring from time to time, 'Beauty!' This narcissistic exercise does more than anything else to make the poem the airless, eventless, self-caressing thing it so dis-agreeably is.[7]

Keats himself thought of *Endymion* as something in which he took 'the bare circumstance' from his earlier poem 'I Stood Tip-toe upon a Little Hill', pieced it out with information from Lemprière's *Classical Dictionary*, and made 4,000 lines of poetry from it. The fable, a mortal's search for the divine ultimately found embodied in the human, was both incapable of realizing the unconscious forces of Keats's genius and of being a spring of life or of realizing the deepest sorts of experience which he was analysing at this time in his letters. Contemporary critics objected to what they saw as the immature sexuality in the poem, and certainly it is unpleasantly fingering and narcissistic:

> Sideway his face reposed
> On one white arm, and tenderly unclosed,
> By tenderest pressure, a faint damask mouth
> To slumbery pout; just as the morning south
> Disparts a dew-lipped rose.

The poem is without any intrinsic distinction, the effect is mellifluous and trivial, and it is difficult to take it seriously in spite of the serious-ness of its intention. There is no leading idea, unless we call Endymion's search for pleasure one, and that is hardly remarkable in the detail. It appears to be the result of no particular pressure, and engages nothing that exists at a deeper level. Its aesthetic insipidity is all too rarely interrupted by the drive of Keats's potent creative energy.

There would be no need to qualify these remarks very radically to have them apply with equal force to *Isabella, or the Pot of Basil* (1820). This is a poetical version of an anecdote drawn from the fourth day in Boccaccio's *Decameron*. *Lamia* (1820) derives from Burton and uses a myth with a long history stretching back in English literature to the late fourteenth- or early fifteenth-century *Thomas of Erceldoune*. But *Lamia* differs from *Isabella* in that it is meant to present a serious idea; it is a poem written to the formula of the 'vast idea'. It is still plangent and melancholy, but slower and fuller in movement. The poem endeavours to represent – but as in a tableau rather than a drama – the conflict between illusory beauty and the hallucination of pleasure and the life of the intellect and moral dignity.

Lycius, the normal man, is caught and destroyed between the two. But there is an excessive disproportion between the important ideas formally involved and the essentially literary idiom and manner.

That discrepancy is abolished in *The Eve of St Agnes* (1819). The poem is much less pretentious than *Lamia*; no vast idea rolls before the poet's eye. He remains within the limitations of a subject which gives him without pressing or manipulation natural opportunities for realizing his extraordinary perception of glow, richness and colour in the physical world. The exigencies of the narrative, slight as they are, control his delight in luxury and give it due subordination as one element in experience. Keats successfully resists the temptation merely to indulge his 'sensual vision'. The figure of Madeline, delicate and uncharacterized as it is, is more than an example of what Keats called the 'tendency to class women in my books with roses and sweetmeats'. Throughout the poem the imagery has, even in those scenes which could easily become occasions for uncritical relaxed indulgence, a certain quality of coolness and crispness, and a scope of metaphorical reference, which keep it from being ludicrous or merely sensual.

> And still she slept an azure-lidded sleep,
> In blanched linen, smooth, and lavender'd,
> While he from forth the closet brought a heap
> Of candied apple, quince, and plum, and gourd;
> With jellies soother than the creamy curd,
> And lucent syrops, tinct with cinnamon;
> Manna and dates, in argosy transferr'd
> From Fez; and spiced dainties, every one,
> From silken Samarcand to cedar'd Lebanon.

'Azure-lidded' is keen and exact; 'blanched' and 'lavender'd' introduce more than the purity of the linen; the gesture of bringing forth the gorgeous fruits from a closet encloses them in reality; the word 'lucent' really lets in light, and 'tinct' is minutely precise – signs that the eye is on the object; the references to Fez and Samarcand have a generalizing, idealizing effect, and 'cedar'd Lebanon' supports the whole with the grave authority of the Bible. The total effect is both rich and severe.

Between *Endymion* (November 1817) and the great Odes (April– May 1819) Keats was, it is clear, astonishingly transformed, advancing from the status of a charming minor talent to that of a genius of the first order. It was not a steady progression or a total transmutation. There was overlapping and backgliding. Still, the progression was extraordinary. As I see it, that development is in essence a brilliant, profound and exemplary exercise in self-education. We can trace in Keats's letters the double course of moral and intellectual development which was entailed for him in the education of his sensibility. Here it is possible only to summarize brutally the luminous evidence in his letters of his intricate, arduous progress in self-discipline. At the roots of it there lay a certain kind of decision. The young poet begins with a primary poetic sensibility, 'the knowledge of contrast, feeling for light and shade, all that information (primitive sense) necessary for a poem'. There is no doubt that there is delight to be had, both for the poet and readers in the uninhibited play of this 'primitive sense'; but it is like the graceful, fluent gestures of childhood, supple but not subtle, free but not disciplined, exquisite but not serious. But no young poet any more than any young person becomes adult by the mere progression of original endowment. It also requires effort, conscience, thought. The man at a certain point in his life, the poet at a certain point in his career – it may be earlier or later – must make a fundamental choice, a moral decision.

For Keats this radical election assumed a variety of forms. 'I think a little change has taken place in my intellect lately – I cannot bear to be uninterested or unemployed, I, who for so long a time, have been addicted to passiveness.' Or again: 'I hope I am a little more of a Philosopher than I was, consequently a little less of a versifying Pet-lamb.' Or in another place: 'Some think I have lost that poetic ardour and fire 't is said I once had – the fact is perhaps I have: but instead of that I hope I shall substitute for it a more thoughtful and quiet power.' Perhaps these words put the choice most nakedly: 'I must choose between despair & Energy – I choose the latter.' Following on this decision there came the long effort 'to refine one's sensual vision' by acquiring the virtues of the disciplined mind. These were, according to Keats's reading of his life, integrity or a consistent moral attitude, generosity and disillusion or tolerance and a tonic sense of reality, energy and patience, independence and a rational humility. And finally, as a result both of these qualities and of the struggle to achieve them, he attained to the recognition and accept-ance of a mature conception of man, the view of man as at least potentially responsible and moral, and therefore tragic and not wholly passive, conformist and perfectible. Some writers, as for example Coleridge with his philosophical bent, take such a development to be a growth in self-knowledge – which of course it is; an increasing understanding both of a common human nature as well as of that peculiar modification of it which makes each individual unique; a deepening apprehension of 'the each in all and the all in each'. But for Keats as poet the ontological preceded the cognitive; being was the ground of recognition. And in Keats's eyes the education of sensibility, the qualities engendered in the course of it, the interplay of various elements of human nature, even the circumstances of our life – all these are preparatory and subordinate not just to a fuller discovery of self but to its actual constitution. Every human life was spent in the struggle to establish what Keats called 'a sense of identity'. Keats thought of the world as a place in which we alter nature, where we construct from our experience and whatever lies to hand a personal identity, in which we school an intelligence and make it a soul. Human life was 'a vale of soul-making'.

The fruit of Keats's maturing mind and sensibility is the set of four odes, *On Melancholy*, *To a Nightingale*, *On a Grecian Urn*, and *To Autumn* written in 1819, the first three during the early months of the year. These poems are different in kind from their predecessors; while the earlier ones are merely decorative, these are enlarged and complicated by a dimension of human experience unknown in the former. Their distance from the earlier poems may be indicated by saying that while Spenser is the dominant influence there, here it is Shakespeare; and not Shakespeare as the supplier of external literary tricks like Shelley's Shakeapeare in *The Cenci*, but a Shakespeare who is grasped, subordinated to Keats's purposes, and dissolved in Keats's own idiom. To say this is not to claim for the poems, or for them all, a complete maturity. F. R. Leavis defined the sort of inadequacy which persists in them when he said, 'It is as if Keats were making major poetry out of minor – as if, that is, the genius of a major poet were working in the material of minor poetry'.[8] And there are, without doubt, positive weaknesses in these poems, remnants of decay, touches of nostalgic softness and moments of regression to a less-disciplined past. I can best illustrate this combination of strength and relaxation, order and impurity, by a detailed consideration of one of these poems, and for this purpose I will choose the *Ode on a Grecian Urn*. But first I must refer to the third great literary influence on Keats's poetic career and to the poem in which it is manifest, to Milton and *Hyperion*, begun in the autumn of 1818 and abandoned in April 1819.

Keats had, says Ian Jack,[9] 'visited the Isle of Wight as the author of *Endymion, A Poetic Romance*: now as he travelled northwards [Jack is referring to Keats's tour of Scotland and Ireland] he travelled as the poet of *Hyperion*, a poet whose mind was becoming the stage for an action of an epic magnitude. Whereas – as Leigh Hunt was to point out – Keats "*luxuriated* in the Isle of Wight", he looked at "the lakes and mountains of the north ... with an *epic* eye"'. It was Milton, of course, who was the exemplar of the epic eye. It is easy to see why Milton should have appealed as a model to a poet of Keats's character, and one engaged like Keats in an effort, intense and sustained, 'to refine his sensual vision'. (Not that Milton appeared as an artist actually undergoing this process of self-redemption, but rather that he showed what might be hoped for at the end of it.) There was a strong Miltonic current running in the eighteenth century, especially among those minor writers who were later to be thought of as the writers of 'true poetry', the predecessors of romanticism. Then with the rejection of Augustanism, Milton came to stand for all that was lofty, epic and severe in the English tradition. He was the solitary giant, looming and self-sufficient, and the distracted second generation romantics were profoundly impressed by his heroic individuality, his calm assumption of the poet's public robes, and the untroubled confidence with which he undertook his enormous theme. Above all, he represented a poet in his role as moral teacher and spiritual healer. But although we can see *why* Milton should have attracted Keats, we can also see *how*, in the event, Keats's choice of Milton as an exemplar was a disastrous one, as Keats himself admitted when he abandoned his project. 'Life to him would be death to me.' No two poets could have been so radically different from, so constitutionally unsympathetic to, one another; no two poetic styles could have been so naturally antagonistic. While Milton was a man of solid certainties whose slightest prejudices were liable to be erected into dogmas, Keats was one who arrived at his convictions with difficulty and held them tentatively and fluidly. Keats's use of language which accommodated itself so easily to the influence of Shakespeare was denuded of all its proper virtue when associated with Milton's. The idiom which Keats elaborated had neither the full 'beautiful curiosity' of Milton's language nor the palpable embodying power characteristic of the best of Keats himself. It was says Leavis, 'a very qualified Miltonic – Miltonic as transformed by a taste for "Spenserian vowels that elope with ease" ... The attitude towards the verse, the handling of the medium, reminds us strongly of Tennyson.'

This is a judgement which the following lines vividly confirm:

> Goddess benign, point forth some unknown thing:
> Are there not other regions than this isle?
> What are the stars? There is the sun, the sun!
> And the most patient brilliance of the moon!

The association of these names, Keats, Milton, Spenser, Tennyson, points to a discrepancy which lies at the heart of this poem. *Hyperion* was intended to be an extension of Keats's poetic experience, an effort in a new direction, and also a stage in his spiritual progress, an exercise in moral discipline; in fact, it turned out to be a contraction of the one and a retrogressive step in the case of the other. What was meant to be as strict and ascetic as Milton proved to be as ornamental as Spenser, as relaxed as Tennyson. What was designed to be a central commentary on human life disclosed itself as merely marginal and elegiac, not a vehicle for wisdom but a symptom of weakness.

The true line of Keats's development is recovered in the great Odes. These are the poems of a sensibility both powerful and exquisite, on the point of attaining its majority, on the point of completing its self-education. And because of this Keats is liable momentarily to be guilty of certain imperfections. But our recognition of these will only make us wonder all the more at the triumph of the spirit, the triumph of the lacerated spirit, which these poems, written at an unpropitious time and in the most tragic conditions, represent.

The *Ode on a Grecian Urn* was written during April 1819, at an agonizing time in Keats's life, when his money was nearly gone, his health undermined, his love-affair a cause of pain, his family dispersed or dead. If at moments the poem's lucidity as a work of art is muddled by unabsorbed personal feeling, this is hardly surprising. Such objectivity is not come by without a rare effort of character, together with an apt choice of the proper technical means.

Earl Wasserman, who believes that in the twentieth century we have lost both the skill and the conceptual understanding to read romantic poems in the way their writers intended them to be read, and who finds in a way surprising to an English critic philosophic leanings and metaphysical tendencies in Keats's odes, makes a sharp division between the *Ode to a Nightingale* and the *Ode on a Grecian Urn*.[10] The *Ode on a Grecian Urn* works out its destiny

in terms of its inherent drama, its own grammar and symbols. Its dynamic force lies within itself and is released and exploited by factors that are the property of poetry alone, and of this poem in particular ...

Ode to a Nightingale, on the other hand, he considers to be

synthetically fashioned: instead of operating within its own framework, it functions only because the poet intervenes and cuts across the grain of his materials to make them vibrant. The first is the work of art; the second the workings of art.

Many will think this an elaborate and overwhelming way of registering a more inward and natural coherence and a greater degree of impersonality and control in the *Ode on a Grecian Urn* than is to be seen in *Ode to a Nightingale*, the more personal and subjective poem. The practical means Keats chose to endow the poem with this more objective status are the remoteness of the subject, the projection of imagination that is needed to realize the Greek element in it, and the whole elaborate and informal structure of the ode.

But these comparatively external conditions imposed by the poet on himself carry only a general and predisposing influence. Closer to the poet's purpose, because more intimate with the substance of the poem, is the structure formed by the different kinds of statement out of which the poem is made. There are three sorts of statement used in the ode: address, question, and something vaguer which I shall call generalization or reflection. These three modes of statement are alike in this, that they all direct the flow of attention on to the object and away from the speaker. A vivid address, a provocative or surprising question, a brooding generalization compose a kind of discourse in which the pivotal points are the second and third persons, and the first is reduced to anonymity. This poetic use of syntax brings to Keats's rich language the authority of a more than subjective validity. It is also an example of what Matthew Arnold spoke of in Keats as 'character passing into intellectual production'.

Of course, when I speak of a statement producing a general effect throughout a poem, I am speaking of a secondary function. The first function of each statement, phrase, or even word, is to produce a precise effect in a particular place. Look at the opening address:

> Thou still unravish'd bride of quietness
> Thou foster-child of silence and slow time.

What this does is to provide a first term for the violent contrast which is the ground of the first stanza and the source of the rest of the poem. The contrast is between the form of the vase, a perfect and unchanging definition, and the tumult of action inscribed upon its surface. The images in the first part of the poem combine to stress – but that is too harsh a word, subtly to present the vase's character of arrested and timeless perfection. In doing so they call, paradoxically, on a contribution from the three dimensions of time: from the immediate, the momentarily present in 'still unravish'd bride'; from the possible and the future in 'foster-child of silence'; and from the past in 'Sylvan historian'. But Keats's symbols, like Shakespeare's, are habitually charged with more than single significance. The word 'still' keeps in simultaneous operation both the notion of enduring in time and that of tranquillity; the phrase 'still unravish'd bride' keeps in play both the idea of the present and that of uncorrupted innocence, a note which is continued in 'foster-child'. It is a foster-child, too, because it is from the hand of man, an artefact adopted by time; a natural object presumably would be just a child of time. The human quality is registered again in 'Sylvan historian', which also alerts the mind to the urn's expressive function, the urn as an organ of communication, something that is consequent on but different from its self or being, the theme of the opening couplet. The narrative or telling function of the vase introduces the next three lines, which present the content of what is told. There is another note sustained in this passage: 'Sylvan' is connected with 'flowery' and 'flowery' with 'leaf-fringed', the frame of the carvings of the urn upon the detail of which the poet's attention is now fixed:

> What leaf-fringed legend haunts about thy shape
> Of deities or mortals or of both
> In Tempe or the dales of Arcady.

'Legend' suggests first the mythical content, a development this of the sense latent in 'historian'; but legend also implies the intricacy of the carving – it is to be read, to be interpreted and not just seen; the lightness of sound of 'legend' is carried on in the aerial and ghostly 'haunts about thy shape', and evokes the fineness and delicacy of the carving, a suggestion which is strengthened by the muted and exact rhythm of the whole phrase and by the sense in 'haunts about thy shape' of hardly touching the surface; the word 'about' involving a slight labial effort in speech and with a full and open sound rounds out for us the circle of the vase's shape.

The next two lines –

> Of deities or mortals or of both
> In Tempe or the dales of Arcady

– make explicit the hint in 'legend'; they also quicken the pulse of the rhythm and prepare us for the extreme agitation of the last three lines; simultaneously, and this is a good example of the use of double and opposed potentialities of words, their cool freshness acts as a foil for the Dionysiac conclusion:

> What men or gods are these? What maidens loth?
> What mad pursuit? What struggle to escape?
> What pipes and timbrels? What wild ecstasy?

These six peremptory questions in a broken and tempestuous rhythm powerfully enforce the sexual suggestiveness of the language, and complete, as it were by opposition, the note announced in 'Thou still unravish'd bride'. At this point the stanza has described a great unerring circle from peace to violence and from innocence to passion.

There is another quality of this magnificent stanza I want to call attention to. That is the marvellously plastic use of language of such a sort that the system of apprehension assumed by the reader in response to the poet's words is a kind of model or metaphor of the physical structure of the vase, from its still centre to its turbulent surface. The language traces in the responsive mind the shape of the vessel. The next stanza has a second example of this essentially poetic power.

Heard melodies are sweet, but those unheard
Are sweeter, therefore, ye soft pipes, play on:
Not to the sensual ear but more endeared
Pipe to the spirit ditties of no tone.

These lines have not only a musical reference but a musical structure. The theme – the pre-eminence of the unrealized possibilities of silence – is announced in a generalization like a ground or bass; it is elaborated in a middle key, quicker, less deliberate; and then pointed in the words, 'Pipe to the spirit ditties of no tone', which have the clear and nimble melodic line of a composition for the flute.

The word 'therefore' in the second line concludes a poetic and not a logical argument, or more correctly it completes a piece of characteristically poetic logic. In the first stanza, silence symbolizes the timeless and unmoving, and music activity and passion. Now the poet reflects that this music carved on the urn is itself soundless, a possibility, never realized, of actual sound, a distillation of silence. At this point, music comes to stand for the perfection of the possible, for all that is superior to 'the sensual ear'. The second half of this stanza and the whole of the third stanza detail the conclusion and connect it with the instances cut in the vase – the fair youth, the trees, the bough, the happy melodist.

In this section, and particularly in the passage beginning 'More happy love! more happy, happy love!', there is, it seems to me, a decided slackening in the tightness of the poem's organization, a softening and blurring of its energy and precision. This is seen in the litter of Keatsean clichés (happy love for ever warm, a heart high-sorrowful and cloyed) and an unwarranted amount of repetition (the word 'happy' occurs six times in the stanza). The shrill insistence of the repetition shows, or rather shows up, the poet's anxiety to project a desperately desired state on to the object; he is betrayed under the pressure of his private condition into deserting his heroic detachment from self and fidelity to the object for the sake of personal psychological relief. There is a corresponding dimming of his critical conscience which leaves him unaware of the touch of caricature, of absurdity, in the table of the lover's symptoms (it seems the right term) which concludes the stanza. Significantly, these are of the hectic and feverish kind associated with Keats's own disease.

We must, I think, be conscious of an inartistic and too personal

presence of the poet's self in this last part of the stanza; but we must
also recognize the supple recovery of poise in the next one. There
we detect the taint of sickness; here we feel vitality and control,
the qualities of health. We are aware of vitality in the intensely
realized, vividly rendered scene, and in the deep, organic movement
of the rhythm; we are aware of control in the poet's pure and disinterested attitude, in the kept distance and the designed succession
of effects. The initial question – 'Who are these coming to the
sacrifice?' – works both within and without the frame of events in
the stanza; it voices both the bystander's awe and the reader's wonder,
and its effect is to place the reader there in the front rank of the
spectators. From that viewpoint he sees the procession as a brilliant
figure on a darker ground – first the priest and the animal, then,
less clearly, the more generalized crowd, 'those coming to the sacrifice', and more distantly still, the town, the generic town, on river
or sea-shore or mountain-built from which the procession comes.
The detail is rich enough to establish the reality of the procession,
and it is complex enough to be a verbal equivalent of the intricate
decoration on the vase. It is also so finely, so economically organized,
as to carry with complete lucidity a complex symbolic meaning.
A commentator can only point clumsily at the meaning the poet
offers with utter precision. I will call it, fumblingly, inadequately,
an association of the natural and the numinous. The business of
associating these two starts at the beginning of the stanza: 'Who'
quietly touches a note of surprise at the unusual; 'these' identifies
them with us, the ordinary natural occupants of the world; 'sacrifice'
is the destination which gives a tone to the whole journey; 'green
altar' fuses the two elements; and 'mysterious priest' intensifies the
feeling of religious solemnity. The association is completed in the
following couplet, when the 'heifer lowing', the familiar farm beast
richly suggestive of terrestrial good, modulates easily into the elected,
sacramental victim, 'all her silken flanks with garlands dressed'.

Keats now turns to contemplate the town, the point of departure
of the procession and the familiar centre of a communal life which
is intimate, explicable, accustomed. The idea connecting the natural
and the numinous here, the small town and the dedicated victim,
is contained in the phrase 'this pious morn'. Piety is a settled, traditional, humanized habit of religion, the bridge between the ultimate

mysteries and the simple immediacy of everyday life, symbolized in the 'little town'. And how tactfully the poet lodges the suggestion that is to be the impulse of the next movement of the poem. The town is desolate, emptied of its folk, and appropriately silent. And it is this image of silence which the poet uses as a means of transferring our attention from the decorated surface of the urn, 'with brede of marble men and maidens overwrought', to its total pattern, the silent form which teases us out of thought and the cold pastoral which holds a permanent communication for men. Keats's reading of that communication, 'Beauty is truth, truth beauty', has been the subject of endless comment. For some it is meaningless, for others an utterance of a New Testament or Dantesque grandeur. But it seems to me that a modest and attentive reader, careful not to import his metaphysics or his prejudices into the poem, can accept it as something neither so outrageous nor so formidable. Keats distinguished between fact and truth; it was the business of the organizing imagination to transfigure the one into the other. And the equivalence of beauty and truth which he asserts here is an elliptical way of making the same assertion, in place at this point in the poem, since this, the transfiguring of brute fact into imagination or poetic truth, is what the poem has been doing all along. There is a relevant remark on this theme in a letter to Bailey – 'What the imagination seizes as beauty must be truth whether it existed before or not ... the Imagination is like Adam's dream – he awoke and found it true.'

But we are, I think, quite rightly disappointed by the intrusive and over-anxious last line and a half:

> ... that is all
> Ye know on earth, and all ye need to know.

Even if we interpret the statement as sympathetically as possible, taking 'that is all' to mean 'that is the finally important thing', it still looks like an effort, ungainly and unjustified, to inflate the dignity of the poem's conclusion. It is ungainly for it suddenly puts on the poet the necessity of taking up quite a new stance and arguing a case directly. It is unjustified because it doesn't issue irresistibly from what has gone before. Keats's design on us may not be palpable at this moment but it certainly leaves us suspicious and uneasy.

The complete maturity so earnestly laboured at in Keats's life, so lucidly and persuasively theorized about in his letters, is wholly realized in Keats's art in the *Ode to Autumn*. In this poem we see genius having at its disposal a perfected sensibility. Keats's meditations on maturity, his efforts to achieve it, here issue into a disciplined poetic act. The poem exhibits, like the best Romantic poems, a radically original, first-hand response to experience, and exhibits it, moreover, with the characteristic Keatsean virtues of density and definition, weight and pressure. Autumn in this poem is neither attenuated by customary perception nor conventional expectation, nor idealized away — as in other Romantic poetry — into a thin and misty abstraction. Keats's art shows us not an ideogram, not the pictured structure of the season, but its dimensions and complex savour. For it gives us not only the fullness and softness of autumn — the ripeness of it — but also its more masculine qualities, the acrid, the rough, and the vigorous. Or rather it embodies a more inclusive conception of ripeness. Not only does it offer mellow fruitfulness and clammy cells, the fume of poppies and the last oozings, but also the moss'd cottage-trees, the granary floor, the brook, the cider press, the stubble plains, the small gnats and the river sallows. By this point in his career it is clear that ripeness had come to be for Keats both a varied and an ordered concept. It represented a rich fund of experience which had been examined and weighed by a scrupulously just and delicately balanced mind. It is no accident that the ripeness which is the theme of the poem should stand in so close an analogy to the maturity which is the theme of Keats's moral and intellectual life.

NOTES

1. *The Letters of John Keats*, 1814–1821, ed. H. E. Rollins, 2 vols (Cambridge, Mass., 1958), Vol. I, 387. (Henceforth cited as *Letters*.)

2. *Letters*, I, 238–9.

3. Jack Stillinger, *The Hoodwinking of Madeline* (Urbana, Ill. 1971) 5.

4. George Santayana, *The Life of Reason* (New York, 1905), Vol, IV, 212.

5. Christopher Ricks, *Keats and Embarrassment* (Oxford, 1974), 7–8, 9–11.

6. George Santayana, *Interpretations of Poetry and Religion* (New York and London, 1957), 256.

7. John Jones, *John Keats's Dream of Truth* (London, 1969), 128–9.

8. F. R. Leavis, *Revaluation* (London, 1936), 251.

9. Ian Jack, *Keats and the Mirror of Art* (Oxford, 1967), 106.

10. Earl Wasserman, *The Finer Tone* (Baltimore, 1953), 179.

LORD BYRON

J. D. JUMP

'Sir, I have quarrelled with my wife; and a man who has quarrelled with his wife is absolved from all duty to his country. I have written an ode to tell the people as much, and they may take it as they list.' The speaker is Mr Cypress, the poet. He is visiting an old friend before leaving England, and he does not hesitate to exhibit his 'lacerated spirit'.

I have no hope for myself or for others. Our life is a false nature; it is not in the harmony of things; it is an all-blasting upas, whose root is earth, and whose leaves are the skies which rain their poison-dews upon mankind. We wither from our youth; we gasp with unslaked thirst for unattainable good; lured from the first to the last by phantoms – love, fame, ambition, avarice – all idle, and all ill – one meteor of many names, that vanishes in the smoke of death.
(*Nightmare Abbey*, XI).

These words echo Byron's *Childe Harold's Pilgrimage* (IV, 124, 126); and Mr Cypress is a portrait of Byron (1788–1824) as he was known to readers in 1818, the year in which Peacock's *Nightmare Abbey* appeared.

By this date, Byron had become famous as the author of *Childe Harold's Pilgrimage* and of a number of tales in verse. He had popularized the Byronic hero, so well described thirteen years later by Macaulay, in his review of Moore's *Life of Byron*, as 'a man proud, moody, cynical, with defiance on his brow, and misery in his heart, a scorner of his kind, implacable in revenge, yet capable of deep and strong affection'. But the poems which seemed to have been written by a Mr Cypress tell only part of the truth about Byron; another very important part finds expression, both before and after 1818, in his incomparable letters and journals.

At their most completely representative, these are obviously unrehearsed in thought and spontaneous in expression. In fact, they probably give a truer impression of Byron's conversation in congenial

company than do most of what purport to be records of his talk.[1]
Here is his version of a story concerning a young British junior officer
who had been separated from the Italian lady he loved by the outbreak of war between England and France; but who, when the fall of
Napoleon a quarter of a century later restored peace, returned as a
colonel to claim her:

Six-and-twenty years ago, Col. [Fitzgerald], then an ensign, being in Italy,
fell in love with the Marchesa [Castiglione], and she with him. The lady
must be, at least, twenty years his senior. The war broke out; he returned
to England, to serve – not his country, for that's Ireland – but England,
which is a different thing; and *she* – heaven knows what she did. In the
year 1814, the first annunciation of the Definitive Treaty of Peace (and
tyranny) was developed to the astonished Milanese by the arrival of Col.
[Fitzgerald], who, flinging himself full length at the feet of Mad. [Castiglione],
murmured forth, in half-forgotten Irish Italian, eternal vows of indelible
constancy. The lady screamed, and exclaimed, 'Who are you?' The Colonel
cried, 'What! don't you know me? I am so and so,' etc., etc., etc.; till, at
length, the Marchesa, mounting from reminiscence to reminiscence, through
the lovers of the intermediate twenty-five years, arrived at last at the recollection of her *povero* sub-lieutenant. She then said, 'Was there ever such virtue?'
(that was her very word) and, being now a widow, gave him apartments
in her palace, reinstated him in all the rights of wrong, and held him up
to the admiring world as a miracle of incontinent fidelity, and the unshaken
Abdiel of absence.

(24 December 1816[2])

This is one of the many occasions on which Byron scoffs at 'sentimental and sensibilitous' (29 June 1811) persons. The romantic lover,
murmuring forth 'eternal vows of indelible constancy', does so in
'half-forgotten Irish Italian'; as the Marchesa peers back into her
love-life, the structure of the sentence ludicrously reflects the stages
by which she mounts to the recollection of her suitor; and it is the
irony of a gay and resourceful *raconteur* which plays upon her praise
of Fitzgerald's 'virtue', her reinstatement of him 'in all the rights of
wrong', and her upholding him 'as a miracle of incontinent fidelity'.
The story is a little satirical comedy characterized by a lightly mocking treatment of human absurdities. It could never have been told by
a Mr Cypress.

The impetuosity of Byron's utterance becomes particularly evident
on the many occasions when he makes humorous use of the catalogue.

In this account of a party at which 'all was hiccup and happiness for the last hour or so', he lists the eight stages of conviviality:

> Yesterday, I dined out with a large-ish party ... Like other parties of the kind, it was first silent, then talky, then argumentative, then disputatious, then unintelligible, then altogethery, then inarticulate, and then drunk. When we had reached the last step of this glorious ladder, it was difficult to get down again without stumbling; and, to crown all, Kinnaird and I had to conduct Sheridan down a damned corkscrew staircase, which had certainly been constructed before the discovery of fermented liquors, and to which no legs, however crooked, could possibly accommodate themselves.
>
> (31 October 1815)

'Altogethery' is a delightful coinage. The passage as a whole owes much to the flexibility, vigour, and raciness of its language. Or, as in a later letter (7 November 1822), Byron's humour can take the form of fanciful and nonsensical inventions appended to reported facts; and then we have delighted observation, exuberant fancy, and cheerful volubility. But Byron's humour can be of a more aggressive kind. Somebody wrote a bad biography of his friend, Thomas Moore. Byron read it and wrote to Moore: 'The biographer has made a botch of your life ... If that damned fellow was to *write my* life, I would certainly *take his*' (9 June 1820).

But he was not always jocose. There was certainly a darker side to his nature. Throughout his life he was subject to feelings of profound gloom. Trying to account for their incidence, he says: 'People have wondered at the Melancholy which runs through my writings. Others have wondered at my personal gaiety.' He quotes his wife as having reconciled the two views by saying, 'at *heart* you are the most melancholy of mankind, and often when apparently gayest'. He goes on to hint at 'the *real* causes which have contributed to increase this perhaps *natural* temperament of mine'. But to tell them 'is impossible without doing much mischief' (*Detached Thoughts*, 73 and 74).

No doubt a hope of escaping from his low spirits partly motivated his persistent search for excitement. He held that 'a little *tumult*, now and then, is an agreeable quickener of sensation; such as a revolution, a battle, or an *aventure* of any lively description' (*Journal*, 22 November 1813). He went further than this. 'The great object of life is sensation – to feel that we exist, even though in pain. It is this "craving void" which drives us to gaming – to battle – to travel – to intemperate, but keenly felt pursuits of any description, whose principal attraction is the agitation inseparable from their accomplishment' (6 September 1813: *Letters*, III, 400). Living in accordance with these doctrines, he spoke scornfully of those who could achieve a placid contentment.

Lord, Lord, [he wrote to Moore] if these home-keeping minstrels had crossed your Atlantic or my Mediterranean, and tasted a little open boating in a white squall – or a gale in 'the Gut' – or the 'Bay of Biscay', with no gale at all – how it would enliven and introduce them to a few of the sensations! – to say nothing of an illicit amour or two upon shore, in the way of essay upon the Passions, beginning with simple adultery, and compounding it as they went along.

(3 August 1814)

Byron had 'no great esteem for poetical persons' (*Journal*, 26 November 1813).

I do think the preference of *writers* to *agents* – the mighty stir made about scribbling and scribes, by themselves and others – a sign of effeminacy, degeneracy, and weakness. Who would write, who had any thing better to do? ... Look at the querulous and monotonous lives of the 'genus'; ... – what a worthless, idle brood it is!

(*Journal*, 24 November 1813)

Apart from Scott, Gifford, and Moore, all the writers he had met had had 'more or less of the author about them – the pen peeping from behind the ear, and the thumbs a little inky, or so' (25 March 1817). Later, he grew less hostile; but he still found writers difficult socially: 'I never know what to say to them after I have praised their last publication' (*Detached Thoughts*, 53).

His preference for agents, or doers, was perfectly sincere. He had himself many of the abilities proper to a man of action; and during his last months he was exercising these in a cause which had his determined support. Even before leaving Italy, he was making severely practical suggestions as to what the Greek insurgents needed: 'first, a park of field artillery – light, and fit for mountain-service; secondly, gunpowder; thirdly, hospital or medical stores' (12 May 1823). These contrast sharply with the high-minded but much less realistic proposals of the committee formed in London to aid the Greeks against the Turks.

Three years earlier, Byron had tried to make a practical contribution to the liberation of Italy from foreign rule. In a diary which he kept for a short time when his hopes in this connection were at their highest, he declares repeatedly his faith in freedom. Even more memorable than these entries is a letter of the same period in which his loathing of tyranny finds haughty and spirited expression. The author of this was, so to speak, an Italian patriot; but he was also an English peer, who wasn't going to sit in silence while menials tampered with his mail.

Of the state of things here it would be difficult and not very prudent to speak at large, the Huns opening all letters: I wonder if they can read them when they have opened them? if so, they may see, in my most legible hand, that I think them damned scoundrels and barbarians, their emperor a fool, and themselves more fools than he; all which they may send to Vienna, for anything I care. They have got themselves masters of the Papal police, and are bullying away; but some day or other they will pay for it all. It may not be very soon, because these unhappy Italians have no union nor consistency among themselves; but I suppose Providence will get tired of them at last, and show that God is not an Austrian.

(23 November 1820)

In his letters and journals, we meet a Byron who is impulsive and exuberant; humorous and observant; liable to moods of profound dejection, from which he seeks relief in violent excitement; enamoured of action; and proud and spirited in his hatred of oppression. Clearly he is much more than a Mr Cypress.

At about the time he was completing *Childe Harold's Pilgrimage*, Byron read J. H. Frere's *Whistlecraft*, I and II (1817), an instalment of a medley poem inspired by the Italian works of Luigi Pulci and others. He sensed at once the opportunities offered by its metrical form to the writer who intends to 'be either droll or pathetic, descriptive or sentimental, tender or satirical, as the humour strikes' him. Byron quotes these words in his 'Preface' to the first two cantos of *Childe Harold's Pilgrimage* (1812) in order to indicate an intention which few if any readers would otherwise have discerned in the Spenserian stanzas narrating the travels of his 'gloomy Wanderer' (II, 16). But the three poems for which he took over Frere's metre, the Italian *ottava rima*, show him fully realizing precisely this intention of voicing an extraordinarily wide variety of moods. In fact, these poems, in their variety, their exuberance, their informality, and their humour, are palpably the work of the author of the letters and journals.

Beppo (1818) is the earliest of them. Its plot recalls the story of Colonel Fitzgerald and the Marchesa Castiglione, though in the poem the lover who returns after a long absence is the lady's husband. But the plot is barely more important than the long digressions, and what is most important of all is the tone which characterizes the whole work. This is gay, flippant, and irreverent. It is the tone of many of Byron's letters, the characteristic tone of the high-spirited mocking observer of the human comedy; and it is the tone which predominates in Byron's masterpiece, *Don Juan*.

Byron began writing *Don Juan* in the autumn of 1818, and was still adding to it in the spring of 1823, the year when he left Italy for Greece. The poem records principally six major adventures of its hero. It opens with a description of his childhood and his early love-affair with Donna Julia, a married friend of his mother's. The discovery of this intrigue leads to his being bundled out of the country, and the first half of canto II contains an account of his shipwreck and his prolonged sufferings in an open boat. His third adventure involves Haidée, the daughter of a Greek pirate, who finds Juan unconscious on the shore of the island which is her father's home and base. She becomes his lover; but, on her father's unexpected return, Juan is seized and sold into slavery. In Constantinople, he resists the imperious advances of Gulbeyaz, the Sultan's favourite wife. His servitude lasts from late in the fourth to the end of the seventh canto, when he escapes from the Turks and enlists in the army of their enemies, the Russians. Before long, his military prowess and personal charm commend him to the notorious Empress Catherine II, whose favourite he becomes. Towards the end of canto X, she initiates his last adventure by despatching him to England on a diplomatic mission. While mixing in English social life, he attracts the attention of three women: Aurora, a young heiress; Adeline, the restless wife of a haughty politician; and the lax and lavish Duchess of Fitz-Fulke. When Byron breaks off early in canto XVII, the last of these has – temporarily, at least – the start of her rivals.

After finishing five cantos, Byron had told John Murray, his publisher:

The 5th is so far from being the last of *D.J.*, that it is hardly the beginning. I meant to take him the tour of Europe, with a proper mixture of siege, battle, and adventure, and to make him finish as *Anacharsis Cloots** in the French revolution. To how many cantos this may extend, I know not, nor whether (even if I live) I shall complete it; but this was my notion: I meant to have made him a *Cavalier Servente*† in Italy, and a cause for a divorce in England, and a Sentimental 'Werther-faced man'‡ in Germany, so as to show the different ridicules of the society in each of those countries, and to have displayed him gradually *gâté* and *blasé* as he grew older, as is natural. But I had not quite fixed whether to make him end in Hell, or in an unhappy marriage, not knowing which would be the severest.

(16 February 1821)

It would be foolish to suppose from this that Byron had a settled scheme for the entire poem. Eighteen months earlier, he had admitted to Murray that, while he had abundant materials, he had no plan (12 August 1819); and six months before his death he threatened to retaliate for the attacks on the cantos published so far by writing at least a hundred! His general intention, however, was clearly enough defined. *Don Juan* was to be a sort of picaresque novel in verse; and its hero's peregrinations were to provide its author with varied opportunities for satirical comedy.

But the poem contains more than merely a record of Juan's adventures. Byron conceived it on the lines of the Italian medley poems; and the discursiveness of his models seems to have been his authority for an even greater discursiveness on his own part. He allows himself repeated digressions, in which he speaks in his own person and very much in his epistolary manner.

> I rattle on exactly as I'd talk
> With anybody in a ride or walk.
> (XV, 19)

He speaks of love, of fame, of politics, and of poetry; and in so doing he voices explicitly that sardonic but finally compassionate sense of the human comedy which equally informs his presentation of the incidents of his plot.

Juan is at the centre of that plot, but he excites little interest on his own account. He is an amiable paragon; and our attention slips past

---

* A Prussian baron who became a supporter of the French Revolution. Suspected by Robespierre, he was condemned on a false charge and guillotined in 1794.

† Sanctioned lover of a married woman.

‡ Quoted from Thomas Moore. Werther is the hero of a romance by Goethe.

him to the persons he meets and the settings in which he meets them. We are arrested, for example, by the energy and verve of Julia's indignant tirade against her jealous husband, Alfonso; our interest in this is sharpened by the knowledge that Alfonso has good reason for his suspicion and that Julia's professions of virtue are hypocritical; and we are delighted by the irony of the poet who can permit to the unfaithful wife the authentic tone of scornful self-righteousness.

> During this inquisition Julia's tongue
>   Was not asleep – 'Yes, search and search,' she cried,
> 'Insult on insult heap, and wrong on wrong!
>   It was for this that I became a bride!
> For this in silence I have suffered long
>   A husband like Alfonso at my side;
> But now I'll bear no more, nor here remain,
> If there be law or lawyers in all Spain.
>
> 'Yes, Don Alfonso! husband now no more,
>   If ever you indeed deserved the name,
> Is't worthy of your years? – you have threescore –
>   Fifty, or sixty, it is all the same –
> Is't wise or fitting, causeless to explore
>   For facts against a virtuous woman's fame?
> Ungrateful, perjured, barbarous Don Alfonso,
> How dare you think your lady would go on so?'
>
> (I, 145–6)

These are merely the first two stanzas of an overwhelming verbal assault.

In the last line quoted, the furious emphasis upon 'dare' testifies to Byron's mastery both of metre and of dialogue. Other passages exhibit the same skill. Thus, in the slave-market in Constantinople, Juan finds himself next to an Englishman, also offered for sale, whose speech at once characterizes him for us:

> 'My boy!' – said he, 'amidst this motley crew
>   Of Georgians, Russians, Nubians, and what not,
> All ragamuffins differing but in hue,
>   With whom it is our luck to cast our lot,
> The only gentlemen seem I and you;
>   So let us be acquainted, as we ought:
> If I could yield you any consolation,
> 'Twould give me pleasure. – Pray, what is your nation?'

When Juan answered – 'Spanish!' he replied,
　'I thought, in fact, you could not be a Greek;
Those servile dogs are not so proudly eyed:
　Fortune has played you here a pretty freak,
But that's her way with all men, till they're tried;
　But never mind, – she'll turn, perhaps, next week;
She has served me also much the same as you,
Except that I have found it nothing new.'

'Pray, sir,' said Juan, 'if I may presume,
　What brought you here?' – 'Oh! nothing very rare –
Six Tartars and a drag-chain —'

(V, 13–15)

This conversation continues for some time, and the Englishman becomes an important secondary character. But already he has made himself felt as a blunt and somewhat fatalistic man of action, carelessly assured of his superiority to those whom he dismisses colloquially as 'ragamuffins', 'servile dogs', 'and what not'.

His tone differs sharply from that adopted by Juan's mother, a priggish bluestocking, when she learns that Juan has become the favourite of the Empress Catherine (X, 31–3). Her letter to him, a compound of religiosity, worldly wisdom, sententiousness, and complacency, gives Byron occasion to cry out:

Oh for a *forty-parson power* to chant
　Thy praise, Hypocrisy!

(X, 34)

The exclamation would be equally appropriate after Byron's ironical report of the arguments used by Adeline's husband, Lord Henry Amundeville, to justify his continued placid enjoyment of the profits of government sinecures (XVI, 70–7).

In these and other instances, Byron's dramatic presentation of his characters is completely successful. But more typically he shows them to us without making any pretence of removing himself from the stage. On the contrary, his unconcealed presence there as a witty, cynical, worldly observer and commentator is more than anything else responsible for the distinguishing flavour of *Don Juan*.

Occasionally he sentimentalizes. He is more liable to do this in the first third of the poem than later: the 'Ave Maria!' passage (III, 101–3), for example, in his treatment of Juan and Haidée, is a literary equivalent of a well-known strain in tea-room music. On the other hand, he writes of Haidée's death (IV, 71–2) with unforced tenderness. Normally, however, his fundamental compassion for his characters shows itself only intermittently through the high-spirited mockery which is more obviously typical of him; and when it does show itself he usually snaps out of it as quickly as possible by a deliberately bathetic return to his habitual tone. The episode of cannibalism in the open boat (II, 67–83) provides striking instances of this.

His mockery becomes keenest when Juan, in the last six cantos, is admitted to British polite society:

> In the great world, – which, being interpreted,
>   Meaneth the West or worst end of a city,
> And about twice two thousand people bred
>   By no means to be very wise or witty,
> But to sit up while others lie in bed,
>   And look down on the Universe with pity, –
> Juan, as an inveterate patrician,
> Was well received by persons of condition.
>
> . . . But Juan was a bachelor – of arts,
>   And parts, and hearts: he danced and sung, and had
> An air as sentimental as Mozart's
>   Softest of melodies; and could be sad
> Or cheerful, without any 'flaws or starts',
>   Just at the proper time: and though a lad,
> Had seen the world – which is a curious sight,
> And very much unlike what people write.
>
> (XI, 45, 47)

In the second of these stanzas, a graceful and lilting rhythm almost subdues the expected metrical pattern while Byron is speaking of Juan's charm; when that pattern eventually reasserts itself, it serves to accentuate the sardonic, knowing chuckle with which the final couplet is delivered. This effect of spontaneous, varied, and expressive talk is wonderfully sustained throughout *Don Juan*.

Shortly after the stanzas just quoted, Byron describes a typical day in his hero's London life, ending with his attendance at a ball. A catalogue of lookers-on, nicely graduated in order of decreasing interest in the proceedings, with the 'mere spectator' giving the final signal of tedium, recalls the humorous catalogues in Byron's prose:

> There stands the noble hostess, nor shall sink
>   With the three-thousandth curtsy; there the waltz,

The only dance which teaches girls to think,
    Makes one in love even with its very faults.
Saloon, room, hall, o'erflow beyond their brink,
    And long the latest of arrivals halts,
'Midst royal dukes and dames condemned to climb,
And gain an inch of staircase at a time.

Thrice happy he who, after a survey
    Of the good company, can win a corner,
A door that's *in* or boudoir *out* of the way,
    Where he may fix himself like small 'Jack Horner',
And let the Babel round run as it may,
    And look on as a mourner, or a scorner,
Or an approver, or a mere spectator,
Yawning a little as the night grows later.

(XI, 68–9)

In these lines, Byron is less concerned to describe any particular ball attended by Juan than to evoke the social life of the London season as he had himself known it. Such personal reminiscence, accompanied by a predominantly satirical commentary, occupies much of the last third of the poem. Thus, the fact that Juan at no point becomes entangled with a 'cold coquette' does not discourage Byron from devoting a stanza to the type:

Such is your cold coquette, who can't say 'No',
    And won't say 'Yes', and keeps you on and off-ing
On a lee-shore, till it begins to blow –
    Then sees your heart wrecked, with an inward scoffing.
This works a world of sentimental woe,
    And sends new Werters yearly to their coffin;
But yet is merely innocent flirtation,
Not quite adultery, but adulteration.

(XII, 63)

To feel 'sentimental woe' on account of such creatures is as ridiculous in Byron's eyes as to sentimentalize the sort of 'sweet Friendship' that he later treats with blighting sarcasm:

There's nought in this bad world like sympathy:
    'Tis so becoming to the soul and face,
Sets to soft music the harmonious sigh,
    And robes sweet Friendship in a Brussels lace.
Without a friend, what were Humanity,

337

> To hunt our errors up with a good grace?
> Consoling us with – 'Would you had thought twice!
> Ah! if you had but followed my advice!'
>
> (XIV, 47)

Byron directs his satire in *Don Juan* as much against the 'sentimental and sensibilitous' as against the respectable and censorious. Donna Julia's tirade illustrates this perfectly. On the one hand, its tone of haughty and yet shrewish self-righteousness ironically parodies a tone of the unco' guid; on the other, Byron has been careful to show us Julia as a person of sensibility, and her whole speech is for him an instance of the radical dishonesty of such persons. This is in his first canto. He expresses the same aversion in his last, when he praises a distressed woman because

> she was not a sentimental mourner
> Parading all her sensibility.
>
> (XVI, 65)

His preference for sense as against sensibility marks him as an anti-romantic; and *Don Juan* is, in its total effect, a great anti-romantic poem. Byron never tired of insisting that its virtue was that it was truthful. Like his hero, he had seen the world and knew that it was 'very much unlike what people write' (XI, 47). Informed by experience,

> I mean to show things really as they are,
> Not as they ought to be: for I avow,
>   That till we see what's what in fact, we're far
> From much improvement.
>
> (XII, 40)

Whatever his outraged critics might assert, he was serious in his use of that last word. For he believed that by fastening upon the truth, or, in Pope's phrase, by stooping to it, he was moralizing his song.

He was quite astonished, he said [to a friend six months before his death], to hear people talk in the manner they did about the book. *He* thought he was writing a most moral book. That women did not like it he was not surprised; he knew they could not bear it because it *took off the veil*; it showed that all their d—d sentiment was only an excuse to cover passions of grosser nature; that all platonism only tended to *that*, and they hated it because it showed and exposed their hypocrisy.

(*Letters and Journals*, VI, 429–30)

The truth to which Byron stoops is a matter of fidelity to what he believes to be observable facts. Accordingly, he more than once expresses a sceptic's impatience with metaphysical and theological speculation (XI, 5–6; XV, 88–92). In all this, he aligns himself rather with his Augustan predecessors than with his Romantic contemporaries.

His literary judgements are in keeping with this association. His poetic decalogue opens with the commandments:

> Thou shalt believe in Milton, Dryden, Pope;
>   Thou shalt not set up Wordsworth, Coleridge, Southey;
>   (I, 205)

and he never tires of ridiculing the Lake poets.

> We learn from Horace, 'Homer sometimes sleeps';
>   We feel without him, – Wordsworth sometimes wakes, –
> To show with what complacency he creeps,
>   With his dear '*Waggoners*', around his lakes.*
> He wishes for 'a boat' to sail the deeps –
>   Of Ocean? – No, of air; and then he makes
> Another outcry for 'a little boat',
> And drivels seas to set it well afloat.[3]
>
> If he must fain sweep o'er the ethereal plain,
>   And Pegasus runs restive in his 'Waggon',
> Could he not beg the loan of Charles's Wain?
>   Or pray Medea for a single dragon?
> Or if, too classic for his vulgar brain,
>   He feared his neck to venture such a nag on,
> And he must needs mount nearer to the moon,
> Could not the blockhead ask for a balloon?
>
> 'Pedlars', and 'Boats', and 'Waggons'! Oh! ye shades
>   Of Pope and Dryden, are we come to this?
> That trash of such sort not alone evades
>   Contempt, but from the bathos' vast abyss
> Floats scumlike uppermost, and these Jack Cades†
>   Of sense and song above your graves may hiss –
> The 'little boatman' and his *Peter Bell*
> Can sneer at him who drew 'Achitophel'!
>
>   (III, 98–100)

---

* Byron alludes to Wordsworth's poem, *The Waggoner*.
† Demagogues.

The invocation to Pope and Dryden in the last stanza compels us to recall the difference between their Augustanism and Byron's. Pope and Dryden seem characteristically to write as the spokesmen of a coherent and civilized social group. The members of this may not hold identical religious, political, and other beliefs; but they do share, and their poets share, a deep respect for the fundamental Augustan virtues of good sense, reasonableness, and moderation. Byron writes with an equally keen awareness of his public, and he writes likewise as an exponent of good sense. But, so far from seeming to feel his public sustaining him, he evidently draws very much more exclusively on his own resources, and even at times has to defy what he supposes to be a canting, a moralistic and sensibilitous, world. In the passage last quoted, for instance, he speaks with the insolence of an aristocrat and the irresponsibility of an exile; he speaks, in short, for himself.

At the same time, we must not doubt the genuineness of his admiration for and indebtedness to the work of Pope. He declared that he had always regarded Pope 'as the greatest name in our poetry' (3 May 1821). His early satire, *English Bards, and Scotch Reviewers* (1809), shows him using the master's couplet with remarkable vigour and accomplishment; and near the beginning of canto XIV of *Don Juan* he gives us the Byronic equivalent of the famous *apologia* – 'Why did I write?' etc. – from the *Epistle of Dr Arbuthnot*. Nor was his admiration confined to Pope among the poets of the previous century. 'Rough Johnson, the great moralist' (XIII, 7), had a large share of it; and the basic theme of *Don Juan* is none other than that of Johnson's finest poem, *The Vanity of Human Wishes*.[4]

Byron rightly denied the accusation that he was misanthropic (IX, 20–21). His sense of 'the nothingness of Life' (VII, 6), his conviction that, 'vanity of vanities, all is vanity', is expressed sardonically, wryly, sometimes theatrically; but it is expressed with a pity for, rather than a detestation of, his fellow-men. His most explicit statements of the theme occur in certain of his digressions: at the opening of canto VII, for example, and at the close of canto XI. One of the stanzas devoted to it early in the poem illustrates the characteristic manner of delivery:

> What are the hopes of man? Old Egypt's King
> Cheops erected the first Pyramid
> And largest, thinking it was just the thing

> To keep his memory whole, and mummy hid;
> But somebody or other rummaging,
>   Burglariously broke his coffin's lid:
> Let not a monument give you or me hopes,
> Since not a pinch of dust remains of Cheops.
>
>   (I, 219)

After the idiomatic casualness of the third line, alliteration and rhyme focus attention upon the phrase 'mummy hid' as defining the ludicrous and pathetic means by which Cheops tried to eternize himself. The extravagant 'burglariously', following the familiar 'rummaging', admits a gust of boisterous and jovial laughter. Finally, the ingenious feminine rhyme accentuates the sardonic hilarity with which the stanza ends.

The Vision of Judgment, Byron's third poem in *ottava rima*, was written in 1821, during an interval in the composition of *Don Juan*. George III had died early in the previous year, old, blind, and insane. In the spring of 1821, the Poet Laureate, Robert Southey, published *A Vision of Judgment*, describing the dead king's admission to celestial bliss. The poem simply asked for ridicule; and Byron so disliked Southey, both as a convert to Toryism and as a suspected slanderer of himself, that he was more than ready to supply it.

But ferocious ridicule of Southey's poem is only a part of his achievement in *The Vision of Judgment*. Within ten stanzas of its opening, he is imagining the royal funeral and telling what he believes to be the unqualified truth about it. In his view, George III had been a political calamity to his country and to mankind; and the funeral had been insincere and theatrical.

> It seemed the mockery of hell to fold
> The rottenness of eighty years in gold.
>
>   (10)

From this, Byron plunges recklessly into reflections on the doctrine of eternal punishment.

> 'God save the king!' It is a large economy
>   In God to save the like; but if he will
> Be saving, all the better; for not one am I
>   Of those who think damnation better still:
> I hardly know too if not quite alone am I
>   In this small hope of bettering future ill
> By circumscribing, with some slight restriction,
> The eternity of Hell's hot jurisdiction.
>
>   (13)

Having thus committed himself, he pretends to go on to the defensive; in the next stanza, the series of clauses beginning, 'I know ...', 'I know ...', 'I know ...', is such as would normally introduce a piece of self-justification. But his irony becomes more and more marked as the stanza proceeds. His acknowledgement that one may be damned for resisting the doctrine of eternal punishment is so phrased as to make such resistance seem plain charity; the crude forcefulness of 'crammed ... till we quite o'erflow' carries a hint that 'the best doctrines' are unlikely to be voluntarily and sincerely embraced; and the final couplet, with its colloquial emphasis on '*damned*' and its ludicrous feminine rhyme, rounds off the whole with hearty, scornful laughter.

> I know this is unpopular; I know
> 'Tis blasphemous; I know one may be damned
> For hoping no one else may e'er be so;
> I know my catechism; I know we're crammed
> With the best doctrines till we quite o'erflow;
> I know that all save England's Church have shammed,
> And that the other twice two hundred churches
> And synagogues have made a *damned* bad purchase.
>
> (14)

But this, though typical in its tone, is a digression from the main plot of *The Vision of Judgment*. As that develops, we see the Archangel Michael and his antagonist Satan claiming George III for heaven and hell respectively. Wilkes and Junius give their testimony. Then Southey arrives. He delivers a speech of absurd self-advertisement, concluding with an offer to 'save the Deity some worlds of trouble' (101) by reading aloud his own *Vision of Judgment*. All present, celestial and infernal, fly in consternation; and, says Byron,

> All I saw farther, in the last confusion,
>   Was, that King George slipped into Heaven for one;
> And when the tumult dwindled to a calm,
> I left him practising the hundredth psalm.
>
> (106)

This plot enables Byron severely to castigate an official Tory bard and a royal instrument of political oppression. But his severity is not such as to preclude wit and humour. In *The Vision of Judgment*, as in *Don Juan*, he is conspicuously the Whig aristocrat in exile, self-assured, responsible to nobody, reckless, voluble, exuberant, wickedly ironical, and deceptively informal. Above all, in both of these poems he manifests a tremendous and infectious vitality. Few will claim that Byron achieves a balanced and comprehensive view of human existence. Nevertheless, in the best of his verse and prose, he voices the insights of a disillusioned though not misanthropic man of the world with a zest and a vitality which are the more welcome today in direct proportion to their rarity among our defeatists 'waiting for Godot'.

NOTES

1. Nearly all the extant records of Byron's conversation have been collected by Ernest J. Lovell in *His Very Self and Voice* (New York, 1954).

2. Throughout this essay dates given in full refer to letters or, where indicated, journal entries in R. E. Prothero's six-volume edition of Byron's *Letters and Journals* (London, 1898–1901).

3. Wordsworth's *Peter Bell* opens with the lines:

> There's something in a flying horse,
> There's something in a huge balloon;
> But through the clouds I'll never float
> Until I have a little Boat,
> Shaped like the crescent-moon.

4. See in this connection Byron's diary entry dated 9 January 1821.

THE LETTERS AND JOURNALS
OF THE ROMANTICS

GILBERT PHELPS

As might be expected in an age which rejoiced in the liberation of the Self, letter-writing and diary-keeping had a special attraction for the Romantics. The best letters and journals, indeed, besides their obvious value in conveying information about the life, character and milieu of the writer, can act as an unusually sensitive gauge both to the oscillations of his own sensibility and to those of the period in which he lives. Yet no area has been more vaguely charted, or less subject to responsible critical control. Only too often both forms have served as an excuse for the most self-indulgent sort of responses, which throw undue emphasis on the quaint, the trivial, or the sensational.

This has particularly been the case with diaries.* One of the reasons for their appeal, of course, is that they provide a creative outlet for the amateur. As Arthur (Lord) Ponsonby, who in the 1920s made a notable collection of lost or forgotten specimens, pointed out:

> People of all ages and degrees who may never have ventured to write a line for publication and who may be quite incapable of any literary effort, are able to keep a diary the value of which need not in any way suffer from their literary incapacity.

Undoubtedly such a diary can be valuable for the writer concerned and in some cases it can also be so for those who read it. But if it *is* published, then the same criteria must be applied to it as to any other piece of writing, and the word 'value' takes on different connotations. It is true that the naive and the artless can possess a certain attraction, and even at times achieve telling effects. It is amusing and sometimes illuminating, for example, to read in the Reverend John Woodeforde's Diary (which he kept almost unremittingly from 1758 to 1803) the details of the meals he ate, the walks he took, or

---

* The terms diary and journal are more or less interchangeable, though the former perhaps suggests a greater degree of privacy.

the neighbours he visited; or to encounter such innocent juxtaposi-
tions as this from an entry for 28 September 1792 in his niece
Nancy's diary: 'Mr and Mrs Custance sent us a brace of partridges.
Dreadful times in France. Many are fled for refuge here.'

Obviously, too, social historians can derive considerable profit
from such diaries (the whole Woodeforde family were inveterate
diarists over a period of nearly two hundred years). But none of this
can alter the fact that the diaries of Parson Woodeforde and his niece
are in nearly every respect the smallest of small beer. The truth of the
matter is that, with very few exceptions, the only diaries (and letters)
of any genuine *literary* value are the products of highly intelligent,
cultured and complex minds and personalities. The diary of Samuel
Pepys is of special relevance in this connection. The first selection
(after his obscure form of shorthand has been deciphered) was
published in 1825 (one of several instances of the resuscitation of this
kind of material during the period of the Romantic revival), and
from then on the diary was continually being culled for the spicy
passages, and continually advanced as the perfect example of artless,
unpremeditated utterance. Indeed the word Pepysian came to stand
for these qualities. Ironically enough, recent research has shown that it
is not at all an appropriate adjective to apply to Pepys himself.
There is convincing evidence that he took considerable pains with his
diary[1] – often, for example, making rough drafts of his entries – and
that he came to regard it as a genuine creation, as something that
had, over the years, engaged his best faculties; and in any case it was
the work of a man who was possessed of outstanding taste, originality
and distinction of mind, and of narrative gifts that might have made
him a great novelist.

Letters and diaries can, of course, intermingle and overlap: the
letter-journal which Byron wrote for his half-sister Augusta in
Switzerland in 1816 (after his divorce and virtual ostracism) is one
instance, and the letter-journals which Keats sent to his brother in
America between 1818 and 1819 are another. The two genres,
however, have different origins and traditions. The earlier examples
of both, it is true, were alike in that both were directed to the
external rather than the internal world. The letters were mostly ex-
changes of a public nature, concerned with business, political or
diplomatic affairs, and the diaries dealt with travel, military annals

and public transactions of various kinds, with only the occasional personal aside.

It was the rise of the Puritan sects in the seventeenth century, with their advocacy of a daily examination of the state of the soul, that provided the real impetus to private diary-keeping. Most of the diaries that resulted consist of a series of monotonous breast-beatings, confessions of minor peccadilloes, and self-exhortations, but the Quaker George Fox's *Journal* (1694), with its forceful style, shot through from time to time with visionary gleams, is in quite a different category – and John Bunyan's superb *Grace Abounding to the Chief of Sinners* (1666) almost certainly grew out of just such a diary.

It was hardly surprising that the Augustans, with their urbane values and their conviction that the 'proper study of mankind is man', should have found the letter and the journal particularly congenial. Among the cultured few who were the arbiters of taste letters were formal pieces of writing, composed within the prevailing conventions of good taste and decorum, and often begged back from the recipients for further polishing. All the same, even those letters which were most carefully related to the tastes and standards of polite society (like those of Lord Chesterfield to his son, in his less cynical moments) were in some degree symptomatic of the beginnings of the movement away from a classical orientation towards something more subjective and personal. Thomas Gray's careful composition of his letters, for example, did not exclude either personal charm or those genuinely felt responses to the natural scenery of the Lake District and the Alps which looked forward to the Romantics. William Shenstone, too, could not keep out the personal note from his loving accounts of his experiments in landscape gardening, any more than Gilbert White could from his on the natural history of Selborne.

Far more important, however, in modifying the Augustan restraints and initiating those changes in taste and sensibility that helped prepare the way for the Romantic revival, was the extension of the letter-writing habit beyond the limits of what the Augustans conceived as 'polite society'. Among the more obvious factors which contributed to this process were the growing prosperity of the middle classes, resulting in increased leisure, especially for women; the growth of literacy; and vastly improved communications and postal services. At these levels of society the letter was a liberating force, both socially and emotionally. Again this applies particularly to women. Still cut off, by class and custom, from many intellectual satisfactions, including the supposedly superior conversation of exclusively masculine society, letter-writing provided them with an alternative that might itself be superior, as Richardson suggested when, in a letter to one of his women correspondents, he contrasted the 'goose-like gabble' of ordinary conversation with the more solid delights that await the lady who makes 'her closet her paradise' by conducting a correspondence. It was, of course, Richardson's realization of these facts that led him first to begin his 'little volume of letters, in a common style, on such subjects as might be of use to country readers who are unable to indite for themselves', and then to turn aside from the project (though he completed it later) in order to write his epistolary novel *Pamela, or Virtue Rewarded* (1740).

What Richardson called the 'common style' appropriate to a letter – and to his novels – together with its loose, frequently disjointed and helter-skelter form and approach, undoubtedly helped to undermine the Augustan ideal of decorum, and with it (as Fielding was quick to recognize) the whole concept of Classicism in literature. In effect, between them Richardson's 'familiar' letter and his epistolary novels began two processes which were to have profoundly important consequences in the future: the democratization of literature, and its feminization – not merely, of course, in the sense that there were to be more women writers but, far more important, in the release of feminine modes of feeling and being as an essential component of general human experience.

As the eighteenth century advanced, diaries too (although still essentially private) began to register changes in attitude and sensibility which, on the whole, were not yet apparent in other literary forms. The Puritan origins of the genre were still very much in evidence, and especially the principle of regular self-examination. Sometimes this operated in a specifically religious context: various non-conformist divines still kept diaries of the old breast-beating type, and (at a higher level of achievement) it was in 1725 that John Wesley began the record of his evangelical travels which he sustained for an astonishing sixty-six years, right up to the year of his death in 1793.

The principle operated, however, just as strongly among lay diarists. Dr Johnson urged his young protégé Boswell to use his diary primarily as a means of spiritual and moral self-improvement, and made sporadic attempts to keep one himself. Boswell's diaries,[2] of course, contain a good deal of material of a far from edifying nature, as his *London Journal* of 1763, with its descriptions – often brilliantly funny and attended by narrative skill of a high order – of his sexual adventures and misadventures, make abundantly clear. At the same time, Boswell is continually upbraiding himself, and as continually noting his failures to live up to the standards, social as well as moral, that he has set himself. His diaries, in fact, are of particular interest in registering the gradual change-over that was taking place, from the 1760s onwards, from a predominantly Augustan sensibility to a predominantly Romantic one. They illustrate, above all, the increasing tensions between the demands of self-government, social as well as moral, and those of unrestricted self-expression. In this respect at least Boswell was half a Romantic.

Towards the end of the eighteenth century, and on into the nineteenth, there was a considerable increase in both letter-writing and diary-keeping. Both point to an accelerating retreat from the old Augustan restraints, in many respects along the lines indicated by Boswell's example. Both also make it clear that immediacy of response to experience was now, on the whole, valued above a considered appraisal. The tendency was to write while the emotion was at its peak, to pour the feelings directly into language.

The more formal traditions of letter-writing, it is true, were not completely superseded. As a young man Robert Burns, for example, conducted a literary correspondence with some of his friends almost along the lines of a competition in essay-writing, and, Richardson-like, helped his semi-literate neighbours with their correspondence. Some of his later letters to strangers or to the socially elevated are also formal compositions. On the other hand, when he is caught up in his creative work of transmuting old Scottish songs and ballads his approach becomes easy, vivid and very much to the point. In a letter to George Thomson, compiler of the *Collection of Scottish Songs and Airs*, of September 1794, Burns writes:

... I shall withdraw 'O'er the seas and far away' altogether; it is unequal and unworthy of the work. Making a poem is like begetting a son: you cannot know whether you have a wise man or a fool, until you produce him to the world and try him.

For that reason I send you the offspring of my brain, abortions and all; and as such, pray look over them, and forgive them and burn them ...

And when he is writing to his special cronies, Burns's epistolary style is energetically colloquial, while there was certainly no sign of Augustan restraint in the more scandalous letters, which shocked even Byron by their freedom of expression. The letters of William Cowper, whose frame of mind and mode of life removed him to some extent from the Romantic mainstream, are also frequently Augustan in tone and approach, but in addition to their considerable charm his letters often display an ease of style and a moving directness of response, especially in connection with nature and his relationships with his friends, that relate him to the new age rather than the old.

As far as diaries were concerned, though, the break with the conventions of the past *was* almost complete. There are two partial exceptions. One of these is the persistence of the travel journal, which became even more popular – hardly surprising in view of the appeal that exotic, far-away places had for the romantic imagination. James Cook's *A Voyage towards the South Pole and round the world*, published in 1777, had a second lease of life, and *A Voyage to the Pacific Ocean*, published in 1784, was equally popular. These travel books, old and new, entered into some of the greatest poetry of the period: Coleridge, for example, drew on some of them in his *Rime of the Ancient Mariner* (1798), as did Byron in several episodes of *Don Juan*. The other was the survival of the journal of high society. A connecting link here is Fanny Burney (Madame d'Arblay) who was still keeping a diary (the earlier part of which includes lively accounts of her life at Court from 1786 to 1791) and did so until the year of her death in 1840. Politicians of the period, like Charles Cavendish Fulke Greville, were also busy setting down their inside view of the political life of the times, and reporting at length the conversations of the great and the notorious – a strongly marked feature of this type of journal in the nineteenth century.

The old Puritan impetus, however, which had in effect launched the diary genre, survived only in John Wesley and a few like-minded clergymen. The regular, patient recording of events as the groundwork for the writer's thoughts and reflections also became rarer, often to be replaced by long soliloquies unrelated, or only tenuously so, to any particular occasion; by confessions of varying degrees of frankness; or by what Gray had called 'the pleasures of recollection' – nostalgia in fact is a notable feature of diaries after about 1800. As, moreover, self-realization was now something to be cultivated and encouraged, the idea of eventual publication (of letters as well as of diaries) became the rule rather than the exception. When, for example, Sir Walter Scott, in his mid-fifties and with a solid reputation behind him, began a diary in 1825, he assumed a potential reader from the start, sometimes addressing him directly, and projecting a persona of bluff geniality which he assumed was already familiar to his public.

Another feature of the period was the increase of diaries devoted to its great literary figures, and here the general picture of greater freedom and spontaneity of expression has to be considerably modified. At a time when the beginnings of a Literary Establishment were already apparent, as well as the symptoms of modern publicity, the minor writers and the hangers-on of the literary scene often combine a sense of solemn literary performance with straightforward journalistic opportunism. Literary gossip and anecdotage, in consequence, form the staple of many of the diaries of this kind. Henry Crabb Robinson, author of no less than thirty-five closely written diaries and a vast mass of related material, is a striking example. A few interesting and useful glimpses of Wordsworth, Coleridge and their circle emerge, but the bulk of the diaries consists of little more than literary chit-chat, devoid of any real illumination or critical judgement, while the style is for the most part pedestrian in the extreme.

In some cases what was regarded as a peripheral activity by the writers concerned, today seems to have more continuing vitality than their main works. The letters of Robert Southey, for example, can be read with greater profit and pleasure than most of his verse. Sydney Smith has enjoyed a great reputation as a wit, but some of the funniest – and least self-conscious – of his drolleries are to be found in his letters. But the letters and journals of the period of the Romantic revival are so numerous that it is impossible to mention more than a handful. Four examples, however, must be singled out for rather more detailed comment.

One of these is the diary of Benjamin Haydon, the painter, whose huge canvases on historical and biblical subjects earned him a great reputation in the early years of the nineteenth century, and convinced him that he was the great Romantic Genius, destined to be the saviour of English art, but who quarrelled with the Royal Academy, fell out of popular favour, and committed suicide in 1846 at the age of sixty. The diary which Haydon kept from the age of twenty-two, right up to the day of his death, has some intrinsic merits. He was the friend of many contemporary writers (among them John Keats), and the descriptions he gives of various literary gatherings have a liveliness and humour beyond anything that Crabb Robinson could achieve, and some of his comments on the old masters are also succinct and to the point. But the main importance of his vast Diary is that it presents a highly significant case, probably the most complete portrait of the Artist as Romantic, in its most inflated form, that the period has to offer.

In many ways Haydon can be seen as a later counterpart to Boswell. Both men were egocentric to an extravagant degree; both were obsessed by the marvellous uniqueness of their own personalities; and both used the diary as a vehicle for immortalizing their own stories. But there the likenesses end. For whereas Boswell draws back from time to time to make rueful comments and self-assessments, Haydon never falters in his adherence to the Romantic image he has made for himself, pouring out a torrent of vehement self-justification and self-glorification, increasingly paranoid as his early fame falls from him, and creating a series of Romantic tableaux with himself at their centre as the Martyred Hero, right up to his final dramatic farewell penned shortly before his suicide. The tone of this entry is typical:

> I have never suited my labour to existing tastes. I know what is right and do it. So did the early Christians, and so do all great men. Suffering is the consequence, but it must be borne. Should I have shaken the nation if I had not?

There could hardly be a greater contrast than that between Haydon's feverish diary with its romantic purple passages, and the quiet, unemphatic *Journals* of Dorothy Wordsworth. Whereas Haydon is always at the centre of his own drama, her attention is almost entirely directed outwards, to the world around her, to other people, and, above all, to her brother William. Brother and sister shared the same sensibility to such a remarkable degree that her journals often seem to be his poetic workshop.[3] The best-known example is Dorothy's entry in her *Grasmere Journal* of 15 April 1802, made some two years before Wordsworth wrote his famous poem on the same subject:

... I never saw daffodils so beautiful, they grew among the mossy stones about and about them, some rested their heads upon these stones as on a pillow for weariness and the rest tossed and reeled and danced and seemed as if they verily laughed with the wind that blew upon them over the lake, they looked so gay, ever glancing, ever changing ...

There are in fact numerous echoes in Wordsworth's poetry of his sister's journals. It was not only Wordsworth, moreover, who benefited from Dorothy's observations and insights. Their close friend Coleridge took note of this entry (from the *Alfoxden Journal*) for 7 March 1798: 'Only one leaf upon the top of a tree – the sole remaining leaf – danced round and round like a rag blown by the wind' – and transmuted it in his poem *Christabel*:

> The one red leaf, the last of its clan
> That dances as oft as dance it can ...

Dorothy Wordsworth is so intent upon serving her brother and his friends that her journals sometimes provoke exasperation and frustration. At the same time it would be quite wrong to see them as a mere poetic filter or medium for her brother's needs. In spite of her self-effacement there is a genuine, even a tough, underlying personality and, above all, a strong sense of realism. It is not only that there are numerous details of ordinary domestic life – shelling peas, making giblet pie, darning socks and so on – but a large proportion of the *Grasmere Journal* is devoted to the revelation of a very unromantic England. Beggars of all kinds – wounded and discharged soldiers and sailors, abandoned wives and children, the destitute throw-outs of the Industrial Revolution, as well as gypsies and professional 'travellers' – probably occupy as much space as the better-known evocations of nature. William drew on many of these entries, too, of course (as with his sister's description of the old leech-gatherer), and the poetry that resulted was some of his best, but it was her initial realism of observation that helped to give it much of its fibre.

Dorothy Wordsworth's journals often exhibit what one might call the quintessential quality of the diary and its main justification – a kind of temporal immediacy that can only rarely be captured by any other form. There is, for example, this entry:

6th May Thursday 1802. A sweet morning. We have put the finishing touch to our Bower and here we are sitting in the orchard. It is one o'clock. We are sitting upon a seat under the wall which I found my brother building up when I came to him with his apple ...

Those few sentences illustrate perfectly that proclamation 'I am here, and it is now' which must be central to any worthwhile diary, and it is not an effect that is achieved by accident, but by an unerring choice of the right words and a rigorous exclusion of inessentials. The same economy and precision inform her descriptions of nature. Coleridge rightly wrote of her (in June 1797):

Her eye watchful in minutest observation of nature; and her taste a perfect electrometer. It bends, protrudes, and draws in, at subtlest beauties and most recondite faults.

Her ear was as sensitive – and realistically selective – as her eye, and she had the rare gift of seeing and feeling natural objects in their independent essence. She frequently refers to the shapes of things beneath their appearances. A birch tree is not to her a representative of a genus, but 'a tree in shape with stem and branches' at the same time that it is 'like a Spirit of Water'. As she sees separate objects in their individual uniqueness, she also sees them in relation to other entities. The passage about the daffodils, for instance, ends with a few sentences which remind the reader that the daffodils are close to the human world, and at once broaden out and concretize the scene:

There was here and there a little knot of daffodils and a few stragglers a few yards higher up but they were so few as not to disturb the simplicity and unity and life of that one busy highway.

This sense of a living unity is one of the distinguishing features of the true creative imagination. There are times, indeed, when Dorothy's combination of simplicity, realism and lyricism contrasts favourably with the kind of abstractions which marked large tracts of William's later poetry. When she said, in describing the effect a quiet evening beside Rydal Water had upon her, that 'it made me more than half a poet', she was pointing to a self-evident truth.

The personal record which most obviously invites comparison with Benjamin Haydon's is that of Lord Byron, in the sense that both are concerned with archetypal Romantic figures. The great difference is that whereas in his diaries Haydon surrendered to and obsessively acted out his Romantic image, the letters and journals of Byron are almost completely at variance with it. They exhibit a far more various, intelligent and likeable man than the earlier, typically Byronic poems would suggest. One of the most stimulating features of his letters, indeed, is the critical self-awareness they reveal. His assertion that for him poetical composition was really a subordinate activity was not, as is so commonly supposed, an affectation but a realization that the kind of poetry which had made him famous was not of the first quality, as a letter of 10 June 1822, written in the wake of the cool reception afforded to the first published cantos of *Don Juan*, makes clear:

> At present I am paying the penalty of having helped to spoil the public taste, for, as long as I wrote in the false exaggerated style of youth and the times in which we live, they applauded me to the very echo; and within these few years, when I have endeavoured at better things and written what I suspect to have the principle of duration in it ... all men ... have risen up against me and my later publications ...

His scoffing use of the word 'poeshie' in another letter to denote that 'false, exaggerated style', so common among some of the Romantics, is symptomatic of the same realism. His contempt for this kind of verse led him to extremes and to lack of judgement in his attacks on Wordsworth and Keats in some of the letters, but it was the same distrust of the Romantic mode that also gave rise to many excellent comments on Pope, for him 'the touchstone of taste'.

Practically every one of Byron's letters, from the earliest onwards, is impregnated with his complex personality. To read them is to be convinced that their writer was a genuine man of genius, who is living his life energetically and reflecting deeply upon it. At their best they are alive with intelligence and wit, very close in tone and approach, in fact, to *Don Juan*. The letter-journals which intersperse the ordinary correspondence tend to be rather more fragmentary, often consisting of brief notes separated by dashes, but they can be just as vivid and witty, as in this extract from his Swiss journal addressed to Augusta:

Arrived at the Grindenwald; dined, mounted again, and rode to the higher Glacier – twilight, but distinct – very fine Glacier, *like a frozen hurricane*. Starlight, beautiful, but a devil of a path! Never mind, got safe in; a little lightning; but the whole of the day as fine in point of weather as the day on which Paradise was made. Passed *whole woods of withered pines, all withered*; trunks stripped and barkless, branches lifeless; done by a single winter, – their appearance reminded me of me and my family.

It is, however, the letters written from Venice which are the most brilliant in style and approach, if frequently scandalous in subject-matter. There are passages recounting his amorous adventures which display a command of narrative verve and pace (again very close to *Don Juan*) which any novelist would envy. In fact Byron wrote the first canto of his masterpiece in the midst of his Venetian debaucheries. His own life, of course, was stranger than fiction, and taken together the letters almost read like a large, rambling, picar-esque autobiographical novel. It is seldom that a body of correspon-dence contains so many disparate materials and yet somehow succeeds in conveying a sense of unity.

Byron's correspondence would be read with pleasure and profit if he had never written a line outside it, but by far the greatest letters of the period (and indeed in English literature as a whole) – letters which rise, time after time, to the heights of the creative imagination – are those of John Keats. This is all the more remarkable in view of the fact that the two hundred or so letters that have survived were crowded into a period of little over four years. At one level there are some valid comparisons between Keats's letters and those of Byron. Keats could be just as flippant and light-hearted, and his letters to friends and members of his family (especially his younger sister, Fanny) are full of puns and jokes. What distinguishes letters like these is the almost uncanny sensation they create of the voice of the writer, with its individual timbre and intonations, speaking directly, more than a century and a half later, into the ear of the reader. In his letters Keats, too, shows himself (paradoxical though it may sound of the greatest of all the Romantic poets) an anti-Romantic, in the sense that he came to realize, as the letters so abundantly illustrate, that there was much in Romanticism – and in his own earlier poems – that was false and unreal and had to be worked through, as he grappled with the unromantic realities of his own short life, determined to find their true poetic correlatives.

But the great difference between the two bodies of correspondence is that Keats's is almost continually the workshop of a poet (and it must be added, a far greater poet) not only because it contains so many ideas that were on the brink of poetic expression, as well as from time to time the first drafts of actual poems, but also because of the boldness with which it tackles some of the most difficult and profound issues of aesthetics and philosophy.

Keats's letters contain so many brilliant *aperçus* that have since passed into the general language of criticism, forming the themes and even in many cases the titles of numerous essays and books, that ironically they have engendered the very danger of abstraction which Keats set himself so firmly against. What Keats was fundamentally concerned with in his letters was his *practice* as a poet, in direct relation to his experience of living, and not with aesthetic theory. In them he insists time after time that true poetry cannot be imposed from the outside, that it has nothing to do with preconceived theories. 'If poetry comes not as naturally as leaves to a tree,' he declares, 'it had better not come at all', and in consequence the ideas that belong to aesthetic or intellectual systems are valid for the poet only when they have themselves become the stuff of personal experience – for 'axioms in philosophy are not axioms until they are proved upon our pulses'.

The letters are in effect a poet's pilgrimage, charting his growing critical self-awareness and his deepening realization that his creative salvation must come from within himself. After the hostile reception of his long poem *Endymion* in 1818 Keats wrote to his publisher:

It is as good as I had power to make it – by myself . . . I have written independently *without Judgment*. I may write independently *with Judgment*, hereafter. The Genius of Poetry must work out its own salvation in a man: It cannot be matured by law and by precept, but by sensation and watchfulness in itself, – that which is creative must create itself – in 'Endymion' I leaped headlong into the sea, and thereby have become better acquainted with the soundings, the quicksands, and the rocks, than if I had stayed upon the green shore and piped a silly pipe and took tea and comfortable advice.

And in an astonishingly short space of time the letters are revealing a full and mature understanding that the challenge that faced him as a poet was to extend his natural capacity for sensuous absorption to the embodiment of the tragic experiences both of his own life and of humanity in general – and they do so in language and imagery that often rival those of the great poems themselves.

Letters and diaries are not, of course, at the centre of an age's creative effort. But they demand the same kind of attention, and if they are approached at a level higher than that belonging to mere gossip or journalistic entertainment they can provide an important supplement to the literature itself, always illuminating, if at times only in a negative sense, and sometimes intrinsically and even profoundly rewarding.

NOTES

1. See 'The Diary as Literature', William Matthews, one of the introductory essays to Vol. 1 of the complete edn. of Robert Latham and William Matthews (eds), *The Diary of Samuel Pepys*, 11 vols (London, 1970–75).

2. James Boswell's *London Journal* of 1762–3, ed. F. A. Pottle (London, 1950). Since then Professor Pottle, in collaboration with other editors, has published all of Boswell's private diaries.

3. *The Journals of Dorothy Wordsworth*, ed. Mary Moorman (Oxford, 1971), consisting of the *Alfoxden* and *Grasmere Journals*, contains an Appendix of Wordsworth's shorter poems mentioned in the text, and in addition another Appendix consisting of two of Dorothy Wordsworth's own poems.

LANDSCAPE PAINTING FROM
BLAKE TO BYRON

GEOFFREY GRIGSON

The painters between Blake and Byron whom we now admire –
chiefly landscape painters – worked for the most part against the open
dictates and tastes and desiderata of the period. On either side of 1800
the artist was markedly insecure in his role, and so divided in his
aims. A motive strong in the foundation of the Royal Academy (a
late-comer among European academies under royal patronage) had
been, so to say, the manumission of the artist. He wished for a place
in society such as was granted traditionally to the poet. He wished
his art to be emancipated and dignified and made independent. He
wanted not only place and patronage and sales, but encouragement
(though with misgivings, since the profounder pressure of his art was
towards paintings of emotion, naturalism, and spontaneity) for work
which was more elevated, more noble, more polite and various, and
larger in scale than incessant portraiture. Since he was insecure, he
could not make his own terms. Since he was ill-paid (except for portraits and then for domestic subjects) and dependent upon patronage
and upon the few exhibiting societies of his profession, it was dangerous to be moved too much by the deeper, more authentic pressures
of his art, and difficult to resist the rewarding pressures of conformity.

The Academy was founded in 1768, when William Blake was
eleven years old. Nearly a hundred years later, in 1863, Lord Elcho,
presiding over a Royal Commission on its activities, asked the president, Sir Charles Locke Eastlake, 'What are the privileges of the
Royal Academicians', and recieved an answer which was still relevant: 'I might mention, first, the distinction of their writing themselves *Esqr.*' Artists again and again spoke feelingly, often bitterly, of
their position. Blake jabbed down his view in the margin of the *Discourses* of Sir Joshua Reynolds, whom he condemned so angrily as the
'doll' of the connoisseurs. He declared:

358

The Enquiry in England is not whether a Man has Talents & Genius, But whether he is Passive & Polite & a Virtuous Ass & obedient to Noblemen's Opinions in Art and Science. If he is, he is a Good Man. If Not, he must be starved.

Blake set that down some forty years after the foundation of the Academy and some four years after the foundation of the Old Water-colour Society in 1804. Artists whom he would certainly have impounded among the virtuous, passive, obedient asses were no less aware than himself of the difficulties of independence. 'The position of the painter is not much thought of in England,' said the portrait-painter James Northcote (1746–1831) in his old age. And he recalled how his old master, Sir Joshua Reynolds, had felt this inferiority and how Reynolds's sister had 'always claimed more respectability from being the daughter of a poor clergyman' than from being related so closely even to so famous a painter. Northcote was buttressed from ill-fortune by his membership of the exclusive Academy. A younger Academician and conformist, William Collins (1788–1847), father of the novelist Wilkie Collins, said that only the Academy prevented artists from being 'treated like journeymen'.

Blake was certainly not alone in his view that Edmund Burke in his *Enquiry into the Origin of our Ideas of the Sublime and Beautiful* (1757) and Reynolds in his *Discourses* had 'mocked inspiration and vision'. The *Discourses* were both Augustan and politic. They were part of the campaign to raise the social position of painting and painter. Based on the time-honoured theory of mimesis, they preached moderation, composure, dignity, reason and common sense, and rules. Art, said Reynolds, is 'intrinsically imitative', genius is not inspiration but 'the effect of close observation and experience'. 'Damn'd Fool!' answered Blake. 'In the midst of the highest flights of fancy and imagination, reason ought to preside from first to last,' said Reynolds. 'If this is True,' said Blake, 'it is a devilish Foolish Thing to be an Artist.' 'Mere Enthusiasm will carry you a little way,' said Reynolds. 'Mere Enthusiasm,' Blake answered, 'is the All in All.'

In other words, Reynolds in the *Discourses*, delivered between 1769 and 1791, contradicted not only much of his own inclination, but what were to be the inclinations of the livelier artists in a half-century. When G. F. Watts, as a Victorian idealist, maintained that he painted ideas not objects, he was in some sense still submitting himself (with the most unlively results) to this programme which Reynolds offered as a dignified, time-warranted answer to such questions as *What is Art?* and *Why should Art be respected?* The better artists of the half-century or so between Blake and Byron might have gained if there had been someone to think for them and make pronouncements clearly and persuasively on their behalf in contradiction to Reynolds.

In some points J. H. Fuseli (1741–1825) was the antidote and supplement to Reynolds which the age required. He was intelligent, energetic, and fearless, acting something of the part of a Wyndham Lewis in our own century. 'His look is lightning, his word a thunderstorm; his jest is death, his revenge hell', his friend Lavater said about the young Fuseli of 1773. He was not one of the public's painters, and he placed art above subservience to patrons. The twelve lectures which Fuseli delivered as Professor of Painting at the Academy between 1801 and 1825, and the aphorisms collected by his biographer Knowles in the *Life and Writings* (1831), recognized certain freedoms for the artist. Fuseli was not a 'romantic'. In many ways he was a thoroughgoing man of the eighteenth century. But whereas Reynolds, for example, still insisted that invention in painting did not imply the invention of the subject, since subjects were 'commonly supplied by the Poet or the Historian' (*Ut pictura poesis*), Fuseli in his lecture to Academy students propounded the question: 'Whether it be within the artist's province or not, to find or to combine a subject from himself, without having recourse to tradition or the stores of history and poetry?'

'Why not?' was his reply:

if the subject be within the limits of art and the combinations of nature; though it should have escaped observation? Shall the immediate avenues of the mind, open to all its observers, from the poet to the novelist, be shut only to the artist? Shall he be reduced to receive as alms from them what he has a right to receive as common property? (1801)

If Reynolds made rules, Fuseli also could point to Rembrandt, who contradicted rules no less than Shakespeare – 'Shakespeare alone excepted no one combined with so much transcendent exellence, so many in all other men unpardonable faults – and reconciled us to them' (1801). Every artist, he also declared,

has or ought to have, a character or system of his own; if, instead of referring that to the test of nature [by nature he still meant 'a collective idea', 'the general and permanent principles of visible objects'] you judge him by your own packed notions, or arraign him at the tribunal of schools which he does not recognize – you degrade the dignity of art, and add another fool to the herd of Dilettanti.

Fuseli did much to dignify and emancipate art, not for the patron and the public, not for the herd of Dilettanti, but for the true artist. No wonder so able, fiery, fearless, and positive a lecturer and teacher (in the Academy schools, as Keeper of the Academy, as well as Professor of Painting) energized, as he did, the young painters of the time. Benjamin Robert Haydon said with justice, after his death, that no one else had Fuseli's power 'of rousing the dormant spirit of youth'. He was one of the first to see the abilities of Turner and Constable. Samuel Palmer,[1] in a later generation, admired no painter with more fervency.

In spite of intellectual aid from Fuseli, painters of all degrees of 'vision and inspiration' had still to rely rather too much, when it came to justifying their practice and their inclination (not always identical), upon their own heart's affections. This is especially true of landscape. Pure landscape was neither popular with patrons nor particularly rewarding to artists. The drawing and painting, though, of what may be called impure landscape or landscape as an adjunct to topography, gained popularity in response to the discovery and exploration of countryside and continent. When Thomas Gray had visited Malham and Gordale Scar in the limestone wilderness of the West Riding in the autumn of 1769, he found that the topographical artists Francis Vivares, Smith of Chichester, and William Bellers had been there before him. Smith and Bellers had engraved prints of Gordale, and the age of topographical illustration, the age of impure landscape, had begun.

There were ripostes and reactions. Reynolds (who placed landscape below domestic scenes and portraiture in a scale of increasing inferiority) had spoken in his Fourth Discourse against Dutch and Flemish representations of 'an individual spot', contrasting 'views' by Rubens with the 'style of general nature' adopted by Claude in his landscapes for the production of 'beauty' (1771). Gainsborough had spoken from the older theory – rejecting with Reynolds the particulars of here and now – when he politely refused Lord Hardwicke's request for an example by himself of English scenery. 'With regard to

real Views from Nature in this Country,' Gainsborough wrote to
Lord Hardwicke in the third person, 'he has never seen any Place that
affords a subject equal to the poorest imitation of Gaspar or Claude'.
Gainsborough added a little scornfully that Paul Sandby (1725–1809)
– who like himself had been one of the first Academicians – was 'the
only Man of Genius ... who has employ'd his Pencil that way'.
Fuseli in his Academy lectures was kinder to landscape than Reynolds
had been. He amplified Reynolds's protest, inveighing against landscape as an illustration of travels or particular views – against 'the
last branch of uninteresting subjects – that kind of landscape which is
entirely occupied with the tame delineation of a given spot'. What
are commonly called 'Views', he pronounced, 'if not assisted by
nature, dictated by taste, or chosen for character, may delight the
owner of the acres they enclose, perhaps the antiquary or traveller,
but to every other eye they are little more than topography' (1805);
and when he declared in the same lecture that 'the landscape of Titian,
of Mola, of Salvator, of the Poussins, Claude, Rubens' – in spite of
Reynolds – 'Elzheimer, Rembrandt, and Wilson, spurns all relation
with this kind of map-work', he was perhaps thinking of Paul Sandby's early connection with the military survey of Scotland and the
military drawing department in the Tower of London. The Poussins,
Claude, Elsheimer – to such artists, Fuseli added, 'nature disclosed her
bosom in the varied light of rising, meridian, setting suns; in twilight, night, and dawn. Height, depth, solitude, strike, terrify, absorb, bewilder in their scenery. We tread on classic or romantic
ground through the characteristic groups of rich congenial objects.'
As for the Dutch – 'The usual choice of the Dutch school, which frequently exhibits no more than the transcript of a spot, borders, indeed, nearer on the negative kind of landscape.'

Many, indeed most, connoisseurs would have agreed with Fuseli
in condemning such 'map-work'; and they would have preferred
most of the painters in his list to the new practitioners of landscape-
at-home. But some of the new practitioners – Crome, Turner, Constable, Cotman, Bonington, Samuel Palmer – would have agreed as
well. They had to steer between the emptiness of 'map-work' and the
extreme frill or artifice of too much classic or romantic ground; between the refreshment which even topography, in Fuseli's sense,
would bring (through the direct contact of artist and environment)

and the neutralizing numbing effect of too much of the particularity of here and now. To help them in their manoeuvre artists turned especially to that poem which so widely directed sensation for more than a hundred years, Thomson's *Seasons*. This now underestimated work (of which there were above twenty editions between 1730 and 1830) offered neither stale artifice nor map-work, neither remoteness nor tame delineation of a given – or named – spot, for its own sake. In every line *The Seasons* were familiar, for example, to Turner and to Constable, men of one generation with only a year between them (Turner was born in 1775, Constable in 1776). Thomson's sentiments of a landscape pervaded by the Universal Soul and the visual experience of these two painters coalesce again and again in their pictures, exhibited at the Academy so often with the apposite quotation from *Spring, Summer, Autumn,* or *Winter.* Constable wrote to his friend Fisher in 1826, quoting *The Seasons* (*Summer*, II, 1654–6), not out of the book, but inaccurately out of a memory stocked with favourite passages.

I have dispatched a large landscape to the Academy – upright, the size of my Lock – but a subject of very different nature – inland – cornfields – a close lane, kind of thing – but it is not neglected in any part. The trees are more than usually studied and the extremities well defined – as well as their species – they are shaken by a pleasant and healthful breeze – '*at noon*' – 'while now a fresher gale, *sweeping with shadowy gust the fields of corn*'.

The picture – the famous *Cornfield* in the National Gallery – was exhibited, not as one of a given spot, but first of all as *Landscape*, then as *Landscape: Noon*.

Turner, as a second to James Thomson and *The Seasons*, drew upon Milton for his picture texts, changing in his old age rather to Lord Byron. It was to Milton also that Samuel Palmer turned (partly in deference to Fuseli's Miltonic canvases) as warrant for his paradisaical scenery, so dependent upon moons, stars, rich velvet shadows, and tufted foliage – to Milton, and to the pastoralism of Fletcher's *Faithful Shepherdess*, which embodied, Palmer said, all his 'dearest landscape longings'; but he, as well, knew *The Seasons*, which was inescapable reading.

Painters of landscape must also have derived some warrant from abroad – from one of the writings of the 'Swiss Theocritus', the painter and poet Salomon Gessner (1730–88), who was Fuseli's godfather, as gentle as Fuseli was extreme. Available to them was Gessner's by no means unimportant *Letter to M. Fuslin on Landscape Painting*, which had been translated (by W. Hooper in *New Idylles By Gessner*) in 1776. Gessner went to nature, he declared, for his one model, his one master; correcting too much niggling detail by studying masses, effects, and disposition in the painters, especially in the two Poussins and Claude. He had a word for Daniel Webb's *Inquiry into the Beauties of Painting* (1760), which departs especially in the matter of colour from too strict a neo-Classicism, and he praised Thomson's *Seasons* as a source for subjects, seeing in him 'sometimes the simplicity of Berchem, of Potter, of Roos; sometimes the grace and amenity of Lorrain [i.e. *Claude*]; frequently the great and noble character of Poussin; and then, by that contrast so important in the effect, the gloomy and savage tone of Salvator Rosa'. '*How I pity the unfeeling landscape painter, whom the sublime pictures of Thomson cannot inspire!*'

He explained that he 'delivered himself to his own ideas' and prescribed himself his own subjects; he sketched constantly to record 'ideas whose rapid and slight impression would otherwise have been infallibly lost'; he emphasized the revolutionary value of first impressions, first ideas, first illuminations – thoughts 'conceiv'd in the first warmth', effects 'with which we are struck at the first view', which are 'never so well express'd as by the strokes that are drawn at that instant'. (There, incidentally, more than in mechanical explanations, more than in a mere development from topographical tinting and 'map-work', is the explanation of the English delight in water-colour. Water-colour catches the first view, the thought conceived in the first warmth. Though difficult to handle, it is quick, it is the colour-sketcher's medium, answering to spontaneity and to things as they appear; well suited to effects of brilliance demanded by that reinstatement and refreshment of colour which also mark the change from the smoother and more sombre 'imitation' of the Augustan aesthetic.)

How familiar Gessner's remarks were to English painters, one cannot say. Gessner, though, was one of the most popular of the sentimental authors of the time; and his *Letter* was certainly read with pleasure and profit by Constable in his student days in London in 1796. His *Letter*, too, is addressed to painters, in contrast to other expositions of landscape – for example, by William Gilpin (1724–1804), brother of the considerable artist Sawrey Gilpin, and by Sir Uvedale Price (1747–1829) – which were differently aimed. Gilpin and Price's examination of the picturesque (that which is rough, irregular, and sudden in variation), supplementing Burke's categories of the beautiful (which is smooth, polished, and gradual in variation) and the sublime (which is rugged and vast), had more to do with landscape in actuality than with landscape in the frame. It was concerned more with the art of the established masters as a model for the improvement of a gentleman's acres than with art on its own living account in contemporary practice.

Gilpin and Price appealed more to connoisseurs than to artists. From the picturesque, though, proliferated those many books for amateurs on how to sketch landscape in water-colour; of which the best remembered is David Cox's *Treatise on Landscape Painting and Effect in Water Colours* (1813), illustrated, the publishers said, with 'an unusual variety of the most picturesque Scenes in England and Wales'.

Of course it would be unreasonable to look back and expect to find quite clear programmes, thought out and laid out, for all the mixed strains of painting in this period of Blake to Byron. Yet pure landscape could have done with a strong critical justification as convincing to patrons as it might have been comforting to artists. In the absence of such justification pure landscape was little rewarded or encouraged. The young painter was apt to be confused between inclination and the kinds of painting which would bring him credit and livelihood. There might in the air be a strong extroversion to nature, to environment, light, colour, particularity. In this nature it might be possible to find oneself, to find the substance of one's yearnings, or to come close to the Universal Soul, or merely to detect lessons of morality; but many of the better artists cast their eye backward and yearned persistently also for those grandeurs of History Painting or High Art, which would dignify the new English school; while the painters' public wanted neither the one nor the other, neither the landscape nor the history. The public expected painters to paint faces; beyond which – at any rate in the first thirty years of the nineteenth century – they asked for little, and were prepared to reward the painter for little, except pictures of sentiment, particularly if it were domestic, of a Dutch cast.

How did the would-be painter of landscape settle this dilemma or tackle it? He might illustrate books, especially topographical books; he might paint, against his inclination, as many faces as possible; he might mix styles and subjects, or catch at whatever fashions arose of a sudden; he might paint landscape obstinately, and struggle, and live by teaching young ladies the formulae of sketching the picturesque, or the medieval, or the primitive — ruins, cottages, cows, or donkeys — which was the fate in Norwich, for example, of John Crome (1768–1821) and John Sell Cotman (1782–1842).

The aspiring painter of landscape or 'history' had to rely, so far as exhibitions went, upon the exhibiting societies. He could send his pictures to the annual exhibitions of the Academy (where they had first to be approved by a jury of the exclusive body of Academicians), and of the British Institution, established in 1805 'to encourage and reward the talents of the artists of the United Kingdom', and later still of the Society of British Artists (1823); which was the way to the possible chances of a rich patron. The commercial possibilities of acting as intermediary between artist and purchaser were not exploited by a new, objurgated tribe of picture dealers until early in Victoria's reign. One-man exhibitions, such as Fuseli's Milton Gallery of canvases painted from Milton's poems, which he opened in 1799 and again in 1800, or William Blake's famous exhibition of 'poetical and historical inventions' at his brother's shop in 1809, or Benjamin Robert Haydon's exhibitions at the Egyptian Hall were uncommon. They were likely to cost more than the artist could afford or recover.

The three exhibitions just mentioned belonged to history painting, that persistent dream of the age. Painters and public complained that High Art was not encouraged, painters aspired or were exhorted to High Art, through all the years, from Reynolds to the Victorians. 'The Painters of England are unemploy'd in Public Works,' Blake complained in the *Descriptive Catalogue* of his exhibition; and yet painters could make England, like Italy, 'an Envied Storehouse of Intellectual Riches'. The student at the Academy schools finished his student-life by composing an historical picture from a subject chosen by his instructors. The British Institution, in its endeavours to encourage English artists, awarded its considerable premiums to often vast and always abortive essays in history — Pocock's *Thomas à Becket*

(1807), Haydon's *Assassination of Dentatus* (1810), Bird's *Death of Eli* (1813), James Ward's *Battle of Waterloo, in an Allegory* (1817), John Martin's *Belshazzar's Feast* (1821). The Art Union, which established in 1837 an annual lottery for prizes expendable only upon works of art from the exhibitions, earnestly desired its reluctant prize-winners, by a minute of 1842, 'to give a preference to Historical pictures illustrative of the Bible, British History, or British literature'; which accorded with the Union's declared purpose of forwarding the 'highest historical and poetical efforts of the Painter and Sculptor'; and twelve months later, in 1843, the dream of history painting by English artists reached its climax of still-birth and pretentiousness when 141 cartoons for frescoes in the new Houses of Parliament were exhibited in competition in Westminster Hall. The artists had been told by the Fine Arts Commission, newly established, to take their subjects from British History, or from the works of Spenser, Shakespeare, or Milton.

Their subjects – subject was indeed fatally demanded of the artist. Constable complained in 1824 that he had to combat from high quarters, even from the President of the Academy (Sir Thomas Lawrence[2]), 'the seeming plausible arguments that subject makes the picture'. The British public, declared Lady Eastlake, 'had scarcely ever advanced beyond the lowest steps of the aesthetic ladder, the estimate of a subject'. The subjects most in demand were domestic and sentimental. The axis of the art of the exhibitions was sentiment; the most popular artist of the day – in practice mawkishly sentimental, in person (according to the painter David Scott) a most uninspired looking man 'cut out of red cheese' – was David Wilkie (1785–1841), a mediocre draughtsman rapidly made an R.A., and knighted in 1836 after a career of such genre paintings as *The Blind Fiddler* (1807), *Blind Man's Buff* (1812), and *The Penny Wedding* (1818), which by their subject immediately stroked the soft underbelly of the feelings. 'Wilkie in such subjects seemed as if he were guided by the precept of Polonius,' one of his biographers remarked without guile, *'be thou familiar, but by no means vulgar.'* 'No artist's works are better known and loved than Wilkie's,' said Felix Summerly (Sir Henry Cole), in his *Handbook to the National Gallery*, in 1843. 'For the last thirty years, every print-shop has exhibited one or more engravings of his pictures to millions of admiring spectators.'

The influence upon Wilkie and others was Dutch. Thus from 1818 onwards Sir Robert Peel, patron and politician, collected Dutch genre paintings which held a neutral or negative mirror to existence. He exhibited his Dutch pictures for the delectation of a public which liked Dutch genre reflected in turn in a mirror of English sentiment, and for the instruction of artists – such as Wilkie (who was patronized by Sir Robert), Mulready, Collins (two painters whose work began with landscape), Webster, Leslie, Landseer – who all too willingly catered for that liking. Sir Robert, in the meantime, opposed the purchase for the new National Gallery (founded in 1824) of Italian masters of the *Quattrocento*. 'I think,' he would say, 'we should not collect curiosities.' Dutch example justified subject if not sentiment, though it must be admitted that Dutch painting of the seventeenth century offered as well that detail of nature, that honest and refreshing objectivity which were increasingly favoured. Even Samuel Palmer, for all his admiration of Blake, Fuseli, Claude, and Elsheimer, could not escape an early and to himself valuable reverence for Cuyp, Potter, Hobbema, and Ruysdael. To admit as much, though, is not to deny that sentiment or sentimental piety spread like a fungus, infecting painting of all kinds, history, portraiture, landscape. Everything in the exhibitions tended centripetally to sentiment; and sentiment obstructed the self-projection of the time and for all its Dutch tone put a limit to the new extroversion, the new realism or objectivity, the new directness of eye, which now struggled for life. Benjamin Robert Haydon, the friend of Wordsworth and Keats and the most violent devotee of High Art, might trust for fame, at his exhibition at the Egyptian Hall in 1832, to *Xenophon and the Ten Thousand, first viewing the Sea*; for bread he trusted to *The Sabbath Evening of a Christian* and *The First Start in Life, or Take Care, my Darling*. Or the different elements would mix not merely in the exhibition but inside the frame. William Etty (1787–1849), for example, an R.A. so given to mythologies in Venetian colour, would concoct a revel rout, in the caustic words of Constable, of 'satyrs and lady bums', of satyrs among nymphs, who on a second glance proved only to be young ladies of the London drawing-room without, for a while, some of their silk and bombazine. Or large history would dwindle to small domestic sentimental history – the costume pieces of such a painter as C. R. Leslie (1794–1859), Constable's timid biographer. Sentiment, contrariwise, would attempt to add to itself a little dignity by edging towards history in a penny wedding between low and high. Wilkie, in this way, painted for the Duke of Wellington in 1822 his *Chelsea Pensioners* (sentiments aroused by old age, duty well done, recollections of youthful prowess) *receiving the Gazette announcing the Battle of Waterloo*; this has been called the most popular work ever exhibited at the Royal Academy.

Painters more in earnest or more talented either allowed themselves prudential degrees of compromise or worked, for the most part, well away from the brightness of celebrity and eminence. Of the older generation Blake's friend and enemy, Thomas Stothard (1755–1834), painted some of the most remarkable landscapes in unexpected combinations of water-colour. Yet he could only make his living and his name by an alliance of neo-classicism and sentiment; particularly in book illustrations which share with the designs of John Flaxman the sculptor (1755–1826) or the painter Henry Howard (1769–1847), an obvious, if mild, affinity to the designs of Blake. So far as pure landscape is concerned, not a single one of the better landscape painters had a public career which it is comforting to analyse. In 1782 Richard Wilson had died in retirement and poverty. J. R. Cozens (1752–99) died obscure and insane; the great John Crome (1768–1821) and the able J. S. Cotman (1782–1842) lived provincial lives of difficulty, anxiety, and distress. The overrated Thomas Girtin (1775–1802) died young on the apparent outskirts of greatness; which was the case also of R. P. Bonington (1801–28). James Ward (1769–1859), a massive, nearly ludicrous failure in the world's eye, was sustained only by relentless energy and an application to most of the possible kinds of studio painting. His masterpiece of landscape and the sublime *Gordale Scar* (1812), now in the Tate Gallery, lay for much of his life rolled up in the basement of the British Museum. Francis Danby (1793–1861) survived less by a talent expressed in early innocent and objective combinations of genre and landscape, and intermittently in later landscapes of individual power, than by excursions, in the wake of Turner, into sensationalism and fairy-fancy and nymphatics. Samuel Palmer in his creative time from 1825 to 1830 produced landscapes which were a remarkable fusion and more remarkable transmutation of elements – the neo-classicism of Stothard and Flaxman, the poetries of Blake and Fuseli, the 'primitivism' (as he felt it to be) of

Dürer and Lucas van Leyden, and the new naturalism of the period, as if in a head-on crash between past and present. Though he exhibited year after year, his landscapes of nature (in his own words) 'received into the soul', landscapes of a Christian nature mysticism which are among the most wonderful and moving works of the English school, they received, so far as is known, only a single notice. A critic in the *European Magazine*, in his review of the Academy's summer exhibition of 1825, spoke of two pictures 'by a Mr Palmer' so 'amazing' that the painter should have exhibited himself alongside at a shilling a look.

The most gigantic artist of the time, J. M. W. Turner (1775–1851), succeeded, in the worldly sense, less by his pure landscape than by work for the publishers and by canvases which astutely blended – and varied – traits of history, sensationalism, sentiment, and piety. The purest of his landscape (such as the Thames oils of 1807) was little known or regarded. The extreme dissolution of static form into catherine-wheels of shimmering colour which he achieved in the independence of his old age, in canvases which are the triumphs of his vision, appeared incomprehensible. Critics and public treated it as a yearly joke of the Academy exhibition. John Constable (1776–1837), whose canvases of freshness and sparkle were, as he called them, his acts, a painter for whom expression and conception, means and subject, were at last inseparable, continued like a thunderstorm, in Kierkegaard's definition of genius, to go resolutely against the common winds of his time, supported by conviction, feeling and character (and private means) against half-praise, neglect, contempt, and misinterpretation.

Looking back now only to those works of art which retain an affective energy, to us much of the period of Blake and Byron certainly appears as one of great landscape painting. Looking back, though, from 1830 or 1840, as a disappointed landscape painter or an equable clear-eyed observer, one's view would have been different. One would have seen the period as the aged Mulready saw it somewhat later, when he gave evidence before the Commission on the Royal Academy of 1863 – as a time in which the painters, for a long while isolated by the French wars, had continued to paint what their public called for, 'portraits demanding the respectful observance of individual character and pictures of subjects drawn from familiar life'; to which was added as well a sentimental spice of fairyland and the seraglio. 'The Devil,' wrote Constable in 1829, when the Academy exhibition came around, 'must vomit pictures all over London.' But not landscapes. Landscape was 'below zero' in the London of 1837, according to W. B. Scott. Its practitioners had had reason to be glad of strange markets. The public would look at panoramas, the public would buy annuals. Girtin in 1802 exhibited a vast panorama of London, the 'Eidometropolis', in the Great Room at Spring Gardens, and planned to follow it with a panorama of Paris. Beginning with the *Forget-me-not* of 1823, annuals proliferated on the sentimental model of the German *taschenbücher*, and called for designs of sugared landscape well fitted to the poems of Samuel Rogers or Tom Moore, the more shallow of Byron's excesses, or the more flimsy, footling, and airy-fairy gestures of a Shelley or a George Darley.

And the topographical market endured. Travel at home and abroad, coupled with the search for the picturesque and the medieval and the 'primitive', increased both a patron's and a publisher's demand for landscape of the given spot; resulting, for example, in albums of the scenery of the Lakes, in the highly professional and agreeable aquatints made by William Daniell (1769–1837), for the massive volumes of *A Voyage Around Great Britain* (1814–25), or in Cotman's etchings for his *Architectural Antiquities of Norfolk* (1818) and his *Architectural Antiquities of Normandy* (1822). Travel in the East resulted also in the *Oriental Scenery* (1808) of Thomas Daniell (1749–1840), assisted by William Daniell (who was his nephew), records of Oriental architecture which, in turn, influenced the architectural exoticism and charm of the Prince Regent's Royal Pavilion at Brighton. If, indeed, there is a rift between landscape and topography, between pure landscape and that tame map-work Fuseli had so decried in his lecture of 1805, topography must none the less have its acknowledgement. The impulsion to trudge and travel after topographical drawings and illustrations did have the great result, as I have suggested, of refreshing landscape as a style and inspiring in some artists a more piercing and more touching vision; much as the sententious hill and prospect poems of the period opened a way (by their own admission) for the wider, more penetrative, more humane insights of Coleridge and Wordsworth.

Outside landscape William Blake, as an artist, bravely made his own lifelong obscured counter-journey, for all his technical deficiencies. One should point also to a little-recognized and at the time little-rewarded change in portraiture after 1800, mainly from the hand and eye of lesser painters who looked their sitters again (unlike the fashionable Sir Thomas Lawrence) in the wart and the crease and the flesh, as though they, too, were natural objects; and to the work, now mostly transferred from England to Swiss collections, of the Anglo-Swiss artist, Jacques-Laurent Agasse (1767–1849), a pupil of David's, influenced over here by Stubbs; a painter not only of riders, horses, and other animals, but of genre subjects of English life which show that 'domestic' art can have qualities of structure, colour, innocence, and appeal without a mawkishly unimaginative, Wilkie-like dependence upon point and title and subject. 'He was of independent, unconciliating manners,' it was said of Agasse. He 'lived poor and died poor'.

Upon a broad view, drawing was the deficiency of the best artists of the time (comparable to a loosening or softening of the articulation of poetry between Dryden and Shelley), while colour, as the vehicle of emotion, was their triumph. Gravelot, the French draughtsman who taught Gainsborough, remarked to the engraver Basire that 'De English may be very clever in deir own opinions, but dey do not draw de draw'. Yet they drew de draw with more dexterity and precision from Thornhill to Rowlandson than in the colourists' period from Blake to Turner and Palmer, partly because of closer associations with France and a strictness of early work for Huguenot goldsmiths and silk-weavers whose influx had followed the revocation of the Edict of Nantes in 1685.

Per contra, a self-delivery to nature, an uprush and outrush of feeling, a championship of spontaneity and the first impression favoured colour (in water-colour especially) rather than the draughtsman's line; all the more so in a period fascinated by the inquiries of Newton, Goethe, Thomas Young, and others into the constitution and mysteries of colour and light.

NOTES

1. Palmer and some of his circle of 1825–30 also made copies for themselves of Blake's marginalia on Reynolds.

2. Lawrence's opinion was that 'high merit in art consists not so much in sensation as in thought'.

NOTES

PART IV

PART IV

APPENDIX

VOLUME 5

COMPILED BY HILDA D. SPEAR

List of Abbreviations

E.&S.	Essays and Studies by Members of the English Association
E.C.	Essays in Criticism
E.L.	Everyman's Library edition
E.L.H.	English Literary History
E.L.N.	English Language Notes
M.L.N.	Modern Language Notes
M.L.R.	Modern Language Review
M.P.	Modern Philology
N.C.B.E.L	The New Cambridge Bibliography of English Literature
P.M.L.A.	Publications of the Modern Language Association of America
P.Q.	Philological Quarterly
R.E.L.	Review of English Literature
R.E.S.	Review of English Studies
W.C.	World's Classics
abr.	abridged
b.	born
c.	circa
ch.	chapter
d.	died
ed.	edited, editor
edn	edition
pt.	part
repr.	reprinted
rev.	revised
trans.	translated
vol.	volume

Under each author, the aim has been to list first the standard or a reliable biography, secondly standard editions and where possible good selections, and thirdly a selection of books and articles for further study.

FOR FURTHER READING
AND REFERENCE

The Social and Intellectual Setting

I. HISTORIES: GENERAL AND POLITICAL

Aspinall, A. and Smith, A. E. (eds.) *English Historical Documents, 1785–1832,* 1959

Bartlett, C. J. *Castlereagh,* 1966

Brewer, J. *Party Ideology and Popular Politics at the Accession of George III,* 1976

Briggs, A. *The Age of Improvement,* 1959

Brooke, J. *King George III,* 1972

Brown, L. M. and Christie, I. R. (eds.) *Bibliography of British History 1789–1851,* 1977

Bryant, A. *The Age of Elegance,* 1950
> *The Years of Endurance,* 1942
> *Years of Victory,* 1944

Cannon, J. *Parliamentary Reform, 1640–1832,* 1973
> (ed.) *The Whig Ascendancy,* 1981

Dickinson, H. T. *Britain and the French Revolution 1789–1815,* 1989

Ehrman, J. *The Younger Pitt, The Years of Acclaim,* 1969

Ferguson, W. *Scotland, 1689 to the Present,* 1968

Foord, A. S. *His Majesty's Opposition 1714–1830,* 1964

Gash, N. *The Age of Peel,* 1968

Hanham, H. J. (ed.) *The Nineteenth Century Constitution 1815–1914,* 1969

Hibbert, C. *George IV, Prince of Wales, 1762–1811,* 1972
> *George IV: Regent and King,* 1973

Hinde, W. *George Canning,* 1973

Hone, J. A. *For the Cause of Truth: Radicalism in London, 1796–1821,* 1982

Keir, D. L. *The Constitutional History of Modern Britain, 1485–1937,* 1938; 8th edn, 1966

Kemp, B. *King and Commons, 1660–1832,* 1957

Lenman, B. *Integration, Enlightenment, and Industrialization: Scotland 1746–1832,* 1981

Mitchell, L. G. *Charles James Fox,* 1992

379

O'Gorman, F. *Voters, Patrons and Parties: The Unreformed Electorate of Hanoverian England 1735–1832*, 1989

Plumb, J. H. *England in the Eighteenth Century*, 1950
　　The First Four Georges, 1956

Smith, E. A. *Whig Principles and Party Politics: Earl Fitzwilliam and the Whig Party, 1748–1833*, 1975

Smout, T. C. *A History of the Scottish People*, 1969

Stevenson, J. (ed.) *London in the Age of Reform*, 1977

Thompson, E. P. *Whigs and Hunters: The Origin of the Black Act*, 1975

II. THE SOCIAL AND ECONOMIC BACKGROUND

See under *Authors*: Cobbett, Mill, Southey, Wollstonecraft.

Ackermann, R. *The Microcosm of London*, 3 vols., 1808–11; repr., 1904

Ashton, T. S. *The Industrial Revolution: 1760–1850*, 1948

Bagwell, P. S. *The Transport Revolution in Britain from 1770*, 1974

Bovill, E. W. *English Country Life, 1780–1830*, 1962

Boyer, G. R. *An Economic History of the English Poor Law, 1750–1850*, 1990

Bumsted, J. M. *The People's Clearance, 1770–1815: Highland Emigration to British North America*, 1983

Campbell, R. H. *Scotland since 1707*, 1965

Chaloner, W. *The Social and Economic Development of Crewe, 1780–1923*, 1950

Chambers, J. D. *Population, Economy and Society in Pre-Industrial England*, 1972
　　The Vale of Trent, 1760–1800, 3rd Supplement to *The Economic History Review*, 1957

Chapman, S. D. and Chambers, J. D. *The Beginnings of Industrial Britain*, 1970

Cole, G. D. H. *A Short History of the British Working Class Movement, 1789–1947*, 3 vols., 1925–7; rev. edn, 1948

Deane, P. *The First Industrial Revolution*, 1965

Dicey, A. V. *Lectures on the Relation between Law and Public Opinion in England during the Nineteenth Century*, 1905; repr., 1948

Emsley, C. *British Society and the French Wars, 1798–1815*, 1979

Flinn, M. W. *The Origins of the Industrial Revolution*, 1966

Foster, J. *Class Struggle and the Industrial Revolution: Early Industrial Capitalism in Three English Towns*, 1974

Fulford, R. *Samuel Whitbread, 1764–1815: A Study in Opposition*, 1967

George, M. D. *London Life in the Eighteenth Century*, 1925

Gregg, P. *A Social and Economic History of Britain, 1760–1950*, 1950

Hadfield, C. *British Canals: An Illustrated History*, 1950; rev. edn, 1959

Hammond, J. L. and B. *The Skilled Labourer, 1760–1832*, 1919
　　The Town Labourer, 1760–1832, 1917

Harrison, M. *Mass Phenomena in English Towns, 1790–1835*, 1988

Hobsbawm, E. J. *Industry and Empire: An Economic History of Britain Since 1750*, 1968

Horn, P. *Life and Labour in Rural England, 1760–1850*, 1987

Jones, E. L. *Agriculture and the Industrial Revolution*, 1974

Landes, D. S. *The Unbound Prometheus*, 1969

Laver, J. *The Age of Illusion: Manners and Morals 1750–1848*, 1972

Low, D. A. *That Sunny Dome: A Portrait of Regency Britain*, 1977

MacDonagh, O. *The Inspector-General: Sir Jeremiah Fitzpatrick and the Politics of Social Reform, 1783–1802*, 1981

Marshall, D. *English People in the Eighteenth Century*, 1956

Mathias, P. *The First Industrial Nation: An Economic History of Britain, 1700–1914*, 1969

Mingay, G. E. *English Landed Society in the Eighteenth Century*, 1963
    (ed.) *The Agrarian History of England and Wales, Vol. VI, 1750–1850*, 1989

Owen, D. *Philanthropy in England, 1660–1960*, 1965

Parker, R. A. C. *Coke of Norfolk: A Financial and Agricultural Study, 1707–1842*, 1975

Patterson, A. T. *Radical Leicester, 1780–1850*, 1954

Pawson, E. *The Early Industrial Revolution*, 1979

Perkin, H. J. *The Origins of Modern English Society, 1780–1880*, 1969

Prothero, I. J. *Artisans and Politics in Early Nineteenth-Century London: John Gast and His Times*, 1981

Quinault, R. and Stevenson, J. (eds.) *Popular Protest and Public Order: Six Studies in British History, 1790–1920*, 1974

Rostow, W. W. *The Stages of Economic Growth*, 1960

Taylor, A. J. (ed.) *The Standard of Living in Britain in the Industrial Revolution*, 1975

Thompson, E. P. *The Making of the English Working Class*, 1963

Thompson, F. M. L. (ed.) *The Cambridge Social History of Britain, 1750–1950*, 3 vols., 1990

Tranter, N. *Population Since the Industrial Revolution*, 1973

Turley, D. *The Culture of English Anti-Slavery, 1780–1860*, 1991

Webb, R. K. *The British Working-Class Reader, 1790–1948*, 1955

White, R. J. *From Waterloo to Peterloo*, 1957

Williams, E. *Capitalism and Slavery*, 1944

Youngson, A. J. *The Making of Classical Edinburgh, 1750–1840*, 1966

III. INDUSTRIAL HISTORY

Ashton, T. S. *An Eighteenth Century Industrialist, Peter Stubs of Warrington, 1756–1806*, 1939
    Iron and Steel in the Industrial Revolution, 1924

Ashton, T. S. and Sykes, J. *The Coal Industry of the Eighteenth Century*, 1929

Barker, T. C. and Harris, J. R. *A Merseyside Town in the Industrial Revolution: St Helens, 1750–1900*, 1954

Court, W. H. B. *The Rise of the Midland Industries, 1600–1838*, 1938

Crouzet, F. *The First Industrialists*, 1985

Edwards, M. M. *The Growth of the British Cotton Trade, 1782–1815*, 1967

Fitton, R. S. and Wadsworth, A. P. *The Strutts and the Arkwrights, 1758–1830*, 1959

Frow-Smith, R. *A History of British Livestock Husbandry, 1700–1900,* 1959

Hamilton, H. *The English Brass and Copper Industries to 1800,* 1967

Hudson, K. *Industrial Archaeology,* 1963

Hyde, C. K. *Technological Change and the British Iron Industry, 1700–1870,* 1977

Lee, C. H. *A Cotton Enterprise 1795–1840: a History of M'Connel Kennedy fine cotton spinners,* 1972

Mann, J. de L. *The Cloth Industry in the West of England 1640–1880,* 1971

Miles, D. *Francis Place, 1771–1854: The Life of a Remarkable Radical,* 1989

Pollard, S. *The Genesis of Modern Management: A Study of the Industrial Revolution in Great Britain,* 1965

Raistrick, A. *Dynasty of Ironfounders: The Darbys and Coalbrookdale,* 1953

Randall, A. *Before the Luddites: Custom, Community and Machinery in the English Woollen Industry, 1776–1809,* 1991

Read, D. *Press and People, 1790–1850,* 1961

Rimmer, W. G. *Marshalls of Leeds, Flax Spinners, 1788–1886,* 1960

Sigsworth, E. *Black Dyke Mills,* 1958

IV. PHILOSOPHY, RELIGION, SCIENCE AND EDUCATION

See under *Authors:* Bentham, Coleridge, Edgeworth, Godwin, Mill, P. B. Shelley, Wollstonecraft.

Bates, E. *Rural Philosophy, or, Reflections on Knowledge, Virtue and Happiness* rev. and enlarged edn, 1804

Brougham, Lord H. *Practical Observations upon the Education of the People,* 1825

Davy, H. *Elements of Chemical Philosophy,* 1812

Paine, T. *The Rights of Man,* 2 vols., 1791–2

Paley, W. *Natural Theology,* 1802

Stewart, D. *Outlines of Moral Philosophy,* 1793

Cobban, A. *Edmund Burke and the Revolt against the Eighteenth Century,* 1929; 2nd edn, 1960

Grave, S. A. *The Scottish Philosophy of Common Sense,* 1960

Lyons, D. *In the Interest of the Governed,* 1973

Plamenatz, J. *Man and Society,* Vol. I, ch. 9 and Vol. II, ch. 1, 1963

Willey, B. *The Eighteenth Century Background,* 1940

Bossy, J. *The English Catholic Community, 1570–1850,* 1976

Coupland, R. *The British Anti-Slavery Movement,* 1933

Henriques, U. *Religious Toleration in England, 1787–1833,* 1961

Semmel, B. *The Methodist Revolution,* 1974

Ward, W. R. *Religion and Society in England, 1790–1850,* 1972

Wilbur, E. M. *A History of Unitarianism,* 1952

Willams, B. *The Making of Manchester Jewry,* 1976

Bernal, J. D. *Science and Industry in the Nineteenth Century,* 1953

Christie, J. and Shuttleworth, S. (eds.) *Nature Transfigured: Science and Literature, 1700–1900*, 1989

Clow, A. and N. *The Chemical Revolution*, 1952

Desmond, A. *The Politics of Evolution: Morphology, Medicine and Reform in Radical London*, 1989

Olson, R. *Scottish Philosophy and British Physics, 1750–1880: A Study in the Foundations of the Victorian Scientific Style*, 1975

Singer, C. *et al.* (eds.) *The History of Technology, IV: The Industrial Revolution*, 1958

Winsor, M. P. *Starfish, Jellyfish and the Order of Life in Nineteenth-Century Science*, 1976

Wolf, A. *A History of Science, Technology and Philosophy in the Eighteenth Century*, rev. D. McKie, 1952

Adamson, J. W. *English Education, 1789–1902*, pt. 1, 1930

Cruse, A. *The Englishman and his Books in the Early Nineteenth Century*, 1930

Laqueur, T. W. *Religion and Respectability: Sunday Schools and Working Class Culture, 1780–1850*, 1976

Silver, H. *English Education and the Radicals, 1780–1850*, 1976

Smith, J. W. A. *The Birth of Modern Education*, 1954

Stewart, W. A. C. and McCann, W. P. *The Educational Innovators, 1750–1880*, 1967

V. DIARIES, LETTERS AND PERSONAL REMINISCENCE

See under *Authors*: Austen, Bentham, Blake, Bowles, Burns, Byron, Clare, Cobbett, Coleridge, Darley, De Quincey, Edgeworth, Godwin, Haydon, Hogg, Hood, Hunt, Keats, Lamb, Moore, Reynolds, Robinson, Scott, M. Shelley, P. B. Shelley, Southey, Wollstonecraft, Wordsworth.

Aspinall, A. (ed.) *The Correspondence of George, Prince of Wales, 1770–1812*, 8 vols., 1963–72

  The Later Correspondence of George III, 1783–1810, 5 vols., 1962–70

  The Letters of George IV, 1812–1831, 3 vols., 1938

Byng, J., Viscount Torrington *The Torrington Diaries* ed. C. B. Andrews, 4 vols., 1934–8

Castle, E. (ed.) *The Jerningham Letters, 1780–1843*, 1896

Cockburn, H. *Memorials of his Time* ed. H. A. Cockburn, 1909

Fremantle, A. (ed.) *The Wynne Diaries, 1789–1820*, 3 vols., 1835–40; abr., 1952

Holland, Lady E. *The Journal of Elizabeth, Lady Holland* ed. Earl of Ilchester, 2 vols., 1909

Maxwell, H. (ed.) *The Creevy Papers*, 2 vols., 1903–4

Pool, B. (ed.) *The Croker Papers, 1808–1857*, 1967

Romilly, S. *Memoirs of the Life of Sir Samuel Romilly*, 3 vols, 1840

Strachey, L. and Fulford, R. (eds.) *The Greville Memoirs*, 1938

Thale, M. (ed.) *The Autobiography of Francis Place, 1771–1854*, 1972

Woodforde, J. *The Diary of a Country Parson, 1758–1802* ed. J. D. Beresford, 5 vols., 1924–30; abr., 1978

Fothergill, R. A. *Private Chronicles: A Study of English Diaries*, 1974

Todd, W. M., III *The Familiar Letter as a Literary Genre in the Age of Pushkin*, 1976

VI. THE NON-LITERARY ARTS

See under *Authors*: Blake, Haydon, Hazlitt.

Gilpin, W. *Remarks on Forest Scenery and Other Woodland Views*, 2 vols., 1791

Price, U. *An Essay on the Picturesque, as Compared with the Sublime and the Beautiful*, 2 vols., 1794–8

Ford, B. (ed.) *The Cambridge Guide to the Arts in Britain. 5: The Augustan Age*, 1991; *6: Romantics and Early Victorians*, 1990

Allen, B. S. *Tides in English Taste, 1619–1800*, 2 vols., 1937

Artz, F. B. *From the Renaissance to Romanticism: Trends in Style in Art, Literature and Music, 1300–1830*, 1962

Clark, K. M. *The Gothic Revival: An Essay in the History of Taste*, 1928; rev. edn, 1950

Edwards, R. and Ramsey, L. G. G. (eds.) *The Connoisseur Period Guides.* IV: *The Late Georgian Period, 1760–1810*; V: *The Regency Period, 1810–1830*, 1956–8

Sitwell, S. *British Architects and Craftsmen: A Survey of Taste, Design and Style: 1600–1830*, 1945; rev. edn, 1947

Steegman, J. *The Rule of Taste from George I to George IV*, 1936

Andrews, M. *The Search for the Picturesque: Landscape Aesthetics and Tourism in Britain 1760–1800*, 1989

(ed.) *The Picturesque: Literary Sources and Documents*, vols. II and III, 1994

Barbier, C. P. *William Gilpin: His Drawings, Teaching, and Theory of the Picturesque*, 1963

Barrell, J. *The Political Theory of Painting from Reynolds to Hazlitt: 'The Body of the Public'*, 1986

Bicknell, P. *Beauty, Horror and Immensity: Picturesque Landscape in Britain, 1750–1850*, 1981

Boase, T. S. R. (ed.) *Oxford History of English Art* X: *1800–1870*, 1959

Brion, M. *Art of the Romantic Era* trans. D. Carroll, 1966

Caudwell, H. *The Creative Impulse in Writing and Painting*, 1951

Clark, K. M. *Landscape into Art*, 1949

Cundall, H. M. *A History of British Water Colour Painting*, 1908; rev. edn, 1929

Fawcett, T. *Art in the English Provinces: Artists, Patrons, and Institutions outside London, 1800–1830*, 1974

Grigson, G. *The Harp of Aeolus*, 1947

Klingender, F. D. *Art and the Industrial Revolution*, 1947; rev. A. Elton, 1968

Piper, J. *British Romantic Artists*, 1942

Quennell, P. *Romantic England: Writing and Painting, 1717–1851*, 1970
Ray, G. N. *The Illustrator and the Book in England from 1790 to 1914*, 1976
Tait, A. A. *The Landscape Garden in Scotland, 1735–1835*, 1980
Tinker, C. B. *Painter and Poet: Studies in the Literary Relations of English Painting*, 1938
Wilenski, R. H. *English Painting*, 1933; rev. edn, 1954

George, M. D. *Hogarth to Cruikshank: Social Change in Graphic Satire*, 1967
Hill, D. *Mr Gillray, The Caricaturist*, 1965
   (ed.) *Fashionable Contrasts, Caricatures by James Gillray*, 1966

Chalklin, C. W. *The Provincial Towns of Georgian England: A Study of the Building Process, 1740–1820*, 1974
Davis, T. *The Architecture of John Nash*, 1960
Gotch, J. A. *The English Home from Charles I to George IV*, 1918
Hill, F. *Georgian Lincoln*, 1966
Hussey, C. *English Country Houses: Late Georgian, 1800–1840*, 1958
Olsen, D. J. *Town Planning in London in the Eighteenth and Nineteenth Centuries*, 1965
Penny, N. *Church Monuments in Romantic England*, 1977
Smith, W. H. *Architecture in English Fiction*, 1934
Stillman, D. *English Neo-Classical Architecture*, 1988
Summerson, J. *Architecture in Britain, 1530 to 1830*, 1953
   Georgian London, 1945

Cornforth, J. *English Interiors, 1790–1848: The Quest for Comfort*, 1978
Gow, I. *The Scottish Interior*, 1991
Jourdain, M. *English Interior Decoration, 1500–1830*, 1950
Jourdain, M. and Rose, F. *English Furniture: The Georgian Period, 1750–1830*, 1953

Abraham, G. (ed.) *The New Oxford History of Music*, vol. 8, 1982
Blom, E. *Music in England*, chs. VII–VIII, 1942
Temperley, N. (ed.) *The Athlone History of Music in Britain*, Vol. 5: *The Romantic Age, 1800–1914*, 1981

The Literature

VII. BIBLIOGRAPHIES

Annual Bibliography of English Language and Literature, annually since 1921
Fogle, R. H. *Romantic Poets and Prose Writers*, 1967
Houtchens, C. W. and L. H. (eds.) *The English Romantic Poets and Essayists*, 1957; rev. edn, 1966
Jackson, J. R. de J. *Romantic Poetry by Women: A Bibliography, 1770–1835*, 1993
Raysor, T. M. (ed.) *The English Romantic Poets*, 1950; rev. F. Jordan, 1972

The Romantic Movement: A Selective and Critical Bibliography in E. L. H.,
    1937–49, P.Q., 1950–64, E.L.N., 1965–78, Garland Publishing Inc.,
    1979–94 and currently published annually by Locust Hill Press, CT
Royle, T. *The Macmillan Companion to Scottish Literature,* 1983
Ward, W. S. *British Periodicals and Newspapers, 1789–1832: A Bibliography of
    Secondary Sources,* 1972
    (ed.) *Literary Reviews in British Periodicals 1798–1826: A Bibliography,* 4
    vols., 1972–9
Watson, G. (ed.) N.C.B.E.L. II–III, 1969–71
The Year's Work in English Studies, annually since 1919

VIII. GENERAL STUDIES

Abrams, M. H. *Natural Supernaturalism: Tradition and Revolution in Romantic
    Literature,* 1971
Bate, J. *Shakespeare and the English Romantic Imagination,* 1986
Bate, W. J. *From Classic to Romantic,* 1946
Bowra, C. M. *The Romantic Imagination,* 1950
Butler, M. *Romantics, Rebels and Reactionaries,* 1981
Cafarelli, A. W. *Prose in the Age of Poets: Romanticism and Biographical Narrative
    from Johnson to De Quincey,* 1990
Collins, A. S. *The Profession of Letters, 1780–1832,* 1928
Cooke, M. G. *The Romantic Will,* 1976
Craig, D. *Scottish Literature and the Scottish People, 1680–1830,* 1961
Hayter, A. *Opium and the Romantic Imagination,* 1968
Hazlitt, W. *The Spirit of the Age,* 1825; W.C., 1904
Hilles, F. W. and Bloom, H. (eds.) *From Sensibility to Romanticism: Essays
    Presented to Frederick A. Pottle,* 1965
Hoeveler, D. L. *Romantic Androgyny: The Women Within,* 1990
Jack, I. and Renwick, W. L. *Oxford History of English Literature,* IX and X, 1963
Jackson, W. *The Probable and the Marvelous: Blake, Wordsworth, and the
    Eighteenth-Century Critical Tradition,* 1978
Kelly, G. *Women, Writing and Revolution, 1790–1827,* 1993
Ker, W. P. *On Modern Literature* ed. T. Spencer and J. Sutherland, 1955
Kinsley, J. (ed.) *Scottish Poetry: A Critical Survey,* 1955
Kovačevič, I. (ed.) *Fact into Fiction: English Literature and the Industrial Scene,*
    1975
Logan, J. V. *et al.* (eds.) *Some British Romantics: A Collection of Essays,* 1966
Mellor, A. K. *Romanticism and Gender,* 1993
Muir, P. *English Children's Books, 1600–1900,* 1954
Perkins, D. *Is Literary History Possible?,* 1992
Pickering, S. *The Moral Tradition in English Fiction, 1785–1850,* 1976
Praz, M. *The Romantic Agony* trans. A. Davidson, 1933; rev. edn, 1951
Rodway, A. *The Romantic Conflict,* 1968
Sales, R. *English Literature in History, 1780–1830,* 1983
Selincourt, E. de. *Wordsworthian and other Studies,* 1947

Smith, O. *The Politics of Language, 1791–1819*, 1991
Speirs, J. *Poetry Towards Novel*, 1971
Stillinger, J. *Multiple Authorship and the Myth of Solitary Genius*, 1991
Sutherland, D. *On Romanticism*, 1971
Ward, G. *Guide to Romantic Literature from 1790 to 1830*, rev. edn., 1994
Willey, B. *The Eighteenth Century Background*, 1940
    Nineteenth Century Studies, 1949
Williams, R. *The Country and the City*, 1973

IX. POETRY

Abrams, M. H. (ed.) *English Romantic Poets: Modern Essays in Criticism*, 1960; rev. edn, 1975
Armstrong, I. *Language as Living Form in Nineteenth-Century Poetry*, 1982
Bloom, H. *The Anxiety of Influence: A Theory of Poetry*, 1973
Bradley, A. C. *English Poetry and German Philosophy in the Age of Wordsworth*, 1909
Bush, D. *Mythology and the Romantic Tradition in English Poetry*, 1937
Christiansen, R. *Romantic Affinities: Portraits from an Age, 1780–1830*, 1988
Curran, S. *Poetic Form and British Romanticism*, 1986
Fairchild, H. N. *Religious Trends in English Poetry* III, *1780–1830*, 1949
Grierson, H. J.C. *The Background of English Literature: Classical and Romantic*, 1934
Harvey, A. D. *English Poetry in a Changing Society, 1780–1805*, 1980
Hough, G., *The Romantic Poets*, 1953
James, D. G. *The Romantic Comedy*, 1948
Knight, G. W. *The Starlit Dome*, 1941
Kroeber, K. *Romantic Narrative Art*, 1960
Leavis, F. R. *Revaluation*, 1936
Mellor, A. K. *English Romantic Irony*, 1980
Read, H. *The True Voice of Feeling: Studies in English Romantic Poetry*, 1953
Sickels, E. M. *The Gloomy Egoist: Moods and Themes of Melancholy from Gray to Keats*, 1932
Thorpe, C. D. et al. (eds) *The Major Romantic Poets: A Symposium in Reappraisal*, 1957
Watson, J. R. *English Poetry of the Romantic Period: 1789–1830*; rev. edn., 1992
Woodring, C. *Politics in English Romantic Poetry*, 1970

X. THE NOVEL

Allen, W. *The English Novel*, 1954
Birkhead, E. *The Tale of Terror, A Study of the Gothic Romance*, 1921
Block, A. *The English Novel, 1740–1850: A Catalogue*; rev. edn, 1961
Campbell, I. (ed.) *Nineteenth-Century Scottish Fiction*, 1979
Colby, V. *Yesterday's Woman: Domestic Realism in the English Novel*, 1974

Howells, C. A. *Love, Mystery and Misery: Feeling in Gothic Fiction*, 1978
Kelly, G. *English Fiction of the Romantic Period, 1789–1830*, 1989
    The English Jacobin Novel, 1780–1805, 1976
Kiely, R. *The Romantic Novel in England*, 1972
Leavis, Q. D. *Fiction and the Reading Public*, 1932
MacCarthy, B. G. *The Later Women Novelists: 1744–1818*, 1947
Mayo, R. D. *The English Novel in the Magazines, 1740–1815*, 1962
Summers, M. *The Gothic Quest*, 1938
Tompkins, J. M. S. *The Popular Novel in England, 1770–1800*, 1932
Wagenknecht, E. *Cavalcade of the English Novel*, 1943

XI. THE LITERARY PERIODICAL

Blunden, E. *Leigh Hunt's 'Examiner' Examined, 1808–1825*, 1928
Clive, J. *Scotch Reviewers: 'The Edinburgh Review', 1802–1815*, 1957
Clive, M. *'Blackwood's' in Midwest Quarterly*, XV, 1974
Copinger, W. A. *Bibliographiana II: On the Authorship of the First Hundred Numbers of the Edinburgh Review*, 1895
Cox, R. G. 'The Great Reviews', I–II in *Scrutiny*, VI, 1937
Graham, W. *Tory Criticism in the Quarterly Review, 1809–1853*, 1921
Hayden, J. D. *The Romantic Reviewers 1802–1824*, 1969
Hildyard, M. C. *Lockhart's Literary Criticism*, 1931
Joyce, M. *Edinburgh, The Golden Age, 1769–1832*, 1951
Montluzin, E. L. de *The Anti-Jacobins, 1798–1800, The Early Contributors to the Anti-Jacobin Review*, 1988
Reiman, D. H. (ed.) *The Romantics Reviewed: Contemporary Reviews of British Romantic Writers*, 9 vols., 1972
Roper, D. *Reviewing before the 'Edinburgh', 1792–1802*, 1979
Sullivan, A. (ed.) *British Literary Magazines II: The Romantic Age, 1789–1836*, 1983

XII. DRAMA

Booth, M. R. *et al. The Revels History of Drama in English. Vol. VI 1750–1880*, 1975
Conolly, L. W. *The Censorship of English Drama, 1737–1824*, 1976
Donkin, E. *Women Playwrights in London, 1776–1829*, 1997
Donohue, J. W. *Dramatic Character in the English Romantic Age*, 1970
Fletcher, R. M., *English Romantic Drama, 1795–1843; A Critical History*, 1967
Nicoll, A. *A History of Early Nineteenth Century Drama* IV, *1800–1850*, 1930; rev. edn, 1955
    A History of Late Eighteenth Century Drama, 1750–1800, 1927; rev. edn, 1952

XIII. CRITICISM

Abrams, M. H. *The Mirror and the Lamp: Romantic Theory and the Critical Tradition*, 1953

FOR FURTHER READING AND REFERENCE

Babcock, R. W. *The Genesis of Shakespeare Idolatry, 1766–1799*, 1931

Foakes, R. A. (ed.) *Romantic Criticism, 1800–1850*, 1968

Hodgart, P. and Redpath, T. (eds.) *Romantic Perspectives. The Work of Crabbe, Blake, Wordsworth and Coleridge as Seen by their Contemporaries and by Themselves*, 1964

Jordan, F. *The English Romantic Poets: A Review of Research and Criticism*, 1985

Redpath, T. (ed.) *The Young Romantics and Critical Opinion, 1807–1824*, 1973

Saintsbury, G. *Essays in English Literature, 1780–1860* 1890

Smith, D. N. (ed.) *Shakespeare Criticism, 1623–1840*, 1916

Wellek, R. *A History of Modern Criticism, 2: The Romantic Age*, 1955

AUTHORS AND WORKS

Collections and Anthologies

Bernbaum, E. (ed.) *An Anthology of Romanticism and Guide through the Romantic Movement*, 5 vols., 1929–30; rev. edn, 1948–9

Bloom, H. and Trilling, L. (eds.) *The Oxford Anthology of English Literature*, 2 vols., 1973

Mahoney, J. *The English Romantics: Major Poetry and Critical Theory*, 1978

Scott, A. F. (ed.) *Every One a Witness: The Georgian Age*, 1970

Auden, W. H. and Pearson, N. H. (eds.) *Poets of the English Language*, IV, 1952

Breen, J. (ed.) *Women Romantic Poets, 1785–1832: An Anthology*, 1992

Jerrold, W. and Leonard, R. M. (eds.), *A Century of Parody and Imitation*, 1913

McGann, J. J. (ed.) *The New Oxford Book of Romantic Period Verse*, 1994

Rice-Oxley, L. (ed.) *Poetry of the Anti-Jacobin*, 1924

Warburg, J. (ed.) *The Industrial Muse: The Industrial Revolution in Poetry*, 1958

Wright, D. (ed.) *English Romantic Verse*, 1970

Wu, D. (ed.), *Romantic Women Poets: an Anthology*, 1997

Bald, R. C. (ed.) *Literary Friendships in the Age of Wordsworth. An Anthology*, 1932

Bellringer, A. W. and Jones, C. B. (eds.) *The Romantic Age in Prose: An Anthology*, 1980

Grabo, C. H. (ed.) *Romantic Prose of the Early Nineteenth Century*, 1927

Lynam, R. (ed.) *The British Essayists*, 30 vols., 1827

Macintyre, C. F. and Ewing, M. (eds.) *English Prose of the Romantic Period*, 1938

Rodway, A. E. (ed.) *Godwin and the Age of Transition*, 1952

Williams, R. (ed.) *The Pelican Book of English Prose II. From 1780 to the Present Day*, 1970

Woodring, C. (ed.) *Prose of the Romantic Period*, 1961

Cox, J. N. (ed.) *Seven Gothic Dramas: 1789–1825*, 1992
Nicoll, A. (ed.) *Lesser English Comedies of the Eighteenth Century*, 1927
Smith, D. Nichol (ed.) *Eighteenth Century Essays on Shakespeare*, 1903

Authors

AUSTEN, JANE (1775–1817): Novelist; b. Steventon, Hampshire; daughter
of clergyman; various schools; uneventful life; moved with family to Bath,
1801; Southampton, 1806; Chawton, 1809; *Sense and Sensibility* published
1811; *Pride and Prejudice*, 1813; *Mansfield Park*, 1814; *Emma*, 1815 (post-dated
1816); *Northanger Abbey* and *Persuasion* published posthumously, 1818.

Life by E. Jenkins, 1938
Jane Austen, Facts and Problems, R. W. Chapman, 1948
The Novels of Jane Austen ed. R. W. Chapman, 5 vols., 1923
The Works of Jane Austen: Minor Works ed. R. W. Chapman, 1954
Jane Austen's Letters ed. R. W. Chapman, 1932; enlarged edn, 1952
See:
H. S. Babb, *Jane Austen's Novels: the Fabric of Dialogue*, 1962
F. W. Bradbrook, *Jane Austen and Her Predecessors*, 1966
A. C. Bradley, 'Jane Austen' in E.&.S. II, 1911
M. Butler, *Jane Austen and the War of Ideas*, 1975
W. A. Craik, *Jane Austen, the Six Novels*, 1965
P. De Rose and S. W. McGuire, *A Concordance to the Works of Jane Austen*,
    3 vols., 1982
D. D. Devlin, *Jane Austen and Education*, 1975
E. M. Forster, 'Jane Austen' in *Abinger Harvest*, 1936
D. Gilson, *A Bibliography of Jane Austen*, 1982
J. D. Grey, *The Jane Austen Handbook*, 1986
J. Halperin (ed.), *Jane Austen: Bicentenary Essays*, 1975
B. Hardy, *A Reading of Jane Austen*, 1975
D. Kaplan, *Jane Austen Among Women*, 1992
Q. D. Leavis, 'A Critical Theory of Jane Austen's Writings' in *Scrutiny*, X:
    1–3, 1941–2; repr. in *A Selection from Scrutiny*, II ed. F. R. Leavis, 1968
R. Liddell, *The Novels of Jane Austen*, 1963
A. W. Litz, *Jane Austen: A Study of Her Artistic Development*, 1965
J. McMaster (ed.), *Jane Austen's Achievement: Papers Delivered at the Jane
    Austen Bicentennial Conference at the University of Alberta*, 1976
M. Mudrick, *Jane Austen: Irony as Defense and Discovery*, 1952
B. C. Southam (ed.), *Critical Essays on Jane Austen*, 1969
V. Woolf, 'Jane Austen' in *The Common Reader*, 1925
A. Wright, *Jane Austen's Novels: A Study in Structure*, 1953

BEDDOES, THOMAS LOVELL (1803–49): Poet and dramatist; b. Clifton;
son of doctor: nephew of Maria Edgeworth; Charterhouse, 1817–20; Pem-
broke College, Oxford, 1820; B.A., 1825; studied at Göttingen and Würz-

burg, 1825–32; *The Bride's Tragedy* published, 1822; began *Death's Jest Book, or The Fool's Tragedy*, 1825; this was eventually published posthumously in 1850; committed suicide, 1849.

Life by H. W. Donner, 1935
Plays and Poems of Thomas Lovell Beddoes ed. H. W. Donner, 1950
Selected Poems of Thomas Lovell Beddoes ed. J. Higgens, 1976
See:
E. Blunden, 'Beddoes and his Contemporaries' in *Votive Tablets*, 1931

BENTHAM, JEREMY (1748–1832): Lawyer, philosopher and writer; b. London; son of attorney; a precocious child; Westminster School; Queen's College, Oxford, 1760; B.A., 1764; propagated Utilitarian philosophy; *Fragment on Government* published anonymously, 1776; *Introduction to Principles of Morals and Legislation*, 1780; started *Westminster Review*, 1823; helped to found London University; by will, left his body to University College, London.

Life by C. W. Everett, 1966
Collected Works of Jeremy Bentham: 1. *The Correspondence, 1752–1788* ed. T. L. S. Sprigge and I. R. Christie, 10 vols., 1968–94: in progress; 2. *Works* ed. J. H. Burns, 9 vols., 1970–93: in progress
See:
D. Baumgardt, *Bentham and the Ethics of Today*, 1953
J. Dinwiddy, *Bentham*, 1989
D. C. Long, *Bentham and Liberty: Jeremy Bentham's Ideas of Liberty in Relation to his Utilitarianism*, 1977
G. L. Nesbitt, *The First Twelve Years of the Westminster Review, 1824–1836*, 1934
M. Mack, *Jeremy Bentham: An Odyssey of Ideas*, 1962

BLAKE, WILLIAM (1757–1827): Poet, painter and engraver; b. London: son of haberdasher; early in life showed a prophetic turn of mind and saw visions; drawing-school in Strand, 1767; apprenticed to engraver, 1772; student at Royal Academy, 1778; married Catherine Boucher, 1782; *Poetical Sketches*, 1783; after father's death set up print-shop, together with fellow apprentice, 1784–7; deeply affected by death of brother, Robert, from consumption; issued *Songs of Innocence* by his own invented method of 'Illuminated Printing', 1789; *Songs of Experience*, 1794; began great prophetic books, *c.* 1797; an enthusiastic admirer of the French Revolution; acquainted with William Godwin, Mary Wollstonecraft and Tom Paine; moved to Felpham, 1800; returned to London, where he lived in poverty, 1803–27; friendship with John Linnell, the landscape painter, and his circle began in 1818 and continued until Blake's death; throughout his life he was a visionary and his great prophetic books have their origin in his visions.

Life by A. Gilchrist 1863; ed. R. Todd, 1942; rev. edn, 1945; K. Raine, 1970

The Complete Writings of William Blake ed. Sir G. Keynes, 1957; rev. edn, 1966

The Prose and Poetry of William Blake ed. D. V. Erdman, 1965, 3rd edn rev., 1980

The Complete Poems of William Blake ed. W. H. Stevenson, 1989

The Illuminated Blake: All of William Blake's Illuminated Works with a Plate-by-Plate Commentary ed. D. V. Erdman, 1974; rev. edn, 1975

Blake's Illuminated Books ed. M. D. Paley et al., 6 vols., 1997

The Letters of William Blake ed. Sir G. Keynes, 1956, rev. edn, 1982

The Notebook of William Blake ed. D. V. Erdman, 1973

See:

G. E. Bentley, *Blake Books*, 1977
    (ed.), *William Blake: The Critical Heritage*, 1975

B. Blackstone, *English Blake*, 1949

M. Bottrall, *The Divine Image: A Study of Blake's Interpretation of Christianity*, 1950

J. Bronowski, *A Man Without a Mask*, 1943; rev. as *William Blake and the Age of Revolution*, 1965; rev. edn, 1972

S. Cox, *Love and Logic: The Evolution of Blake's Thought*, 1992

S. F. Damon, *A Blake Dictionary: The Ideas and Symbols of William Blake*, 1965

M. Eaves, *The Counter-Arts Conspiracy: Art and Industry in the Age of Blake*, 1992

D. V. Erdman (ed.), *A Concordance to the Writings of William Blake*, 1968
    Blake: Prophet against Empire, 1954; rev. edn, 1970

R. N. Essick, *William Blake, Printmaker*, 1980

M. Ferber, *The Social Vision of William Blake*, 1985

N. Frye, *Fearful Symmetry: A Study of William Blake*, 1947

D. Fuller, *Blake's Heroic Argument*, 1988

W. Gaunt, *Arrows of Desire*, 1956

D. G. Gillham, *Blake's Contrary States: The Songs of Innocence and of Experience as Dramatic Poems*, 1966

R. F. Gleckner, *The Piper and the Bard: A Study of William Blake*, 1959

G. Keynes, *Blake Studies*, 1949; rev. and enlarged edn, 1971

R. Lister, *William Blake: An Introduction to the Man and to his Work*, 1968

H. M. Margoliouth, *William Blake*, 1951

M. D. Paley, *Energy and the Imagination*, 1969
    William Blake, 1978

M. D. Paley and M. Phillips (eds.), *William Blake: Essays in Honour of Sir Geoffrey Keynes*, 1973

D. Saurat, *Blake and Modern Thought*, 1929

A. C. Swinburne, *William Blake*, 1868; ed. H. J. Luke, 1970

E. P. Thompson, *Witness Against the Beast: William Blake and the Moral Law*, 1993

J. Viscomi, *Blake and the Idea of the Book*, 1993

J. Wicksteed, *Blake's Innocence and Experience*, 1928

BOWLES, WILLIAM LISLE (1762–1850): Poet, clergyman and antiquarian; b. King's Sutton; son of clergyman; Winchester, 1776–81; Trinity College, Oxford, 1781; B.A., 1792; *Fourteen Sonnets written chiefly on Picturesque Spots during a Journey*, 1789; these sonnets interested Coleridge, who wrote a sonnet in praise of them; married Magdalene Wake, 1797; vicar of Bremhill, Wiltshire, 1804–50; edition of Pope, 1807; *Invariable Principles of Poetry*, 1819; these two publications angered Byron who defended Pope against Bowles' strictures.

Life by G. Gilfillan as Introduction to Vol. II of *Poetical Works*, 1855
Poetical Works ed. G. Gilfillan, 2 vols., 1855
A Wiltshire Parson and his Friends: The Correspondence of W. L. Bowles ed. G. Greever, 1926
See:
J. J. Van Rennes, *Bowles, Byron and the Pope Controversy*, 1927

BURNS, ROBERT (1759–96): Poet, farmer and excise-officer; b. Alloway, Ayrshire; son of tenant farmer; educated at home and day-school; met Jean Armour, 1784, by whom he had several children before he married her in 1788; first volume, *Poems Chiefly in the Scottish Dialect*, published, 1786; *Tam O'Shanter*, 1790; continued to lead promiscuous life; gave up farming; became excise-officer in Dumfries, 1791; severe attack of rheumatic fever, 1795.

Life by J. Mackay, 1992
The Poems and Songs of Robert Burns ed. J. Kinsley, 3 vols., 1968
The Songs of Burns (with the contemporary music) ed. D. A. Low, 1993
Burns: Poetry and Prose ed. R. Dewar, 1929
The Letters of Robert Burns ed. J. de L. Ferguson, 2 vols., 1931; rev. edn by G. R. Roy, 1985
See:
R. Crawford (ed.), *Robert Burns and Cultural Authority*, 1996
T. Crawford, *Burns: A Study of the Poems and Songs*, 1960
D. Daiches, *Robert Burns*, 1952; rev. edn, 1966
M. Lindsay, *The Burns Encyclopaedia*, 1959; rev. and enlarged edn, 1970
D. A. Low (ed.), *Critical Essays on Robert Burns*, 1975
    Robert Burns: The Critical Heritage, 1974
F. B. Snyder, *Robert Burns: His Personality, His Reputation and His Art*, 1936

BYRON, GEORGE GORDON, LORD (1788–1824): Poet; b. London; b. with lame foot; son of dissolute, profligate and spendthrift member of noble family; unhappy childhood; became sixth Lord Byron, 1798; Harrow, 1801–5; infatuation with Mary Chaworth, 1803; Trinity College, Cambridge, 1805; M.A., 1808; publication of first volume of poems, *Fugitive Pieces*, which was immediately suppressed, 1806; *English Bards and Scotch Reviewers*, 1809; Albanian tour, 1809–11; friendship with Thomas Moore began, 1811; first two cantos of *Childe Harold*; intrigue with Lady Caroline Lamb, 1812; married Annabella Milbanke, 1815; separation from wife; scandal over clandestine relationship with half-sister, Augusta Leigh; left

England for good; met with Shelley in Switzerland, 1816; lived as libertine in Italy; began writing *Don Juan* 1818; went on expedition to assist Greek revolution, 1823; d. from fever in Missolonghi; buried in family vault at Hucknall Torkard.

Life by L. A. Marchand, 3 vols., 1958
Lord Byron: The Complete Poetical Works ed. J. J. McGann, 7 vols., 1980–93
Byron's Letters and Journals ed. L. A. Marchand, 12 vols., 1973–82
George Gordon, Lord Byron: A Selection from his Poems ed. A. S. B. Glover, 1954
His Very Self and Voice: Collected Conversations ed. E. J. Lovell, 1954
Lady Blessington's Conversations of Lord Byron ed. E. J. Lovell, 1969
Thomas Medwin: Conversations of Lord Byron ed. E. J. Lovell, 1966
See
F. L. Beaty, *Byron the Satirist*, 1985
B. Blackstone, *Byron: A Survey*, 1975
T. A. J. Burnett, *The Rise and Fall of a Regency Dandy: The Life and Times of Scrope Berdmore Davies*, 1981
W. J. Calvert, *Byron: Romantic Paradox*, 1935
J. Christensen, *Lord Byron's Strength: Writing and Commercial Society*, 1992
R. F. Gleckner, *Byron and the Ruins of Paradise*, 1968
T. A. Hoagwood, *Byron's Dialectic: Skepticism and the Critique of Culture*, 1993
M. K. Joseph, *Byron the Poet*, 1964
J. D. Jump (ed.) *Byron: A Symposium*, 1975
F. R. Leavis, 'Byron's Satire' in *Revaluation*, 1936, 1964
A. Levine and R. N. Keane (eds.), *Rereading Byron*, 1992
L. A. Marchand, *Byron's Poetry*, 1965
J. J. McGann, *Fiery Dust: Byron's Poetic Development*, 1968
H. Read, *Byron*, 1951
A. Rutherford, *Byron: A Critical Study*, 1961
   (ed.) *Byron: Augustan and Romantic*, 1990
   (ed.) *Byron: The Critical Heritage*, 1970
P. West, *Byron and the Spoiler's Art*, 1960

CAMPBELL, THOMAS (1777–1844): Poet; b. Glasgow; son of merchant; Glasgow Grammar School; Glasgow University, 1791; went to Edinburgh to study law 1797; *Pleasures of Hope* published, 1799; continental tour 1800–1801; married Matilda Sinclair, 1803; settled in London; employed in journalism and lecturing, 1803–26; *Poems*, 1805; editor of *New Monthly Magazine*, 1820–30; rector of Glasgow University, 1826–9.

Life by W. Beattie in *Life and Letters of Thomas Campbell*, 3 vols., 1849–50
Complete Poetical Works ed. J. L. Robertson, 1907
See:
A. M. Turner, 'Wordsworth's influence on Thomas Campbell' in P.M.L.A., XXXVIII, 1923

CLARE, JOHN (1793–1864): Poet and farm-labourer; b. Helpston, Northants; son of farm-labourer; helped on farm from age of seven; apprenticed to gardener at Burghley House, 1810; joined Northamptonshire Militia, 1812; returned to gardening, 1814; married Patty Turner; first volume, *Poems Descriptive of Rural Life and Scenery*, 1820; *The Village Minstrel and Other Poems*, 1821; severe mental illness, 1823; *Shepherd's Calendar*, 1827; *The Rural Muse*, 1835; increase of mental delusions and removal to private asylum, 1837–41; certified insane and taken to Northampton General Lunatic Asylum, 1841; in times of lucidity he suffered profound distress at his condition and at his separation from his old life.

Life by J. W. and A. Tibble, 1932; rev. edn, 1972
The Early Poems of John Clare ed. E. Robinson et al., 2 vols., 1989
The Later Poems of John Clare ed. E. Robinson and D. Powell, 2 vols., 1984
The Poems of John Clare ed. J. W. Tibble, 2 vols., 1935
The Selected Poems and Prose of John Clare ed. E. Robinson and G. Summerfield, 1967
The Prose of John Clare ed. J. W. and A. Tibble, 1951
John Clare, Letters ed. M. Storey, 1986
John Clare: The Journal, Essays, The Journey from Essex, 1980
The Midsummer Cushion ed. A. Tibble and R. K. R. Thornton, 1978
See:
J. Barrell, *The Idea of Landscape and the Sense of Place, 1730–1840: An Approach to the Poetry of John Clare*, 1970
E. Blunden, *Nature in English Literature*, 1929
T. Chilcott, '*A Real World and Doubting Mind*': *A Critical Study of the Poetry of John Clare*, 1985
G. Crossan, *A Relish for Eternity: The Process of Divinization in the Poetry of John Clare*, 1976
T. R. Frosch, 'The Descriptive Style of John Clare', in *Studies in Romanticism*. pp. 137–49, 1971
J. Goodridge (ed.) *The Independent Spirit: John Clare and the Self-Taught Tradition*, 1994
M. Storey *The Poetry of John Clare: A Critical Introduction* 1974
     (ed.) *Clare: The Critical Heritage* 1973

COBBETT, WILLIAM (1762–1835): Political essayist and journalist; b. Farnham; son of farmer; educated at home; joined army, 1783; sent to Canada, 1784–91; married Ann Reid whilst in Canada; procured discharge from army, 1791; lived in America, 1792–1800; began *Cobbett's Weekly Political Register*, 1802; *Grammar of the English Language*, 1818; journeyed through southern England and published accounts of his journeys as 'Rural Rides' in the *Political Register*, 1820–30; *Advice to Young Men*, 1829; M.P., 1832–5.

Life by G. D. H. Cole, 1924; G. Spater, 2 vols., 1982
The Autobiography of William Cobbett ed. W. Reitzel, 1933; repr., 1967
William Cobbett: Selections ed. A. M. D. Hughes, 1923
Rural Rides ed. G. Woodcock, 1967

Rural Rides ed. James Paul Cobbett, 1853; repr. with an introduction by Asa
Briggs, 1957

The Opinions of William Cobbett [selections] ed. G. D. H. and M. Cole,
1945

See:

E. Blunden, 'Rural Rides' in *Votive Tablets*, 1931

I. Dyck, *William Cobbett and Rural Popular Culture*, 1992

J. W. Osborne, *William Cobbett: His Thoughts and His Times*, 1966

J. Sambrook, *William Cobbett*, 1974

COLERIDGE, SAMUEL TAYLOR (1772–1834): Poet, critic and philosopher;
b. Ottery St Mary, Devonshire, youngest son of clergyman; orphaned,
1781; Christ's Hospital (friendship with Lamb), 1782–91; Jesus College,
Cambridge, 1791–4; ran away to join Dragoons, Dec. 1793–April 1794; met
Southey, planned 'Pantisocracy', 1794; met Wordsworth; married Sara
Fricker; public lectures, 1795; published *Poems*; settled at Nether Stowey,
1796; began *Ancient Mariner*, 1797; annuity from Wedgwoods; German
tour with William and Dorothy Wordsworth; published *Lyrical Ballads*
with Wordsworth, 1798; met and fell in love with Sara Hutchinson, 1799;
political journalism, 1799–1802; moved to Keswick, 1800; bad health, 1801;
published 'Dejection', 1802; in Malta and Italy, 1804–6; separation from
wife and from Sara Hutchinson, *c.* 1807; literary lectures, 1808; weekly
publication of *The Friend*, 1809–10; quarrel with Wordsworth, 1810; *Remorse* acted, 1813; under care for opium addiction, 1814; settled with Dr
Gillman at Highgate; published *Christabel, Kubla Khan, The Statesman's
Manual*, 1816; *Biographia Literaria*, 1817; enlarged *The Friend*, 1818; elected
with annuity to Royal Society of Literature, 1824; *Aids to Reflection*, 1825;
published *Poetical Works*, 1828; *Church and State*, 1829; attended first meetings of the British Association, 1831.

Life by J. D. Campbell, 1894; W. J. Bate, 1968

The Life of S. T. Coleridge: The Early Years, L. Hanson, 1938; *Coleridge and
Sara Hutchinson*, G. Whalley, 1955; *Coleridge the Talker*, R. W. Armour
and R. F. Howes (eds.), 1940

Collected Works ed. K. Coburn *et al.*, Bollingen editions, 16 vols.,
1969–94

Collected Letters of S. T. Coleridge, 1785–1834 ed. E. L. Griggs, 6 vols.,
1956–71

The Notebooks of S. T. Coleridge, 1794–1819 ed. K. Coburn, 5 vols., 1957–90:
in progress

Poetical Works ed. J. D. Campbell, 1893; ed. E. H. Coleridge, 1912; *Poems* ed.
J. B. Beer 1963

For extensive list of writings see N.C.B.E.L. III, 211–26

See:

M. M. Badawi, *Coleridge: Critic of Shakespeare*, 1973

J. B. Beer, *Coleridge the Visionary*, 1959

Coleridge's Poetic Intelligence, 1977

(ed.), *Coleridge's Variety: Bicentenary Studies*, 1974

R. L. Brett, 'Coleridge's Theory of Imagination,' *English Studies*, The English Association, 1949

(ed.), *Writers and their Background: S. T. Coleridge*, 1971

K. Coburn, *The Self-Conscious Imagination* (on the *Notebooks*), 1974

(ed.), *Coleridge: A Collection of Critical Essays*, 1967

J. Colmer, *Coleridge, Critic of Society*, 1959

G. Dekker, *Coleridge and the Literature of Sensibility* (on *Dejection*), 1978

R. H. Fogle, *The Idea of Coleridge's Criticism*, 1962

N. Fruman, *Coleridge, The Damaged Archangel*, 1971

T. Fulford and M. D. Paley (eds.), *Festschrift, Coleridge's Visionary Languages: Essays in Honour of John Beer*, 1993

L. M. Grow, *The Prose-Style of Samuel Taylor Coleridge*, 1976

P. Hamilton, *Coleridge's Poetics*, 1983

J. R. de J. Jackson (ed.), *Coleridge: The Critical Heritage*, 2 vols., 1970–1991

E. Kessler, *Coleridge's Metaphors of Being*, 1979

F. R. Leavis, 'Coleridge in Criticism,' *Scrutiny*, IX, 1940

(ed.), *Mill on Bentham and Coleridge*, 1950

T. H. Levere, *Poetry Realized in Nature: Samuel Taylor Coleridge and Early Nineteenth Century Science*, 1981

L. S. Lockridge, *Coleridge the Moralist*, 1977

J. L. Lowes, *The Road to Xanadu*, 1927; rev. edn 1951

T. McFarland, *Coleridge and the Pantheist Tradition*, 1969

A. H. Nethercot, *The Road to Tryermaine* (on *Christabel*), 1939

M. D. Paley, *Coleridge's Later Poetry*, 1996

C. de Paolo, *Coleridge: Historian of Ideas*, 1992

S. Prickett, *Coleridge and Wordsworth: the Poetry of Growth*, 1970

H. Read, *Coleridge as Critic*, 1949

I. A. Richards, *Coleridge on Imagination*, 1934

C. R. Sanders, *Coleridge and the Broad Church Movement*, 1934

E. Schneider, *Coleridge, Opium and 'Kubla Khan'*, 1953

A. D. Snyder, *Coleridge on Logic and Learning*, 1929

C. M. Wallace, *The Design of 'Biographia Literaria'*, 1983

W. Walsh, *Coleridge: the Work and the Relevance*, 1967

K. Wheeler, *Sources, Processes and Methods in Coleridge's 'Biographia Literaria'*, 1980

B. Willey, *S. T. Coleridge*, 1972

C. R. Woodring, *Politics in the Poetry of Coleridge*, 1961

CRABBE, GEORGE (1754–1832): Poet and clergyman; b. Aldeburgh, Suffolk; eldest son of Custom House warehouse-keeper; apprenticed to surgeon, 1768; practised as surgeon-apothecary intermittently, 1775–9; took interest in botany and other branches of natural history; abandoned his profession and went to London, intending to live by his writing, 1779; became protégé of Edmund Burke; took Holy Orders, 1781; chaplain to Duke of

Rutland, 1782; married Sarah Elmy; *The Village*, 1783; *Poems*, 1807, in which *The Parish Register* appeared; *The Borough*, 1810; held various Church livings, 1787–1814; *Tales*, 1812; became Rector of Trowbridge, 1814; *Tales of the Hall*, 1819; was acquainted with Thomas Campbell, Thomas Moore, Samuel Rogers, Scott, Southey and Wordsworth.

Life by his son, G. Crabbe, 1834; ed. E. M. Forster, 1932; ed. E. Blunden, 1947
Selected Letters and Journals of George Crabbe ed. T. C. Faulkner, 1985
George Crabbe: Poems ed. A. Ward, 3 vols., 1905–7
New Poems by George Crabbe ed. A. Pollard, 1960
George Crabbe: Tales, 1812 and other Selected Poems ed. H. Mills, 1967
See:
T. Bareham and S. Gatrell, *A Bibliography of George Crabbe*, 1978
P. Cruttwell, 'The Last Augustan' in *The Hudson Review*, VII, 1955
G. Edwards, *George Crabbe's Poetry on Border Land*, 1990
E. M. Forster, 'George Crabbe and Peter Grimes' in *Two Cheers for Democracy*, 1951
L. Haddakin, *The Poetry of Crabbe*, 1955
P. New, *George Crabbe's Poetry*, 1976
A. Pollard (ed.), *Crabbe: The Critical Heritage*, 1972
O. F. Sigworth, *Nature's Sternest Painter: Five Essays on the Poetry of George Crabbe*, 1965
J. Speirs, 'Crabbe as Master of the Verse Tale' in *The Oxford Review*, 2, 1966
F. Whitehead, *George Crabbe: A Reappraisal*, 1995

DARLEY, GEORGE (1795–1846): Poet, critic and mathematician; b. Dublin; Trinity College, Dublin, 1815; quarrelled with his family and settled in London; *The Errors of Ecstacie*, 1822; wrote dramatic criticism for *London Magazine* and later for *The Athenaeum; The Labours of Idleness* published under the pseudonym of Guy Penseval, 1826; wrote a number of mathematical works; *Nepenthe*, 1839; edited Beaumont and Fletcher, 1840.

Life by C. C. Abbott in *The Life and Letters of George Darley*, 1928
The Complete Poetical Works of George Darley ed. R. Colles, 1908
See:
E. Blunden, 'George Darley and his Latest Biographer' in *Votive Tablets*, 1931
L. Brisman, 'George Darley: The Poet as Pygmy' in *Studies in Romanticism*, XV, 1976
R. A. Streatfeild, 'A Forgotten Poet: George Darley' in *Quarterly Review*, CXCVI, 1902

DE QUINCEY, THOMAS (1785–1859): Essayist and critic; b. Manchester; son of merchant; Bath Grammar School, 1797; Manchester Grammar School, 1800; ran away from school; went to London, 1802; Worcester College, Oxford, 1803; began taking opium, 1804, and soon became an addict; met Coleridge, 1807; left Oxford without taking a degree, 1808;

went to live at Grasmere, 1809; married Margaret Simpson, 1816; editor of *Westmorland Gazette*, 1819–20; *Confessions of an English Opium-Eater* published in *London Magazine*, 1821, and in book form, 1822; published papers in various magazines, 1821 onwards; *Autobiographical Sketches*, 1834–40; complete works published in America, 1851–5.

Life by G. Lindop, *The Opium-Eater*, 1981

The Collected Writings of Thomas de Quincey ed. D. Masson, 14 vols., 1889–90

The Confessions of an English Opium Eater and Other Writings ed. G. Lindop, 1985

Reminiscences of the English Lake Poets ed. J. E. Jordan, 1961

Selected Essays on Rhetoric ed. F. Barwick, 1968

De Quincey as Critic ed. J. E. Jordan, 1973

De Quincey to Wordsworth: A Biography of a Relationship (Letters) ed. J. E. Jordan, 1962

See:

M. H. Abrams, *The Milk of Paradise*, 1934

J. Barrell, *The Infection of Thomas De Quincey*, 1991

G. T. Clapton, *Baudelaire et De Quincey*, 1931

A. Goldman, *The Mine and the Mint: Sources for the Writings of Thomas De Quincey*, 1965

J. E. Jordan, *Thomas De Quincey, Literary Critic: His Method and Achievement*, 1952

R. L. Snyder (ed.), *Thomas de Quincey: Bicentenary Studies*, 1985

L. Stephen, 'De Quincey' in *Hours in a Library* 1, 1874

J. C. Whale, *Thomas de Quincey's Reluctant Autobiography*, 1984

V. Woolf, 'De Quincey's Autobiography' in *The Common Reader*, 2nd series, 1932

EDGEWORTH, MARIA (1767–1849): Novelist; b. Oxfordshire; daughter of writer; interested in education; went to live in paternal home in Ireland, 1782; *Castle Rackrent* published anonymously, 1800; published *Practical Education*, in collaboration with father, and *Belinda*, 1801; continental tour, 1802; visited London and became popular among literary figures, 1803; *Ormond*, 1817; visited Scott at Abbotsford, 1823.

Life by her stepmother, F. A. Edgeworth, 3 vols., 1867; M. Butler, 1972

The Works of Maria Edgeworth ed. M. Butler *et al.*, 12 vols., 1997

Letters from England, 1813–1844 ed. C. Colvin, 1971

Maria Edgeworth in France and Switzerland: Selections from the Edgeworth Family Letters ed. C. Colvin, 1979

See:

O. E. M. Harden, *Maria Edgeworth's Art of Prose Fiction*, 1971

M. Hurst, *Maria Edgeworth and the Public Scene: Intellect, Fine Feeling and Landlordism in the Age of Reform*, 1969

E. E. MacDonald (ed.), *The Education of the Heart: the Correspondence of Rachel Mordecai Lazarus and Maria Edgeworth*, 1977

FRERE, JOHN HOOKHAM (1769–1846): Diplomat and poet; b. London; son of merchant; Eton; Caius College, Cambridge; B.A., 1792; contributor to the *Anti-Jacobin*; M.P., 1796; various government posts abroad, 1800–1809; married Dowager Countess of Erroll, 1816; retired to Malta, 1820; helped to found *The Quarterly Review*; the so-called Byronic stanza was used by Frere in 'King Arthur and his Round Table' before Byron used it.

Life by A. von Eichler, 1905
The Works of John Hookham Frere with memoir by Sir B. Frere, 2 vols., 1872; rev. edn, 3 vols., 1874
The Poetry of the Anti-Jacobin, ed. J. Wordsworth, 1991
See:
G. Festing, *J. H. Frere and His Friends*, 1899
H. Walker, *English Satire and Satirists* chs. XI–XII, 1925

GIFFORD, WILLIAM (1756–1826): Journalist, satirist, critic and editor; b. Ashburton; son of glazier; apprenticed to shoemaker, but later sent to Exeter College, Oxford; B.A., 1782; satirized the Della Cruscans in the *Baviad*, 1791 and *Maeviad*, 1795; became editor of the *Anti-Jacobin*, 1797; *Epistle to Peter Pindar*, 1800; editor of the *Quarterly Review*, 1809–1824.
See:
R. B. Clark, *William Gifford, Tory Satirist, Critic and Editor*, 1930
J. M. Longaker, *The Della Cruscans and William Gifford*, 1924

GODWIN, WILLIAM (1756–1836): Philosopher and political writer; b. Wisbech, son of clergyman; day-school and tutors; Dissenting College at Hoxton, 1773–8; became minister in succession at Ware, Stowmarket and Beaconsfield, 1778–83; *Life of Chatham* published; left ministry, 1783; became a political journalist; *Political Justice*, 1793; *Caleb Williams*, 1794; *The Enquirer*, 1797; fell in love with Mary Wollstonecraft, and married her, March 1797; she died later that year in childbirth; *St Leon*, 1799; married Mrs Clairmont, 1801; *The Life of Geoffrey Chaucer*, 1803; *Fleetwood*, 1805; the Juvenile Library opened and run by Godwin, 1805–24; met Shelley who had previously been greatly influenced by Godwin's philosophical and political thought, 1811; *Mandeville*, 1818; *Thoughts on Man*, 1831.

Life by C. K. Paul, 1876; D. Fleisher, 1951
The Collected Novels and Memoirs of William Godwin ed. M. Philp et al., 8 vols., 1992
Political and Philosophical Writings of William Godwin ed. M. Philp, 7 vols., 1993
Godwin and Mary, Letters of William Godwin and Mary Wollstonecraft ed. R. M. Wardle, 1966
See:
H. N. Brailsford, *Shelley, Godwin and their Circle*, 1913, 2nd edn, 1951
J. P. Clark, *The Philosophical Anarchism of William Godwin*, 1977
F. A. Lea, *Shelley and the Romantic Revolution*, 1945

D. H. Monro, *Godwin's Moral Philosophy*, 1953
W. St Clair, *The Godwins and the Shelleys: A Biography of a Family*, 1991

HAYDON, BENJAMIN ROBERT (1786–1846); Historical artist and art critic; b. Plymouth; son of publisher; Plymouth Grammar and Plympton St Mary Schools; Royal Academy, 1807; friendships with Hazlitt, Keats, Lamb, Wordsworth and other literary figures of the time; a difficult, often quarrelsome man, best remembered for the portraits of the age contained in his journals. Committed suicide, 1846

Life by himself, *Autobiography* ed. E. Blunden, 1927; E. George 1948; rev. edn, 1967
The Diary of Benjamin Robert Haydon, 1808–1846 ed. W. B. Pope, 5 vols., 1960–63
Neglected Genius: The Diaries of Benjamin Robert Haydon (A selection) ed. J. Joliffe, 1990
See:
C. Olney, 'John Keats and Benjamin Robert Haydon' in P.M.L.A., XLIX, 1934
V. Woolf, 'The Genius of Benjamin Robert Haydon' in *The New Republic*, XLIX, 1926; republished in *The Moment and Other Essays*, 1947

HAZLITT, WILLIAM (1778–1830): Essayist and critic; b. Maidstone; son of Unitarian Minister; Ireland, 1780; America, 1783–7; day-school and tutors, 1787–93; Hackney Theological College to train for ministry, 1793; abandoned idea of becoming a minister and left college, 1794; spent time reading, writing and painting; became apostle of French Revolution; met Coleridge, 1798; Paris, 1802–3; met Lamb and became one of Lamb circle; *Essay on the Principles of Human Action*, 1805; married Sarah Stoddart, 1808; contributed to a number of periodicals and gave several series of lectures; *Characters of Shakespeare's Plays*, 1817; divorced in Scotland, 1823; married a widow, Mrs Bridgewater, 1824; separated from her soon afterwards; *The Spirit of the Age*, 1825.

Life by H. Baker, 1962
Complete Works ed. P. P. Howe, 21 vols., 1930–34
The Letters of William Hazlitt ed. H. M. Sikes *et al.*, 1978
See:
W. P. Albrecht, *Hazlitt and the Creative Imagination*, 1965
    William Hazlitt and the Malthusian Controversy, 1950
C. Brinton, *The Political Ideas of the English Romanticists*, 1926
S. P. Chase, 'Hazlitt as a Critic of Art' in P.M.L.A., XXXIX, 1924
J. A. Houck, *William Hazlitt: A Reference Guide*, 1977
G. Keynes, *Bibliography of William Hazlitt* 1931, 2nd edn rev., 1981
J. Kinnaird, *William Hazlitt: Critic of Power*, 1978
E. Schneider, *The Aesthetics of William Hazlitt*, 1933
C. D. Thorpe, 'Keats and Hazlitt: A Record of Personal Relationship and Critical Estimate' in P.M.L.A., LXII, 1947

R. M. Wardle, *Hazlitt*, 1971

HOGG, JAMES, 'THE ETTRICK SHEPHERD' (1770–1835): Poet and shepherd; b. Ettrick, Selkirkshire; son of shepherd; became a shepherd himself, 1777; met Scott, 1802; *The Mountain Bard* published on Scott's recommendation, 1807; settled in Edinburgh, 1810; settled in farm at Yarrow by Duke of Buccleuch, 1817; married Margaret Phillips, 1820; *The Private Memoirs and Confessions of a Justified Sinner*, 1824; *The Shepherd's Calendar*, 1829; *Scottish Pastorals*, 1831.

Life by E. C. Batho, *The Ettrick Shepherd*, 1927
The Works of the Ettrick Shepherd ed. T. Thomson, 2 vols., 1865–6
The Collected Works of James Hogg ed. D. S. Mack *et al.*, 6 vols., 1997–8: in progress
James Hogg: Selected Poems and Songs ed. D. Groves, 1986
James Hogg: Selected Stories and Sketches ed. D. S. Mack, 1982
The Private Memoirs and Confessions of a Justified Sinner ed. J. Carey, 1969
The Three Perils of Man ed. D. Gifford, 1972
Tales of Love and Mystery ed. D. Groves, 1985
James Hogg: Memoirs of the Author's Life and Familiar Anecdotes of Sir Walter Scott ed. D. S. Mack, 1972
See:
D. Gifford, *James Hogg*, 1976
L. Simpson, *James Hogg: A Critical Study*, 1962

HOOD, THOMAS (1799–1845): Poet and wit; b. London; son of bookseller; father d. 1811; day-school; entered counting-house, 1812; removed because of ill-health and sent to father's relations in Dundee, 1815; returned to London, 1818; assistant editor of *London Magazine*, 1821; met Clare, De Quincey, Lamb and other literary figures; married Jane Reynolds, 1824; *Odes and Addresses to Great People* published anonymously with J. H. Reynolds, his brother-in-law, 1825; *Comic Annual* begun, 1830; lived on continent, 1835–40.

Life by J. C. Reid, 1963
The Works of Thomas Hood ed. by his son, T. Hood, 7 vols., 1862
Selected Poems of Thomas Hood ed. J. Clubbe, 1970
The Letters of Thomas Hood ed. P. F. Morgan, 1973
See:
E. Blunden, 'The Poet Hood' in R.E.L., I, 1960
V. S. Pritchett, 'Our Half-Hogarth' in *The Living Novel*, 1946
C. B. Shaw, 'This Fellow of Infinite Jest' in *Poetlore*, XL, 1929

HUNT, JAMES HENRY LEIGH (1784–1859): Poet, essayist and journalist; b. Southgate; son of impoverished preacher, immigrant from America; Christ's Hospital, 1791–9; *Juvenilia*, 1801; employed in War Office, 1805–8; *The Examiner* begun, 1808; married Marianne Kent, 1809; *The Reflector*, 1810–

11; imprisoned for libel against Prince Regent, 1813–15; *The Story of Rimini*, 1816; friendship with Hazlitt, Lamb, Keats and Shelley; *The Indicator*, 1819–21; The Liberal, 1822–3; went to Italy to join Byron and Shelley, 1822–5; *The Tatler*, 1820–32; *Leigh Hunt's London Journal*, 1834–5; *A Legend of Florence* produced at Covent Garden, 1840; awarded a Civil List pension, 1847.

Life by E. Blunden, 1930
The Poetical Works of Leigh Hunt ed. H. S. Milford, 1923
Leigh Hunt's Dramatic Criticism ed. L. H. and C. W. Houtchens, 1950
Leigh Hunt's Literary Criticism ed. L. H. and C. W. Houtchens, 1956
Leigh Hunt's Political and Occasional Essays ed. L. H. and C. W. Houtchens, 1962
The Correspondence of Leigh Hunt ed. T. Hunt, 1862
See:
E. Blunden, *Leigh Hunt's 'Examiner' Examined*, 1928
R. S. Edgecombe, *Leigh Hunt and the Poetry of Fancy*, 1994
M. Roberts, 'Leigh Hunt's Place in the Reform Movement, 1808–1810' in R.E.S., XI, 1935
G. D. Stout, *The Political History of Leigh Hunt's 'Examiner'*, 1949
J. R. Thompson, *Leigh Hunt*, 1977

JEFFREY, LORD FRANCIS (1773–1850): Lawyer, critic and editor; b. Edinburgh; son of law-court clerk; Edinburgh High School, 1781–7; Edinburgh, Glasgow and Oxford Universities, 1787–92; called to Bar, 1794; helped to found the *Edinburgh Review* and became its first editor, 1802; challenged to duel by Moore for a hostile review, but prevented from fighting by being arrested, 1806; later established friendship with Moore; became Lord Advocate, 1830–34; M.P., 1831.

Life by P. Flynn, 1978
Contributions to the Edinburgh Review, 4 vols., 1844
Jeffrey's Criticism: A Selection (ed.) P. F. Morgan, 1985
See:
R. C. Bald, 'Francis Jeffrey as a Literary Critic' in *The Nineteenth Century*, XCVII, 1925
M. Y. Hughes, 'The Humanism of Francis Jeffrey' in M.L.R., XVI, 1921
P. F. Morgan, 'Principles and Perspectives in Jeffrey's Criticism' in *Studies in Scottish Literature*, IV, 1967

KEATS, JOHN (1795–1821): Poet; b. London; son of manager of livery stables; father d. 1804; mother d. 1810; under guardianship of Richard Abbey; apprenticed to a surgeon, 1811; appointed as dresser at Guy's Hospital, 1815; gave up surgery for poetry; *Poems*, 1817; profoundly affected by death of youngest brother, Tom, from consumption; *Endymion*, 1818; went to live with Charles Armitage Brown in Hampstead; it now became obvious that Keats's own lungs were affected and his health swiftly deteriorated; met and fell in love with Fanny Brawne; *Lamia, Isabella, The Eve of St Agnes and Other Poems*, 1820; went to Italy for winter, with Joseph Severn, in hope of recovering health; d. Rome.

Life by S. Colvin, 1917; R. Gittings, 1968
The Poems of John Keats ed. J. Stillinger, 1978
John Keats, The Complete Poems ed. J. Barnard, 1973
The Letters of John Keats ed. H. E. Rollins, 2 vols., 1958
The Letters of John Keats (selection) ed. R. Gittings, 1970
See:
H. de Almeida, *Romantic Medicine and John Keats*, 1990
W. J. Bate, *The Stylistic Development of Keats*, 1945
A. W. Crawford, *The Genius of Keats*, 1932
M. Dickstein, *Keats and his Poetry: A Study in Development*, 1971
F. Edgcumbe (ed.), *The Letters of Fanny Brawne to Fanny Keats*, 1937
W. H. Evert, *Aesthetic and Myth in the Poetry of Keats*, 1965
R. H. Fogle, *The Imagery of Keats and Shelley: A Comparative Study*, 1949
G. H. Ford, *Keats and the Victorians: A Study of his Influence and Rise to Fame, 1821–1895*, 1945
N. F. Ford, *The Prefigurative Imagination of John Keats*, 1951
H. W. Garrod, *Keats*, 1926
I. Jack, *Keats and the Mirror of Art*, 1967
K. Muir (ed.), *John Keats: A Reassessment*, 1958
J. M. Murry, *Keats and Shakespeare*, 1926
     Studies in Keats, 1930; rev. edn, 1955
C. Ricks, *Keats and Embarrassment*, 1974
M. R. Ridley, *Keats' Craftmanship*, 1933
H. E. Rollins (ed.), *The Keats' Circle*, 2 vols., 1948; rev. by W. J. Bate, 1965
R. M. Ryan, *Keats: The Religious Sense*, 1976
S. M. Sperry, *Keats the Poet*, 1973
J. Stillinger, *The Texts of Keats's Poems*, 1975
H. Vendler, *The Odes of John Keats*, 1983
W. Walsh, *Introduction to Keats*, 1981
E. R. Wassermann, *The Finer Tone: Keats' Major Poems*, 1953
S. J. Wolfson, *The Questioning Presence: Wordsworth, Keats and the Interrogative Mode in Romantic Poetry*, 1986

LAMB, CHARLES (1775–1834): Essayist, poet, and clerk in East India Company; b. London; son of assistant to Bencher of Inner Temple; lifelong friendship with Coleridge began at Christ's Hospital, 1782–9; clerk at South-Sea House, 1791; at East India House, 1792; attack of madness, 1795; sister murdered mother in an attack of insanity, 1796; on death of father, Mary Lamb made her home with her brother, 1799; *Tales from Shakespeare* published with Mary's collaboration, 1807; *Essays of Elia* published in the *London Magazine*, 1820–25; first volume in book form, 1823; retirement from East India Company, 1825; *The Last Essays of Elia*, 1833; a kindly and lovable man who had many friends.

Life by E. V. Lucas, 2 vols., 1905; rev. edn 1921; *Young Charles Lamb* by
   W. F. Courtney, 1982
The Works of Charles and Mary Lamb ed. E. V. Lucas, 7 vols., 1903–5
The Essays of Elia, Including Elia and the Last Essays of Elia ed. M. Elwin,
   1952
Tales from Shakespeare ed. W. Macdonald, 1903
Lamb's Criticism ed. E. M. W. Tillyard, 1923
The Letters of Charles and Mary Anne Lamb ed. E. W. Marrs, 3 vols., 1976–8
See:
G. L. Barnett, *Charles Lamb: The Evolution of Elia*, 1964
E. Blunden, *Charles Lamb and his Contemporaries*, 1933
      'Elia and Christ's Hospital' in E. & S., XXII, 1936
      'Lamb's Select Criticism' in *Votive Tablets*, 1931
F. S. Boas, 'Charles Lamb and the Elizabethan Dramatists' in E. & S., XXIX,
   1943
G. Gordon, 'Charles Lamb' in *The Discipline of Letters*, 1946
M. H. Law, *The English Familiar Essay in the Early Nineteenth Century*, 1934
W. Pater, 'Charles Lamb' in *Appreciations*, 1889
C. A. Prance, *Companion to Charles Lamb: A Guide to People and Places,
   1760–1847*, 1983
F. V. Randel, *The World of Elia: Charles Lamb's Essayistic Romanticism*, 1975

LANDOR, WALTER SAVAGE (1775–1864): Poet and essayist; b. Warwick;
son of doctor; Rugby, 1785; removed to avoid expulsion, 1791; Trinity
College, Oxford, 1793; rusticated, 1794, and did not return; left home after
differences with father; first volume, *The Poems of Walter Savage Landor*
published, 1795; *Gebir*, 1798; *Poetry, by the author of Gebir*, 1802; married
Julia Thuillier, 1811; France, 1814; Italy, 1815–35; *Imaginary Conversations*,
1824–9; quarrelled with wife, left her and returned to England, 1835; settled
at Bath, 1837; *Last Fruit off an Old Tree*, 1853; sued for libel and left
England, 1858; a man who united a perverse and often violent temper with
exceptional courtesy, sympathy and generosity.

Life by R. H. Super, 1954
The Works of Walter Savage Landor ed. T. E. Welby and S. Wheeler, 16
   vols., 1927–36
Imaginary Conversations and Poems: A Selection ed. H. Ellis, 1933
Poems of Walter Savage Landor (a selection) ed. G. Grigson, 1964
See:
R. Pinsky, *Landor's Poetry*, 1968
C. L. Proudfit (ed.) *Landor as Critic*, 1979
      The Wordsworth Circle (*Landor* issue) VII. i, 1976
R. H. Super, 'The Fire of Life' in *Cambridge Review*, January, 1965
P. Vitoux, *l'Oeuvre de Walter Savage Landor*, 1964
S. Wheeler and T. J. Wise, *A Bibliography of the Writing in Prose and Verse of
   W. S. Landor*, 1919

MILL, JAMES (1773–1836): Utilitarian philosopher and historian; b. Forfarshire; son of shoemaker; day-school and Montrose Academy; Edinburgh University, 1790; studied divinity and philosophy; married Harriet Burrow, 1805; settled in London; disciple of Jeremy Bentham; contributed to various periodicals, 1806 onwards; *Elements of Political Economy*, 1821; *An Analysis of the Phenomena of the Human Mind*, 1829.

Life by L. Stephen, *The English Utilitarians*, II, 1900
Analysis of the Phenomena of the Human Mind ed. J. S. Mill, 2 vols., 1869
Selected Economic Writings ed. D. Winch, 1966
Essay on Government ed. E. Barker, 1937
See:
W. H. Burston, *James Mill on Philosophy and Education*, 1973
E. Halévy, *The Growth of Philosophical Radicalism* trans. M. Morris, 1928; new and corrected edn, 1958
J. Hamburger, *James Mill and the Art of Revolution*, 1963

MOORE, THOMAS (1779–1852): Poet; b. Dublin; son of grocer; day-school; began to publish poems in periodic literature, 1793; Trinity College, Dublin, 1794; studied at Middle Temple and was called to the Bar, but never practised; *Translations from Anacreon*, 1800; *Poetical Works of the Late Thomas Little*, 1802; tour of North America, 1804–6; *Epistles, Odes and Other Poems*, 1806; *Irish Melodies* published intermittently, 1807–34; friendship with Byron began; married Bessie Dyke, 1811; *The Twopenny Postbag*, 1812; *Lalla Rookh*, 1817; *Life of Byron*, 1830; decline of mental powers before death; a man of generous instincts and noble mind.

Life by H. H. Jordan, 2 vols., 1975
Poetical Works, 10 vols., 1840–41
Moore's Poetical Works ed. A. D. Godley, 1910
The Journals of Thomas Moore ed. W. S. Dowden, 6 vols., 1983–91
The Letters of Thomas Moore, 1793–1847 ed. W. S. Dowden, 2 vols., 1964

PEACOCK, THOMAS LOVE (1785–1866): Novelist, poet and official of the East India Company; b. Dorset; son of glass merchant; private school, 1791; clerk in London merchant-house, 1800; first volume, *Palmyra and Other Poems*, 1805 (post-dated, 1806); friendship with Shelley; *Headlong Hall*, 1815 (post-dated, 1816); *Melincourt*, 1817; *Rhododaphne* and *Nightmare Abbey*, 1818; appointment in East India Company, 1819; married Jane Gryffydh; *The Four Ages of Poetry*, 1820; *Maid Marian*, 1822; *The Misfortunes of Elphin*, 1829; *Crotchet Castle*, 1831; retired from East India Company, 1856; last book, *Gryll Grange*, serialized in *Frazer's Magazine*, 1860; satirized contemporary figures and topical ideas in novels in which the plot is insignificant and the conversations between the characters are all-important.

Life by H. F. B. Brett-Smith in Vol. 1 of the Halliford Edition of *The Works*, 1934

The Works of Thomas Love Peacock, Halliford Edition, ed. H. F. B. Brett-Smith and C. E. Jones, 10 vols., 1929–34
The Novels of Thomas Love Peacock ed. D. Garnett, 1948; repr. in 2 vols, 1963
See:
B. Burns, *The Novels of Thomas Love Peacock*, 1985
M. Butler, *Peacock Displayed: A Satirist in His Context*, 1979
C. Dawson, *His Fine Wit: A Study of Thomas Love Peacock*, 1970
A. M. Freeman, *Thomas Love Peacock: A Critical Study*, 1911
J. L. Madden, *Thomas Love Peacock*, 1967
H. Mills, *Peacock: His Circle and his Age*, 1969

RADCLIFFE, MRS ANN (1764–1823): Novelist; b. London; daughter of William Ward, a merchant; married, 1787; *The Castles of Athlin and Dunbayne*, 1789; *A Sicilian Romance*, 1790; *The Romance of the Forest*, 1791; *The Mysteries of Udolpho*, 1794; *The Italians*, 1797; lived remainder of life in retirement.

The Italian ed. F. Garber, 1968
The Mysteries of Udolpho ed. B. Dobrée, 1966
See:
E. Birkhead, *The Tale of Terror* ch. 3, 1921
R. D. Havens, 'Ann Radcliffe's Nature Descriptions' in M.L.N., LXVI, 1951
C. F. McIntyre, *Ann Radcliffe in Relation to her Time*, 1921
A. S. S. Wieten, *Mrs Radcliffe: Her Relation towards Romanticism*, 1926

REYNOLDS, JOHN HAMILTON (1794–1852): Poet; b. Shrewsbury; son of schoolmaster; St Paul's School; entered Insurance office; *Safie, an Eastern Tale* and *The Eden of the Imagination*, 1814; friendship with Keats began, 1816; *The Garden of Florence*, 1821; married Eliza Drewe, 1822; Reynolds is remembered today, not because of his own work, but because of his friendship with Keats.

Life by G. L. Marsh as Introduction to *Poetry and Prose*, 1928
The Letters of John Hamilton Reynolds ed. L. M. Jones, 1973
See:
E. Blunden, 'Friends of Keats' in *Votive Tablets*, 1931

ROBINSON, HENRY CRABB (1775–1867): Diarist and journalist; b. Bury St Edmunds; son of tanner; private schools; travelled widely on continent as correspondent of *The Times*, 1800–1809, entered Middle Temple, 1813; helped to found Athenaeum Club and University College, London; famous as a conversationalist; his friendships with most of the important literary figures of his time make his journals and letters a fascinating contribution to literary history.

Life by E. J. Morley, 1935

Diary, Reminiscences and Correspondence of Henry Crabb Robinson ed. T. Sadler, 3 vols., 1869; rev. edn, 2 vols. 1872

The Diary of Henry Crabb Robinson abr. and ed. D. Hudson, 1967

Blake, Coleridge, Wordsworth, Lamb, etc., being Selections from the Remains of Henry Crabb Robinson ed. E. J. Morley, 1922

Henry Crabb Robinson on Books and their Writers ed. E. J. Morley, 3 vols., 1938

The Correspondence with the Wordsworth Circle, 1808–1866 ed. E. J. Morley, 2 vols., 1927

ROGERS, SAMUEL (1763–1855): Poet; b. London; son of banker; private school and tutors; poor health in childhood and youth enabled him to have long holidays which he spent reading; *The Pleasures of Memory*, 1792; father's death in 1793 resulted in the poet having independent means; *Human Life*, 1819; began to move in literary world and made friendships with Byron, Moore, Wordsworth and others; *Italy*, 1822; declined Laureateship, 1850; his famous breakfasts where brilliant conversation and wit abounded were attended at various times by most of the important figures of contemporary London.

Life by P. W. Clayden, *The Early Life of Samuel Rogers*, 1887 and *Rogers and his Contemporaries*, 2 vols., 1889

The Poetical Works of Samuel Rogers ed. E. Bell, 1891

See:

C. P. Barbier (ed.) *Samuel Rogers and William Gilpin: Their Friendship and Correspondence*, 1959

A. Dyce, *Recollections of the Table-Talk of Samuel Rogers* ed. M. Bishop, 1952

SCOTT, SIR WALTER (1771–1832): Novelist and poet; b. Edinburgh; son of lawyer; lame in right leg through infantile paralysis; Edinburgh High School, 1778–83; Edinburgh University, 1783; apprenticed in father's office, 1786; called to the Bar, 1792; joined Royal Edinburgh Light Dragoons as Quarter-Master; married Charlotte Charpentier, 1797; appointed Sheriff-deputy of Selkirkshire, 1799; *Minstrelsy of the Scottish Border*, 1802; *The Lay of the Last Minstrel*, 1805; became Clerk of Session in Edinburgh, 1806; went to London where he was lionized, 1807; became regular contributor to *The Quarterly Review* from its inception; founded publishing firm of John Ballantyne and Company, 1809; settled at Abbotsford, 1812; offered Laureateship, which he refused, 1813; friendship with Byron, 1815; illness, 1817–19; first novel, *Waverley*, published anonymously, 1814; *Guy Mannering*, 1815; *The Heart of Midlothian*, 1818; became a baronet, 1821; financial ruin, 1826; Scott wrote with great rapidity and after a rather late start as a novelist he produced novels at brief intervals until his death.

Life by his son-in-law, J. G. Lockhart, 3 vols, 1837–8; E. Johnson, 1970

The Poetical Works ed. J. L. Robertson, 1904

Selected Poems ed. T. Crawford, 1972

The Waverley Novels, Abbotsford Edition, 12 vols., 1842–7

The Edinburgh Edition of the Waverley Novels ed. D. Hewitt *et al.*, 9 vols., 1993–7: in progress

Miscellaneous Prose Works, 30 vols., 1834–71

The Journal of Sir Walter Scott ed. W. E. K. Anderson, 1972

The Letters of Sir Walter Scott ed. H: J. C. Grierson *et al.*, 12 vols., 1932–7

Sir Walter Scott on Novelists and Fiction ed. I. Williams, 1968

For extensive list of writings see N.C.B.E.L., III, 670–9

See:

J. H. Alexander and D. Hewitt (eds.), *Scott in Carnival: Selected Papers from the Fourth International Scott Conference*, 1993

M. Ball, *Sir Walter Scott as a Critic of Literature*, 1907; repr. 1966

A. Bell (ed.), *Scott Bicentenary Essays, Selected Papers read at the Sir Walter Scott Bicentenary Conference*, 1973

H. P. Bolton, *Scott Dramatized*, 1992

D. Brown, *Walter Scott and the Historical Imagination*, 1979

A. O. J. Cockshut, *The Achievement of Walter Scott*, 1969

J. C. Corson, *A Bibliography of Sir Walter Scott: A Classified and Annotated List of Books and Articles Relating to His Life and Works, 1797–1940*, 1943

C. F. Fiske, *Epic Suggestion in the Imagery of the Waverley Novels*, 1940

R. C. Gordon, *Under Which King? A Study of the Scottish Waverley Novels*, 1969

H. J. C. Grierson *et al.*, *Sir Walter Scott Lectures, 1940–1948*, 1950

J. T. Hillhouse, *The Waverley Novels and their Critics*, 1936

A. N. Jeffares (ed.), *Scott's Mind and Art*, 1969

R. Mayhead, *Walter Scott*, 1973

J. Millgate, *Walter Scott: The Making of the Novelist*, 1984

E. Muir, *Scott and Scotland: the Predicament of the Scottish Writer*, 1936; repr., 1982

C. O. Parsons, *Witchcraft and Demonology in Scott's Fiction*, 1964

J. Rubenstein, *Sir Walter Scott, A Reference Guide*, 1978

   Sir Walter Scott: An Annotated Bibliography of Scholarship and Criticism: 1975–1990 (a sequel to the Reference Guide above), 1994

A. Welsh, *The Hero of the Waverley Novels*, 1963

SHELLEY, MARY WOLLSTONECRAFT (1797–1851): Novelist; daughter of William Godwin and Mary Wollstonecraft; fell in love with Shelley and went with him to Switzerland and Italy, 1814; married him after death of his wife, Harriet, 1816; *Frankenstein*, 1818; edited Shelley's works, 1839–40.

Life by E. Sunstein, 1991

The Novels and Selected Works of Mary Shelley, ed. N. Crook and P. Clemit, 8 vols., 1996

Journals of Mary Shelley ed. P. H. Feldman and D. Pugh, 2 vols., 1985

The Letters of Mary Wollstonecraft Shelley ed. B. T. Bennett, 3 vols., 1980–88

See:

J. Blumberg, *Mary Shelley's Early Novels: 'This Child of Imagination and Misery'*, 1993

R. Florescu, *In Search of Frankenstein*, 1975

W. H. Lyles, *Mary Shelley: An Annotated Bibliography*, 1975

W. E. Peck, 'The Biographical Elements in the Novels of Mary Wollstonecraft Shelley' in P.M.L.A, XXXVIII, 1923

SHELLEY, PERCY BYSSHE (1792–1822): Poet; b. Sussex; son of rich landowner; Eton, 1804–10; University College, Oxford, 1810; friendship with Thomas Jefferson Hogg; publication of *The Necessity of Atheism* for which he was sent down from Oxford, March 1811; married Harriet Westbrook, August, 1811; *Queen Mab*, 1813; fell in love with Mary Godwin with whom he went to Switzerland, 1814; *Alastor and Other Poems*; second visit to Switzerland; met Byron; death of Harriet; married Mary Godwin, 1816; removal to Italy, 1818; *The Cenci*, 1819; *Prometheus Unbound*, 1820; drowned in bay of Spezia, 1822.

Life by N. I. White, 1940; 2 vols, 1947

Shelley's Poetry and Prose: Authoritative Texts; Criticism eds D. H. Reiman and S. B. Powers, 1977

Shelley Poems and Prose, ed. T. Webb, 1995

The Prose Works of Percy Bysshe Shelley, ed. E. B. Murray, vol. 1, 1993: in progress

The Letters of Percy Bysshe Shelley ed. F. L. Jones, 2 vols, 1964

The Esdaile Notebook ed. K. N. Cameron, 1964

See:

C. H. Baker, *Shelley's Major Poetry: The Fabric of a Vision*, 1948

N. Brown, *Sexuality and Feminism in Shelley*, 1979

P. Butter, *Shelley's Idols of the Cave*, 1954

K. N. Cameron, *Shelley: The Golden Years*, 1974

K. N. Cameron and D. H. Reiman (eds.), *Shelley and his Circle, 1773–1822*, 8 vols., 1961–86

J. Chernaik, *The Lyrics of Shelley*, 1972

T. Clark, *Embodying Revolution: The Figure of the Poet in Shelley*, 1989

P. M. S. Dawson, *The Unacknowledged Legislator: Shelley and Politics*, 1980

Durham University Journal (Special Issue on Shelley, ed. M. O'Neill), N. S. 54.2, 1993

C. Grabo, *The Magic Plant: The Growth of Shelley's Thought*, 1936
    A Newton Among Poets, 1930

A. M. D. Hughes, *The Nascent Mind of Shelley*, 1947

B. P. Kurtz, *The Pursuit of Death. A Study of Shelley's Poetry*, 1933

S. Norman, *Flight of the Skylark: The Development of Shelley's Reputation*, 1954

C. E. Pulos, *The Deep Truth: A Study of Shelley's Scepticism*, 1954

C. E. Robinson, *Shelley and Byron: The Snake and Eagle Wreathed in Fight*, 1976

N. Rogers, *Shelley at Work: A Critical Enquiry*, 1956; rev. edn, 1967

B. Shelly, *Shelley and Scripture: The Interpreting Angel*, 1994

F. Stovall, *Desire and Restraint in Shelley*, 1932

E. R. Wasserman, *Shelley, A Critical Reading*, 1971

B. Weaver, *Toward the Understanding of Shelley*, 1932

T. Webb, *Shelley: A Voice Not Understood*, 1977
    The Violet in the Crucible: Shelley and Translation, 1977

N. I. White, *The Unextinguished Hearth: Shelley and his Contemporary Critics*, 1938

SOUTHEY, ROBERT (1774–1843): Poet and biographer; b. Bristol; son of draper, brought up for greater part of his childhood by maiden aunt; Westminster School, 1788; expulsion, 1792; Balliol College, Oxford, 1793; admirer of French Revolution; friendship with Coleridge and formulation of idea of 'Pantisocracy'; left Oxford without taking a degree, 1794; dismissed from aunt's house, penniless; temporary estrangement from Coleridge; married Edith Fricker, 1795; given annuity of £160 by a friend, 1796; visit to Spain and Portugal with uncle; began legal studies at Gray's Inn, 1797; secretary to Irish Chancellor of Exchequer in Dublin, 1801–2; settled at Greta Hall, Keswick, with the Coleridges, 1803; *Letters from England by Don Manuel Espriella*, 1807; became regular contributor to *The Quarterly Review* from its inception, 1809; *Life of Nelson;* became Poet Laureate, 1813; *Life of Wesley*, 1820; *A Vision of Judgement*, 1821; insanity of wife, 1834; *The Doctor*, 1834–7; wife's death, 1837; married Caroline Bowles, 1839; failure of mind soon after.

Life by J. Simmons, 1945; K. Curry, 1975

The Poetical Works of Robert Southey, 10 vols, 1837–8

Poems of Robert Southey ed. M. H. Fitzgerald, 1909

Life of Nelson ed. E. R. H. Harvey, 1953

Life of Wesley ed. M. H. Fitzgerald, 2 vols, 1925

The Doctor ed. M. H. Fitzgerald, abr. edn, 1930

Essays Moral and Political, 1822; repr., 2 vols., 1971

Letters from England ed. J. Simmons, 1951

Letters of Robert Southey. A Selection ed. M. H. Fitzgerald, 1912

New Letters of Robert Southey, 1792–1838 ed. K. Curry, 2 vols, 1965

See:

G. Carnall, *Robert Southey and His Age*, 1960

K. Curry, *Robert Southey: A Reference Guide*, 1977

E. L. Griggs, 'Robert Southey and the Edinburgh Review' in M.P., XXX, 1932

L. Madden, *Robert Southey: The Critical Heritage*, 1972

J. Raimond, *Robert Southey: L'Homme et son temps; L'œuvre; Le rôle*, 1968

H. G. Wright, 'Three Aspects of Southey' in R.E.S., IX, 1933

WILSON, JOHN 'CHRISTOPHER NORTH' (1785–1854): Poet, scholar, and essayist; b. Paisley; son of manufacturer; Paisley Grammar School; Glasgow and Oxford Universities, 1797–1807; B.A., 1807; married Jane Penny, 1811; *The Isle of Palms*, 1812; called to Bar, 1815; *The City of the Plague*, 1816; began to contribute to *Blackwood's Magazine* as 'Christopher North', 1817; Professor of Moral Philosophy at Edinburgh University, 1820; *Noctes Ambrosianae* written in collaboration with Maginn and others, published in *Blackwood's*, 1822–35; *Lights and Shadows of Scottish Life*, 1822; *The Trials of Margaret Lyndsay*, 1823; *The Foresters*, 1825.

Life by Mrs Gordon, 2 vols, 1862; E. Swann, 1934
Works ed. J. F. Ferrier, 12 vols, 1855–8
Noctes Ambrosianae ed. R. S. Mackenzie, 5 vols, 1863–6
See:
M. Munday, 'John Wilson and the Distinction between Fancy and Imagination' in *Studies in Romanticism*, XIII, 1974
M. O. Oliphant, *William Blackwood and his Sons: Their Magazine and Friends* 2 vols., 1897
A. L. Strout, 'John Wilson, "Champion" of Wordsworth' in M.P., XXXI, 1934

WOLLSTONECRAFT, MARY, MRS GODWIN (1759–97): Writer; b. London; daughter of profligate and wastrel; left home after death of mother, 1780; ran a school with help of sister, 1783–5; *Thoughts on the Education of Daughters*, 1787; met William Godwin; *Vindication of the Rights of Woman*, 1792; went to Paris, where she met and fell in love with Gilbert Imlay, 1792; lived as his wife and had a daughter, Fanny, by him, 1794; separated from Imlay because of his infidelity; lived with Godwin whom she married, 1797; d. in childbirth; the daughter born at this time later married Shelley.

Life by her husband, W. Godwin, *Memoirs of the Author of a Vindication of the Rights of Woman*, 1798; ed. W. C. Durrant, 1927; B. M. Wardle, 1966
The Works of Mary Wollstonecraft ed. M. Butler and J. Todd, 7 vols., 1989
Collected Letters of Mary Wollstonecraft ed. R. M. Wardle, 1979
See:
Z. R. Eisenstein, *The Radical Future of Liberal Feminism*, 1981
G. Kelly, *Revolutionary Feminism: The Mind and Career of Mary Wollstonecraft*, 1992
C. K. Paul, *William Godwin, his Friends and Contemporaries*, 1876
J. M. Todd, *Mary Wollstonecraft: An Annotated Bibliography of her Works and Criticism*, 1975
V. Woolf, 'Four Figures. III Mary Wollstonecraft' in *The Common Reader*, 2nd Series, 1932

WORDSWORTH, WILLIAM (1770–1850): Poet; b. Cockermouth, Cumberland; son of attorney-at-law; Hawkshead Grammar School, 1778–1787; St John's College, Cambridge, 1787; an enthusiastic admirer of French Revolution; grand tour of Alps, 1790; B.A., 1791; went to France, 1791–2; affair with Annette Vallon, which resulted in a daughter being born to him after his return to England; *An Evening Walk* and *Descriptive Sketches*, 1793; disillusioned with Napoleon and the Revolution; settled with sister, Dorothy, at Racedown, Dorsetshire, and afterwards at Alfoxden; friendship with Coleridge began, 1795; started writing *The Prelude c.* this time; visit to Germany with Dorothy and Coleridge; publication of *Lyrical Ballads*, 1798; settled at Dove Cottage, Grasmere, 1799; married Mary Hutchinson, 1802; in 1805 the first draft of *The Prelude* was finished, but Wordsworth went on revising it for the rest of his life; estranged from Coleridge, 1810, but reconciled later; appointed Distributor of Stamps for Westmorland and Cumberland, 1813; granted Civil List pension, 1842; Poet Laureate, 1843.

Life by G. M. Harper, 2 vols., 1916; M. Moorman, 2 vols., 1957–65
The Poetical Works of William Wordsworth ed. E. de Selincourt and H. Darbishire, 5 vols, 1940–49
The Prose Works of William Wordsworth ed. W. J. B. Owen and J. W. Smyser, 3 vols., 1974
The Cornell Wordsworth ed. S. Parrish *et al.*, 16 vols., 1975–92: in progress
Poems ed. J. O. Hayden, 2 vols, 1977
Literary Criticism of William Wordsworth ed. P. M. Zall, 1966
The Prelude (A Parallel Text) ed. J. C. Maxwell, 1971
The Letters of William and Dorothy Wordsworth ed. E. de Selincourt, 6 vols., 1935–9: rev. by C. L. Shaver *et al.*, 8 vols., 1967–93
The Love Letters of William and Mary Wordsworth ed. B. Darlington, 1981
See:
F. W. Bateson, *Wordsworth: A Re-interpretation*, 1954
E. Batho, *The Later Wordsworth*, 1933
J. Beer, *Wordsworth and the Human Heart*, 1958
Bicentenary Wordsworth Studies in Memory of John Alban Finch, 1970
A. C. Bradley, 'Wordsworth' in *Oxford Lectures on Poetry*, 1909
H. Darbishire, *The Poet Wordsworth*, 1950
H. S. Davies, *Wordsworth and the Worth of Words*, 1987
D. Ferry, *The Limits of Mortality: An Essay on Wordsworth's Major Poetry*, 1959
F. Garber, *Wordsworth and the Poetry of Encounter*, 1971
H. W. Garrod, *Wordsworth's Lectures and Essays*, 1923; rev. edn 1927
G. H. Hartman, *Wordsworth's Poetry, 1787–1814*, 1964
R. D. Havens, *The Mind of a Poet*, 1941
M. Jacobus, *Tradition and Experiment in Wordsworth's 'Lyrical Ballads' (1798)*, 1976
L. M. Johnson, *Wordsworth's Metaphysical Verse: Geometry, Nature and Form*, 1982
J. Jones, *The Egotistical Sublime*, 1954
J. E. Jordan, *Why the Lyrical Ballads?*, 1977
　　(ed.), *De Quincey to Wordsworth: A Biography of a Relationship*, 1962

F. D. McConnell, *The Confessional Imagination*, 1974

T. McFarland, *William Wordsworth: Intensity and Achievement*, 1992

H. G. Margoliouth, *Wordsworth and Coleridge, 1795–1834*, 1953

F. Marsh, *Wordsworth's Imagery. A Study in Poetic Vision*, 1952

S. E. Meisenhelder, *Wordsworth's Informed Reader: Structures of Experience in his Poetry*, 1989

M. Moorman (ed.), *Journals of Dorothy Wordsworth*, 1971

W. J. B. Owen, *Wordsworth as Critic*, 1969

H. Read, *Wordsworth*, 1930

M. L. Reed, *Wordsworth: The Chronology of the Middle Years*, 2 vols., 1967–75

C. L. and A. C. Shaver, *Wordsworth's Library: A Catalogue*, 1979

P. D. Sheats, *The Making of Wordsworth's Poetry, 1785–1798*, 1973

J. C. Smith, *A Study of Wordsworth*, 1944

N. P. Stallknecht, *Strange Seas of Thought: Studies in Wordsworth's Philosophy of Man and Nature*, 1945; rev. edn, 1958

C. Woodring, *Wordsworth*, 1968

J. Wordsworth, *The Music of Humanity*, 1969

    William Wordsworth: The Borders of Vision, 1982

NOTES ON CONTRIBUTORS

JOHN BARRELL Professor of English, University of Sussex. Author of various books on art and literature, most recently *The Political Theory of Painting from Reynolds to Hazlitt* (1986), and *Poetry, Language and Politics* (1988)

MALCOLM BRADBURY Professor of American Studies at the University of East Anglia. His critical works include *The Modern American Novel* (1984), *No, Not Bloomsbury* (1987) and *The Modern World: Ten Great Writers* (1988). He edited *The Penguin Book of Modern British Short Stories* and co-edited *Modernism, 1890–1930* (1976). Novels include *The History Man* (1975), *Rates of Exchange* (1985) and *Cuts* (1987).

PATRICK CRUTTWELL Emeritus Professor of English, Carleton University, Ottawa. Author of *The English Sonnet* (1966) and *The Shakespearean Moment and its Place in Poetry in the 17th Century* (1970)

GEOFFREY GRIGSON (d. 1985) Poet, critic, writer and editor. His books include *Samuel Palmer: The Visionary Years* (1947), *Britain Observed* (on landscape painting of England) (1975), *Oxford Book of Satirical Verse* (ed.) (1980), *Collected Poems* (1982).

D. W. HARDING Emeritus Professor of Psychology in the University of London. Author of *Experience into Words: Essays on Poetry* (1963), *Words into Rhythm: English speech rhythms in verse and prose* (1976), and others.

JOHN D. JUMP (d. 1976) Was Professor of English Literature in the University of Manchester. Author of *Matthew Arnold* (1955) and *Byron* (1972); general editor of *The Critical Idiom* series.

G. D. KLINGOPULOS Was Senior Lecturer in English, University College, Cardiff. Contributor to *Scrutiny*.

NORMAN PAGE Professor of Modern English Literature, University of

Nottingham. His recent publications include *A. E. Housman: A Critical Biography* (1983), *A Dickens Companion* (1984), *E. M. Forster* (1988), and *Muriel Spark* (1990).

GILBERT PHELPS Formerly BBC Third Programme producer; is now a free-lance writer, lecturer and broadcaster. Author of *The Russian Novel in English Fiction* (1956), *A Survey of English Literature* (1965) and *From Myth to Modernism: A Short Guide to the World Novel* (1988). His eight novels include *The Winter People* (1963), *The Old Believer* (1973) and *The Low Roads* (1975).

EDGELL RICKWORD (d. 1982) Poet and literary critic. Founder and co-editor with Douglas Garman of *The Calendar of Modern Letters, 1925–7*. Associate editor of *Left Review* and *Our Time*. His books include *Rimbaud the Boy and the Poet* (124), *Essays and Opinions* (1972), *Literature in Society* (1978), and collected poems, *Behind the Eyes* (1976).

LEO SALINGAR Fellow of Trinity College and formerly Lecturer in English, Cambridge University. Author of *Shakespeare and the Traditions of Comedy* (1974) and *Dramatic Form in Shakespeare and the Jacobeans* (1986).

HILDA D. SPEAR Retired as Senior Lecturer in English at Dundee University in 1993, where she is presently an Honorary Research Fellow. Her recent publications include *Iris Murdoch* (1995), *Forster in Egypt: A Graeco-Alexandrian Encounter* (1987) and *Remembering, We Forget: A Background Study to the Poetry of the First World War* (1979); she has also edited several editions of nineteenth- and twentieth-century poetry.

JOHN SPEIRS (d. 1979) Was Reader in English, Exeter University. Author of *The Scots Literary Tradition* (1940), *Chaucer the Maker* (1951), *Medieval English Poetry, the Non-Chaucerian Tradition* (1957), and *Poetry towards Novel* (1971).

GEOFFREY STRICKLAND Reader in French at Reading University. Author of *Stendhal: the Education of a Novelist* (1974) and *Structuralism or Criticism?* (1981). He is an editor of *The Cambridge Quarterly*.

CHRISTOPHER THACKER Senior Lecturer in French, Reading University until 1984. 1984–8 Garden Historian with English Heritage. Author of *Voltaire* (1971), *Masters of the Grotto: Joseph and Josiah Lane* (1976), *The History of Gardens* (1979), and *The Wildness Pleases: the Origins of Romanticism* (1982).

LIONEL TRILLING (d. 1975) Was Professor of English and Comparative Literature at Columbia University in New York; critic and writer of fiction. A 12-vol. Uniform Edition of his work, edited by his wife Diana, is published in America by Harcourt Brace Jovanovich and in England by Oxford University Press.

WILLIAM WALSH Was Professor of Commonwealth Literature and formerly Acting Vice-Chancellor at Leeds University. His books include: *F. R. Leavis* (1980), *Introduction to Keats* (1981), and *A Manifold Voice* (1970). He has also written widely on the literature of many Commonwealth countries, particularly India, Australia and Canada.

FRANK WHITEHEAD Was Reader in English and Education at the University of Sheffield. Author of *The Disappearing Dais* (1966), and co-author of the Schools Council Research Study *Children and their Books* (1977).

R. O. C. WINKLER (d. 1962) Was in the Civil Service. Contributor to *Scrutiny*.

INDEX

Addison, Joseph 202, 209, 216
   Cato 210, 211
   On the Royal Exchange 202
Agasse, Jacques-Laurent 372
Ainsworth, Harrison
   Rookwood 146
Akenside, Mark 246
Alfieri, Vittorio, Count 223
Anson, George, Baron Anson
   Voyages 45
Anti-Jacobin, The 44, 53
Arnold, Matthew 162, 311, 312, 321
Augustan Age and literature,
   stability 15; emotional expression
   52; Crabbe 88, 91, 129; and
   Gothic novel 112–13; Scott 128,
   129, 131, 138; and nature 302;
   Byron 339; Pope and Dryden
   340; letters and journals 346;
   Richardson and 347; Reynolds'
   Discourses 359
Austen, Jane, motivation of her
   novels 29; and moral
   judgement 54–61; and Crabbe
   95; terminology 142; language
   146–9; irony 154–5, 157, 167,
   170, 171, 183–4; antagonism
   to 156–7; advice to her niece
   165; vulgarity 168; society and
   moral life 170, 173; Henry
   James on 172, 173; notes on 391
   Emma 29–30, 55, 58, 60–61, 147,
   148, 155, 157, 168, 172–86
   Mansfield Park 55, 57, 58, 147,
   155–6, 158–71

Northanger Abbey 50, 112, 126,
   147, 148
Persuasion 55–60 passim, 146,
   161, 168, 172, 175
Pride and Prejudice 55–9 passim,
   154, 158, 159, 161, 166, 168
Sanditon 149
Sense and Sensibility 54, 58, 59,
   60, 146, 147, 148, 155

Bamford, Samuel 17–18
Beattie, James 229, 309
Beckford, William
   Vathek 111, 126
Beddoes, T. L. 391
Bentham, Jeremy 191, 207, 392
Bewick, Thomas 18–19
Blackwood's Edinburgh Magazine 53,
   313
Blair, Hugh 147–8
Blair, Robert
   The Grave 112
Blake, William, and new technology 20; later genius 31; and
   testing of values 37–8;
   importance of childhood 40;
   and social code 61; language
   65, 80; problem of obscurity
   69–70, 77; symbolic books 72;
   short poems 72–8; prophetic
   writings 79, 81–2, 84; attitude
   to Innocence and Experience
   79–80; poems of self-analysis
   80–82; letters 82, 86;
   influences on 85; and Milton